D1091241

Studies in Public Regulation

MIT Press Series on the Regulation of Economic Activity

General Editor
Richard Schmalensee, MIT Sloan School of Management

Studies in Public Regulation

Edited by Gary Fromm

The MIT Press
Cambridge, Massachusetts
London, England

This book was set in Times New Roman by Asco Trade Typesetting Ltd., Hong Kong and printed and bound by Murray Printing Company in the United States of America.

Library of Congress Cataloging in Publication Data

Conference on Public Regulation (1977: Washington, D.C.)
  Studies in public regulation.
  Sponsored by National Bureau of Economic Research.
  Includes bibliographic references and index.
  Contents: Regulation in theory and practice, Paul L. Joskow and Roger G. Noll; Income-distribution concerns in regulatory policymaking, Robert D. Willig and Elizabeth E. Bailey; Theory of solvency regulation in the property and casualty insurance industry, Patricia Munch and Dennis Smallwood; [etc.]

  1. Trade regulation—United States—Congresses. 2. Trade regulation—Congresses. I. Fromm, Gary. II. National Bureau of Economic Research. III. Title.
HD3616.U47C544   1977   353.0082   81-9442
ISBN 0-262-06074-4   AACR2

Contents

Foreword

Government regulation of economic activity in the United States has grown dramatically in this century, radically transforming government-business relations. Economic regulation of prices and conditions of service was first applied to transportation and public utilities, and has recently been extended to energy, health care, and other sectors. In the 1970s, explosive growth occurred in social regulation focusing on workplace safety, environmental preservation, consumer protection, and related goals. The expansion of regulation has not proceeded in silence. Critics have argued that many regulatory programs produce negative net benefits, while regulation's defenders have pointed to the sound rationales for and potential gains from many of the same programs.

The purpose of the MIT Press Series on Regulation of Economic Activity is to inform the ongoing debate on regulatory policy by making significant and relevant research available to scholars and decisionmakers. The books in this series will present new insights into individual agencies, programs, and regulated sectors, as well as the important economic, political, and administrative aspects of the regulatory process that cut across these boundaries.

The individual essays in this collection are notable for the exceptionally high quality of analysis and for their concern with matters of importance for public policy. Several have already become standard references. Moreover, the whole is greater than the sum of its parts; by skillfully illuminating different aspects of the economics of regulation, these essays together give us new insights about the regulatory process in general, as well as new awareness of the strengths and weaknesses of traditional methods of analyzing that process and its effects.

Richard Schmalensee

Preface

The essays in this volume were presented at a Conference on Public Regulation sponsored by the National Bureau of Economic Research (NBER) under a grant awarded by the National Science Foundation through the Research Applied to National Needs program. The purpose of the conference was to advance the theory and practice of regulation.

Papers to be presented were selected in an open competition. A call was issued and more than 150 abstracts were received. These were reviewed by a steering committee of experts on public regulation. The committee discussed the merits of the leading candidates so as to choose papers that would make significant contributions toward formulating, analyzing, and evaluating regulatory policies. After the conference the committee critiqued the papers presented, offered suggestions to the authors, and decided which papers were to be included in the proceedings volume.

Much is owed to the committee for the high quality of these essays. The results from some are applicable immediately to regulatory issues, while others suggest promising paths for additional research. Members of the committee were Gary Fromm (chairman), of SRI International and the National Bureau of Economic Research; William Baumol, of Princeton University; William Baxter, of Stanford University; Peter Bloch, of the American Bar Association; Darius Gaskins, of the Interstate Commerce Commission; Michael Gort, of the State University of New York at Buffalo; George Hay, of Cornell University; Paul Joskow, of the Massachusetts Institute of Technology; Marvin Kostors, of the American Enterprise Institute; Bruce Smith, of Teknek, Inc.; Harvey McMains, of the University of Texas; Sam Peltzman, of the University of Chicago; Laurence Rosenberg, of the National Science Foundation; Frederick M. Scherer, of Northwestern University; Michael Spence, of Harvard University; Harry Trebing, of Michigan State University; and Leonard Weiss, of the University of Wisconsin.

Thanks especially are due to Bruce Smith, formerly of the National Science Foundation, and to Laurence Rosenberg, who enthusiastically supported the project and helped arrange for its funding. Readers of this volume, too, benefit from the able editing of the papers by Sarah J. Gaston and by the staff of The MIT Press.

The National Bureau of Economic Research was organized in 1920 to consider, in an objective and impartial manner, issues bearing on economic problems. The NBER concentrates on topics of national interest that are susceptible to scientific treatment.

Gary Fromm

Studies in Public Regulation

Regulation in Theory and Practice: An Overview

Paul L. Joskow
Roger C. Noll

During the past twenty-five years the amount of research on the economics of government regulation has increased enormously. The study of public-policy approaches to problems in industrial organization was once limited almost exclusively to antitrust policy and the regulation of a few industries with natural monopoly characteristics. This area of inquiry has been transformed as new administrative agencies with powers to set prices, restrict entry, and control what products are produced, and how, have come to affect the efficiency of industrial markets and the distribution of production and income throughout the economy.

The increased attention to the economics of administrative regulation is due to a number of factors. First, research has benefited considerably since the late 1950s from the application of modern statistical analysis and the mathematics of constrained optimization. Although technically unsophisticated by contemporary standards, the classic works by Averch and Johnson (1962), Caves (1962), Meyer et al. (1959), and Stigler and Friedland (1962) represent a watershed in the study of economic regulation by administrative agencies. What economists now know about the effects of government regulation on economic activity that they did not know twenty years ago is, for the most part, attributable to the kinds of analytical techniques that were first used in a handful of classic papers such as these.

A second reason for the expansion of scholarly interest in this area is the increasing importance of administrative regulation in the U.S. economy. Regulation spread to more and more sectors of the economy, and the relative importance of such heavily regulated sectors as transportation, energy, and telecommuncications has also increased. The impact of environmental, safety, and health regulations cuts across the entire economy. It is now almost impossible to study any important industrial market in the U.S. economy without taking account of the effects of the many restrictions on the behavior of economic agents that have been established and are administered by one or more regulatory agencies.

Third, economists have had to come to grips with important contradictions between theoretical prescriptions to remedy market imperfections so as to increase economic welfare and the actual behavior and performance of regulatory agencies. Implementation of theoretical schemes designed to ameliorate market imperfections has often proved to be difficult and costly, and the regulatory process has often created its own imperfections. In addition, what regulatory agencies attempt to do and how they go about it are influenced by political and bureaucratic processes which economists rarely, if ever, considered in suggesting regulatory policies to deal with market imperfections.

We have been asked to begin this compendium by presenting an overview of the large and rapidly expanding scholarly literature on regulation. An initial reluctance to engage in such an endeavor has been replaced by the conviction that a critical overview of this literature is especially appropriate at this time. No comprehensive review of the recent literature exists in any easily available form. For anyone interested in the field—especially students—this makes life fairly difficult. More important is the possibility that research on the economics of regulation may well be at a crossroads. In particular, applying the traditional theoretical and empirical tools to study the traditional regulated industries has reached the point of rapidly diminishing returns. In some cases strong qualitative results have emerged. Additional research can refine the quantitative significance of these results, but it is not likely to change any basic conclusions about the effects or desirability of government regulation. In other areas, the traditional tools have not yielded strong quantitative results, and there is little hope that they will. In these areas new conceptual tools and empirical techniques appear necessary if significant progress is to be made. Research on regulation may be at a crossroads on an even more basic level, in that changes are taking place in the perspective from which scholars ask questions about regulation. Most of the empirical literature on regulation is motivated by some variant of the question of regulation versus deregulation: Is regulation socially desirable? A negative response implies reliance on a real or imaginary free market. In our opinion, very few situations in which there is a clear "yes" or "no" answer to this question have not already been well worked over, and even these are sufficiently similar to those that have been exhaustively studied that the results of the studies can be easily generalized to them.

Many areas of research in which there are few clear theoretical or empirical results also cannot effectively be attacked by comparing regulation with the absence of regulation, because a completely unregulated market is not a viable, practical alternative. The issues in these areas often involve problems of evaluating different regulatory instruments, regulatory processes, and extents of regulation, and determining the distribution of costs and benefits throughout the population that results from a particular set of regulatory activities. Indeed, even in cases in which there is a clear case for deregulation, distribution must be explored to make the case in the political arena as well as to structure a politically acceptable transition from a regulated to an unregulated state.

We shall develop these arguments further in this article. The bulk of the discussion is devoted to the original assignment: a summary and a critical evaluation of the more important areas of contemporary research on the economics of regulation. We supplement this discussion with some suggestions and speculations about promising directions for future research in regulatory economics. No attempt is made to cover everything that might reasonably be included under the heading of regulatory economics. Our focus is on regulatory activities conducted by administrative agencies, either independent or within the executive branch of government, that have been delegated regulatory responsibility by statute. We exclude antitrust policy and regulatory activities administered directly by the courts (such as property law, liability law, and contract law). These policy instruments are alternatives to administrative regulation, for they define the basic institutional context in which a market, free from administrative regulation, operates. It is in this context that we believe these instruments should be evaluated, and the task of doing so is well beyond the scope of this paper.

Government Regulation of Industry: An Overview

Studies of regulation, whether theoretical or empirical, normally fall into three areas: price and entry regulation in industries with competitive market structures, price and entry regulation in monopolistic industries, and (for want of a better term) "qualitative" regulation, which attempts to cope with various kinds of market-failure problems that are only indirectly linked to prices, profits, and market structure. In the third category are environmental, health, occupational-safety, and product-quality regulation. We shall examine the research results in each of these areas separately. In addition, no overview of this field would be complete without considering theories of regulation that seek to answer very general questions about the behavior of regulatory agencies as a class of government institutions. This section concludes with a review of various theories of regulation.

Price Regulation in Industries with Competitive Market Structures

If economics has any scientifically settled issues, one is surely that price and entry regulation in perfectly competitive industries generates economic inefficiencies. As a theoretical matter, the result is trivial: Under standard neoclassical assumptions about human motivation, frictionless markets, and production technologies, an externally imposed constraint upon the actors in an otherwise perfectly competitive market can do no better than leave the market as efficient as it was before the constraint was imposed. And, because implementing the constraint must consume some resources, society must always operate more efficiently if a competitive market is simply left alone.

The contribution of the literature on regulating competition is that the data confirm the theory in several key economic sectors that nearly all nations attempt to regulate. Economic research has demonstrated convincingly that price and entry regulation in agriculture (an industry we shall henceforth ignore, because of our ignorance about the research on it), transportation, and oil and natural-gas production creates economic inefficiencies. Usually this inefficiency is manifested in higher prices, higher production costs, and slower technological progress than would occur without regulation. In a few instances, such as regulation of hydrocarbon fuels, the inefficiency is created by prices that are too low to clear markets, which leads to inefficient patterns of commodity utilization.

In the 1960s, the standard approach to estimating the inefficiencies of regulating competition was to compare equilibrium prices, costs, and quantities in regulated and unregulated situations. These comparisons could be based upon direct observation when unregulated and regulated markets operated simultaneously, or when relatively recent changes in the nature of regulation permitted easy intertemporal comparisons. Examples of research of this type include the analysis by Snitzler and Byrne (1958, 1959) of the agricultural exemption in trucking, the study by Joskow (1973b) of state regulation of property and liability insurance, the research by Stigler (1971) on occupational licensing, MacAvoy's (1973) and Pindyck's (1974) studies of the effects of imposing natural-gas field-price regulation, the comparisons of interstate and California intrastate airline service by Levine (1965), Jordan (1970), and Keeler (1972), and the study of gas pipelines by MacAvoy and Noll (1973). Montgomery's 1978 examination of FEA controls of petroleum applied the same approach to a more recent regulatory development. Each of these studies found that efficiency losses due to regulation were large in proportion to total transactions in regulated markets. Owing to their base in relatively recent empirical information, these studies have to be taken seriously in current debates about public policy. For example, the Interstate Commerce Commission (1976) felt called upon to attempt a formal rebuttal of a study by Moore (1975) that was based upon the same methods and some of the same data as the Snitzler and Byrne papers.

One difficulty with the comparative approach to studying the effects of regulation is that, in some instances, regulation has been in force for so long that studies of the effects of the imposition of regulation or of unregulated markets have questionable current quantitative value. MacAvoy (1956) and Spann and Erickson (1970) examined the effects of the early actions of the ICC on railroad prices and identified efficency losses of the same sort that more recent studies have found in airlines, trucking, and hydrocarbon fuels. However, such studies have less immediacy in current policy debates, because of the impossibility of directly extrapolating findings from the 1880s into the present. Ideally, we would like to have matched samples of contemporary regulated and unregulated firms to enable us to make clear comparisons between regulated and unregulated industry behavior and performance. Unfortunately, we rarely have this opportunity. Often, lacking data on unregulated firms, we must infer what the unregulated industry would look like.

Several studies, beginning with Meyer et al. (1959), have attempted to infer the inefficiencies of existing ICC regulation solely from data dealing with regulated operations, without the benefit of comparisons between regulated and unregulated states of the world. One feature of regulated competition has been that regulators have tended to set prices on the basis of uniform formulas for particular categories of service that apply across several firms and markets. Because regulators apparently are loath to take actions to weed out inefficient operations, these prices are usually set high enough so that considerable variability in the cost of providing service can be observed among economically viable firms and technologies. Thus, one approach to estimating the cost of regulation is to measure the cost penalty associated with the protective price umbrella that regulators constructs for the inefficient. For example, Meyer et al. (1959), Friedlaender (1969), and Harbeson (1969) argued that one cost of ICC regulation is a misallocation of freight transport among competing modes. They estimated its magnitude by comparing the cost of shipping different categories of commodities various distances by competing modes. A conceptually similar approach was taken by MacAvoy and

Sloss (1967) and Gellman (1971) in arguing that ICC price-setting policies and formulas had prevented or retared warranted cost-reducing innovations such as the unit train, the "Big John" hopper car, and truck-rail piggybacking.

Until about 1970, the studies that have been discussed so far were generally regarded as providing relatively good quantitative estimates of the costs of regulating a variety of markets with competitive market structures. But all of these studies share the assumption that the nature of a regulated industry's product is homogeneous. Although variable product quality was mentioned in several earlier studies (notably, Caves 1962 and Eads 1972), Douglas and Miller (1974) (for airlines) and Boyer (1977) and Levin (1978) (for surface transportation) demonstrated that this assumption could lead to overestimation of the cost of price regulation. A key observation is that regulatory agencies are more effective in controlling prices than in establishing the quality of service offered by a regulated firm. As a result, in multifirm regulated markets the firms compete by varying the quality of service. In the airline industry this takes the form of competition in flight frequency, choice of aircraft, and (where not controlled directly) service amenities such as meals, seat width, and lounge facilities. Competition in dimensions other than price leads to excessive service quality, and therefore to higher average costs and prices, while continually driving earned rates of return to competitive levels.

The analytical treatment by Douglas and Miller (1974), Eads (1975), and DeVany (1974) of competitive rivalry where minimum prices are fixed has widespread potential application. The general point is that prices, costs, and price-cost margins in a regulated multifirm market cannot give a correct measure of the inefficiency caused by regulation because service quality is lower in unregulated markets. One must evaluate the price-quality combination and compare it with the optimum in order to estimate the cost of regulation. This general insight is applicable to other examples of multifirm regulation, such as trucks, taxis, insurance, banking, and occupational licensing. Ideally, with observations on regulated and unregulated firms, cost could be estimated relatively easily by comparing price, cost, and quality outcomes in the two markets. An example is the common comparison of interstate airline markets regulated by the Civil Aeronautics Board with similar unregulated routes in California and Texas. Unfortunately, in many industries such comparisons cannot be made, and the regulated price, cost, and quality equilibrium must be inferred from simulations of competitive equilibrium.

Boyer (1977) and Levin (1978) recognized the importance of product quality in measuring the costs associated with the misallocation of freight among competing transport modes due to price regulation. Both argued that the relative-cost approach of Meyer et al. (1959) and subsequent studies leads to serious overestimation of the amount of traffic that is not now shipped by the least costly mode. The relative-cost method overlooks important differences in the attributes of service quality among modes. Boyer and Levin concluded that intermodal substitution possibilities are far more limited than the previous studies had implicitly assumed, and cited as evidence the small price elasticities of demand that they estimated from econometric models of the freight-transport sector. Their studies led to estimates of the cost of intermodal misallocation of freight resulting from price regulation that are an order of magnitude lower than estimates based on relative-cost studies.

Unlike the studies of the airline industry that deal with service quality, Boyer's and Levin's retained the assumption that service quality is exogenous to regulation. A next step in this line of research is to attempt to determine whether regulation affects the relative service qualities of freight-transportation modes, and, in particular, whether the structure of regulation has caused part of the spread in service quality among competing modes. If so, the true cost of price regulation would lie somewhere between the estimates derived from the relative-cost approach, which implicitly assumes that the modes are perfect substitutes, and the calculations provided by Boyer and by Levin.

Relaxing the implicit assumption that product quality is invariant with respect to changes in regulation creates difficult theoretical and empirical problems. The likelihood that quality of service has more dimensions in surface freight transport than in passenger air transport makes the required theoretical and empirical analysis more difficult. The problem is greater still in other sectors, for in transportation the most important facets of service quality have to do with speed, frequency of service, and freight-damage rates, all of which are easier to model and to quantify than are the elements of quality that are important in other sectors of the economy. Endogenizing quality may be important in numerous competitive regulated markets in which the dimensions of quality are more ephemeral and the task of the research scholar in estimating the effects of regulation is therefore exceptionally difficult.

Nevertheless, new research along these lines is unlikely to change the conclusions of economists about the wisdom of subjecting competitive industries to price and entry regulation. In many cases, variable product quality is not a potentially important issue. Hydrocarbon fuels, for example, are relatively homogeneous; moreover, regulation attempts (not completely successfully) to account for physical differences in the composition of fuels from different sources. In cases in which quality is potentially important, more sophisticated research will change numerical estimates of the cost of regulation; however, in the absence of a case for regulatory interventions designed to affect quality directly, regulation can only lead to a departure from efficient combinations of price, quality, cost, and output. In an era when economists are often accused of being unable to agree on anything, we find comfort in the virtually unanimous professional conclusion that price and entry regulation in several multifirm markets is inefficient and ought to be eliminated.

In light of the surprising consensus among economists about the appropriate direction for public policy in a number of important industries with competitive market structures, the question remains why efforts to eliminate price and entry controls have met with such stiff resistance. Gradual deregulation of interstate airline rates and entry was accomplished after years of debate. Deregulation of surface freight transportation has faced much stiffer resistance, as have similar efforts in telecommunications. To most regulatory economists, "regulatory reform" means the elimination of regulation in these markets, and the failure of public officials to move quickly in response to these findings is a great disappointment that leads to skepticism about the policy impact of economic research. We believe that there are a number of reasons why the economic analyses of these industries has not helped as much as it might have in advancing the cause of regulatory reform. But we also believe that the concerns about the impotence of economic analysis in affecting regulatory reform reflect a misperception of the application of scholarly research to the implementation of public policy.

Two basic problems invariably arise in the political debate over major changes in regulatory policy. First, with any major change in government regulation that has important impacts on price, market structure, cost, and product quality, some groups will gain while others lose. On balance, economics research provides a strong case that the financial benefits to those who gain will exceed the cost to those who lose. But, lacking some type of compensation scheme, those who expect to lose are likely to resist a change in policy. If the gainers are widely dispersed and the losers are well organized, the stage is set for the losers to mount an effective political campaign against reform. When it is unclear who is to gain and who is to lose, and how much money is involved, it may become even easier for the losers to magnify the extent of the potential losses and their distribution. The uncertainty associated with the distribution of gains and losses is compounded by the inherent uncertainty associated with deriving the outcome of deregulation from inference rather than comparison. Unfortunately, economists have devoted little if any consideration to the distribution of costs and benefits associated with existing regulations and proposed regulatory reform. Research on the distributional consequences of deregulation would facilitate the development of workable compensation schemes that would allow an effective political consensus to emergy. Such research would also undermine the ability of the losers to convince others (or their repressentatives) that they will lose too.

The second problem concerns the transition between regulated and unregulated states of the world. Most economic analysis compares long-run equilibria. But legislators, who are naturally cautious about making major policy changes in key sectors of the economy, are going to look carefully at the short-run response to the elimination of regulatory controls. The greater the inefficiency associated with prevailing regulatory instruments, the greater the likelihood that severe short-run economic dislocations will arise from their elimination. Such short-run dislocations could easily abort a regulatory reform program before it had a chance to achieve a long-run equilibrium. Again, economists have done little research on the dynamic characteristics of transition from a regulated to an unregulated regime. Such research would alert policymakers to the possibility of important short-run industry behavior and performance, as well as contributing to policies that might make the transition smoother and more politically acceptable.

Although further research on the incidence of regulation and deregulation and the nature of the transition path between a regulated and an unregulated regime would add useful information to the policy debate, it is ridiculous to place the burden of proof for regulatory reform on the shoulders of academic economists. Economists can provide an analytical and empirical framework in which the issues can be discussed sensibly, help to identify potential gainers and losers, and suggest transition schemes to smooth out short-run economic dislocations. And they can, of course, make all this information freely available to the public by publishing it. What academic economists can do beyond this is severely limited.

From this perspective, academic research on regulation in industries with competitive market structures has had an important impact. It has been used extensively by congressmen and the executive branch in the debates on airline deregulation, trucking deregulation, telecommunications policy, and many other regulatory issues. Though such research has not made and will never make the case on its own, it has made an important contribution to elevating the level of public discourse in numerous policy arenas.

Price Regulation of Monopoly

The economics literature is ambivalent about the desirability of regulating monopolies. Because economic theory is firm in concluding that monopolies create economic inefficiency, social intervention to prevent, undo, or control monopoly is potentially attractive. However, because social interventions generate direct and indirect costs through the peculiar kinds of inefficiencies they cause, attempting to deal with monopoly may be at least as costly as leaving it alone. One of the more embarrassing features of the literature on economic regulation is that, after a century of trying, the profession is still unable to reach a consensus on what, to an outsider, must appear to be one of the best-defined and most central issues on which economists ought to have something to say. Where progress has been made, it has generally been in response to an examination of the effects of alternative regulatory mechanisms and in the development of schemes to make price regulation more effective.

Whereas the study of regulated competition has produced essentially one interesting theoretical development—the models of quality competition when prices are set above the competitive level—several interesting microtheoretic developments have come from the study of the regulated monopoly firm. We shall examine three of these.

The A-J Model The so-called A-J literature began with the seminal work of Averch and Johnson (1962) and, in our opinion, culminated in a series of papers by Klevorick (1971, 1973). The A-J models examine a monopoly firm that produces output via a neoclassical production technology using two resources: capital and labor. The firm is assumed to seek to maximize some objective, usually profits. A regulatory commission comes into the picture by imposing a constraint on the firm's behavior. It is normally assumed that the firm is constrained to earn on its capital stock some "fair" rate of return that is greater than the cost of capital but less than the unconstrained, profit-maximizing rate of return. Implicitly, the objective of the regulatory commission is assumed to be to keep earned rates of return no higher than the allowed rate of return. The primary result of the basic model is that such a constrained firm will produce output at greater than minimum cost. In particular, the expansion path of the constrained firm traces a locus of capital-labor ratios that is higher than a cost-minimizing producer would use.

Extensions of the basic A-J model have included the examination of different firm objective functions and different types of regulatory constraints (Bailey and Malone 1970). Not surprisingly, changing the nature of the objective and the constraints alters the basic conclusion. Because a firm can never do better than minimize cost, changing the model either changes the size or the direction of the production inefficiency or returns the firm to the cost-minimizing expansion path. As a result, most work continues to be based on the assumptions of profit maximization and a binding rate-of-return constraint.

Some richness has been added to this model by consideration of the intermittency of regulatory review. A number of attempts to introduce "regulatory lag" into the model have been made. These models normally assign an active (deterministic or probabilistic) role to the regulatory agency. During the "lag" period, the firm is allowed some relaxation of the regulatory constraint (depending on the particular model) but the regulatory commission is always ready to pounce on the firm to force its earned rate of return back to the allowed rate. Such pouncing may occur at set intervals or probabilistically according to some probability distribution known to the firm (Bailey and Malone 1970; Bailey and Coleman 1971; Klevorick 1973).

The welfare implications of rate of return regulation are examined in papers that seek to determine the optimal fair rate of return (Klevorick 1971; Sheshinski 1971). In these models, the optimal rate of return is derived by replacing the maximization of profit by some social-welfare objective. The idea is then to pick the allowed rate of return that yields a constrained welfare maximum. Klevorick (1971), Bailey (1973), and Sheshinski (1971) indicated that some regulation of natural monopoly will always be optimal. This strain of the literature is important because it recognizes that cost minimization cannot be the only criterion for judging a regulatory system. If it were, society would be satisfied with no regulation, because a neoclassical monopoly firm uses its inputs efficiently.

The A-J explanation for the metafact that regulated monopolies appear to be excessively capital-intensive industries has become conventional fare in the economics literature. Whether the predictions of the model are verified by reality is an empirical question that we shall discuss below; however, eschewing Freidman's methodological advice, we shall offer some opinions on the assumptions and structure of the model, some of which appear in the work of Joskow (1973a, 1974). The A-J results depend on several assumptions that are at variance with the reality of the world of regulated monopoly. Some of these are the standard assumptions of microeconomic models, such as the existence of a continuously differentiable production function, factor and product market prices that are certain, and homogeneous inputs and outputs with exogenously determined characteristics. Other assumptions pertain to the nature of the regulatory process itself, and it is these that we wish to examine more fully.

First, the regulatory agency is assumed to regulate profits only; however, what regulators actually do is regulate prices. The calculation of an allowed profit is a way station along the road to determining how much of an increase in prices will be allowed. Once set, the regulated firm's prices—not its rate of return—are fixed, pending subsequent regulatory review (except for the effects of automatic-adjustment clauses). This fact has important implications for the behavior and performance of regulated firms and regulatory agencies when costs and demand conditions are changing rapidly and there is regulatory lag.

Second, the A-J model ignores the fact that one of the issues in a regulatory proceeding is the determination of allowed costs. Although, admittedly, a regulatory agency is unlikely to be sufficiently expert and to have enough data to exercise very close scrutiny of management decisions in a regulated firm, the agency does review the expenditures and investments of the firm and has the power to identify and disallow costs associated with serious production inefficiencies.

Third, the A-J model implicitly assumes that the planning horizon for capital investments is short in comparison with the interval between regulatory reviews, or at least that the outcome of regulatory reviews is sufficiently predictable over the investment-planning horizon that the firm can select an appropriate investment plan in response to it. In fact, the time spent in constructing a major capital investment is often several times as long as the time between regulatory reviews. A firm's ability to respond quickly to unanticipated changes in the regulatory constraint is, as a result, quite limited. Moreover, the A-J-model literature presumes that the frequency of regulatory reviews is exogenous to the firm. As Joskow (1973a) pointed out, the profits of the firm are an important cause of regulatory review: Low profits and rising nominal costs lead a firm to ask for a price increase, or (less frequently) declining nominal costs and growing profits cause the regulator or an intervenor to review the performance of a firm in search of a justification for a price reduction. Only when the firm is near the profit rate at which it expects to trigger a regulatory review will it have an incentive to produce inefficiently, for otherwise any increase in profits that is due to a cost reduction will be retained by the firm. Obviously, the fact that actions by the agency and by the firm depend on actions taken by the other introduces the possibility of strategic behavior by both.

In the mid-1970s several empirical tests of the A-J model appeared in the literature. All dealt with the electric utility industry. One (Boyes 1976) found no evidence of the capital-intensivity bias, but the result is suspect because the author tested the A-J hypothesis by examining capital-fuel ratios of new generating plants during the electrical conspiracy of the late 1950s. Spann (1974), Courville (1974), and Peterson (1975), using data from other periods, all found inefficiently capital-intensive generation equipment and concluded that the A-J effect had been confirmed. McKay (1976) showed that the conclusions of these studies are unjustified. Peterson's finding that unregulated firms spend relatively less on capital for electricity generation is explained by the fact that most of the unregulated firms in his sample used facilities that burned natural gas, while most of his regulated firms burned other fuels. What Peterson was actually measuring was the lower capital costs of gasburning generators and the consequences of interstate price regulation of gas. Boyes, Courville, and Spann all misspecified the nature of the tradeoff between capital and fuel by using expenditures, rather than energy efficiency, as the measure of capital. McKay found that when the appropriate measure of the efficiency frontier between equipment design and fuel consumption is used, the A-J effect can no longer be detected.

Negative empirical findings do not disprove the A-J hypothesis, for excessively capital-intensive processes could be introduced in many ways other than through the substitution of thermodynamic efficiency for fuel. Nevertheless, in light of the comments already set forth about the extent to which the model incorporates real aspects of the decision problem facing regulated firms, we believe that further empirical work to test the A-J theory (especially studies limited to the electric utility industry) is unlikely to be very productive. In our view, the A-J model is useful primarily in illustrating the implications of one approach to regulating monopolies. The model is interesting not because it represents the way monopolies actually are regulated, but because it calls attention to the value of attempting to represent institutional arrangements in a formal microtheoretic model for the purpose of determining the incentive structure that such arrangements create. Recent efforts by state utility commissions to monitor utility supply decisions more closely recognize implicitly that rate-of-return regulation may produce incentives that lead a firm to depart from least-cost production in a variety of ways, especially in the current economic environment.

A potentially fruitful line of theoretical inquiry is to formulate models that more faithfully represent the regulatory process. For example, Burness et al. (1980) have formulated a model in which a firm faces a price fixed by the regulator, a requirement to serve all comers, and upper and lower bounds on its rate of return that, when reached, trigger a costly regulatory process that resets prices. This model is intended to capture some of the properties of the regulatory process suggested by Joskow (1974). (See also Hendricks 1975.) Because their model is motivated by questions about the risk-taking propensities of regulated firms, Burness et al. examine only one issue: the attitudes of a regulated firm toward the selection between a negotiated fixed-price contract and a cost-plus contract for constructing new capital facilities. They find that the Joskow model reaches the opposite conclusions as the A-J model: In the A-J world firms pick the fixed-price contract, while in the Joskow world they opt for cost-plus. Burness et al. then examine the history of nuclear steam systems, and find that sales of nuclear power plants increased substantially when the manufacturers switched from a fixed-price system to a cost-plus system, although there are reasons other than the effects of regulation why the switch may have occurred. In any case, this paper is a step along a path that has not been much traveled, and one that holds some hope of shedding substantial light on the efficiency of the production and market decisions of regulated monopolies.

Sustainability of Natural Monopoly Beginning with the paper by Faulhaber (1975), economists at New York University and Bell Labs have published a series of interesting papers that deal with a fundamental issue concerning the regulation of natural monopoly: whether optimal (second-best) prices (or, for that matter, any set of prices that cover total costs) can prevent entry into the market of a regulated natural monopoly, even if such entry would increase total production costs and lead to higher prices for some consumers.

Natural monopoly over several commodities can arise from global subadditivity of the cost function—that is, the situation where the cost of producing all commodities together is less than the cost of producing the same amount of each separately. Contrary to the conventional wisdom, natural monopoly does not guarantee the existence of a vector of break-even prices that will preclude entry (the natural monopoly may not be sustainable for any break-even price vector) even if the natural monopoly is producing output efficiently and charging efficient prices. Very simply, a break-even monopoly may have to set the prices for some services higher than is necessary to recover the "stand-alone" costs of serving some coalition of consumers. If firms enter in response to these price-cost margins, the result will be increases in the total costs of production and in the prices charged for other commodities or to those customers not included in the new coalition.

Panzar and Willig (1977) showed that the presence or the absence of any sustainable (entry-blocking) price vector that covers the natural monopolist's cost of production depends on interproduct-substitution effects on the demand side, product-specific economies of scale, and economies of joint production. In order for a natural monopoly to be unsustainable, some product-specific economies of scale, or else the economies of joint production, must have been exhausted, so that further increases in the output of some product must raise either its own or some other product's average cost. If diseconomies of joint production are being experienced at the margin, then greater interproduct-substitution effects and product-specific scale economies will make the existence of sustainable prices less likely. If product-specific diseconomies of scale are present, greater economies of joint production will make the existence of sustainable prices more likely. Baumol et al. (1977) showed that Ramsey-optimal prices will be sustainable under very strong conditions.

To date, the sustainability literature has skirted three major issues that are directly related to its principal theoretical results. First, the models presume perfect regulation that manages to force monopolists to produce at least cost and at zero economic profit. Second, entrants are confined to producing some subset of the products that are being offered by the monopolist, rather than offering other products that are not colocated in goods-characteristic space with the products of the monopolist. Because *ex ante* the monopolist offers all feasible commodities, the question of the optimal product mix is not addressed. Once the product mix is allowed to become variable, the optimal market structure, even with pervasive economies of scale and scope, could be monopolistic competition rather than monopoly. Third, the question of the response of the monopolist to entry—and, therefore, the viability of the entrant—is left hanging. Even in the frictionless world of traditional comparative statics, the original firm can cut its losses by reducing its own product mix, and in so doing undermine the position of the entrant. In a world in which an incumbent firm has an advantage because of established business patterns and information costs, an incumbent could undermine the position of an entrant simply by duplicating its product mix.

Although the authors of these papers (especially Panzar and Willig) exercise caution in drawing policy conclusions from their theoretical results, we are concerned about the improper policy inferences that might be drawn from this literature. The primary policy inference is that entry should be carefully scrutinized to ensure that society captures all the benefits of natural monopoly. In the context of a specialized model in which Ramsey prices are sustainable, Baumol et al. (1977) suggest that "the public interest is served by encouraging a monopolist to price in *anticipation* of entry rather than in *response* to it" (p. 360).

We have a number of problems with such policy prescriptions. As an empirical matter, strict global subadditivity is not likely to be convincingly demonstrated (or refuted), even in a world without technological change. That is, a single firm's natural monopoly over all commodities and all output vectors normally cannot be verified on the basis of the data that are likely to be available. Indeed, this is the heart of the problem. Theoretical analysis can assume subadditivity, but policy application requires that regulators know whether a monopoly is natural over the relevant commodity space. If the monopoly is natural, a single regulated firm can be more efficient and an exclusive franchise may make sense (with the assumption that the regulated monopolist will be efficient). However, if the cost function is not known with certainty, as seems likely in most cases in which the issue arises, the imposition of entry restrictions may allow the monopolist to provide products that would be provided more efficiently by separate firms. This is of particular concern in a world in which the potential for process and product innovations is great and where a regulated firm's profits are not regulated perfectly. In addition, requiring a potential entrant to prove that the monopolist does not have a cost function that exhibits strict global subadditivity is a burden of proof that is likely to be almost impossible to meet.

Another difficulty with erecting entry barriers is that a protected monopolist has less reason to engage in efficient practices. For example, Ramsey-optimal prices are not likely to be preferred to some other break-even price vector. Moreover, when demand functions are not independent, Ramsey-optimal prices will be extremely difficult for a regulatory agency to calculate and enforce. In addition, entry restrictions reduce the impetus for least-cost production and cost-reducing technological change that might result from the threat of competitive entry. Even if a potential entrant intended to produce a new product, bearing the burden of proof that the product was indeed new would not only impose costs and delays but also would provide information that would help the monopolist prepare a competitive response.

In short, the theoretical results that have been derived in these papers do not sustain a general argument for entry restrictions into markets presently served by regulated monopoly firms. As yet, the theory is too specialized and insufficiently operational to support such a strong policy conclusion.

The only empirical application of the sustainability models that we are aware of is a paper by Baumol and Braunstein (1977) on the industry that publishes academic journals. That study found that the cost function in this industry is subadditive, and that costs could be reduced by concentrating the industry. The authors did not propose the establishment of a regulated monopoly for publishing academic journals; the absence of such a conclusion, for obvious reasons, illustrates the difficulty of deriving general policy implications from the sustainability literature. To have policy significance the model must be extended to incorporate complementary operational theories and empirical results on the issues of optimal product mix, relationship of product mix to market structure, and effect of market structure on rate and direction of technical change. The current value of the sustainability model is that it eliminates a shibboleth from the economics literature by demonstrating that one cannot prove theoretically that natural monopolies do not need a franchising process that protects them from entry. Whether entry restrictions are justified in any particular case is a largely empirical matter that depends on static and dynamic aspects of costs and product mix.

Variable Pricing   In the literature on monopoly pricing, the one great practical triumph of theory is the work on peak-load (variable) pricing. (We prefer the latter term because recent developments in this literature have generalized the results beyond the case of the time-variant demand.) Beginning with papers by Houthakker (1951) and Boiteux (1951; 1960), a series of articles has steadily advanced the state of knowledge about an important practical problem: pricing in a situation in which short-term supply and demand conditions fluctuate so that, even when investments are perfectly efficient, an invariant price in all periods will produce quantitatively important and recurring mismatches between demand and capacity (see Kahn 1970, chapters 3 and 4).

In complete detail the variable-pricing problem is very complex. On the demand side, the position of the demand curve varies continuously over time. Some sources of time-dependent demand are regular and predictable, but others are not; thus, the quantity demanded at a given price is a random variable, drawn from a distribution function with time-dependent parameters. On the supply side, the firm has several different technologies it can use to produce output, each of which has unique long-run and short-run cost characteristics. Supply, too, is a random variable in that, in the short run, a particular technology may be operational only at less than full capacity; a plant may shut down unexpectedly, or the sun may fail to shine on solar collectors.

The institutional constraints on the pricing problem can also vary. The goal may simply be economic efficiency, but it may include upper and lower bounds on the profitability of the enterprise. Moreover, the firm may be allowed to adopt price structures of varying complexity— for example, by adopting multipart tariffs, or by segmenting customers into various groups, each of which faces a different price structure. And, of course, each of the institutionally feasible pricing systems has an implementation cost, such as the metering devices necessary to initiate time-dependent pricing. Finally, institutional arrangements to deal with excess demand must be incorporated into the model if prices and demand cannot vary instantaneously; examples of this are random rationing, preplanned rationing based upon value of service, and temporary elimination of service to some users.

As stated, the variable-pricing problem has not been solved, although several problems that bite off a large chunk of it have been. One strain of papers, including Houthakker 1951, Boiteux 1951 and 1960, Steiner 1957, Hirschleifer 1958, Turvey 1968, Wenders 1976, and Panzar 1976, established the basic peak-load-pricing results. These papers deal with cost functions and variable-demand relations in which time dependence is known with certainty. They address pricing problems that are concerned only with economic efficiency, unconstrained by revenue limits, but with the institutional constraint that in each period a single price applies to all units of output. (This price can vary from period to period.) These papers provide successively more refined definitions of the appropriate concept of marginal cost and versions of the basic result that prices ought to equal marginal cost in each period.

The most interesting generalization of the basic peak-load problem is the incorporation of random variation in demand and supply. French utility economists, especially Boiteux, have investigated this problem since the early 1950s. (See Dreze's excellent summary [1964]; see also Balasko 1974 and Joskow 1976.) Their concern, as well as that of Crew and Kleindorfer (1976), is to incorporate two additional features of demand into the optimal pricing model: the uncertainty attached to the quantity demanded at a given price at any time, and the social costs associated with a failure to satisfy all demand at the going price. This extension of the model produces two useful results: a marginal-cost pricing rule that incorporates expected marginal operating costs and expected marginal rationing costs, and an optimal-investment rule that, on average, produces excess capacity (the optimal reserve margin) even in peak periods.

The significance of variable-pricing theory lies in its practical importance. Pricing schemes derived primarily from variable-pricing models are employed in several European countries to sell electricity (see Acton and Mitchell 1977). In France, for example, the year is separated into five periods (winter peak, winter shoulder, summer shoulder, winter off-peak, and summer off-peak) with differing probabilities that demand will exceed capacity. Customers buy capacity rights for each period at different prices, and face an additional use charge per kilowatt-hour which also varies by period. The capacity rights specify the maximum amount of instantaneous power a customer is permitted to demand in each period, and revenues from the sale of capacity rights are an important factor in investment decisions. Inexpensive control and metering devices, and even continuous digital home displays of current and total energy use, are in widespread use. The U.S. government has financed peak-load-pricing experiments in ten states, and in about twenty states time-of-day rates have been either ordered by regulators commissions or proposed voluntarily by utility companies (see Joskow 1979a, 1979b).

The atypical success of the variable-pricing literature, in terms of its practical impact, is worth trying to explain. Most economists who work in applied areas such as the economics of regulation believe that economics has something important to say to practitioners, yet they often are frustrated by the snail's pace at which economic rationality creeps into actual practice. Park (1973) even assembled a book of essays that constitutes a lament for the impotence of economists in another area (cable television policy)—a lament that is equally appropriate to numerous other regulatory issues.

The reasons for the success of the variable-pricing literature are numerous, and no attempt will be made here to detail them (for details see Joskow 1979a, 1979b). But one interesting element is that well over half of the references cited in this section were written by people who were willing to work with utility managers and whose research is to some degree the result of successive confrontations of theory with reality. Most of the French authors work for Electricité de France, and in the United States many papers in recent years have been written by economists associated with one or more peak-load-pricing experiments or with Bell Labs. These economists have carried on the theoretical search for a general theory of optimal pricing, but their work has demonstrated two additional features: Great attention has been paid to bringing the assumptions of the models ever closer to the realities of operating a utility, and nearly all of the papers recognize the problems and costs associated with implementing a perfect pricing scheme and even provide some additional analysis on locating (in the manner of Baumol and Quandt 1964) the "optimally imperfect" scheme. Perhaps it is accidental that a literature with successes in practical application also has these characteristics, but we doubt it.

Before concluding our discussion of the regulation of natural monopolies, we must note that Demsetz (1968) questioned the basic natural-monopoly justification for regulation. He suggested that, even where technological considerations indicate that a single producer would be most efficient, the use of some form of competitive franchise bidding could prevent a natural monopoly from behaving like a classical monopolist. Williamson (1976) and Goldberg (1976) criticized this approach because of its simplistic and idealized notion of private contracting and the problems that might arise in structuring and enforcing private contracts for natural monopolies. Both of these papers try to examine the nature of the private contracting problems that may result, and suggest that many of the problems that may arise are similar to the kinds of problems that regulatory agencies must deal with. They suggest that regulatory agencies may be an efficient substitute for private contracting in certain circumstances.

The more expansive conceptualization of private contracting institutions introduced by Williamson and Goldberg raises serious questions about the utility of comparing the performance of actual regulated markets with idealized models of competitive market behavior that ignore the costs of private contracting. More extensive empirical investigation of the nature of private contracts in different economic environments and of the costs of negotiation and enforcement would be useful for advancing our understanding of the costs and benefits of alternative institutional arrangements.

Environmental, Product-Quality, and Health Regulation

The most vigorous recent extensions of government intervention are actions intended to improve the quality of the environment, of consumer products, and of workplaces. Agencies such as the Environmental Protection Agency, the Food and Drug Administration, the Consumer Product Safety Commission, and the Occupational Safety and Health Administration are having increasingly important effects on the economy. Rapid extensions of rate and entry regulation in the health-care sector by states and by the federal government have been accompanied by regulatory control, yet relatively little useful research on the behavior and performance of these agencies has been forthcoming.

A substantial amount of theoretical research into externalities, information costs, product quality, consumer misperceptions, and moral hazards underlies a theoretical case for government intervention in many of these areas. The empirical relevance of these market imperfections has proved difficult to document because the information that is needed to measure it cannot be easily inferred from market transactions. Even in the case of environmental externalities, which most economists agree require some form of government intervention, there is disagreement about the particular instruments to be used and the ability of government regulatory agencies to deal with the problem effectively.

Environmental Regulation   The best-developed theoretical models in the area of noneconomic regulation deal with environmental external diseconomies. The theoretical characterization of the environmental problem is borrowed directly from the public-finance literature on collective goods, and is a straightforward application of Samuelson's classic paper (1954). What is special about the theory of environmental externalities is the rather interesting array of institutional interventions by government that have been explored in the theoretical literature.

If perfect information were available about the benefits and costs of alternative abatement strategies for every source of pollution, the problem, in both theory and practice, would be relatively uninteresting. With perfect, costless information, optimal source-specific standards could be legislated. The interesting aspects of the problem are related to the imperfect information about sources of emissions, the amount of pollution at each point of reception, and the costs and benefits of abatement that a regulator faces. A regulator can know only imperfectly where pollution is created and received and whether a source is in compliance with a regulatory rule. Moreover, regulatory interventions generate more information about the relevant facts of environmental problems, so that changes in regulatory constraints have two objectives: to produce a more efficient result in their own right and to generate more information to guide further alterations in the regulations.

Most economic-policy analyses of environmental problems propose the use of negotiations and corrective taxes to "internalize the externality." Baumol and Oates (1971) set up the problem in a straightforward partial-equilibrium format, regarding pollution abatement as having costs to abaters (which generate a surrogate supply function) and benefits to recipients (which generate a surrogate demand function). The policy problem is seen as imposing an emission tax that balances at the margin the costs and benefits of abatement. Ayres and Kneese (1969) and Leontief (1970) set up specialized linear general equilibrium models which include environmental externalities and in which the appropriate taxes appear as shadow prices. The implementation of emissions taxes may have been advocated most cogently in the public policy arena in a series of monographs by Kneese and others at Resources for the Future (see, for example, Kneese and Schultze 1975).

A less popular "economist's solution" to environmental problems, and one that also relies on decentralized processes to achieve efficiency, is to create tradable licenses to pollute. Coase (1960) saw externalities as a problem in incomplete specification of property rights, over which polluters and recipients could, in principle, negotiate once rights were defined and enforced. Dales (1968) provided a discussion of tradable pollution licenses that is rich in examples of how such a system might be implemented. Montgomery (1972) formalized the theory of tradable licenses and showed the conditions under which a given amount of pollution abatement is accomplished at least cost by creating tradable licenses.

The fascination of economists with marketlike mechanisms to deal with environmental problems is particularly interesting in light of the largely negative theoretical results on the effectiveness of decentralized processes that have appeared in the literature. One set of problems, emphasized by Davis and Whinston (1962), Montgomery (1974), and others, has to do with the thinness of each artificial market for a pollutant. As Arrow (1970) pointed out, the appropriate expansion of the set of commodities subject to market transactions that would allow a competitive solution to the problem of efficient abatement is a separate market for each pollutant that is delivered to each receptor. If the number of receptors at one point is greater than one or if the number of polluters in any particular market is small, price-taking (Cournot) behavior is not likely to conform to actual firm behavior. This undermines the efficiency of both markets in licenses and iterative tax processes.

The second set of problems is that not all equilibria that are reached by an iterative tax scheme or private negotiations over well-specified rights are efficient, and that not all efficient equilibria are stable even if Cournot behavior is followed. The difficulty is that pollutants that reduce the productivity of other production processes (including "consumption" production processes of the type hypothesized by Lancaster [1966]) can never drive the marginal productivity of resources in other processes to zero, because firms (or people) can exit. This means that, in some range, pollution abatement must involve economies of scale and discrete exit or entry points (which must make the problem amenable to corner solutions). Noll and Trijonis (1971) pointed out that the earlier approach to calculating prices from general equilibrium models required one to assume either that pollution costs are independent of output or that the marginal costs of abatement are independent of pollution. Their extension of the Ayres-Kneese and Leontief models admits the possibility of unbounded effects of pollutants on costs. As Starret (1972) demonstrated in a more realistic model, an iterative tax can reach an equilibrium at relatively small amounts of abatement, yet the equilibrium may be dominated by higher levels of abatement (achieved with higher taxes) that capture the gains from scale economies. Moreover, Montgomery (1976) showed that the necessary conditions for an efficient solution to a bargaining process requires that pollutants enter all production and cost functions separately, and that this condition is inconsistent with the conditions for the existence in equilibrium of more than one pollution-producing and pollution-receiving firm.

In terms of the practicality of implementing environmental policies, the second set of criticisms is probably more important than the first. Because the full extension of the commodity space contemplated by Arrow (1970) is impractical, problems of thin markets are unlikely to loom large in comparison with other difficulties. Moreover, no one has seriously proposed (although the demand-revealing mechanism of Groves and Ledyard [1977] may be waiting in the wings) that receptors will be responsible for collectively deciding on pollution taxes or on the number of licenses to pollute that will be issued, except through the imperfect mechanism of the representative political process. The practical problem is whether a sequence of tax or license messages to polluters will produce minimum-cost responses so that decisionmakers, using whatever magic is at hand, can measure the consequences of these iterations and locate an equilibrium that works efficiently, notwithstanding the effects of imperfections in political processes for aggregating preferences and in the definitions of separate pollution markets.

The economists' traditional scheme for using market mechanisms to correct externalities has rarely been utilized. Corrective-tax and tradable-license schemes have almost entirely taken a back seat to direct control of effluents or specification of particular control technologies (Jacoby and Steinbrunner 1973; Mills and White 1978). Part of the problem is that the economists who advocate these policy instruments have usually ignored the problems of information costs, administrative feasibility, and uncertainty that characterize the real world in which these policies must be applied. When economists have considered these factors, they have identified circumstances that lead to a preference for standards—even input standards—rather than decentralized market processes (Spence and Roberts 1976; Spence and Weitzman 1978). But this cannot be the entire explanation. Mills and White (1978) provided a fascinating analysis of the historical evolution of auto emission controls, and presented a convincing case that a workable tax scheme has been available and would have been superior to the course followed by Congress and the EPA. For some reason, there appears to be an administrative and political bias towards rules and standards and away from markets in the area of environmental control. Exactly why such a bias exists is unclear, but eliminating it appears to be a prerequisite to implementing decentralized methods in this area.

Health, Safety, and Performance Standards   Economists have yet to invent a felicitous term for the grab bag of regulatory policies that fall under this heading. Nevertheless, such disparate regulatory activities as occupational licensing, product-safety standards, occupational-health regulation, and truth-in-packaging requirements do have a unifying theme: All seek to protect parties to private market transactions from making decisions that they will regret. In individualistic microeconomics, the conceptual basis for these interventions lies in market imperfections that are due to costly and inexact information about the consequences of economic decisions.

Conventional microeconomic theory was built upon the assumption of costless and perfect information about the characteristics of jobs and products and about the prevailing set of wages and prices. But, as Arrow (1963), Stigler (1961), and others have taught us, information is itself a commodity in that it requires resources to produce and can have economic value to decisionmakers. Moreover, the production and evaluation of information is empirically a very important economic activity, as demonstrated by Machlup (1962) and Porat (1977).

Economists have taken two theoretical approaches to exploring the microeconomic foundations that might, in principle, provide a rationale for various forms of protective regulation: to postulate an exogenously determined state of imperfect information that cannot be affected by individual economic agents, and to make information an endogenous commodity that enters production and consumption decisions.

In a model developed by Spence (1977), consumers misperceive the hazards of products and therefore take more risks than they would take if fully informed. A similar model of a labor market for hazardous jobs would yield too-ready acceptance of risky occupations. This approach has a hint of paternalism, in that the informational difficulty is really ignorance, and in such a state consumers or workers would not know what they wanted regulated—the better-informed would have to tell them. The exception is Hinich's (1975) model of food regulation, which incorporates an insurance system or a similar risk-spreading mechanism to pay for health care. As long as sellers of insurance cannot tell the difference between ignorant and informed individuals (see Arrow 1963), excessive risk taking (moral hazard) by the former will impose a pecuniary external diseconomy on the latter. Thus, the informed group pushes for banning risky products and workplaces in order to save the cost of subsidizing the medical care of the ignorant. One is left with the problem of explaining why regulation, rather than a change in the institutions for financing medical care, is imposed.

Oi (1973) took an approach similar to that of Hinich, but asked a different question with a different set of specialized assumptions. Oi assumes that producers may be legally liable for injuries suffered by consumers, but that they have no mechanism for knowing the damage costs associated with individual consumers. Consumers, on the other hand, are assumed to have perfect information about product risks, to know their expected damage costs, and to be able to obtain actuarily fair insurance at negligible cost. As a result, producer liability leads to an inefficient outcome because producers essentially must homogenize a combined product and insurance policy across heterogeneous consumers. Strict consumer liability allows the consumer to purchase the optimal quality of product and the optimal insurance policy separately.

The analyses of Hinich, Oi, and Spence, though each is obviously specialized, clearly point the way for a more general theoretical model of the informational problem that could underpin protective regulation. Such a model would take account of the following two considerations: First, insurance companies might have as much difficulty as producers in separating individuals into homogeneous risk pools, and may be unable to write insurance contracts that avoid moral hazard. Second, producers might know nothing about differences among consumers in their susceptibility to damage, and consumers might be unable to figure out the *ex ante* risks of products or even which product was responsible *ex post* if they suffered an injury or illness.

The main weakness of models with exogenous information states is that they ignore the process by which agents gather and evaluate information. Facing a positive marginal cost of information, a rational agent purchases information up to the point at which the marginal gains from more informed decisions are balanced by the marginal cost of information. If the market for information is perfectly competitive, decisions will be "optimally imperfect" in the sense of Baumol and Quandt 1964. Unfortunately, as Davis and Kamien (1970) pointed out, the market for information does have one theoretical difficulty: Information is not completely a private good. Once knowledge is produced for one person, it need not be produced independently for others who might want to use it. Thus, if knowledge is priced to recover its full cost, its price exceeds marginal cost and some people may be excluded from using it who would be willing to pay the marginal cost of making it available to them.

In addition to the fact that it may support some sort of public provision of subsidization of information about product quality and workplace safety, the preceding discussion also admits the possibility that standards and bans make sense. The reasoning is that decisionmaking that is based upon the processing of complex information is time-consuming, and thereby has some shadow price. Moreover, if numerous individuals make essentially the same decision on the basis of the same information, and if the tastes of the individuals are identical, it would pay the group to elect one person to process the information, make the decision, and tell everyone else what to do (Colantoni et al. 1976). Of course, if preferences are not identical, delegation of decision power creates consumption inefficiencies because the person making the decision will lead others to consume qualities of products and experience risks at work that are not the same as if each person had made an independent decision. Thus, standardization of workplaces and products to remove certain types of risks saves information-processing costs at the expense of creating some inefficiencies and administrative costs. The point at which a regulatory policy balances these costs at the margin represents what Cornell et al. (1976) identify as the optimal delegation of decisionmaking authority.

The empirical importance of these theoretical arguments is critical, yet is still largely unresolved, and perhaps unresolvable. If a public agency can collect, evaluate, and disseminate information more efficiently than can the private market, we have an argument for regulation in the form of public provision of information. But as a practical matter, to make the measurements required for such a judgment *ex ante* is quite difficult. Even *ex post* it would be difficult to determine whether the public provision of information is beneficial. The net effect of beneficial regulation should be to shift the demand for the regulated products outward by reducing the gross cost of the product to the consumer through a reduction in information-gathering expenses. If the increase in welfare at the prevailing market price is greater than the costs of providing the information through a public authority, society will presumably be better off. However, isolating demand shifts that are due to a reduction in the costs of information borne by consumers from changes in demand that arise from a myriad of other causes is likely to be a very difficult empirical task. On the other hand, while it will be difficult to determine a hard point estimate of the benefits of the public provision of information, a good upper-bound estimate for the net costs of such interventions ought to be possible. As long as the public agency does not provide incorrect or misleading information, the administrative costs of collecting, evaluating, and distributing the information will provide an upper-bound estimate of the costs of regulation.

The situations in which a theoretical case for standards can be made present even more difficult problems for evaluation in practice. The regulation of product quality (including the banning of certain products) requires us to know not only that a public authority can collect and evaluate the relevant information more efficiently than can individual agents in the market, but also that the more efficient use of these results is to set a standard or ban rather than to provide the information directly to consumers. This is a difficult case to make. Regulators are more likely to set the wrong standard than to provide incorrect information, for several reasons. First, with the information available, it may be extremely difficult to determine the "right" product quality for all consumers. Second, agencies with responsibility and political accountability for regulating risky products are likely to be extremely averse to approving a product that results in some injuries or deaths, even if approval is an efficient decision. Third, the standard-setting process is likely to be more easily captured by some particular interest group, whether a consumer group that thinks people ought not to eat hotdogs even if they want to or a producer group that can use the standards as a means to help cartelize an industry by making entry and product differentiation difficult. In addition, standard setting is likely to be more costly, because it requires an enforcement mechanism to be effective.

We suspect that, in most situations in which public collection and evaluation of information is more efficient than the private market, the direct provision of this information to consumers will be a regulatory alternative superior to the establishment of standards and bans on products. Standard setting makes sense only in those situations in which a strong case can be made that the dissemination of information is extremely costly, or that consumers will find it difficult to use the information effectively. Thus, we find troublesome the propensity of agencies such as the Consumer Product Safety Commission to opt for setting standards rather than providing information.

In analyzing the effects of the 1962 amendments to the Food and Drug Act, Peltzman (1973) developed the following hypothesis about protective regulation: Effective regulation should reduce the amount of learning about product quality that takes place during the first few years a product is marketed. In particular, Peltzman argues that the demand for a new drug will decline more slowly with effective regulation because the agency will already have done some of the learning about the quality of the drug before it is marketed. McGuire et al. (1975) correctly pointed out that almost nothing can be concluded from an analysis of the aggregate demand for new drugs. Among other things, they question Peltzman's assumption that all consumers make the same kind of error when purchasing new drugs. For example, without FDA scrutiny, physicians may not prescribe a new drug until more evidence of its effects are known. Such behavior would lead, over time, to movements of individual demand functions that would be just the opposite of those proposed by Peltzman, and could simply cancel out the behavior of those individuals who behave as Peltzman suggests when the aggregate demand function is observed.

We also believe that Peltzman's analysis assumes that the linkage between consumer preferences and observed drug purchases is much the same as that in a typical commodity market, such as the market for new soft drinks. This ignores a number of important, special characteristics of the drug market. First, individuals do not make direct decisions about what drugs to consume; their physicians do. While physicians, prescribing behavior is an unsettled area, serious questions have been raised about the ways in which physicians respond to drug prices and how they evaluate the information available about drug quality. Second, patients generally buy a package of medical-care services from a doctor or a hospital, with a large portion of the total cost borne by third parties. Consequently, the connection between consumer preferences and observed drug demand is indirect.

Peltzman raises another issue, concerning the effects of regulation on innovation. If a regulatory intervention requires prior approval before a new product can be marketed, the effect is to increase the cost of product innovations directly by requiring more research and indirectly by delaying initial marketing (see Grabowski and Vernon 1976). Peltzman (1973) argued that the supply reductions caused by the 1962 drug amendments led to a reduction in the growth of demand for drugs after 1962. We infer that the source of a connection between supply limitations and the position of the demand curve that Peltzman has in mind is that some areas of the product space have been excluded by regulation, so that an aggregated-demand curve for all drugs in the two periods actually spans a different product set. A reduction in the number of drugs on the market, according to this conceptualization of the problem, would cause the representative consumer to find a greater distance in product space between the most desirable drug in principle and the closest approximation to it in reality. Even if this is so, to conclude that a backward shift in the demand curve for drugs represents a loss in welfare is not justified. Because drugs are supposed to treat illness, one source of the reduction in the demand for drugs could be that drugs are more effective, on average, in curing treatable illnesses. Or, perhaps fewer people have to be treated for illnesses arising from taking bad drugs. In short, an improvement in the quality of drugs does not necessarily mean that drug sales will increase, particularly if the improvements take the form of replacements for less effective drugs that required greater dosages.

Data problems have plagued attempts to evaluate consumer-protection regulation in areas other than drugs. Starting in the late 1960s in the Food and Drug Administration and continuing since 1973 in the Consumer Product Safety Commission, the federal government has collected a great amount of information on hospital admissions and emergency treatments for injuries sustained in connection with the use of an extremely wide array of consumer products, encompassing even athletic equipment used in organized sports. Though some accident reports are followed by intensive investigations of the cause of the injury, for the most part the data leave open the cause of an accident. For example, an accident would be chalked up to the "processed foods" category if a person broke a toe by dropping a can of corn as well as if the can exploded without apparent provocation. Moreover, because data on the use of products are not collected, neither scholarly research nor safety-regulatory agencies have been successful in allocating the change in accidents associated with a product among changes in the hazards inhering in a product (such as might occur when a regulatory rule is imposed) and changes in the use of a product (such as might occur if safety regulations increased the price of the product substantially). (This argument was advanced by Cornell et al. [1976].)

Even in the area of automobile safety, which has somewhat better data spanning a longer period of time, the empirical analysis of the effects of safety regulation is controversial. The most detailed study (Peltzman 1976a) attempts by time-series analysis to detect the effect of safety regulations on automobile accidents. Peltzman's interesting insight—which is applicable to all safety and health regulation—is that the imposition of protective regulations might cause consumers to engage in more risky behavior, thereby offsetting some of the potential effectiveness of the regulations. The difficulty in trying to test the empirical importance of this argument is that it requires a complete specification of the process by which the riskiness of an activity is determined. In the case of auto safety, not only can cars change, but so can the physical layouts of roads, the attentiveness of the driver, the amount of safety-related maintenance the car receives, the driver's selection of driving speed and route (a safe, indirect interstate or a dangerous but direct county road?), and, for reasons other than safety of the automobile, the composition of the driving force. The task of convincingly taking account of all of these factors is monumental, and the discussion by Manne and Miller (1976) of Peltzman's attempt reveals that consensus was not reached.

In the area of occupational safety, relating workplace hazards to wages and relating safety standards to injuries have proved easier to accomplish, and economists are in general agreement that OSHA has probably generated more costs than benefits. Although some empirical work on the effects of OSHA regulations has been undertaken, the professional consensus on the effect of the agency rests primarily on more indirect evidence. R. Smith (1976) summarized a series of studies that he and others carried out for the Assistant Secretary of Labor for Policy, and presented some new information that attempted to quantify the aggregative impact of OSHA standards on industrial accidents. He found no measurable impact. R. Smith and the staff of the Council on Wage and Price Stability also undertook several benefit-cost analyses of specific OSHA standards, and concluded that the price tag on these regulations is also probably too high. For example, Smith (1976) estimated that workers would have to value reductions in hearing due to current noise at approximately $15,000 to make the standards worthwhile.

One difficulty with these empirical studies is that the data on industrial accidents are notoriously poor. Experience rating for workmen's-compensation insurance gives employers an incentive to pay off injured workers and not report accidents. The problem of analyzing the impact of OSHA regulations was compounded by a change in Department of Labor injury-reporting procedures that occurred approximately at the same time OSHA was created. Even with reliable injury statistics, estimating the costs of accidents and of avoidance strategies is difficult. As an example of the empirical problems on the benefit side, the evaluation of the noise abatement standards uses data on the relationship of values of property near airports to decibels of noise from airplanes to measure the disutility of noise in the workplace. A few of the assumptions implicit in this approach are that the undesirability of noise in properties near an airport is the same as the undesirability of noise in a workplace; that the disutility of noise is measured by a scalar (loudness) and is unrelated to frequency, intermittancy, and other measures of noise; and that a linear relationship exists between the monetary value and the amount of noise (this last assumption is known to be inaccurate, for example with respect to the relationship between hearing loss and noise). Yet, even after these criticisms have been made, one is at a loss to propose a distinctly better method. One can expect to obtain only indirect evidence on the disutility of noise or most other sources of work-related injuries by observing transactions in labor, product, and property markets. Consequently, benefit-cost analyses of proposed standards, though useful as a device to organize thought and evidence, are unlikely to prove definitive in determining the value of a standard.

The best economic arguments against OSHA have to do with the agency's selection of regulatory targets and with the enforcement of its standards. Cornell et al. (1976) inferred from theoretical arguments in favor of regulatory interventions that the more complex the problem of processing information about a hazard, the more likely that a standard (rather than an informational requirement) ought to be adopted. They concluded that OSHA appears to select regulatory targets not on this basis but by the frequency and severity of injuries. Because workers and employers are more likely to have given attention to dealing with frequent, severe accidents, the likely regulatory impact here can be expected to be small, especially if the problem is relatively easily comprehended. These authors and R. Smith (1976) point out that the theoretical case for intervention is stronger for long-term occupational health problems, but that OSHA has focused relatively little attention on these. Both studies also discuss the feeble incentives for complying with OSHA standards that existing enforcement policies provide. Although the situation varies from industry to industry, most firms can expect an OSHA inspection about once a decade. For firms found out of compliance, fines average about $170 (for an average of about six violations). Compared to the costs of compliance, the expected losses from being found out of compliance are minuscule; consequently, there is little reason to expect much compliance, or much of an effect of OSHA regulations on injury rates.

One approach to the use of incentives to deal with occupational safety problems is to raise fines for noncompliance and rely primarily on an inspection system. Another is to tax injuries, as proposed by R. Smith (1974), and rely on injury reporting to establish the basis for the tax. Because accurate reporting of injuries is problematical, this too would require checking, although perhaps the costs of inspection would be lower for checking injury reports. Nevertheless, the primary advantage of the tax approach is said to be that the regulator does not need to know the details of injury-prevention technology, just as the environmental regulator need not know the details of abatement technology, to impose a tax on performance. This raises the issue of whether a tax equilibrium is necessarily efficient, if regulators adopt the same sort of iterative procedure that was proposed for emissions taxes. To our knowledge, this problem has not been addressed in the literature on occupational safety. We conjecture, however, that a tax equilibrium would be efficient except for two eventualities: The cost function for injury reduction may not be convex, so that tax equilibria may be a local but not a global optimum, and the pecuniary externality associated with the cost-sharing features of health and liability insurance may introduce a further nonconvexity with the same effect as the real external effect on production that is associated with pollution. In addition, the problems raised by Spence and Weitzman (1978) remain, and under certain circumstances these could tip the balance in favor of standards.

The remaining major area of product quality regulation is occupational licensing. The public-interest rationals for occupational licensing is the protection of poorly informed consumers from incompetent practitioners. Economists have long been skeptical of the value of entry barriers in any market, and occupational licensing, especially by self-regulatory processes such as qualifications exams, is no exception. Stigler (1971) argued that occupational licensure is solely a device to restrict entry so that the practitioners of licensed professions can earn more. Benham (1972) and Benham and Benham (1975) showed that eyeglass prices are higher in states that regulate or prohibit advertising by optometrists, and Plott (1965) found that licensing dry-cleaning establishments has a similar effect.

Because the public-interest purpose of occupational licensing is to raise the quality of service, the effects on prices and wages that have been found are not surprising. The key to whether this form of regulation benefits only members of the protected occupational group is whether service quality is higher in states with stricter regulation and, if it is, whether consumers are being denied access to lower-quality services, which, with the relevant information, they would prefer to purchase.

On a priori grounds one would suspect that quality is not improved by entry restrictions, because so little of the regulatory effort is directed at issues of quality. Occupational licensing is usually for a lifetime, whereas a system designed primarily to ensure that practitioners were competent would subject professionals to periodic examinations. Moreover, as Benham (1972) pointed out, the American Optometric Association places very little weight on indexes of professional competence in deciding whether a member is in good standing; instead it allocates most of the weight to whether the member abstains from advertising.

Nevertheless, scientific evidence on the quality issue is surprisingly sparse. McCarthy et al. (1977) examined the quality effects of board certification of surgeons by investigating the frequency of nonconfirmed recommendations for elective surgery based on second-opinion reviews. The rate of nonconfirmation does not differ significantly between board-certified surgeons and those without board certification in their sample, indicating that licensing has little effect on this aspect of quality. Benham (1972) reported some comparisons of the cost of filling a given prescription for eyeglasses in regulated and unregulated states, but his evidence must be regarded as anecdotal. Benham and Benham (1975) entered measures of the absence of regulatory control into their equation for the demand for eyeglasses. Although they estimated this equation for other purposes, one use of such a specification would be to test for quality improvements due to regulation. Better service might be expected to increase the demand for eyeglasses, in that a greater number of marginal cases would opt for glasses and people from adjacent jurisdictions would seek the higher quality available in the regulated state. On the other hand, because glasses are durable goods and because eyesight changes over time, better service might lead to glasses that provided acceptable correction for a longer period of time, thereby reducing the time rate of demand. Benham and Benham (1975) found that measures of the absence of regulatory controls, while not significant by conventional standards (t statistics of 1.2), all have positive signs—that is, demand at a given price is higher in states with less regulation. They also found that the price effects of regulation reduce sales by about one-third. Though these results argue against the possibility that quality effects due to regulation offset the price effects, they are not definitive; the greater sales in the absence of regulation could be lemons.

In the absence of additional studies of the actual effects of licensing in particular professions, the case against professional licensing remains scientifically unproved. On the other hand, for many occupations, serious skepticism continues to be warranted, especially where quality does not appear to be a condition of the license.

Conclusions on Environmental, Product-Quality, and Health Regulation

Research associated with issues of the environment, health, and product quality is, in a very real sense, the frontier of regulatory research. On a practical level, these are the areas in which regulatory efforts have expanded the most in recent years. On the theoretical level, an increasing amount of research effort has gone into evaluating the behavior of economic agents in regimes where information is costly or imperfect or where consumers may be misinformed about the attributes of the products they are purchasing. These efforts have served to identify a variety of situations in which some form of collective action appears to be appropriate or where changes in existing liability rules may be called for. The possible instruments for government intervention vary widely and include the collection and dissemination of information, the establishment of standards, the use of taxes or subsidies, and more reliance on producer liability. The particular instrument favored depends (not surprisingly) on the particular assumptions made in the theoretical work.

Empirical work directed toward identifying situations in which additional government intervention may be called for and toward evaluating existing regulatory efforts has made less progress. Some valiant efforts have been made to come to grips empirically with the costs and benefits of these forms of government regulation in certain industries; however, the data required for making a convincing case are extremely difficult to obtain from information on market transactions. In addition, the empirical work has not kept pace with theoretical developments to the extent that the particular types of market imperfections that regulation might be directed toward have not been adequately incorporated into the empirical analyses that seek to test whether the benefits of regulation outweigh the costs. The empirical difficulties are associated with the need to include price, quantity, *and* quality space. The relevant quality attributes are difficult to measure, and optimal price, quantity, and quality combinations are difficult to infer from market transactions if informational and perceptual imperfections contaminate unregulated-market transactions.

The existing theoretical and empirical work is not without value. Although research has not provided much information on whether regulation is appropriate, it has helped to answer the question whether, if some set of transactions are to be regulated in response to some perceived market imperfection, there are better and worse ways of going about it. In the noneconomic regulatory areas, the tools available to the economist appear to be better suited to identifying means for improving regulation than to arguing whether regulation should be imposed. The theoretical and empirical work done thus far is directly relevant to the former issue, as is much of the work by economists and other scholars on other regulatory agencies that attempts to identify the kinds of thing that administrative agencies do relatively well and those things that they do relatively poorly. Indeed, we advance the general proposition that far too much of the effort of economists has been directed toward asking whether there should or should not be regulation, and far too little effort directed at how to improve the performance of regulatory policies.

Theories of Regulation

The litany of possible market failures contained in the preceding sections constitutes a normative theory of regulation that had great appeal among economists until the 1960s, and still is often the beginning assumption of research on regulation. The essence of this normative analysis as a positive theory is that one begins an analysis of a regulatory process with the assumption that its purpose is to maximize some universal measure of economic welfare, such as consumers' surplus or total surplus.

As a positive theory of regulation, the normative theory of welfare economics is obviously incorrect. Economists have demonstrated that regulatory agencies make numerous decisions that reduce conventional measures of economic welfare. The reasons for the failure of the normative theory are two: First, individuals have objectives, such as guarantees of procedural fairness, constitutional freedoms, and pleasant human relations, that are affected by the actions of regulatory institutions but are not yet accounted for in applied welfare economics. Second, political agents are economic actors, as are producers and consumers, and they respond to incentives created by political institutions and administrative processes. For both reasons, a rational regulator would be unlikely to seek to maximize conventional measures of economic welfare.

General theories of regulation tend to be either legislative or bureaucratic, in that they select either the electoral process and the incentives operating on politicians or the bureaucratic process and the incentives operating on regulators as the focus of analysis. In the first category is the "Chicago School" of regulatory theory, the outstanding proponents of which are Stigler (1971), Posner (1971, 1974), and Peltzman (1976b). The essence of their theory is that regulation is a device for transfering income to well-organized groups if the groups will return the favor with votes and contributions to politicians. The theory predicts that regulators will use their power to transfer income from those with less political power to those with more. Precise *a priori* predictions of the direction of this income redistribution are impossible, because it depends on the costs and benefits of regulation as perceived by different interest groups and their ability to exercise their power in the political arena.

In a world with perfect information and self-interested voters, there is no natural reason why regulatory intervention is a majority-rule equilibrium (assuming preferences are distributed in such a way that such an equilibrium exists). In politics, organizations and contributions matter because they affect voter information and motivation; consequently, a legislative theory of regulation must have some theoretical connections to the electoral process. Once that connection is made, the door is opened to political entrepreneurs who seek power rather than economic payoff, and who pay the informational costs of communicating messages to the unorganized voters who are "done in" by the Chicago School regulator. This possiblity limits the extent to which regulation can impose costs on the general population, but does not completely offset it because the costs would have to exceed some minimum amount before voters could be induced to make them a primary motive for political participation.

Of the theories of regulation that focus on the agencies themselves, most also predict outcomes favorable to organized interests. Noll (1971) argued that the committee structure in Congress, the mechanism of judicial review, and the administrative process all favor well-organized interests. Arguing one's case in a congressional, regulatory, or judicial hearing is expensive, so organized groups that possess resources to expend in this manner can be expected to influence policies to the extent that the outcomes depend upon the information presented in these processes. Bernstein (1955) propounded a life-cycle theory of agencies in which they "age" from active advocates of generalized consumer interests to passive conduits of the interest of organized groups. Eckert (1972) proposed a more direct form of capture: that regulators expect to become employees of organized interests when their regulating days are over. The U.S. Senate Committee on Government Operations (1977), after examining data on employment histories of regulators, concluded that conflict of interest of this sort was enough of a problem to warrant proposing to prohibit employment of former regulators in regulated industries for one year after their terms expire.

Not all structural theories of regulation are pinned to interest-group aggregation. Michelman (1967) proposed that judicial processes, like administrative reviews, serve an important psychological function by giving people their "day in court." Williamson (1970) applied this general framework to price regulation. The argument is that normal market processes (because of the variability of market equilibrium) and governmental interventions to improve efficiency can cause arbitrary and capricious redistribution of income. Administrative processes are a mechanism for ameliorating these redistributions, but they are also processes for defusing destructive psychological responses to capricious redistribution. Through participation in administrative processes, people derive benefits through reduced demoralization should they have their say and still lose. The interesting, unique feature of this theory is that it attempts to incorporate noneconomic aspects of individual welfare into a theory of economic welfare, setting up the possibility of a tradeoff between economic efficiency and psychological well-being. The theory is not inconsistent, therefore, with theories emphasizing bureaucratic and procedural bias in favor of well-organized groups. The latter could be viewed as the cost of providing other forms of noneconomic benefits.

Because bureaucracies are created and supported by legislatures, a complete process theory of regulation must be connected to electoral politics. For theories oriented toward interest-group influence, the key issue is why legislators want to create regulatory institutions that are excessively oriented toward the welfare of well-organized groups. Thus, one way to view bureaucratic theories is as natural extensions of a legislative theory. Questions concerning the operation and organization of agencies would then no longer be central to the concern of the political economist, just as questions about the structure of a competitive firm are not very interesting to the economists who studies a perfectly competitive industry.

A second electoral connection, separated from a pure model of interest-group politics, was proposed by Fiorina and Noll (1978). They argued that a national legislature composed of representatives from single-member legislative districts creates a prisoner's dilemma for voters and legislators: A legislator becomes one of many voters on public-policy issues affecting the welfare of all voters, but is a monopolist in filling the role of an ombudsman for constituents (that is, in providing information about public activities and intervening informally in government processes by virtue of oversight activities on behalf of the home district). To be a good facilitator for constituents, the legislator must be in a position to reward helpful bureaucracies, and therefore must not be a consistent opponent of bureaucratic policy. A voter in a district can be in a prisoner's dilemma if the electoral choice is between an opponent of regulation and a proponent who is a good facilitator. The former, as one small voice in the legislature, is unlikely to effect a change in policy; hence, the payoff to the voter is greater if the proponent of an undesirable policy is elected because in that case, the voter will receive at least some return from the policy (though not enough to offset its cost).

The structure of the regulatory process assumes importance in this model, because it determines the extent to which the congressman/ombudsman can influence its outcome by informal interventions. Administrative law can be interpreted as an attempt to escape from the prisoner's dilemma—a set of formal procedural and evidentiary rules that limit the ability of a representative to convert regulation into porkbarrel, but that raise the costs of participating in the process.

General theories of regulation have two major conceptual difficulties. First, they are extremely difficult to separate from even more general positive theories of representative democracy. Regulation is typical of government policies in that regulatory actions affect both economic efficiency and the distribution of income, in that an important part of both effects is on some well-organized groups, and in that regulation is carried out by a bureaucracy according to the tenets of administrative law. General theories have not yet explained why politicians sometimes choose regulation but at other times choose other instruments of public policy to distribute the favors of a pluralistic democracy, nor why the inefficiencies of a regulatory bureaucracy differ from those of bureaucracy generally. The second problem is that the inherent inefficiencies of regulation that flow from these theories have no natural normative consequence, although one would not deduce this from the tone of the literature. That regulation fails to reach a Pareto optimum is fairly uninteresting if no institutions exist that can reach a point that Pareto-dominates regulation. For regulatory interventions that deal with empirically important market imperfections, the departure of regulatory equilibrium from perfect competition is not normatively compelling.

General theories of regulation face an empirical problem as well. The pluralist theories are built upon comparisons of the economic stakes, the degree of organization, and the resources of the interest groups, yet these variables have proved especially difficult to measure. Empirical tests of interest-group theories inevitably boil down to an estimate of the distribution of costs and benefits of an interventionist policy that is based on the departure of regulated equilibrium from perfect competition. Examples include the study of railroads by Spann and Erickson (1970) and Stigler's (1971) empirical tests of his initial statement of the Chicago School theory. The way in which these theories have evolved makes rejection of the null hypothesis virtually impossible, because the empirical information that is used to test the theory is also the information available to identify the successful interest groups. In the absence of any clear way to reject the hypotheses presented, the theories can easily become tautological. A nontautological test of interest-group theories would go one step farther, to correlate measures of the *ex ante* political influence of a group with its *ex post* net benefits from regulation. Moreover, it could use influence measures to explain the absence of regulation where that is the case.

Because of these conceptual and empirical problems, theories of regulation must still be accorded less than full scientific status. Social scientists have not yet shown convincingly that they understand what political purposes are served by regulation, why some industries are regulated and others are not, and why regulatory controls rather than other policy instruments are selected. Until answers to questions like these are forthcoming, the theory of regulation serves as a convenient way of organizing historical material, but not one that is particularly rich in predictive value.

Despite these reservations about the theory of regulation, this research has played an important role in shaping our conceptions of regulation. It reminds us of the impossibility of a free lunch. Curing a market failure by regulatory intervention generates costs as well as benefits because, owing to certain features of political and bureaucratic institutions, regulators cannot be expected to stop just at curing the market failure. General theories also raise issues that must be faced by those who would reform, rather than abolish, regulation. Presumably, only by asking fairly general questions about regulation can scholars ascertain what purposes regulation serves from the viewpoint of political and bureaucratic actors. Understanding these purposes is a prerequisite to predicting the effect on policy outcomes of a change in the instruments of policy.

Very little research is available on the comparative outcomes of different regulatory institutions. Scholars have expressed opinions about the importance of such issues as the size of a commission, the location of an agency in governmental hierarchy, the form of procedural and evidentiary rules, financial support for consumerist intervenors, and the subcommittee structure in which congressional oversight takes place; however, little scientific research on these issues has been undertaken. Consequently, political actors who seek to make regulation work better can find very little of interest in the scholarly literature either to show them how to reform the process or to convince them that nothing is really likely to improve matters. For those who believe that regulation is never appropriate the absence of comparative institutional analysis is hardly a loss, but to those who believe some regulation is desirable or simply inevitable the absence of guidelines on how to accomplish it most efficiently is an important void in scholarly research.

Promising Directions for Research

The preceding section summarized and evaluated four main lines of inquiry in the economics of administrative regulation. Certain lines of research have led to important results that provide a deeper understanding of the effects of regulation on firm and industry behavior and generate useful information for making public policy. Other lines of research have been less productive, and represent difficult conceptual and empirical challenges for economists. Because government regulation has become an increasingly important factor in our economy, and many important question remain to be answered, scholarly interest in regulatory economics will continue and even increase in the future.

Because it has been a theme of this article that the returns on the traditional theoretical and empirical tools used for analyzing government regulation are diminishing rapidly, we bear an obligation to discuss what we consider to be fruitful lines of future research. We do not intend to provide a comprehensive research agenda. The discussion reflects our own research interests, and focuses on work that would be responsive to the issues raised above.

Research on regulation has two potential values. One is purely scienti-/ fic: Research can increase knowledge about human behavior and institutions, even if it adds nothing to the ability of humans to control their destiny. The other is practical: Research can help political actors (voters, politicians, and bureaucrats) make decisions about public policy. Research on the economics of regulation generally falls more into the first category than into the second. Scholars have formulated reasons why society might decide to override markets, and considered the problems that society's agents may face in attempting to intervene, But, except for the literature on price regulation of competitive industries and peak-load pricing of public utilities, regulatory research has not contributed much to the debate about how to deal practically with the issues that give rise to a demand for regulation, or even whether in specific situations the issues are important enough to bother with. The one general, practical accomplishment of research on regulation is a healthy skepticism about the ability of regulatory agencies to deal easily and effectively with perceived market imperfections. At the very least, research on regulation has made life more difficult for anyone who suggests a regulatory initiative without carefully thinking through the problems that it might entail in practice. But scholars should be able to accomplish more than this.

The preceding remarks are not intended as an indictment of the research community, for the technical methods necessary to deal with practical regulatory problems are only now being developed. Economics as a predictive, empirical science is a very new and rapidly developing discipline. Political science, which we believe also to be relevant, is even less mature, as is the branch of psychology that deals with decisionmaking. Just as scholars of regulation made substantial breakthroughs a generation ago by applying standard neoclassical welfare economics and statistical methods for socioeconomic data to some issues of regulation, the next generation of regulatory research scholars may advance knowledge (especially practical knowledge) substantially by building on several developing areas of research in economics, in political science, and in psychology.

Information

The most fundamental theoretical problems in research on regulation concern making decisions with incomplete information. Among economic theorists, the decade of the 1970s was the era of the economics of information. Theorists have explored several nuances of two related questions: Given a state of knowledge about contingent events, what action will a rational decisionmaker take? How does a rational decisionmaker decide to stop acquiring more information, which is costly, and make a decision? Both these questions are central to an understanding of regulation. Much regulation is justified on informational grounds, and the very existence of administrative processes is testimony to the uncertainly that pervades regulatory decisionmaking. Consequently, the better the theory of decisionmaking under uncertainty, the better will be research on the rationale, process, and effectiveness of regulation.

Research on the economics of information has progressed since Stigler's path-breaking 1961 paper, but the literature still lacks general results. One major problem is that an optimal search procedure for gathering information has not yet been identified. Gastwirth (1976) showed that sequential-search strategies dominate optimal-sample-size strategies, but the results in sequential models depend upon the existence of a reservation price with which each sample price is compared. In search models it is not clear exactly where reservation prices come from, for buying is an occasional, discrete event (not a continuous rate of consumption, as in consumer theory). Several buying events can occur at different times and prices, and the frequency can be varied to alter time rates of consumption. Thus, there is no natural connection between purchase decisions and the reservation price associated with any particular rate of consumption. Moreover, "comparison shopping" is a nonsequential process, and consumers are known to use it, as Bettman (1977) pointed out. Once one admits nonsequential processes and assumes that consumers do not know in advance the distribution from which samples are being drawn, there is no foundation in preference theory for selecting any particular sampling process. In addition, as Wilde and Schwartz (1979) showed, in order for there to be a competitive equilibrium price in such a model some consumers must be willing to continue to search after they can capture no further gains from additional information—in other words, search must be consumption rather than investment.

Another source of difficulty in the literature on the economics of information is that the two behavioral foundations of the current theory of decisionmaking under uncertainty—expected utility maximization and Bayes's Rule—probably do not properly characterize actual decisionmaking. Grether and Plott (1979) showed that, in situations involving probabilistic risk, fully informed experimental subjects exhibit intransitive preferences, even when the stakes are quite high; Grether (1978) showed that in similar kinds of situations people do not update probability information according to Bayes's Rule. These two papers bring into serious doubt the basic assumptions of both search models and decision theory.

These findings are shocking to economists, but they are well established in experimental psychology. Mathematical psychologists have been attempting to construct a new approach to decision theory that is consistent with these findings since the early 1970s. The most interesting idea thus far—"elimination by aspects"—was proposed by Tversky (1972), who suggested that individuals solve decision problems involving uncertainty by first classifying a problem according to what appear to be its essential features, and then applying a general decision rule that, through experience, has proved effective in that particular category.

This model is similar to the model proposed by March and Simon (1959) in the context of organizational decisionmaking. March and Simon saw as the first step in organizational problem solving the "factoring" of problems into subelements, each given to a responsible individual to suboptimize, and viewed the ultimate decision as an integration of a series of partial solutions. The key feature of both the Tversky individual model and the March-Simon organizational model is the simplification of complex problems into something that is easier to solve but that does not necessarily produce optimal or even consistent results.

The implication of the Tversky hypothesis is that the solution that people will develop to problems involving incomplete information will depend upon the particular context in which the problem arises. One inference to be drawn from this hypothesis is that scholars should concentrate on developing a series of special theories dealing with different types of informational problems without being concerned about logical inconsistencies among the special theories. Thus, a model that describes individual behavior in the face of uncertainties about product quality may have little in common with a model that does a good job in describing job search in the absence of workplace risks, and the latter may have little in common with models that deal adequately with the response of employees to hazards in the workplace. A second inference is that if government intervenes to change the state of information in a substantial way, two effects need to be predicted: how the new information changes performance according to a particular decision rule, and how the new information might change the context of problem solving in a way that would cause individuals to change the decision rule that was applied to the particular situation.

Whether Tversky's hypothesis is ultimately correct or whether a general theory of decisionmaking with incomplete information eventually emerges, the implication for scholars of regulation is pretty much the same. No generally theory is in the offing, important policy issues are now being decided on the basis of presumptions about the role of information in economic decisions, and special theories appear promising in the short run. A special theory of product choice with incomplete information and government regulation would be especially important in this context. Either this or a model of labor-market search (with wages, not hazards, the source of uncertainty) is likely to be the first practical problem in the economics of information to be solved. Substantial information already exists in marketing research on how consumers respond to various kinds of information; product-market-search models are proliferating. The next major step will be to incorporate formal characterizations of regulatory interventions into these search models and to devise methods for empirical tests of the theories.

Dynamics

Another major void in economics that has potentially important implications for the study of regulation is the theory of disequilibrium price dynamics (how fast a disequilibrated market returns to equilibrium, and the path of disequilibrium transactions as equilibrium is approached). Alternative market organizations are inevitably compared in terms of their equilibrium properties. This procedure makes sense if markets spend most of their time on an equilibrium price path; however, if random, exogenous events regularly cause supply-and-demand relations to shift in ways that can only be known in a statistical sense by economic agents, price dynamics can be an important element in determining the efficiency and distributional consequences of a market.

Arrow and Capron (1959) developed a simple theory of disequilibrium price paths when demand is shifting outward. With either a linear Walrasian adjustment process or adaptive expectations, the predicted disequilibrium path of transactions traces a price line that rises at a constant rate that never reaches market equilibrium, and that approaches a constant, limiting proportion of excess demand. V. Smith (1964) tested the theory in an experimental setting in which participants received monetary payoffs that were designed to induce normal market incentives, and found that the three predictions of the theory were not borne out by the results.

One source of the incompleteness of current theory is that the price-dynamics problem involves the formulation of expectations and the consummation of transactions that are based upon uncertain information, which places the problem in the unsettled realm of information economics. But V. Smith (1976) showed that out-of-equilibrium transactions persist in an experimental situation designed to represent perfect competition (one where only buyers reap surplus from market transactions and all actors know the reservation prices of everyone else). Smith hypothesized that when sellers can obtain no surplus, interpersonal comparisons of utility that would otherwise be suppressed begin to enter selling decisions, causing buyers to begin to offer inframarginal prices that differ from equilibrium according to the extent to which they are less favored by sellers.

The importance of this work to scholars of regulation is that different market rules produce different amounts and flows of information among participants in the market, and this, in turn, can affect the pattern of disequilibrium transactions. The key issue is whether a particular method of exchanging price/quantity offers among buyers and sellers allows, in disequilibrium, one side of the market to capture rents from participants on the other side who happen to have relatively intense preference—that is, who stand to capture a large surplus in equilibrium. Institutions that cause disequilibrium price paths to approach equilibrium systematically from a particular direction or that prolong the period of disequilibrium transactions when the price path is biased will alter the distribution of the surplus that the market generates. Moreover, if random shocks occur frequently enough so that equilibrium is only approached but never reached, institutions that slow the adjustment process also reduce the efficiency of the market. The efficiency loss arises because, if equilibrium is never reached, the exchange institution affects the price of all units, not just inframarginal ones, and therefore affects expectations about prices and hence consumption and production plans.

Price regulation has two features that ought to be analyzed in terms of their effects on price dynamics. First, a formal regulatory proceeding in which prices can be adjusted in one or both directions only after a formal review leads to disequilibrium transactions that are stuck at the old equilibrium. In periods when nominal costs are falling, "regulatory lag" and entry controls can produce rents even in a competitive environment by prolonging disequilibrium prices. Second, the nondiscrimination requirements of price regulation eliminate any vestige of an auction process from the market. Presumably, the free exchange of disequilibrium offers adds to the richness of information in a disequilibrated market and speeds the adjustment process, although this conjecture is yet to be proved. If so, the requirement to serve all comers at a posted price, even if the regulated price only binds from above, slows downward price adjustments from the old equilibrium.

Whether price dynamics will be proved to be an important element of market performance remains an open question, but in principle the effect of regulation on price dynamics may create a whole new set of economic and political explanations for regulatory interventions. The economics literature has dealt with intertemporal instability, particularly in agriculture, as a cause for a policy intervention that is designed to stabilize prices. Oi (1961), Massell (1969), and Turnovsky (1976), among others, have analyzed the effects on consumers' or total surplus of being guaranteed an average equilibrium price compared with taking random draws each period from a distribution of equilibrium prices. Although these models deal only with comparisons of equilibrium, their premise is precisely that necessary to make price dynamics a potentially important concern. The obvious next step in this literature is to look at additional features of market performance that arise from the effects of intervention on the number and path of disequilibrium transactions.

As suggested above, price dynamics also may prove important in another area of regulatory policy that has assumed greater importance as deregulation of some industries has become more likely: transition from a regulated to a deregulated state. The case here is a little weaker than the argument for considering price dynamics when supply-and-demand relations are uncertain; if firms know demand relations with certainty and all have the same costs in any given market, prices can be expected to follow the short-run marginal cost curve. But if firms are not certain of the position of the demand curve in the range of the new short-run equilibrium, and if firms have different short-run marginal-cost curves and know with certainty only their own costs, a trial-and-error period of disequilibrium price changes can be expected. Although a period of disequilibrium is unlikely to have consequences so monumental that it alters the case for deregulation, a price path that is substantially at odds with that predicted by economists on the basis of long-run equilibrium analysis could scare politicians, already edgy about the consequences of deregulation, into aborting an experiment with competition. In fact, one such event has already occurred: In Massachusetts, deregulation of automobile insurance was terminated after a few months because the short-run effect was not beneficial to some consumers.

Congressional Regulatory Politics
Like all other public policies, regulation is created and nurtured by Congress. Systematic studies of the influence of Congress on regulatory policies, which remain to be undertaken, may prove important because they may contribute to our understanding of the extent to which the inefficiencies of regulation are endemic to its political environment and because they may uncover important insights about the use of congressional reforms to produce better regulation. In the latter vein, economists are among the most outspoken proponents of "sunset laws" (which force reenactment of regulatory statutes after some fixed amount of time), "sunshine laws" (which require more openness in regulatory proceedings), and mandatory benefit-cost analyses of proposed regulations (such as the Inflationary Impact Statements the Office of Management and Budget and the Council on Wage and Price Stability began requiring for certain regulatory decisions in the mid-1970s). Sunset laws force periodic congressional review of regulatory policy, while sunshine laws and mandatory benefit-cost analysis provide Congress with more information with which to evaluate regulation. In a similar way, the nature of congressional oversight of regulatory agencies might be altered by rearranging the subcommittee structure of Congress, or by instituting direct congressional responsibility for regulatory policy decisions through such means as the proposed one-house veto.

The consequences of these reforms depend upon the likely behavior of members of Congress should the nature and process of congressional oversight be altered. At present the research literature provides little insight into this issue. In general, congressional behavior appears to be purposeful and predictable. Shepsle (1978) showed that the process by which congressmen are assigned to committees is nearly perfect in matching assignments to preferences—even to the point that, when excess demand develops for assignment to a particular committee, the tendency is to expand the committee until a new equilibrium is reached. The implication is that legislative overseers of regulatory policy are overseers by choice, a choice that presumably reflects their perceptions about what matters to their reelectability. Ferejohn (1974) provided one link between committee membership and reelection strategies by hypothesizing that oversight is used to reward the districts that are represented on the oversight committees, and demonstrated that the distribution of the benefits of one program (river and harbors projects) corresponds to the theory.

How the reelectability of a legislator depends upon his regulatory oversight activities remains unknown. All that is known at present is that oversight committees generally do attempt to influence regulatory policy at a fairly detailed level. Weingast (1977) argued that the mechanism of control is the relative distribution of the budget of an agency among functional categories of expenditures, and related historical changes in regulatory activities within several agencies to these distributional changes. He also found that, while Congress is likely to allocate a total budget that is roughly in line with proposals from the agency and the executive-branch budgeters, its allocations among functional categories (particularly in times of changes in regulatory policy) are likely to be substantially different from those proposed. For example, the mechanisms for making a regulatory agency the captive of the regulated industry appears to be to reduce its analytical resources relative to its legislative responsibilities and enforcement capabilities, thus making it more dependent on outside information for decisions but more capable of enforcing compliance with the decisions it makes.

Several important questions about congressional influence on regulatory policy remain to be addressed. One is the connection between the interests of a legislator (presumably, reelection) and his oversight activities: Exactly what stake does a legislator have in overseeing regulatory policy? Anecdotes about Lyndon Johnson's television station in Austin, Texas, and about the "Staggers Special" (a highly unprofitable commuter train between Washington, D.C. and the home district of Congressman Harley Staggers in West Virginia) should be replaced by systematic, quantitative studies of the deliverable currency of regulatory policy.

Another type of study would assess the importance of certain structural features of regulation and oversight. Some subcommittees oversee a single agency whereas others are responsible for several, and among the latter some of the agencies overseen are branches of executive departments whereas others are independent. Do any of these structural features alter the nature of regulatory policy and the payoffs of legislative overseers?

Systematic, quantitative studies of the role of Congress in shaping regulatory policy, based on goal-oriented models of the behavior of politicians, are probably more important to those who would reform regulation than to those who would eliminate it. However, would-be deregulators could find them useful as well. The reason is that regulatory reform of any kind must have the assent of Congress—if not explicitly through legislation, then indirectly through an acceptance of change in appointments and policies in agencies. Reformers are more likely to succeed if the changes they propose do not threaten the interests of the legislators who would oversee the reform. At present, the literature on Congress and on the economics and politics of regulation provides only the bare beginnings of an understanding of how, if at all, this can be accomplished.

The Behavior of Regulatory Commissions

To understand the effects of regulation or to pursue regulatory reform requires not only a better understanding of the relationship between legislators and regulators, but also a better understanding of how the regulatory process itself works.

Most regulatory institutions are established under rather imprecise statutes prescribing authorities, organizational structure, and particular policy instruments. A mandate for a regulatory commission to ensure that rates be "just, reasonable, and nondiscriminatory" does not give much guidance, nor does it detail the procedures the commission should follow in arriving at decisions once some kind of operational meaning is given to the statutory mandates. Once a regulatory organization is established, it develops behavioral patterns and a dynamic of its own that are constrained by Congress, but not completely. The political and economic circumstances that led the legislature to establish the regulatory authority may have very different effects on the actual regulatory organization. Perhaps more important is the possibility that the political, economic, and underlying legal environment may change, in part from forces not subject to the control of the regulatory authority and in part from endogenous political and economic consequences of regulation itself which result from the effects of regulation on the behavior and performance of the regulated industry.

In reality, regulatory commissions have objectives, motivations, and responsibilities far more complex than "setting price equal to marginal cost subject to a profit constraint" or "maximizing the present worth of the incomes of commissioners." In addition, many regulatory commissions are complex organizations. There are regulatory commissioners, who may be appointed or elected and whose terms of office may or may not be coterminous with that of executive, and also a Civil Service staff, including attorneys, accountants, engineers, and other administrative personnel. As in any complex organization or bureaucracy, individuals and groups within the commission have differing conceptions of what they should be doing and what their contribution to the output of the organization is or should be. In addition, regulatory commissions are intimately related to the state and federal judicial systems. Procedures for making decisions on such things as the price of a kilowatt-hour of electricity, the siting of a pipeline, or the location and structural characteristics of a nuclear power plant must be consistent with statutory requirements as interpreted by the courts and must also adhere to complex and changing due-process requirements (Stewart 1975). Regulatory commissions cannot adopt just any procedures they might choose, but are constrained by court-enforced constitutional due-process requirements as well as by the current legislation. To say that the decision of a regulatory commission leads to some inefficiency in a narrow economic sense is not to say very much, unless one considers the constraints of equity, justice, and due process within which decisions must be made. American regulatory procedures and behavior increasingly reflect requirements that the process by which decisions are made be "fair" not only to the regulated firm, but to other concerned parties as well. Stewart (1975) indicated that administrative law has moved steadily away from recognizing the rights of property interests to a more expansive conception of balancing the interests of many different groups affected directly or indirectly by regulatory commission actions.

Complex organizations are often thought to behave according to an internal logic. Organizations do not act independently of the economic environment, but develop stable behavioral patterns to process information and to perform actions, at least in the short run. Organizations such as firms, government agencies, and regulatory commissions develop these decisionmaking rules along with and according to their own concepts of the environment in which they operate. They perceive the environment as having a particular structure, which includes a notion of who the relevant economic actors are, how they behave in response to various stimuli, and how they relate to one another. In addition to the fact that the organizations possess decision rules for processing information, their perception of the structure of the world (or that of its constituent parts) determines what information is observed and processed. For all intents and purposes, the organization's perceptions constitute the reality in which it operates. The structure of the environment that the organization perceives may be quite different from the objective reality; however, this structure or model of the economic and political environment works from the viewpoint of the organization, in that it consistently explains the behavior with which the organization is concerned.

In the longer run, many students of organizations view organizational structure and behavior as adaptive, responding (often slowly) to changes in the external environment in which the organization operates as short-run decision rules no longer seem to work satisfactorily (March and Simon 1959, pp. 168–170; Cyert and March 1963). Decision rules must often change over time, and so must the structural concept of the environment. If decision rules are not easily modified in the context of the organization's perception of the structure of the world, serious adaptive problems can arise. A new concept of the world may arise, leading to a new set of decision rules that are consistent with it. Alternatively, the organization could become dysfunctional if it does not possess the capability to deal effectively with changed circumstances in the real environment.

As Allison (1972) demonstrated nicely, the "conceptual window" through which we view organizations (in particular, bureaucracies) has critical implications for our ability to predict behavior, especially behavior that is not routine. Work by Niskanan (1971) and Downs (1967) dealing with government bureaucracies argues persuasively that the complex patterns of goals and behavior characteristic of government organizations make it extremely difficult to predict the outcomes of such processes by merely looking at the motivating forces behind their initial establishment. Thus, even if one variant of the "market failure" or "capture" theory correctly captures the *raison d'être* for the establishment of regulatory commisions, these theories may not be particularly useful for understanding the behavior of such agencies over time. In addition, the pluralistic character of much regulation in the United States, which involves overlapping and often ambiguous jurisdictions among different regulatory agencies and between regulatory agencies and the judicial, executive, and legislative branches, seems to require a more expansive concept of regulatory processes that would include more of an emphasis on the regulatory tasks and goals with respect to a particular regulated industry, how they are transformed into regulatory procedures, and how they change over time.

Extensive attempts at modeling the behavior of regulatory agencies and regulatory processes have not as yet been forthcoming. Joskow (1972) examined the behavior of the New York State Public Service

Commission with regard to the process of setting the allowed rates of return in formal regulatory proceedings. He found the commission's behavior to be stable and predictable, but uncovered some adaptive behavior in response to problems engendered by rapid inflation. In a more general study of state public-utility regulation, Joskow (1974) presented a model of a passive state regulatory agency whose behavior adapts to pressures from the economic and political environment in which it operates, and showed how rapid inflation and the recognition of environmental groups as intervenors in administrative proceedings change the behavior of the commission and the results of the regulatory process. This study emphasizes the relationship among commission tasks, the economic performance of the regulated firms, and specific regulatory procedures.

Joskow (1973a) also pointed to another important aspect of regulatory behavior that has often been overlooked in analyses of the effects of government regulation on industry behavior and performance. Much of what is known about what regulators do comes from hearings, court cases, commission opinions (MacAvoy 1971), and the statutes authorizing the regulation. These documents and the process they describe represent the *formal regulatory process*, that is, the documented legal process open for public inspection. It represents the occasional contacts between the regulators and the firms they regulate in formal regulatory or court procedures. Joskow 1973a documents the importance of the *informal regulatory process* (the day-to-day contacts between the agency and the firms). This process may involve discrete prior consultation between the firms and the agency regarding the size or timing of a proposed rate increase or the site for a proposed power plant, and may also include moral suasion regarding such matters as service quality or executive salaries. This paper by Joskow points to the price reductions filed by many New York State electric utilities during the 1960s—in the absence of formal regulatory reviews or other overt legal acts by the regulatory commissions—as the result of moral suasion and behind-the-scenes bargaining between the staffs of the commissions and the firms concerned. This informal regulatory process represents an attempt to short-circuit many of the time-consuming due-process procedures of American regulatory institutions. Commissions view such ongoing informal activities as being necessary if they are to perform their tasks efficiently. Commission staffs seem to believe that many of the formal legal procedures waste time without altering any of the final outcomes, and that the informal regulatory process is in the public interest. Without making any normative judgment with respect to the desirability of informal regulatory processes, it must be said that in many cases they are extremely important for understanding both agency behavior and the behavior and performance of regulated firms.

Viewing regulatory commissions as organizations and concentrating on the process of regulatory decisionmaking gives useful insights into what is actually happening. The attempts to model and understand regulation from this perspective often give researchers a more complete static and dynamic structural model of regulation rather than just a reduced form. For those interested in incremental policy reform within the context of prevailing institutions as well as exploring possible institutional alternatives, such structural models are extremely useful for positive policy analysis.

Experiments
The above discussion of unsolved problems in the economics of information and in disequilibrium price dynamics referred to several studies that used small-group experiments to generate data and test hypotheses in these areas. Experimental methods have also been used to study voting behavior, and have provided tests of theoretical propositions in social choice theory, spatial models of political choice, and game theory.

Experimental methods are rarely used in economics and political science; indeed, among the social sciences, only psychology contains a well-developed subfield of experimental methods. In economics, field experiments have been used rather extensively by government to test such institutional innovations in social policy as the negative income tax, school and health-insurance voucher systems, and peak-load pricing of electricity. The advantage of field experiments is that they provide a mechanism to test a major change in policy without imposing a major financial or political risk on the government and without risking the welfare of an entire target population. The disadvantages of field experiments are that they are very expensive and not completely controllable. Consequently, field experiments are bound to be controversial in both execution and results, even though they can produce better information than can analysis of conventional socioeconomic data.

Except for peak-load-pricing experiments, the government has not taken full advantage of using large-scale field experiments to test changes in regulatory policies. Reform, relaxation, and even repeal of regulatory constraints have become more popular in the past few years, but actual policy change is often held up because of uncertainties about the transition problem or fears that expectations about the effects of a change in policy might be incorrect. A potentially useful intermediate stage in the process of changing regulatory policy that could overcome these problems is a series of field experiments, designed and evaluated by economists, to test new and less restrictive forms of regulation. For example, the FCC might deregulate cable television in a few markets, offering compensation (should it prove necessary) to local broadcasters if their stations became economically unviable; or a large city might deregulate taxi service in one section of town; or a state regulatory commission might select a few telephone exchanges in which to experiment with a new form of usage-sensitive pricing of telecommunications services. These and numerous other possibilities might serve an important political function in reforming regulation, as well as providing exciting research opportunities for the economists who would be involved in them.

Except in the case of field experiments, economists normally rely on others (government, firms, etc.) to collect and to aggregate their data. This limits the scope of research in numerous ways: Data are often thoroughly contaminated; all of the economic influences that produce the observed results cannot be measured or controlled for purposes of estimating partial effects, and certain types of questions cannot be asked or must be examined indirectly because the most relevant data are not collected.

Laboratory experiments provide an opportunity to control a decision-making environment so that the researcher can generate the kinds of data that are most closely related to the behavioral hypothesis to be tested. V. Smith (1977) detailed the precepts of useful labortory experiments. One is the notion of induced preferences: The experimenter can finesse much of the problem of differences in tastes among subjects by building strong monetary incentives into the experiment. Another is the idea of parallelism: An experiment should contain all of the potentially important structural features of a real-world decisionmaking institution.

Faithful adherence to these and other precepts of good experimental design are difficult to follow, and a potential entrant into this domain of research can expect to experience considerable frustration in discovering the pitfalls of laboratory experimentation. Nevertheless, the potential payoffs are considerable. First, laboratory experiments permit generation of data that are not observable if one is restricted to the records of real-world market transactions. Bargains and rejected offers can be observed, and the experimenter can determine the amount of information, the risk distribution, and the possible gains from trade facing each participant.

The richer scope of available data and the controllability of factors that are normally unmeasurable in real transactions expands the range of testable hypotheses. Second, laboratory experiments allow the researcher to test the comparative efficiency of institutional arrangements, including arrangements that do not exist in the real world, with other influences held constant. This can have great practical importance to decisionmakers because it allows them to gather information about a proposed institutional change, much as field experiments do, but with greater controllability and lower cost.

Several examples of the second use of experiments have emerged. V. Smith (1977) reported a series of auction experiments that pretested a mechanism that was later adopted by a major corporation and by the French government for marketing bonds. Ferejohn et al. (1979) used experimental procedures to pretest for the Public Broadcasting Service some proposed changes in the mechanism used to acquire television programs. Hong and Plott (1977) used experiments to provide the Department of Transportation with an evaluation of proposed changes in the rules of the Interstate Commerce Commission with regard to the advance posting of price changes in the barge industry.

Experimental methods could provide important new information in several areas. They could be used to generate information and to test hypotheses concerning individual behavior with incomplete information (experiments have already begun to bear fruit in this area). Another is in testing regulatory interventions that are designed to change the amount and type of information that is available to participants in a market. Another is to extend V. Smith's pioneering efforts to compare the performance of different forms of market institutions according to the type and form of communication that is allowed among buyers and sellers. Still another is to test alternative mechanism for dealing with external effects, an issue that Plott (1977) explored in a preliminary fashion. The list goes on; we recommend V. Smith's intriguing 1977 survey as a more complete and very interesting defense of the forecast of an important role for experimental methods in applied economics.

Extensions of Traditional Lines of Research

Having presented some perspectives on possible lines of future research that counsel economists to work on the frontiers of microeconomic theory, economic models of political behavior, organization theory, experimental methods, and even some parts of psychology, we hasten to add that more traditional lines of research can still bear fruit. Certainly, there remain many opportunities for interesting research in the vein of studies discussed in the first section above. We will expand on some of these opportunities here.

Numerous regulated industries (particularly those regulated by state and local governments) have not been studied empirically at all. One potentially important area for regulatory research is the medical-care sector, which consumes nearly 10 percent of the GNP. Since 1970, nearly all of the states have begun to regulate some aspect of the delivery of health care services (usually, prices and/or entry in the hospital industry). Because hospitals have local markets, and because the timing and form of regulation differ among the states, opportunities abound for examining the effects of various types of regulatory rules and the overall effect of regulation. Moreover, because the move toward regulation is recent, scholars have better and more reliable sources of information on the political economy of regulation: the motives and behavior of political actors in setting up these institutions. A thorough, comparative study of hospital regulation in the United States would be a major contribution to the literature.

We anticipate substantial new studies that will evaluate the effects of safety regulation more thoroughly than anything that can be found now in the literature. The form this research will take is extensive studies of the regulation of a particular hazard, like Peltzman's (1976) study of automobile safety. Most of the data for these analyses are available from governmental agencies; the NEISS data from the Consumer Product Safety Commission are one example. Added comprehensiveness will be achieved by attempts to account for the effects of regulation in more sophisticated, multiple-equation models of demand and costs in the regulated industry. We doubt, however, that econometric techniques will be refined enough to succeed in generating uncontroversial conclusions about the magnitudes of the effects of these regulations.

Substantial research opportunities using traditional theoretical and empirical techniques remain in agriculture and in such areas of the financial sector as banking, insurance, and securities. These sectors have largely been ignored by regulatory economists, and are ripe for additional research. Contrary to the elementary textbook concept, agriculture is subject to a wide variety of price, production, and entry regulations for specific commodities. In addition, the administration of these regulations appears to be considerably different from that which characterizes traditional regulatory commissions. In financial markets, differences in regulation across states make comparative analysis possible. Recent changes in banking regulation (such as the allowance of interest payments on demand deposits) are worthy of further study, as are the effects of open competition in the property- and liability-insurance markets and the elimination of fixed minimum commissions in the securities industry. Similarly, as more states relax restrictions on advertising by professional groups and ease entry requirements, additional information should be available to assess the effects of professional licensure and other restrictions on competition in service industries.

Most of the empirical literature on regulation focuses entirely on U.S. industries. Little effort has been made to exploit available data on the costs, prices, quality, and rate of technological change in the same industries in other developed countries. In much the same way as comparisons between publicly and privately owned electric utilities in the U.S. have sought to expand our understanding of the effects of government regulation, comparisons across countries may provide an opportunity to evaluate a more diverse menu of institutional alternatives.

Finally, the tendency of existing empirical work to focus on questions of aggregate economic efficiency has caused the distributional consequences of regulatory policy to be largely ignored. This is quite surprising in light of the fact that all theories of regulation indicate that the distribution of the costs and benefits of regulation are important. As a result, economists have had relatively little to say about a set of issues that are of considerable concern to legislators, regulators, and the public. In much the same way as economists who study taxation have examined the distributional consequences of various tax schemes, regulatory economists could obtain similar types of research results from existing data. Such analyses do not require that scholars identify the "right" income distribution, but will allow us to provide information that will be useful in understanding regulation itself and in explicating the consequences of regulatory reforms. Virtually every industry that has been the subject of regulatory research is a candidate for further work directed at identifying the distributional consequences of existing regulatory policies and regulatory reform proposals.

Conclusion

The past twenty years has been a watershed for the study of government regulation by economists. Modern theoretical and empirical techniques have been brought to bear on the effects of government regulation in a wide range of industries. Although useful incremental additions to knowledge in the traditional areas of government regulation are likely to be forthcoming through traditional analytical techniques, it is our belief that the greatest opportunities lie in areas in which the traditional modes of theoretical and empirical analysis are not likely to be as productive as they have been in the past. The future direction for research that we envision involves the utilization of new theoretical and empirical techniques and a change in emphasis. With regard to techniques, we see information economics, disequilibrium price dynamics, models of political and organizational processes, and the use of large- and small-scale experiments as playing important roles in regulatory research. With regard to emphasis, we see further analyses of the incidence of government regulation (rather than its global-efficiency properties) and an effort to understand how regulation can be made to perform a wide variety of tasks better (rather than whether these tasks are legitimate or not) as targets of opportunity. Furthermore, we see these new directions not as independent of, or replacements for, the important research that has already been done, but as serving to build upon and expand what is already known. However, we do believe that economists know a lot less about government regulation than is sometimes thought, and that a large amount of important research remains to be done.

Professor Joskow acknowledges support from a grant by the Sloan Foundation to the Department of Economics at MIT. Professor Noll gratefully acknowledges support from National Science Foundation grant APR75-16566.

References

Acton, J. P., and Mitchell, B. M. 1977. Peak-Load Pricing in Selected European Electric Utilities. Rand Corp. report R-2031-DWP.

Allison, Graham. 1972. *Essence of Decision: Explaining the Cuban Missile Crisis.* New York: Little, Brown.

Arrow, Kenneth. 1963. "Uncertainty and the Welfare Economics of Medical Care." *American Economic Review* 53: 941–973.

————. 1970. "The Organization of Economic Activity: Issues Pertinent to the Choice of Market Versus Nonmarket Allocation." In R. Haveman and J. Margolis (eds.), *Public Expenditure and Policy Analysis* (Chicago: Rand-McNally), pp. 67–81.

Arrow, K. J., and Capron, W. M. 1959. "Dynamic Shortages and Price Rises: The Engineer-Scientist Case." *Quarterly Journal of Economics* 73: 292–308.

Averch, Harvey, and Johnson, Leland. 1962. "Behavior of the Firm under Regulatory Constraint." *American Economic Review* 52: 1052–1069.

Ayres, R. V., and Kneese, A. V. 1969. "Production, Consumption and Externalities." *American Economic Review* 59: 282–297.

Bailey, Elizabeth. 1973. *Economic Theory of Regulatory Constraint*. Lexington, Mass.: Lexington Books.

Bailey, Elizabeth, and Coleman, Roger D. 1971. "The Effect of Lagged Regulation in the Averch-Johnson Model." *Bell Journal of Economics and Management Science* 2: 278–292.

Bailey, Elizabeth, and Malone, John C. 1970. "Resource Allocation and the Regulated Firm." *Bell Journal of Economics and Management Science* 1: 129–142.

Balasko, Y. 1974. On Designing Public Utilities Tariffs with Application to Electricity. Electricité de France manuscript.

Baumol, William J., and Braunstein, Y. M. 1977. "Empirical Study of Scale Economies and Production Complementarity: The Case of Journal Publication." *Journal of Political Economy* 85: 1037–1048.

Baumol, William J., and Oates, W. E. 1971. "The Use of Standards and Pricing for the Protection of the Environment." *Swedish Journal of Economics* 73: 42–54.

Baumol, William J., and Quandt, R. E. 1964. "Rules of Thumb and Optimally Imperfect Decisions." *American Economic Review* 56: 23–41.

Baumol, William J., Bailey, E. E., and Willig, R. D. 1977. "Weak Invisible Hand Theorems on Pricing and Entry in a Multiproduct Natural Monopoly." *American Economic Review* 67: 350–365.

Benham, Lee. 1972. "The Effect of Advertising on the Price of Eyeglasses." *Journal of Law and Economics* 15: 337–352.

Benham, Lee, and Benham, Alexandra. 1975. "Regulating Through the Professions: A Perspective on Information Control." *Journal of Law and Economics* 18:427–428.

Bernstein, Marver H. 1955. *Regulating Business by Independent Commission*. Princeton, N. J.: Princeton University Press.

Bettman, J. 1977. Consumer Information Acquisition and Search Strategies. Mimeographed. University of California at Los Angeles.

Boiteux, M. 1951. "La tarification au coût marginal et les demands aléatoires." *Cahiers du Séminaire d'Econométrie* no. 1: 56–69.

———. 1960. "Peak-Load Pricing." *Journal of Business* 33: 157–179.

Boyer, K. D. 1977. "Minimum Rate Regulation, Modal Split Sensitivities and the Railroad Problem." *Journal of Political Economy* 85: 493–512.

Boyes, William J. 1976. "An Empirical Examination of the Averch-Johnson Effect." *Economic Inquiry* 14: 25–35.

Burness, H. Stuart, Montgomery, W. David, and Quirk, James P. 1980. "Capital Contracting and the Regulated Firms." *American Economic Review* 70: 342–354.

Caves, Richard. 1962. *Air Transport and its Regulators: An Industry Study*. Cambridge, Mass.: Harvard University Press.

Coase, Ronald. 1960. "The Problem of Social Cost." *Journal of Law and Economics* 3: 1–44.

Colantoni, C. S., Davis, O. A., and Swaminuthan, M. 1976. "Imperfect Consumers and Welfare Comparisons of Policies Concerning Information and Regulation." *Bell Journal of Economics* 7: 602–615.

Cornell, Nina W., Noll, Roger G., and Weingast, Barry. 1976. "Safety Regulation." In H. Owen and C. L. Schultze (eds.), *Setting National Priorities: The Next Ten years* (Washington, D.C.: Brookings Institution), pp. 457–504.

Courville, Leon. 1974. "Regulation and Efficiency in the Electric Utility Industry." *Bell Journal of Economics and Management Science* 5: 53–74.

Crew, M. A., and Kleindorfer, P. R. 1976. "Peak Load Pricing with a Diverse Technology." *Bell Journal of Economics* 7: 207–231.

Cyert, Richard, and March, James. 1963. *A Behavioral Theory of the Firm.* Englewood Cliffs, N.J.: Prentice-Hall.

Dales, J. H. 1968. *Pollution, Property and Prices.* University of Toronto Press.

Davis, O. A., and Kamien, M. I. 1970. "Externalities, Information and Alternative Collective Action." In R. Haverman and J. Margolis (eds.), *Public Expenditure and Policy Analysis* (Chicago: Rand-McNally), pp. 82–104.

Davis, O. A., and Whinston, A. 1962. "Externalities, Welfare, and the Theory of Games." *Journal of Political Economy* 70: 241–262.

Demsetz, Harold. 1968. "Why Regulate Utilities?" *Journal of Law and Economics* 11: 55–66.

DeVany, A. S. 1974. "The Revealed Value of Time in Air Travel." *Review of Economics and Statistics* 56: 77–82.

Douglas, George, and Miller, James III. 1974. *Economic Regulation of Domestic Air Transport.* Washington, D.C.: Brookings Institution.

Downs, Anthony. 1967. *Inside Bureaucracy.* Boston: Little, Brown.

Dreze, J. 1964. "Some Postwar Contributions of French Economists to Theory and Public Policy." *American Economic Review* 54: 4–64.

Eads, George C. 1972. *The Local Service Airline Experiment.* Washington, D.C.: Brookings Institution.

————. 1975. "Competition in the Domestic Trunk Airline Industry: Too Much or Too Little?" In Almarin Phillips (ed.), *Promoting Competition in Regulated Markets* (Washington, D.C.: Brookings Institution), pp. 13–54.

Eckert, Ross D. 1972. "Spectrum Allocation and Regulatory Incentives." In *Conference on Communications Policy Research: Papers and Proceedings* (Washington, D.C.: Office of Telecommunications Policy).

Faulhaber, G. R. 1975. "Cross-Subsidization: Pricing in Public Enterprise." *American Economic Review* 65: 966–977.

Ferejohn, John A. 1974. *Pork Barrel Politics.* Stanford, Calif.: Stanford University Press.

Ferejohn, John A. Forsythe, Robert E., and Noll, Roger G. 1979. "An Experimental Analysis of Decisionmaking Procedures for Discrete Public Goods: A Case Study of a Problem in Institutional Design." In Vernon L. Smith (ed.), *Researches in Experimental Economics* (Greenwich, Conn.: JAI), vol. 1, pp. 1–58.

Fiorina, Morris P., and Noll, Roger G. 1978. "Voters, Bureaucrats and Legislators: A Rational Choice Perspective on the Growth of Bureaucracy." *Journal of Public Economics* 9: 239–254.

Friedlaender, Anne. 1969. *The Dilemma of Freight Transport Regulation.* Washington, D.C.: Brookings Institution.

Gastwirth, J. 1976. "On Probabilistic Models of Consumer Search for Information." *Quarterly Journal of Economics* 90: 38–50.

Gellman, Aaron J. 1971. "Surface Freight Transportation." In William M. Capron (ed.), *Technological Change in Regulated Industries* (Washington, D.C.: Brookings Institution), pp. 166–196.

Goldberg, V. P. 1976. "Regulation and Administered Contracts." *Bell Journal of Economics* 7: 426–448.

Grabowski, H. G., and Vernon, J. M. 1976. "Structural Effects of Regulation in the Drug Industry." In R. T. Masson and P. Qualls (eds.), *Essays in Industrial Organization: In Honor of Joe S. Bain* (Cambridge, Mass.: Ballinger), pp. 181–205.

Grether, David M. 1978. "Recent Psychological Studies of Behavior Under Uncertainty." *American Economic Review, Papers and Proceedings* 68: 70–74.

Grether, David M., and Plott, Charles R. 1979. "Economic Theory of Choice and the Preference Reversal Phenomenon." *American Economic Review* 69: 623–638.

Groves, T., and Ledyard, J. 1977. "Optimal Allocation of Public Goods: A Solution to the 'Free-Rider' Problem." *Econometrica* 45: 783–809.

Harbeson, Robert. 1969. "Toward Better Resource Allocation in Transport." *Journal of Law and Economics* 12: 321–338.

Hendricks, W. 1975. "The Effect of Regulation on Collective Bargaining in Electric Utilities." *Bell Journal of Economics* 6: 451–465.

Hinich, M. J. 1975. A Rationalization for Consumer Support for Food Safety Regulation. Department of Economics, Virginia Polytechnic Institute.

Hirshleifer, J. 1958. "Peak Loads and Efficient Pricing: Comment." *Quarterly Journal of Economics* 72: 451–452.

Hong, James T., and Plott, Charles R. 1977. "Implications of Rate Filing for Domestic Dry Bulk Transportation on Inland Waters: An Experimental Approach. Social science working paper 164, California Institute of Technology.

Houthakker, H. S. 1957. "Electricity Tariffs in Theory and Practice." *Economic Journal* 61: 1–25.

Interstate Commerce Commission. 1976. A Cost and Benefit Evaluation of Surface Transport Regulation. Statement 76–1.

Jacoby, Henry, and Steinbrunner, John. 1973. "Salvaging the Federal Attempt to Control Auto Pollution." *Public Policy* 21: 1–48.

Jordan, William. 1970. *Airline Regulation in America: Effects and Imperfections.* Baltimore: Johns Hopkins University Press.

Joskow, Paul. 1972. "The Determination of the Allowed Rate of Return in a Formal Regulatory Proceeding." *Bell Journal of Economics and Management Science* 3: 632–644.

————. 1973a. "Pricing Decisions of Regulated Firms: A Behavioral Approach." *Bell Journal of Economics and Management Science* 4: 118–140.

————. 1973b. "Cartels, Competition and Regulation in the Property and Liability Insurance Industry." *Bell Journal of Economics and Management Science* 4: 375–427.

————. 1974. "Inflation and Environmental Concern: Structural Change in the Process of Public Utility Price Regulation." *Journal of Law and Economics* 17: 291–328.

————. 1976. "Contributions to the Theory of Marginal Cost Pricing." *Bell Journal of Economics* 7: 197–206.

————. 1979a. "Electric Utility Rate Structures in the United States: Some Recent Developments." In W. Sichel (ed.), *Public Utility Ratemaking in An Energy Conscious Environment* (Boulder, Colorado: Westview).

————. 1979b. "Public Utility Regulatory Policy Act of 1978: Electric Utility Rate Reform." *Natural Resources Journal* 19: 787–809.

Kahn, Alfred. 1970. *The Economics of Regulation.* New York: Wiley. (Two volumes.)

Keeler, Theodore. 1972. "Airline Regulation and Market Performance." *Bell Journal of Economics and Management Science* 3: 399–424.

Klevorick, Alvin. 1971. "The Optimal Fair Rate of Return." *Bell Journal of Economics and Management Science* 2: 122–153.

———. 1973. "The Behavior of a Firm Subject to Stochastic Regulatory Review." *Bell Journal of Economics and Management Science* 4: 57–88.

Kneese, A. V., and Schultze, C. L. 1975. *Pollution, Prices, and Public Policy.* Washington, D.C.: Brookings Institution.

Lancaster, K. 1966. "A New Approach to Consumer Theory." *Journal of Political Economy* 74: 132–157.

Leontief, W. 1970. "Environmental Repercussions and the Economic Structure: An Input-Output Approach." *Review of Economics and Statistics* 52: 262–271.

Levin, R. C. 1978. "Allocation in Surface Freight Transportation: Does Rate Regulation Matter?" *Bell Journal of Economics* 9: 18–45.

Levine, Michael E. 1965. "Is Regulation Necessary? California Air Transportation and National Regulatory Policy." *Yale Law Journal* 74: 1416–1447.

MacAvoy, Paul. 1971. "The Formal Work Produce of the Federal Power Commission." *Bell Journal of Economics and Management Science* 2: 379–395.

———. 1973. "The Regulation-Induced Shortage of Natural Gas." *Bell Journal of Economics* 4: 454–498.

MacAvoy, Paul, and Roger G. Noll. 1973. "Relative Prices on Regulated Transactions of the Natural Gas Pipelines." *Bell Journal of Economics* 4: 212–234.

MacAvoy, Paul, and Sloss, James. 1967. *Regulation of Transport Innovation: The ICC and Unit Coal Trains to the East Coast.* New York: Random House.

McCarthy, Eugene, Finkel, Madelon, and Kamons, Ann. 1977. Second Opinion Surgical Program: A Vehicle for Cost Containment. Mimeographed. Paper presented to American Medical Association Commission on Cost of Medical Care.

McGuire, Thomas, Nelson, Richard, and Spavins, Thomas. 1975. "An Evaluation of Consumer Protection Legislation: The 1962 Drug Amendments." (Comment.) *Journal of Political Economy* 83: 655–662.

Machlup, F. 1962. *The Production and Distribution of Knowledge in the United States.* Princeton, N.J.: Princeton University Press.

McKay, Derek. 1976. Has the A-J Effect Been Empirically Verified? Social science working paper 132. California Institute of Technology.

Manne, H. G., and Miller, R. M. (eds.). *Auto Safety Regulation: The Cure or the Problem?* Glen Ridge, N.J.: Horton.

March, James, and Simon, Herbert, 1959. *Organizations.* New York: Wiley.

Massell, B. F. 1969. "Price Stabilization and Welfare." *Quarterly Journal of Economics* 83: 1005–1013.

Meyer, John R., Peck, Merton, Stenason, John, and Zwick, Charles. 1959. *The Economics of Competition in the Transportation Industries.* Cambridge, Mass.: Harvard University Press.

Michelman, Frank I. 1967. "Property, Utility and Fairness: Comments on the Ethical Foundations of 'Just Compensation' Law." *Harvard Law Review* 80: 1165.

Mills, Edwin S., and White, Lawrence, 1978. "Government Policies Towards Automotive Emissions Control." In A. F. Friedlaender (ed.), *Approaches to Controlling Air Pollution* (Cambridge, Mass.: MIT Press).

Montgomery, W. David. 1972. "Markets in Licenses and Efficient Pollution Control Programs." *Journal of Economic Theory* 5: 395–418.

———. 1974. "Artificial Markets and the Theory of Games." *Public Choice* 18: 25–40.

———. 1976. "Separability and Vanishing Externalities." *American Economic Review* 66: 174–177.

Moore, Thomas. 1975. "Deregulating Surface Freight Transportation." In Almarin Phillips (ed.), *Promoting Competition in Regulated Markets* (Washington, D.C.: Brookings Institution), pp. 55–98.

Niskanen, William. 1971. *Bureaucracy and Representative Government*. Chicago: Aldine-Atherton.

Noll, Roger G. 1971. *Reforming Regulation: An Evaluation of the Ash Council Proposals*. Washington, D.C.: Brookings Institution.

Noll, Roger G., and Trijonis, J. 1971. "Mass Balance, General Equilibrium, and Environmental Externalities." *American Economic Review* 61: 730–735.

Oi, W. Y. 1961. "The Desirability of Price Instability Under Perfect Competition." *Econometrica* 29: 58–64.

✓ ———. 1973. "The Economics of Product Safety." *Bell Journal of Economics and Management Science* 4: 3–28.

Panzar, J. C. 1976. "A Neoclassical Approach to Peak-Load Pricing." *Bell Journal of Economics* 7: 521–530.

Panzar, J. C., and Willig, R. D. 1977. "Free Entry and the Sustainability of Natural Monopoly." *Bell Journal of Economics* 8: 1–22.

Park, R. E. (ed.). 1973. *The Role of Analysis in Regulatory Decisionmaking: The Case of Cable Television*. Lexington, Mass.: Heath.

✓ Peltzman, Sam. 1973. "An Evaluation of Consumer Protection Legislation: The 1962 Drug Amendments." *Journal of Political Economy* 81: 1049–1091.

———. 1976a. "The Regulation of Automobile Safety." In H. G. Manne and R. L. Miller (eds.), *Auto Safety Regulation: The Cure or the Problem?* (Glen Ridge, N.J.: Horton).

———. 1976b. "Toward a More General Theory of Regulation." *Journal of Law and Economics* 14: 109–148.

Peterson, H. Craig. 1975. "An Empirical Test of Regulatory Effects." *Bell Journal of Economics and Management Science* 6: 111–126.

Pindyck, Robert S. 1974. "The Regulatory Implications of Three Alternative Econometric Supply Models of Natural Gas." *Bell Journal of Economics* 5: 633–645.

Plott, Charles R. 1965. "Occupational Study of Self Regulation: A Case Study of the Oklahoma Dry Cleaners." *Journal of law and Economics* 8: 195–222.

———. 1977. Externalities and Corrective Policies in Experimental Markets. Social science working paper 180. California Institute of Technology.

Porat, N. U. 1977. *The Information Economy: Definition and Measurement*. Washington, D.C.: U. S. Department of Commerce.

Posner, Richard. 1971. "Taxation by Regulation." *Bell Journal of Economics and Management Science* 2: 22–50.

————. 1974. "Theories of Economic Regulation." *Bell Journal of Economics and Management Science* 5: 335–358.

Samuelson, P. A. 1954. "The Pure Theory of Public Expenditures." *Review of Economics and Statistics* 36: 332–338.

Shepsle, K. A. 1978. *The Grant Jigsaw Puzzle: Democratic Committee Assignments in the U.S. House of Representatives.* University of Chicago Press.

Sheshinski, Eytan. 1971. "Welfare Aspects of Regulatory Constraint: Note." *American Economic Review* 61: 175–178.

Smith, R. S. 1974. "The Feasibility of an 'Injury Tax' Approach to Occupational Safety." *Journal of Law and Contemporary Problems* 38: 730–744.

————. 1976. *The Occupational Safety and Health Act.* Washington, D.C.: American Enterprise Institute.

Smith, Vernon L. 1967. "Effect of Market Organization on Competitive Equilibrium." *Quarterly Journal of Economics* 78: 181–201.

Smith, Vernon L. 1976. "Experimental Economics: Induced Value Theory." *American Economic Review Papers and Proceedings* 66: 274–279.

————. 1977. Relevance of Laboratory Experiments to Testing Resource Allocation Theory. Paper presented to Conference on Criteria for Evaluation of Econometric Models, Ann Arbor, Michigan.

Snitzler, James R., and Byrne, Robert J. 1958. Interstate Trucking of Fresh and Frozen Poultry Under Agricultural Exemption. U.S. Department of Agriculture. Marketing research report 244.

————. 1959. Interstate Trucking of Frozen Fruits and Vegetables Under Agricultural Exemption. U.S. Department of Agriculture. Marketing research report 316.

Spann, Richard. 1974. "Rate of Return Regulation and Efficiency in Production: An Empirical Test of the Averch-Johnson Thesis." *Bell Journal of Economics and Management Science* 5: 38–52.

Spann, Richard, and Erickson, Edward W. 1970. "The Economics of Railroading: The Beginning of Cartelization and Regulation." *Bell Journal of Economics* 1: 227–244.

Spence, A. M. 1977. "Consumer Misperceptions, Product Failure and Producer Liability." *Review of Economic Studies* 44: 561–572.

Spence, A. M., and Roberts, Marc. 1976. "Effluent Charges and Licenses Under Uncertainty." *Journal of Public Economics* 5: 193–208.

Spence, A. M., and Weitzman, Martin. 1978. "Regulatory Strategies for Pollution Control." In A. F. Friedlaender (ed.), *Approaches to Controlling Air Pollution.* Cambridge, Mass.: MIT Press.

Starret, D.C. 1972. "Fundamental Nonconvexities in the Theory of Externalities." *Journal of Economic Theory* 4: 180–199.

Steiner, Peter O. 1957. "Peak Loads and Efficient Pricing." *Quarterly Journal of Economics* 71: 585–610.

Stewart, R. 1975. "The Reformation of American Administrative Law." *Harvard Law Review* 88: 1756.

Stigler, G. 1961. "The Economics of Information." *Journal of Political Economy* 69: 213–225.

————. 1971. "The Theory of Economic Regulation." *Bell Journal of Economics and Management Science* 2: 3–21.

Stigler, G., and Friedland, Claire. 1962. "What Can Regulators Regulate: The Case of Electricity." *Journal of Law and Economics* 5: 1–16.

Turnovsky, S. J. 1976. "The Distribution of Welfare Gains From Price Stabilization: The Case of Multiplicative Disturbances." *International Economic Review* 17: 133–148.

Turvey, R. 1968. "Peak Load Pricing." *Journal of Political Economy* 76: 101–113.

Tversky, A. 1972. "Elimination by Aspects: A Theory of Choice." *Psychological Review* 79: 281–299.

U.S. Senate Committee on Government Operations. 1977. *Study of Federal Regulation.* Volume I: *The Regulatory Appointments Process.* Washington, D.C.: U.S. Government Printing Office.

Weingast, Barry. 1977. A Representative Legislature and Regulatory Capture. Ph.D. diss., California Institute of Technology.

Wenders, J. T. 1976. "Peak Load Pricing in the Electric Utility Industry." *Bell Journal of Economics* 7: 232–341.

Wilde, Louis L., and Schwartz, Alan. 1979. "Equilibrium Comparison Shopping." *Review of Economic Studies* 46: 543–553.

Williamson, Oliver E. 1970. "Administrative Decision Making and Pricing: Externality and Compensation Analysis Applied." In Julius Margolis (ed.), *The Analysis of Public Output.* New York: National Bureau of Economic Research.

————. 1976. "Franchise Bidding for Natural Monopolies: In General and with Respect to CATV." *Bell Journal of Economics* 7: 73–104.

Comment

Alfred E. Kahn

Reading this excellent paper, after more than eight years of absence from the academic economics profession, produced in me an extraordinary variety of reactions—the most prominent was envy. Evidently one either thinks systematically about the phenomenon of regulation, or one practices it; it seems impossible to do both.

So I will have to confine myself to remarking on the portions of this admirable survey, at once encyclopedic and incisive, on which my own recent regulatory experiences have some bearing.

You will understand why I find so congenial Joskow's and Noll's general proposition "that far too much of the effort of economists has been directed toward asking whether there should or should not be regulation, and far too little effort directed at how to improve the performance of regulatory policies"—all too congenial, since of course it describes exactly what I have been trying to do during the last several years.

At the same time, I'm not sure I agree with them. The contribution of the economists who have questioned what seemed to be self-evident cases for regulation has been at least as important as the contribution of those of us who have been trying to make it work better. If I were asked to offer one single piece of advice to would-be regulators, on the basis of my own experience, it is that as they perform their *every single* regulatory action they ask themselves: "Why am I doing this? Is it really necessary?"

Still, I agree enthusiastically with the view that economists can make an important contribution in helping regulators perform at minimum economic cost the tasks that legislators have ordered them to perform. Let me cite a few examples:

• Congress is determined to see to it that more air transportation service is available than an unregulated market would provide to relatively small and isolated communities, over relatively thinly traveled routes; and congressmen are willing to allot as much as $100 million a year of tax money for this purpose. There is no point in my fighting that basic policy, particularly when some case can be made for it on grounds of the external benefits of linking the country together and avoiding even greater urban congestion. But what the Civil Aeronautics Board can do and has done is explain to Congress how it may get what it wants more efficiently, first, by permitting free entry of air taxis and commuter airlines (which can perform these particular services much more efficiently than the certificated carriers), and, second, by developing a plan for specifying the subsidized services we want to purchase and attempting to purchase them at minimum cost (if possible, by competitive bids) rather than, as under the present system, essentially by making good the revenue deficiencies of the carriers certificated for this purpose. (This description does less than justice to the progressive efforts by the Board over the years to refine the methods of subsidy determination, but it will have to suffice.)

• Similarly, legislators seem determined that basic telephone service be provided at less than long-run marginal cost, and (even worse from the efficiency standpoint) through a system of internal subsidization. There is plenty of opportunity, however, within the constraints of that general legislative decision, for careful consideration of what exactly constitutes the "basic service" that is worth subsidizing (should it, for example, include the opportunity to make unlimited local calls, of unlimited duration, at no extra charge; or, at the other extreme, should it embrace only the opportunity to receive unlimited numbers of calls?), and how this subsidy can be provided with minimum distortion.

• In pricing electricity and gas, we need help in devising practicable methods of reconciling marginal-cost pricing with the revenue constraint.

• Another pressing regulatory problem on which we need help is in devising rules that make reasonable economic sense for the regulation of competition between what appear to be natural monopolies (such as the national telecommunications networks and specialized common carriers), or between still partially regulated members of a cartel (for example, the International Air Transport Association and operators of charters.)

• A much narrower but nevertheless extremely challenging problem is assessing the workability of competition in the performance of the retailing function in the travel industry—specifically, assessing the possible desirability of leaving the determination of travel agents' commissions to the free play of competition. This problem is made particularly challenging, and possibly even unsolvable, by the fact that that competition may still, under regulation or international cartelization, be highly imperfect.

• Charting the path from cartel-like regulation, such as the CAB has practiced in the past, to a liberalization and freer play of market forces, which we are (if only for polical reasons) inescapably committed to taking gradually, may be more than challenging. It may well be impossible to shepherd through gradual deregulation, without giving deregulation itself a bad name, an industry that has grown up in a hothouse of protectionism, is subject to the most extraordinarily complicated spiderweb of restrictions carried over from the past, and will continue to be shot through with monopoly power—all this under the watchful eyes of 535 congressmen, each of them watching with a hawk's eye the quality of air service available to every community in his district.

(As I read these remarks from the perspective of February 1980, I am impressed with how rapidly the changes have come during the few intervening months. It has obviously been possible to move to virtual deregulation of the airlines; the market has proved to be a remarkably effective regulator; and the industry, despite its 40 years in a hothouse, has proved remarkably resilient. And the results have been good. It now looks as though we are on the verge of similarly dramatic changes in motor-carrier regulation. And while we are still grappling in common-carrier communications with the problem of how to maintain effective competition among companies with varying degrees of monopoly power, it appears we are on the verge of devising essentially nonregulatory solutions [separate subsidiaries, and requirements of equal and nondiscriminatory access to monopoly facilities] that will permit a breaking down of 45-year-old market barriers (for example, between computers, data processing, and communications; between satellite and cable transmission; between cable TV and telephony) that no longer have any technological justification, and a genuine opening up of the entire technology to competitive exploitation.)

There are, in short, almost unlimited opportunities for intellectually exciting efforts to apply economic logic to concrete regulatory problems, which are just as promising of success as the efforts to which Joskow and Noll rightly refer in the field of variable pricing, particularly of electricity (a success they correctly attribute to the fact that so many economists have been willing to combine theoretical and empirical research with involvement in practical application). If only because this is a field that has heretofore been the almost exclusive preserve of lawyers, accountants, and engineers, there is wide room for the application of economic logic. The rewards, I guarantee, will include a very satisfying— although almost certainly misleading—sense of accomplishment.

It is well not to delude ourselves that these accomplishments, however gratifying, are significant in some macrocosmic sense. On the contrary, it is terribly important that the economist-regulator not take himself excessively seriously. I have had many occasions to observe, mainly to myself, that some of what I have considered my most creative efforts of the last several years (emulating, I thought, Thurman Arnold, who after characterizing the antitrust laws as part of the "folklore of capitalism" undertook the job of Assistant Attorney General for Antitrust with unprecedented vigor) were merely compensations for distortions attributable to the institution of regulated monopoly itself. Let me illustrate briefly:

• Certainly one of my proudest accomplishments was to induce the utility companies I regulated to introduce marginal-cost-related prices, particularly prices embodying peak responsibility principles. Time and again, I had occasion to ask myself why the companies needed pressure from me to do this. Why, particularly in a period of inflation, would an electric company insist on continuously subsidizing sales of electricity on peak, when the result was to add more to its costs than its revenues and to intensify the financial squeeze to which it was in any event being exposed by the combination of inflation and regulatory lag? And why did they have to be forced to reconsider their traditional declining block rates, when it appeared, particularly at times of peak demand, that sales in the ultimate blocks were markedly below marginal cost?

Two important elements of the explanation, I think, must have been bureaucratic inertia and a lingering assumption that it was in their interest to promote additional sales that require additional investment, for the familiar Averch-Johnson reasons. But both of these phenomena are themselves surely the consequence of regulated monopoly—the first of the absence of competition and of regulation on a cost-plus basis, the latter the familiar consequence of basing allowable returns on invested capital. So a plausible case can be made that all this furious activity to reform utility rate structures was itself necessitated by the fact of regulation itself. Unregulated monopolists, lacking a reserve margin of unexploited monopoly power that they could tap only by expanding their rate bases, would presumably have no interest in encouraging sales whose marginal costs exceed their price.

• Similar observations apply, I think, to my efforts to introduce various kinds of management efficiency audits, in an attempt to overcome the familiar defects of cost-plus regulation, or to force surprisingly reluctant separate gas and electric companies to engage in more comprehensive integration of their investment and operations. Unregulated monopolists, it would seem, would have every incentive to buy rather than produce for themselves whenever the marginal costs of buying were less than those of producing.

• I cannot refrain from citing one last example—one in which I took particular pride, but one which illustrates even more clearly than the others the point I am making here. From time to time, we at the New York Public Service Commission found ourselves confronted with requests by small water companies for rate increases in the range of 200 to 300 percent, which, to our astonishment, our staff testified were necessary to enable them to cover their costs and provide a reasonable return on investment. It was very difficult to believe, in these cases, that costs had increased by percentages of that order of magnitude during the period in which the then-current rates had been in effect.

The explanation was not hard to find. Though the companies in question were separate legal and accounting entities, they either were or had been appendages of real estate developers, who got into the water business because most of their customers were unwilling to buy developed lots and houses without an attached water supply. Whatever they earned, they earned not on the water system as such but on the combined operation. Now they were proposing to make the water operation compensatory by conventional regulatory standards.

It proved fairly simple to explicate the sense of injustice expressed by some of their indignant customers. The price that purchasers had paid for the developed lots or houses must have reflected, explicitly or implicitly, the price they were being charged for water, and certain expectations about its future course. It seems a reasonable assumption that the purchasers had no reason to expect their water rates to go up more than costs. If that assumption is correct, the inference is inescapable that to grant a water company associated with a real-estate developer a rate increase of more than the amount by which costs had increased since the time of purchase would as a matter of economic fact have involved permitting a double recovery of the orginal investment— once in the selling prices of the houses, and the second time, by courtesy of the New York Public Service Commission, in the price of the water itself.

The solution we developed was to require applicants for rate increases to justify them in terms of the *increases* in costs they had incurred over some reasonable period in the recent past. This involved establishing a presumption that when the rate increases justified by the rate base/rate of return criterion exceeded those demonstrated cost increases, the differences were *ipso facto* evidence of an attempted double recovery. To put it another way, to the extent water suppliers had been content for some substantial period with rates that were "noncompensatory" by traditional regulatory criteria, that constituted *prima facie* evidence that some portion of the capital dedicated to providing water had already been recovered in the sale prices of the lots and houses. This was a satisfying application of simple economic logic, but one that would have been unnecessary in an unregulated market.

I do not mean by these observations to imply that all such regulation is unnecessary. Like Professors Joskow and Noll, I find that an intellectually intriguing question, but not one to which I want to devote my major efforts—fully recognizing that I may be behaving a little like a rat in a revolving wheel cage. The fact is that suppliers of water may have very substantial reserves of monopoly power, to which consumers are unwilling to be subjected without what appears to them the protection of a regulatory commission.

I should like, in closing, to call attention to one generalization derived from empirical economic research that has proved extremely useful in confronting some of the regulatory problems that now confront me. Research on cartels has demonstrated in many contexts the tendency of collusive price-fixing to inflate costs: If prices are not free to move down to marginal costs and there is a will to compete, marginal costs will increase to the level of price. The airline industry under regulation has become a familiar illustration of this tendency, which J. M. Clark (*Competition as a Dynamic Process* [Washington, D.C.: Brookings Institution, 1961], pp. 252–257) termed "product inflation," a phenomenon that he perceived in some unregulated but highly concentrated markets. Its most striking manifestation has been competitive overscheduling of flights, which has produced an equilibrium of high fares, low load factors, and consequently high unit costs. I have analyzed product inflation as a possible reflection of the "tyranny of small decisions" [*Kyklos* XIX (1966): 39–44], and observed the more general phenomenon of the upward adjustment of cost to an artificially sustained price in my "Combined Effects of Prorationing, the Depletion Allowance and Import Quotas on the Cost of Producing Crude Oil in the United States"[*National Resources* X (1970): 53–61]).

This observation has an interesting corollary for regulatory policy: If a cartel-maintained price induces cost-inflating competition in service, then an active regulatory agency can *control* service quality and costs by an active low-price policy. (I recognize here, as elsewhere, that unregulated competition could do the job without the help of regulation; but that alternative is only partially available to me.) The Civil Aeronautics Board, therefore, has shifted its policy toward discount fares from discouragement to active encouragement, recognizing that if only the offerers are prevented from recouping any resultant net revenue losses by raising their regular fares correspondingly, the effect of the discounts is to raise the airlines' break-even load factors. The encouragement of discount fares, therefore, under suitable safeguards, pushes the carriers toward a new equilibrium of lower average yields, reduced scheduling, higher load factors, and consequently lower average costs.

In short, the observations issuing from economic research, which have been fairly clearly established in the airline field, suggest a very useful tool of regulatory policy itself—a tool, however, like most of the others I have mentioned, that proves helpful as a means of offsetting or correcting the deficiencies in industrial performance caused by regulation itself!

On that note, combining enthusiasm and skeptical self-deprecation, it seems fitting to close.

Comment

George J. Stigler

Joskow and Noll begin their interesting and useful survey of the literature of regulation by carefully avoiding any discussion of what regulation is. I may unintentionally demonstrate with the following remarks that theirs was an eminently wise decision.

Regulation on its face refers to an attempt by the state to use its legal powers to direct the conduct—in our context, especially the economic conduct—of nongovernmental bodies. (Indeed, as James Q. Wilson and Patricia Rachal ["Can the Government Regulate Itself," *The Public Interest* 46 [1977]: 3–14] argue with considerable persuasiveness, the one thing governmental regulators surely cannot regulate is other governmental bodies.) Once this is said, it becomes apparent that public regulation covers the entire interface of public-private relations and includes, besides such old-fashioned fields as public utilities and antitrust policy, the following:

• all public interventions in the resources markets (land use, capital-mobilizing institutions, and labor),

• all money-raising activities of government, except possibly printing money, and those disbursements that do not take the form of purchases in open markets, and

• all public interventions in the production, sale, or purchase of goods and services.

Public regulation therefore includes most of public finance, large parts of monetary and financial economics and international trade, large sectors of labor economics, agricultural and land economics, and welfare economics. Indeed, welfare economics may be defined as that branch of economic theory in which one economist achieves fame by demonstrating a flaw in the price system and a second economist achieves equal fame by discovering the flaw in this demonstration.

Joskow's and Noll's most surprising omission is the economics of legal institutions. If the economic theory of contracts (on which Joskow has written), torts, and property, for example, are not part of the theory of regulation, I don't know where in economics this work belongs. Perhaps I should marvel more at the mysteries of modern communication: Cambridge and Pasadena are closer to each other than to Chicago. The failures of communication, I must emphasize, are *not* on the question of desirable public policy, where on the whole the differences among the three cities appear to be negligible. Rather, the difference is on what are the exciting and important frontiers of research.

Can this vast array of public policies be usefully viewed as a single subject? That is a question that is not answerable by a statement from Joskow and Noll or me or someone else. It is answerable in the affirmative if it can be shown that there is sufficient commonality, in the sources and purposes of regulation, in the techniques that are used, and in the problems that are encountered, to make it useful to analyze all these phenomena *en masse*.

If Joskow and Noll have succeeded in distinguishing in their survey the important themes in the recent literature of regulation, then we can say that the emergence of a specialization of economists in regulation lies well in the future. If, as they believe, the main topics of our literature have been

• regulation of competitive activities (a largely normative subject in their treatment),

• regulation of monopolistic activities (also a largely normative subject, still reeling from an orgy of A-J effects),

• peak-load pricing, and

• a miscellany of producer and consumer-protection laws (again, normatively considered),

then it is amply clear that we have not found a central theoretical scheme on which to hang our researches on regulation.

My conjecture is that if a distinguishable intellectual discipline of regulation is to appear, it will be necessary to formulate our theories in terms of phenomena inherent in the regulatory process. Two of these phenomena are the pervasive control over entry into regulated fields and the peculiar nature of the decisionmaking process in political life (in which, contrary to the clichés of the day, the one thing we are sure of is that each man does not have one vote). I am persuaded that it will be found useful to use the same theory to explain tariffs, controls over energy industries, minimum-wage laws, environmental controls, OSHA, and the structure of the tax system. But this is still only a hope, and we shall see.

I shall make only two comments on the details of Joskow's and Noll's survey of the four main topics they select: regulation of competitive industries, regulation of monopoly, variable pricing, and the collection of protective laws. The first comment is that they make quite a point of the fact that when regulatory policies set a price or limit on entry, large changes can take place in other variables, such as quality of product or service, which substantially alter the outcome from what a simpler theory would predict. I commend to them and to you the work of Yoram Barzel, especially "An Alternative Approach to the Analysis of Taxation" (*Journal of Political Economy* 84 [1976]: 1177–1197). Barzel has generalized the problem of quality change and applied it fruitfully to the oil import quota system and other problems.

My second comment concerns the strong interest Joskow and Noll display in some recent work in price theory, with special reference to stochastic demands and costs, and experimental studies. I must confess that I do not see the special connection between this work and the theory of regulation. Every topic in price theory has implications for regulation, and I assmue that it is only the accident of their own tastes that led Joskow and Noll not to give equal attention to the regulatory problems posed by the theory of rational expectations or the theory of demand-revealing processes.

If I were asked to name the most striking change in the literature of public regulation in the past two decades, I would have chosen not the changes in techniques of analysis but a fundamental change that has occurred in the questions that are asked of regulation: Before 1960 there were extraordinarily few occasions on which anyone asked: Can we estimate empirically the effects of a public policy? The prevalent practice was to appraise the regulatory policy on general theoretical grounds (the standard analysis of monopoly is a leading example), or to judge the policies by an intensive legal-administrative survey of the administering body (Sharfman's volumes on the ICC are the prototype of this approach, which of course still rules in the political science literature). If one wishes to document the prevalent normative, nonquantitative approach to regulation before 1960, he can go to the encyclopedic textbooks—above all, to Clair Wilcox's *Public Policies Toward Business* (Homewood, Ill.: Irwin, 1955), but also to the slightly earlier *Government and Economic Life* by L. S. Lyon et al. (Washington, D.C.: Brookings Institution, 1939–1940) or to the Twentieth Century Fund series.

The consequences of this shift of inquiry have been profound. The shift of focus revealed that the conventional theory of most regulatory policies was incomplete when it was not grossly superficial. When one did not find appreciable regulatory effects in the direction indicated by the preamble to the regulatory policy there was a strong stimulus to look elsewhere, on the not unreasonable ground that public policies are not usefully explained by saying they were a mistake. The inevitable result—

although in my own case the inevitable required ten years to be recognized —was that questions began to be asked as to why we were regulating the activities that we were, and to what ends. These questions lead to an entirely different orientation of the theory of regulation.

One of the main results of this reorientation was the emergence of the beginnings of a theory of regulation: the theory of what regulations will be instituted, and in whose behalf. Joskow and Noll discuss this literature briefly in a manner I find difficult to follow. Part of my difficulty arises because they mix the basic question with another that I consider minor and almost independent, namely, whether it is legislatures or their bureaucratic agents who control regulatory events. They apparently consider it a decisive criticism against the theory of regulation that it does not contain a complete theory of politically effective coalitions; that, at least, is the sense I can read into their complaints at tautological tests of the theory. I only wish the tautological tests had come out better.

To complain at the insufficiency of the work—which after all is only about six years old—in this area is only proper, for on neither theoretical nor empirical sides do we have a mature, confident theory. But Joskow and Noll appear to miss the basic point of the theory of regulation: It poses a fundamental and inescapable problem. If one cannot explain why some regulations appear and some regulations do not appear, one simply cannot deal with the fundamental questions of regulation. Unless I know why New York City has rent controls, I do not know what questions to ask about their effects, what alternative policies are compatible with the coalition strengths that underlie the present rent controls, and where and when rent controls will spread. The theory of regulation is essentially a non-normative theory, and it is possible that Joskow's and Noll's lack of sympathy with it is due to this fact. Certainly the overwhelmingly dominant interest of their paper is in normative questions, which they seldom neglect for even a page.

Joskow and Noll are good enough to devote the last third of their pages to telling us what to work on in the future. On its face this is extraordinarily self-sacrificial behavior: Promising ideas are all that even a rich scholar possesses, and here they are giving away their wealth. Or can it be that these proposed lines of research are not worth their time, but are perhaps worth ours? Rather than pursue the economics of scholarly advice, let me simply say that I have always thought that revealed preference is the only reliable guide to what a scholar believes to be fruitful research problems: If he doesn't work on them, he provides no reason for us to do so.

Their advice is not all that surprising. They tell us that more work should be done on the economics of information; this is about equivalent to telling college students that just because the pill is available is no reason to forget about sex. A second recommended topic for study is economic dynamics. Dynamics is an indispensable item on every list of desirable researches, although its urgency is perhaps less in the context of regulatory processes, which are what economists have in mind when they refer to the long run. A third proposal is that we share the Caltech interest in experimental economics, with which I concur, although the topic is almost conclusive proof that everything in economics has some connection with regulation.

They also commend varied and detailed study of the political and administrative processes. Of course they are right, but I wish their suggestions had been grounded in economic theory instead of reading like the traditional literature of political science.

It is easy to make legitimate points of complaint against a survey of an immense and unsystematic literature, no matter who is making that survey. A literature can be systematized and appraised only when it reaches a period of comparative consensus and hence stability. In the midst of a period of rapid development, varied experimental explorations, and considerable controversy, a survey is inherently incomplete and short-visioned and even *ex parte*. It is indicative of the ambiguity of the current literature that Joskow and Noll devote almost all of their pages to what are really questions of allocational efficiency, whereas if I had been making the survey I would have devoted a large share of the pages to the income-redistribution aspects of regulation. The proper time to survey the literature of regulation, I propose, is after the subject is developed.

2

Income-Distribution Concerns In Regulatory Policymaking

Robert D. Willig
Elizabeth E. Bailey

This paper presents and applies new methodological tools for relating concerns with income distribution to regulatory policymaking. The tools are based on the concept of *social-welfare dominance*, according to which a policy is said to social-welfare-dominate another if it is preferred by all social decisionmakers who subscribe to a certain set of compelling axioms. We present a variety of necessary and sufficient conditions for social-welfare dominance of regulatory policies—conditions that can be tested by means of market data. We demonstrate the feasibility of this new approach to normative analysis by means of pilot studies of some policies toward electric-utility and telephone-service pricing.

Changes in regulatory policies generally benefit some economic agents, while they hurt others. The standard approach to evaluating such policies entails aggregating costs and benefits over all agents and using the algebraic sum as the decision criterion. This methodology views as equivalent dollars of net benefit, irrespective of to whom they accrue. It can only be justified by appeal to costless lump-sum transfers or to social indifference about the distribution of income. In the absence of these unrealistic conditions, state-of-the-art normative analysis conceptualizes possibly different welfare weights applied to the net benefits of different agents. The first section of the article sketches this theoretical development and argues that the numerical values of such welfare weights are arbitrary and can be critical for policy assessment.

Consequently, in the second section we develop qualitative relationships among the welfare weights that are equivalent to three axioms: the Pareto principle, anonymity, and the undesirability of regressive transfers of real income. These axioms underlie the social-welfare-dominance relation between policies.

We show that a policy change is social-welfare-dominant if and only if a series of observable conditions hold. These conditions include the Hicksian dictum that the total net benefits of the change be positive, as well as the Rawlsian dictum that the poorest member of society be made better off. In addition, social-welfare dominance requires the positivity of the net benefits of each group formed by starting from the bottom and working up the scale of real income to any level.

This theory offers a concept of welfare improvement that is far more general than Pareto optimality. Social-welfare-dominating policies can have losers as well as gainers. A policy is social-welfare-dominant as long as losses are counterbalanced by gains to those who are poorer in real income. Such policies can be formed through political linkages between efficient and inefficient components. Such pervasive packaging of regulatory policies makes little sense when analyzed within the usual optimization framework.

The third section presents several additional sets of empirically useful conditions for social-welfare dominance of policies. For example, if the aggregate benefit-cost ratio exceeds unity and if the class-specific benefit-cost ratios decline with income, then the policy change is social-welfare-dominant. First-order necessary conditions for local non–social-welfare dominance are developed.

In the fourth section we discuss philosophical stances from which social-welfare-dominance tools can be utilized in normative and positive studies. The fifth and sixth sections detail pilot applications to seasonal peak-load electricity pricing and to the Ramsey pricing of long-distance telephone services.

Social-Welfare Functions

The current state of the art, by our reading, incorporates income-distribution concerns into normative analysis by means of a Samuelson-Bergson social-welfare function (Samuelson 1963). Policy-setting power is viewed as vested in the hands of a social decisionmaker (SDM). It is assumed that the SDM acts as if he has a complete and continuous preference ordering over social states that obeys the Pareto principle. That is, the SDM respects individual preferences, and views as desirable any change that improves the lots of some people (by their own values) while leaving all others indifferent.

For the sake of concreteness, we limit the discussion to social states that differ only in static, certain allocations of private commodities among neoclassical consumers. Then, social states are represented by vectors

$$(x_{11},\ldots,x_{1m},x_{21},\ldots,x_{2m},\ldots,x_{n1},\ldots,x_{nm}) \in \mathbf{R}_+^{nm},$$

where x_{ij} is the consumption of commodity j by consumer i. The SDM has a complete and continuous preference ordering over $\mathbf{R}_+^{nm}$ that is representable by the ordinal real-valued function $V(x)$, where, for $x', x'' \in \mathbf{R}_+^{nm}$, x' is preferred to x'' if and only if $V(x') > V(x'')$.

If one assumes that each consumer is indifferent about the consumption of others (no extended sympathy), the ith neoclassical consumer's preferences over his own consumptions can be represented by an ordinal, increasing real-valued utility function, $U^i(x_{i1},...,x_{im})$. In accordance with the Pareto principle, the SDM's conditional preference ordering over vectors $(x_{i1},...,x_{im})$, with the consumptions of other consumers held constant, must coincide with the ith consumer's preference ordering and must be independent of the consumptions of others. It follows (Leontief 1947; Debreu 1960) that the variables $x_{i1},...,x_{im}$ are separable in $V(\cdot)$ from its other arguments, that $U^i(x_{i1},...,x_{im})$ can serve as an aggregator of $x_{i1},...,$ x_{im} in $V(\cdot)$, and that, consequently, for $\phi(\cdot)$ which is some real-valued function over $\mathbf{R}^n$,

$$V(x_{i1},...,x_{1m},x_{n1},...,x_{nm}) \equiv \phi(U^1(x_{11},...,x_{1m}),...,U^n(x_{n1},...,x_{nm})). \quad (1)$$

Further, in view of the Pareto principle, $\phi(\cdot)$ is nondecreasing in each of its arguments and is increasing in some of them.

State-of-the-art normative theory proceeds by assuming that each consumer faces a common vector of prices, $\mathbf{p} = (p_1,...,p_m)$, has income m_i, and chooses his own consumption bundle $(x_{i1},...,x_{im})$ to maximize $U^i(\cdot)$ subject to the budget constraint $\Sigma_j x_{ij} p_j \leq m_i$. In such a free consumption market, the ith consumer's maximized utility level is denoted by the indirect utility function

$$l^i(\mathbf{p},m_i) \equiv U^i(X^{i1}(\mathbf{p},m_i),...,X^{im}(\mathbf{p},m_i)), \quad (2)$$

where $X^{ij}(\mathbf{p},m_i)$ is the function giving the market demand for commodity j by consumer i.

The combination of equations (2) and (1),

$$V(\cdot) = \phi(l^1(\mathbf{p},m_1),...,l^n(\mathbf{p},m_n)) \equiv \psi(\mathbf{p};m_1,...,m_n), \quad (3)$$

gives the preferences of the SDM over price vectors, $\mathbf{p}$, and distributions of nominal income, $m_1,...,m_n$, induced by his preferences over allocations of commodities, given the free consumption market. The representation of social preferences given in equation (3) is in a form theoretically applicable to the evaluation of microeconomic policy.[1] For example, the attitudes of the SDM toward changes in regulated prices can be expressed by means of the tradeoffs between prices that are inherent in the function ψ. Such tradeoffs are invariant to ordinal transformations of $V(\cdot)$, $\phi(\cdot)$, and $\psi(\cdot)$. Differentiation of equation (3) gives

$$\frac{\partial \psi}{\partial p_i} \bigg/ \frac{\partial \psi}{\partial p_j} = \sum_k \phi_k \frac{\partial l^k}{\partial p_i} \bigg/ \sum_k \phi_k \frac{\partial l^k}{\partial p_j}, \tag{4}$$

where

$$\phi_k = \frac{\partial \phi}{\partial l^k}.$$

This can be put in a more interpretable form by means of Roy's law:[2]

$$\frac{\partial l^k}{\partial p_j} = -X^{kj} \frac{\partial l^k}{\partial m_k}. \tag{5}$$

Roy's law says that a consumer's rate of substitution between income and the jth price is that consumer's demand for the jth commodity. Substituting (5) into (4) gives

$$\frac{\partial \psi}{\partial p_i} \bigg/ \frac{\partial \psi}{\partial p_j} = \sum_k \left(\phi_k \frac{\partial l^k}{\partial m_k} \right) X^{ki} \bigg/ \sum_k \left(\phi_k \frac{\partial l^k}{\partial m_k} \right) X^{kj}. \tag{6}$$

Equation (6) relates the SDM's tradeoff between prices i and j to two elements:[3] the distribution of demands for goods i and j among consumers and the collection of weighting factors on these demands,

$$\omega_k \equiv \phi_k \frac{\partial l^k}{\partial m_k} = \frac{\partial \psi}{\partial m_k}. \tag{7}$$

Each of the weighting factors measures the marginal social utility, in the view of the SDM, of income to a consumer.

If the SDM were indifferent to small lump-sum transfers of income between any two consumers, then all the ω_ks would be equal. This case would also occur if a costless mechanism for interpersonal lump-sum transfers were available to the SDM. With $\omega_k = \omega$ for all k, equation (6) would reduce to

$$\frac{\partial \psi}{\partial p_i} \bigg/ \frac{\partial \psi}{\partial p_j} = \sum_k X^{ki} \bigg/ \sum_k X^{kj}.$$

Here, the tradeoff between p_i and p_j does not depend on the distribution of demands among consumers. Instead, it is the ratio of total market demands for the goods, which is also the rate of substitution between the prices for market consumers' surplus.

Generally, however, the SDM will not be costlessly able to effect lump-sum transfers, will not be indifferent to transfers, and will not impute equal marginal social utility to each consumer's income. In this case, equation

(6) shows that the larger ω_k is relative to the other weights, the more important is the demand pattern of consumer k for the SDM's view of price tradeoffs. If consumers differ in their demand patterns, then the relative sizes of the weights can become critical for the SDM's decisions on policies affecting prices.

Economic theory can shed little light on the sizes of the welfare weights. Some analysts (for example, Feldstein [1972a] and Atkinson [1970]) have specified functional forms for the behavior of $\psi(\cdot)$ with respect to $m_1,\ldots,$ m_n, and have thus implicitly related the full set of weights to a small set of parameters. However, such procedures are inherently arbitrary. Conceptually, it may be empirically or experimentally possible to determine the ψ function of an SDM, and to proceed to policy analysis on that basis. Such a tack is yet to be carried out successfully.

Here we shall proceed by using the fact that if the SDM would rather not see income transferred from consumer i to j, then $\omega_j \leq \omega_i$. With t representing such a transfer, the SDM's preferences are represented by

$$\phi(\ldots,l^i(\mathbf{p},m_i - t),\ldots,l^j(\mathbf{p},m_j + t),\ldots).$$

Then

$$0 \geq \frac{d\phi}{dt} = -\phi_i\frac{\partial l^i}{\partial m_i} + \phi_j\frac{\partial l^j}{\partial m_j} = -\omega_i + \omega_j, \tag{8}$$

and, at $t = 0$, $\omega_i \geq \omega_j$.

We specify intuitive conditions on the SDM's preferences that are equivalent to such inequalities among the welfare weights, and then ask whether a policy is preferred to another for all weights satisfying the qualitative relationships. Thus, we avoid the need for quantitatively specified weights, while we lose completeness of the preference ordering among policies. The result is a partial ordering that was named social-welfare dominance by Willig and McCabe (1977).

Social-Welfare Dominance

In this section we characterize the social-welfare-dominance partial ordering over policies. One policy social-welfare-dominates another if it is preferred by all SDMs whose social preferences satisfy the three axioms below.[4] (The axioms are expressed in terms of the premises described above: static, riskless allocations of private goods among neoclassical consumers who face a free market without extended sympathy.)

Axiom 1 (Pareto Principle)   The SDM is indifferent to a change that leaves all consumers indifferent. The SDM does not view as desirable a change that no consumer finds desirable. A change that is beneficial to at least one consumer while leaving all others indifferent is viewed as desirable by the SDM.

Axiom 2 (Anonymity)   At prices $\mathbf{p}^0$, the SDM is indifferent to a reversal of nominal incomes between any two consumers.

Axiom 3 (Regressive Transfer Aversion)   At prices $\mathbf{p}^0$, the SDM does not find desirable any transfer of income from a nominally poorer to a richer consumer.

In our context, axiom 1 implies that the social preferences of the SDM can be represented by the function of indirect utility levels, ϕ, defined in equation (3). Because of the forms of axioms 2 and 3, it is convenient to work with the special indirect utility functions, $\mu^k(\mathbf{p}^0|\mathbf{p},m_k)$, which are measured in terms of real income, base $\mathbf{p}^0$. These income-compensation functions, first studied rigorously by Hurwicz and Uzawa (1971), can be defined implicitly by

$$l^k(\mathbf{p}^0,\mu^k(\mathbf{p}^0|\mathbf{p},m_k)) \equiv l^k(\mathbf{p},m_k). \tag{9}$$

They give the nominal income required by consumer k, in facing prices $\mathbf{p}^0$, to be indifferent to income m_k at prices $\mathbf{p}$.

When viewed as a function of $\mathbf{p}$ and m_k, $\mu^k(\mathbf{p}^0|\mathbf{p},m_k)$ is a proper indirect utility function for consumer k. This can be seen from equation (9). Because the function l^k is increasing in its income argument for fixed $\mathbf{p}^0$, the left-hand side of (9) is an ordinal transformation of the function μ^k. Thus, $l^k(\cdot)$ is an ordinal transformation of the function μ^k and can be written for fixed $\mathbf{p}^0$ as

$$l^k(\mathbf{p},m_k) = T^k(\mu^k(\mathbf{p}^0|\mathbf{p},m_k)). \tag{10}$$

Now, for each k, substitute (10) into (3) and define

$$W(z_1,\ldots,z_n) \equiv \phi(T^1(z_1),\ldots,T^n(z_n)).$$

Then,

$$\psi(\mathbf{p};m_1,\ldots,m_n) \equiv W(\mu^1(\mathbf{p}^0|\mathbf{p},m_1),\ldots,\mu^n(\mathbf{p}^0|\mathbf{p},m_n)) \tag{11}$$

yields a particularly convenient representation of the SDM's preferences.

Of course, by axiom 1, $W(\cdot)$ is nondecreasing in all of its arguments and increasing in at least one.

Axiom 2 says that at prices $\mathbf{p}^0$ it is only the vector of nominal incomes, and not their assignment to particular consumers, that matters to the SDM. Thus, $\psi(\mathbf{p}^0;m_1,\ldots,m_n)$ is symmetric in its income arguments. For example,

$$\psi(\mathbf{p}^0;m_1,m_2,m_3,\ldots,m_n) = \psi(\mathbf{p}_0;m_2,m_1,m_3,\ldots,m_n).$$

Note from (9) that

$$\mu^k(\mathbf{p}^0|\mathbf{p}^0,m_k) = m_k. \tag{12}$$

It follows from (12) and (11) that

$$\psi(\mathbf{p}^0,m_1,\ldots,m_n) = W(\mu^1(\mathbf{p}^0|\mathbf{p}^0,m_1),\ldots,\mu^n(\mathbf{p}^0|\mathbf{p}^0,m_n))$$

$$= W(m_1,\ldots,m_n). \tag{13}$$

Consequently, axioms 1 and 2 together imply that $W(\cdot)$ is symmetric in its arguments. This has been established by reference to prices $\mathbf{p}^0$, where $\mu^k = m_k$; it holds as well for other prices where the arguments of $W(\cdot)$ are $\mu^k(\mathbf{p}^0|\mathbf{p},m_k)$.

By axiom 3 and equation (8),[5] $m_i > m_j$ implies that, at prices $\mathbf{p}^0$,

$$\frac{\partial\psi}{\partial m_i} \leq \frac{\partial\psi}{\partial m_j}.$$

In view of (13), $m_i > m_j$ implies that

$$\frac{\partial W(m_1,\ldots,m_n)}{\partial m_i} \leq \frac{\partial W(m_1,\ldots,m_n)}{\partial m_j}.$$

This is a property of the function $W(\cdot)$, whatever the interpretation of its arguments. Thus, under axioms 1–3,

$$\mu^i > \mu^j \text{ implies } \frac{\partial W}{\partial \mu^i} \leq \frac{\partial W}{\partial \mu^j}. \tag{14}$$

Now, consider the social-welfare comparison between policies ρ' and ρ'' that result in $(\mathbf{p}';m_1',\ldots,m_n')$ and $(\mathbf{p}'';m_1'',\ldots,m_n'')$ respectively.

Definition
ρ' social-welfare-dominates ρ'' ($\rho' > \rho''$) if ρ' is preferred to ρ'' by all SDMs whose preferences satisfy axioms 1–3.

Theorem 1

$\rho' > \rho''$ if and only if

$$\sum_{i=1}^{k} \mu^i(\mathbf{p}^0|\mathbf{p}',m_i') > \sum_{i=1}^{k} \mu^i(\mathbf{p}^0|\mathbf{p}'',m_i''), \qquad k = 1,\ldots,n, \tag{15}$$

where the indices i are assigned to possibly different consumers under ρ' and ρ'' so that

$$\mu^1(\mathbf{p}^0|\mathbf{p}',m_1') \leq \mu^2(\mathbf{p}^0|\mathbf{p}',m_2') \leq \cdots \leq \mu^n(\mathbf{p}^0|\mathbf{p}',m_n')$$

and

$$\mu^1(\mathbf{p}^0|\mathbf{p}'',m_1'') \leq \mu^2(\mathbf{p}^0|\mathbf{p}'',m_2'') \leq \cdots \leq \mu^2(\mathbf{p}^0|\mathbf{p}'',m_2'').$$
(16)

(This theorem, proved below, is mathematically analogous to results established by Rothschild and Stiglitz [1973]. A more general version was demonstrated by Willig and McCabe [1977].)

Proof of Theorem 1 Suppose that equation (15) is satisfied. We must prove that it follows that ρ' is preferred to ρ'' by any SDM who satisfies axioms 1–3. Let the SDM's social preferences be represented as in (13). By axiom 2, the consumers can be relabeled to satisfy (16) without changing the relevant values of $W(\cdot)$. For notational convenience, let $Z_i' \equiv \mu^i(\mathbf{p}^0|\mathbf{p}',m_i')$, let $Z_i'' \equiv \mu^i(\mathbf{p}^0|\mathbf{p}'',m_i'')$, and let $\mathbf{Z}'$ and $\mathbf{Z}''$ be the corresponding vectors. Define, with t a scalar, $F(t) = W((1-t)\mathbf{Z}' + t\mathbf{Z}'')$. Then, using the mean-value theorem,

$$W(\mathbf{Z}'') - W(\mathbf{Z}') = F(1) - F(0)$$

$$= \frac{dF(\bar{t})}{dt}$$

$$= \sum_i (Z_i'' - Z_i') \frac{\partial W((1-\bar{t})\mathbf{Z}' + \bar{t}\mathbf{Z}'')}{\partial Z_i}$$

for some $\bar{t} \in [0,1]$.

Since the components of $\mathbf{Z}'$ and $\mathbf{Z}''$ are ordered in an increasing fashion, so too are the components of $(1-\bar{t})\mathbf{Z}' + \bar{t}\mathbf{Z}''$. Then, by axioms 1 and 3 and equation (14),

$$\omega_1 \geq \omega_2 \geq \cdots \geq \omega_n \geq 0,$$

where

$$\omega_i \equiv \frac{\partial W((1 - \bar{t})\mathbf{Z}' + \bar{t}\mathbf{Z}'')}{\partial Z_i}.$$

Using this notation, it follows from algebraic manipulation that

$$W(\mathbf{Z}'') - W(\mathbf{Z}') = \sum_{k=1}^{n-1} \left((\omega_k - \omega_{k+1}) \sum_{i=1}^{k} (Z_i'' - Z_i') \right) + \omega_n \sum_{i=1}^{n} (Z_i'' - Z_i').$$

By equation (15), $\Sigma_{i=1}^{k}(Z_i'' - Z_i') > 0$ for $k = 1,\ldots,n$. Also, $(\omega_k - \omega_{k+1}) \geq 0$. Let j be the largest index such that $\omega_1 = \omega_2 = \ldots = \omega_j$. If $j = n$, then $\omega_n > 0$ by axiom 1 and $W(\mathbf{Z}'') - W(\mathbf{Z}') = \omega_n \Sigma_{i=1}^{n}(Z_i'' - Z_i') > 0$. If $j < n$, then $\omega_j - \omega_{j+1} > 0$ and $W(\mathbf{Z}'') - W(\mathbf{Z}') \geq (\omega_j - \omega_{j+1}) \Sigma_{i=1}^{j}(Z_i'' - Z_i') > 0$. Thus, $W(\mathbf{Z}'') - W(\mathbf{Z}') > 0$ for any SDM in the class.

For the other direction of proof, assume that $\rho' > \rho''$. With consumers ordered according to relations (16), let $W(Z) \equiv \Sigma_{i=1}^{k} Z_i$. Such preferences clearly satisfy axiom 1. At $\mathbf{p}^0$, $Z_i = m_i$, and axiom 2 is immediate. Consider a transfer of $y > 0$ from i to j with $i < j$, and let $G(y)$ be the resulting level of $W(\cdot)$. If $i \leq k$ and $j > k$, then $G(y) = G(0) - y < G(0)$. If $i > k$, $j > k$, and $m_i - y \geq m_k$, then $G(y) = G(0)$, whereas if $m_i - y < m_k$, then $G(y) = G(0) - (m_k - m_i + y) < G(0)$. If $i < j \leq k$ and $m_j + y \leq m_{k+1}$, then $G(y) = G(0)$. If $i < j \leq k$ and $m_j + y > m_{k+1}$, then $G(y) = G(0) - (m_j + y - m_{k+1}) < G(0)$. Thus, $W(Z) = \Sigma_{i=1}^{k} Z_i$ satisfies axioms 1–3 for any k and, for dominance, (15) must hold. Q.E.D.

To interpret theorem 1, note first that in the situations caused by each policy, consumers are relabeled so that consumer 1 is poorer in real income (base $\mathbf{p}^0$) than is 2, who is poorer than 3, and so on. This is permissible, loosely, by virtue of the anonymity axiom. If moving from ρ' to ρ'' does not change the order of consumers' real incomes, then the consumer indexed by i is the same in both situations.

The inequalities in equation (15) say that the sum of the real incomes of the poorest k consumers under ρ' must, for dominance, exceed that under ρ'' for all k. For $k = 1$, equation (15) is the Rawlsian condition that the lot of the poorest consumer be improved. For $k = n$, equation (15) is the Hicksian condition that the sum of the changes in all consumers' real incomes be positive. The novelty and strength of equation (15) is that the condition is required for $k = 1$, for $k = n$, and for all k in between.

It is important to realize that the conditions given in (15) can be checked by means of market data. It was shown by Willig (1973, 1976) that

$\mu(\mathbf{p}^0|\mathbf{p},m)$ is approximated closely by the sum of m and the Marshallian consumer's surplus area (a line integral for multiple price changes) between $\mathbf{p}^0$ and $\mathbf{p}$, if that area is a relatively small portion of m and if the income elasticities of demand are in the usual range. Under such conditions, (15) can be investigated with only small errors by means of sums of consumers' incomes and surpluses. In particular, if $m_i' = m_i''$, then a sum of the form

$$\sum_{i=1}^{k} [\mu^i(\mathbf{p}^0|\mathbf{p}',m_i') - \mu^i(\mathbf{p}^0|\mathbf{p}'',m_i'')]$$

can be well approximated by the sum of the poorest (in real income) k consumers' surpluses between $\mathbf{p}''$ and $\mathbf{p}'$. This sum is independent of $\mathbf{p}^0$, if the identities of the relevant consumers are independent of $\mathbf{p}^0$.

Thus—loosely, or precisely in terms of approximations with well-understood bounds—equation (15) has the following interpretation: A necessary condition for social-welfare dominance is passage of the standard aggregate ($k = n$) consumers' surplus test. The necessary and sufficient conditions for social-welfare dominance are that the policy change increase the aggregated surpluses of the poorest k consumers, for all k.

Of course, in an actual economy, the number of conditions represented by equation (15) is staggeringly large. For practical analysis, it may suffice to partition consumers into a manageable number of income classes, to consider as identical the welfare weights of all consumers within a class, and to apply theorem 1 across classes rather than strictly across consumers. We present below several more easily verified conditions that are either necessary or sufficient for dominance. But let us momentarily digress on the subject of policy packages.

Consider a policy ρ' that does not dominate the status-quo policy, ρ^0. Denote

$$\Delta Z_i = \mu^i(\mathbf{p}^0|\mathbf{p}',m_i') - \mu^i(\mathbf{p}^0|\mathbf{p}^0,m_i^0) \tag{17}$$

as the change in the ith consumer's real income due to the policy, measured against the status-quo base. Then, for at least some k,

$$\sum_{i=1}^{k} \Delta Z_i \leq 0.$$

Suppose that ρ' is efficient in the usual sense in that it increases total surplus:

$$\sum_{i=1}^{n} \Delta Z_i > 0.$$

Then, there may exist an ancillary policy change that, when linked with ρ', makes the policy package dominate the status quo. Such an ancillary change need not itself dominate the status quo, and the policy package need not dominate ρ'. Moreover, the ancillary change may be an inefficient addition to ρ' in that it decreases the gain in aggregate surplus that could have been achieved by ρ' alone.[6]

Thus, the concept of social-welfare dominance can provide a framework for understanding the common regulatory and political process of linking policies together into packages. Such practices have no rationale when analyzed within the usual optimization framework.

Tests for Dominance

To make possible the use of differential analysis, suppose that there are h continuous policy controls, $\theta_1, \ldots, \theta_h$, that are restricted by the feasibility condition that $F(\theta) \geq 0$.[7] Let the status quo be represented by θ^0, with $F(\theta^0) = 0$. Further, let the real income (base $\mathbf{p}^0$) of consumer i be given by $Z_i(\theta)$, where $Z_i(\theta^0) \leq Z_{i+1}(\theta^0)$.

Proposition 1   There exists a feasible policy in the direction V from θ^0 that social-welfare-dominates the status quo θ^0 if

$$\nabla F(\theta^0) \cdot V > 0 \quad \text{and} \quad \left[\sum_{i=1}^{k} \nabla Z_i(\theta^0) \right] \cdot V > 0, \qquad k = 1, \ldots, n, \quad (18)$$

where either $Z_i(\theta^0) < Z_{i+1}(\theta^0)$ or, if $Z_i(\theta^0) = Z_{i+1}(\theta^0)$,[8] there is a $\hat{t}$ such that $Z_i(\theta^0 + tV) \leq Z_{i+1}(\theta^0 + tV)$ for $0 < t \leq \hat{t}$.

Proof of Proposition 1   The functions of t, $F(\theta^0 + tV)$, and $\sum_{i=1}^{k} Z_i(\theta^0 + tV)$ all have positive derivatives with respect to t, at $t = 0$, if relations (18) hold. Then, there is a $\hat{t}$ such that for $0 < t < \hat{t}$,

$$F(\theta^0 + tV) > F(\theta^0) = 0$$

and

$$\sum_{i=1}^{k} Z_i(\theta^0 + tV) > \sum_{i=1}^{k} Z_i(\theta^0).$$

For positive t sufficiently small,

$$Z_i(\theta^0 + tV) \le Z_{i+1}(\theta^0 + tV)$$

and $\theta = \theta^0 + tV$ is a feasible policy that dominates the status quo.

Proposition 1 shows that if local analysis uncovers a feasible dominating direction of policy movement, then there is a feasible dominating policy change that is a finite step in that direction.

Gordon's theorem (Mangasarian 1969) provides a condition that is equivalent to (18) and that is computationally efficient by linear programing methods.

Proposition 2   Relations (18) hold if and only if there is no non-negative, nonzero vector y with

$$\sum_{k=1}^{n} y_k \sum_{i=1}^{k} \frac{\partial Z_i(\theta^0)}{\partial \theta_j} + y_{n+1} \frac{\partial F(\theta^0)}{\partial \theta_j} = 0, \qquad j = 1, \dots, h. \tag{19}$$

Equation (19) has the same form as the first-order conditions for θ^0 to be Pareto-optimal for the n "pseudoconsumers," each of whom is the aggregate of the k poorest actual consumers $(k = 1, 2, \dots, n)$. Such an approach could be used to derive necessary and sufficient conditions for θ^0 to be locally nondominated. However, this tack would require curvature conditions on the functions that are not compelling at this level of generality.

The following mathematical result, proved in Willig and McCabe 1977, is useful in conjunction with Proposition 1 or, directly, with Theorem 1.

Lemma   Let $F(m)$ be an increasing function for $0 \le m \le \bar{m}$. Suppose

$$\int_0^{\bar{m}} g(m) dF(m) > 0. \tag{20}$$

Let $g(m) \equiv b(m) - c(m)$, with $b(m) \ge (0)$, $c(m) > 0$, and with $b(m)/c(m)$ a decreasing function of m for $0 < m < \bar{m}$. Then

$$\int_0^m g(m) dF(m) > 0 \qquad \text{for } 0 < m \le \bar{m}. \tag{21}$$

To apply this lemma to theorem 1, consider a policy move that generates the changes in real income ΔZ_i, where the indexes of consumers increase with real income. We can interpret $F(i)$ as the cumulative (step) density function of consumers, and $g(i)$ as ΔZ_i. Then, $g(i) \equiv b(i) - c(i)$ is a benefit-cost decomposition of the net change in real income, and the lemma establishes the result given in theorem 2.

Theorem 2   A policy move that does not alter the ranking of consumers by real income is social-welfare-dominating if its aggregate net benefit is positive and if it has benefit-cost ratios specific to real income classes that decrease with real income.

Combining the lemma with proposition 1 yields the local test for a dominating policy given as theorem 3.

Theorem 3   With consumers indexed as in proposition 1, there exists a feasible policy in the direction V from θ^0 that social-welfare-dominates the status quo θ^0 if

$$\nabla F(\theta^0) \cdot V > 0,$$

if

$$\sum_{i=1}^{n} \nabla Z_i(\theta^0) \cdot V > 0,$$

and if there exist $b_i \geq 0$ and $c_i > 0$ such that

$$\nabla Z_i(\theta^0) \cdot V = b_i - c_i$$

and b_i/c_i decreases with i.

Theorems 2 and 3 focus attention on benefit-cost ratios that are specific to real income classes of consumers. If these ratios decline with real income for a policy change that leaves intact the ordering of consumers by real income, then the move is social-welfare-dominant if and only if it is efficient in the standard aggregate sense. This result can be useful when data are insufficient for the calculations required by theorem 1 but qualitative information indicates the relationship between income levels and income-class-specific benefit-cost ratios.

Additional tests that are more useful in a different context are discussed in McCabe and Willig 1977.

Positive and Normative Views

Suppose an analyst observes that an SDM has effected a policy move that has resulted in real-income changes, ΔZ_i, that fail to satisfy equations (15) and (16). The move can certainly not be logically criticized on those grounds, even by believers in axioms 1–3. It is possible that the chosen policy was optimal for the SDM's particular preferences, and that those preferences satisfy the axioms. However, a believer in axioms 1–3 would have grounds for protest if the SDM's choice revealed a decision criterion in conflict with the axioms. The inverse of theorem 1 yields the means for such revelation.

Proposition 3   A policy change is weakly preferred by no social preferences that obey axioms 1–3, if and only if the $-\Delta Z_i$ satisfy (15) and (16); that is, if and only if the original policy social-welfare-dominates the new one.

What cogent aspersions may be cast at an SDM who has, with full information, effected a dominated policy? The pros and cons of such arguments are best organized around the defining axioms.

It can be argued that public policy regularly violates the Pareto principle via promotion of merit goods, legally mandatory insurance programs, paternalistic safety rules, legal restrictions on private conduct, and the like. Counterarguments assert that such violations of axiom 1 are in fact Pareto-optimal policies in the face of overlooked externalities, imperfect information, and extended sympathy. The only conclusion that can be drawn here is that without such potentially important complications, imposition on consumers of an SDM's personal tastes is socially counterproductive.

Violations of axiom 2 seem to indicate favoritism based on factors omitted from the explicit normative analysis. The deliberately simple model utilized here does omit many characteristics of individual consumers that might well be included in the evaluation of real income. Among these characteristics could be labor ability, wealth, physical and human capital, health, and family size. Thus, at prices $\mathbf{p}^0$, an SDM might reasonably fail to be indifferent to an interchange of nominal incomes between people whose states of health do not coincide. These matters are given a detailed treatment in Willig 1981, where it is shown that the conditions (15) and (16) can remain robust to such interpersonal differences when the axioms are suitably broadened.

Favoritism in violation of axiom 2 can also be motivated by reciprocal opportunities for the personal financial or political enrichment of the SDM. It is hoped that such violations can be uncovered by the social-welfare-dominance methodology.

The content of axiom 3 depends on the definition of real income. In a more general model than that presented here, real income could include adjustments for abnormal levels of selected characteristics and endowments. Then, for example, in theorem 1, consumer 1 would have the smallest adjusted real income, and the real-income ordering of consumers would depend partially on the set of characteristics for which adjustments are permitted. In this way, the conditions for social-welfare dominance would become less mechanical, less scientific, and more responsive to difficult ethical judgments. Revealed violations of axiom 3 must be viewed in this light. However, there remain wide classes of social-decisionmaking behavior that would fail to satisfy any ethically reasonable version of the axiom. For example, an SDM who acted to maximize his political support or personal finances (see Peltzman 1976; Stigler 1971) would undoubtedly exhibit many instances of preference for policies that are inefficient in the aggregate and that cause regressive transfers of real income. Such behavior can be exposed by analysis based on proposition 3.

In our view, the methodologies presented here can systematically reflect income-distribution concerns in regulatory policymaking. Past regulatory decisions can be reviewed for efficiency and distribution effects within the framework provided by theorem 1 and proposition 3. To narrow the present sets of options, social-welfare-dominated policies can be excluded from consideration with analyses based on proposition 1 or 2 or on theorem 2 or 3. These same methods can underlie a discovery that a regulatory status quo is social-welfare-dominated. Finally, the distributional effects of an innovative policy can be tested and summarized by means of the conceptual tools forged here.

The remaining sections of this article present pilot applications of social-welfare-dominance methods to regulatory policymaking.

Peak and Off-Peak Pricing by Electric Utilities

Until recently, electric utilities in the United States rarely charged differential rates by time of day or by season of the year. Yet, these utilities face demands that exhibit definite peaks and troughs. Electric utilities in the southern and southwestern states, for example, face peaks during the summer months, caused in large part by summer demand for air conditioning. Under seasonal pricing, such an electric utility can cut down the need for additional capacity by instituting a summer surcharge, and can encourage a more efficient utilization of capacity throughout the year by also offering a winter discount. These well-known advantages of peak-load pricing policies have proved to be of substantial economic importance in Europe (Mitchell and Acton 1977).

There is an additional aspect of peak-load pricing that is important in the United States. Public-utility commissioners, who are responsible for approving such policies, often have an interest in the income-distribution consequences of these policies. If seasonal pricing were to have equalizing distributional effects (as may be expected in the case of summer-peaking electric utilities), then commissioners might be particularly disposed to encourage this policy. In contrast, if seasonal pricing were likely to have an adverse effect on low-income families (as may occur in the case of winter-peaking electrics), there would then be hesitation about approval of the policy unless other benefits could be shown to be substantial.

Therefore, as a first application, we examine the income-distribution consequences of a switch from a pricing structure that is uniform throughout the year to one that takes account of seasonal peaks. Since our intent is to illustrate how to test for the existence of a social-welfare-dominant policy, we confine the discussion to a very simple structure in which a summer-peaking electric utility increases its summer block prices by s and decreases its winter block prices by w.[9] We presume that, under the status quo, the seasonally uniform prices exceed marginal cost during the off-peak winter months and are below marginal cost during the summer peak. Thus, we assume that implementation of small positive changes s and w is a move toward marginal-cost pricing that increases aggregate consumers'-plus-producer's surplus.

In the absence of data on demand elasticities, marginal costs, and the ownership of the electric utility, we cannot quantify the effects of price changes on the utility's profit and on the incomes of its owners. Thus, we focus on the welfare effects of various price changes on the consumers of the utility's outputs. We proceed with this pilot application by investigating the income-distribution effects of price changes as if they held the utility's profit constant and had welfare effects on only electricity consumers.

Our data consist of the monthly 1973 electricity usages of the 49 representative households in Gainesville, Florida studied by Roth (1976). Twenty of the households were classified as low-income, 18 as middle-income, and 11 as high-income. The data for households in each income class are summarized in table 2.1 for the summer months (June–September) and for the rest of the year. Note that, while total summer usage is less than total winter usage, monthly output is higher during the peak summer period than it is during the winter.

Table 2.1 Income-distribution consequences of seasonal pricing of electricity, based on data of Roth (1976).

	Income Group		
	Low	Middle	High
Number of households	20	18	11
Average 1970 income	$6,150	$11,125	$19,757
Average 1973 usage, June–Sept.	2,140 kWh	6,389 kWh	13,645 kWh
Average 1973 usage, Oct.–May	4,180 kWh	6,206 kWh	15,318 kWh
Total 1973 usage, June–Sept.	42,800 kWh	115,000 kWh	150,100 kWh
Total 1973 usage, Oct.–May	83,600 kWh	111,700 kWh	168,500 kWh
$r = 0.51$:[a]			
Benefit-cost ratio	1.00	.50	.57
$r = 0.846$:			
Benefit-cost ratio	1.68	.82	.95
Class net benefit	$279	−$204	−$75
Cumulative net benefit	$279	+$75	$0
$r = 1.00$:			
Benefit-cost ratio	1.95	.97	1.12
$r = 1.03$:			
Benefit-cost ratio	2.01	1.00	1.16

a. r = Winter price decrease per kWh/Summer price increase per kWh.

The welfare effects of specific changes of w and s can be analyzed by means of consumers'-surplus methods. However, we lack the requisite monthly demand function for each income class. Consequently, guided by proposition 1, we proceed with local analysis of directions of change in w and s from 0.

If we take the then-current set of prices as the base for real incomes, the derivative of a consumer's 1973 real income with respect to w, evaluated at 0, is his winter 1973 electricity consumption, and that with respect to s is minus his summer 1973 consumption. Thus, with the relative winter and summer price changes denoted by $r = dw/ds$, the rate of change in real income for a particular consumer is

$$\frac{dZ}{ds} = r \times (\text{Winter consumption}) - (\text{Summer consumption})$$

$$= (\text{Winter consumption})\left(r - \frac{\text{Summer consumption}}{\text{Winter consumption}}\right). \tag{22}$$

The ratio of the benefits from the winter price decrease to the costs from the summer price increase is

$$-\frac{\partial Z/\partial w}{\partial Z/\partial s}\frac{dw}{ds} = r \times \frac{\text{Winter consumption}}{\text{Summer consumption}}. \tag{23}$$

Because Roth aggregated his sample of households into three income classes, we can only take the point of view that the welfare weights are the same for all households within the same class. We then consider that axioms 1-3 apply to the different income classes.

Equations (22) and (23) show that the income-distribution effects of price changes in the ratio r depend upon the relative winter and summer consumption of electricity by each of the three income classes. If, for example, relative seasonal consumption were the same for all classes, then, regardless of the absolute levels of usage, the price changes would be distributionally neutral. In particular, the benefit-cost ratio would be identical for each income group.

However, the data displayed in table 2.1 reveal patterns of electricity usage that are very different among income classes. The low-income households have rather equal usage throughout the year, and hence their ratio of consumption during the four summer months to that during the eight winter months is 0.51. The middle-income households use about 50 percent more electricity than the low-income consumers during the winter, but almost three times more in the summer period, presumably because they employ air conditioning. Their ratio of summer to winter usage is 1.03. The high-income households use substantially more electricity than the middle-income consumers throughout the year. Perhaps because they use electric heating in addition to air conditioning, their ratio of summer to winter consumption (0.89) is smaller than that of the middle-income group.

Combining equation (22) with the summer-winter usage ratios shows that if r (the ratio of winter price decrease to summer price increase) exceeds 1.03, then all income classes of consumers will benefit. However, such a large relative price decrease may cause infeasible losses for the utility company.

The normative methodology presented here shows that more moderate decreases in the winter price, relative to the summer price, would social-welfare-dominate the status quo, provided that they did not decrease vendor profit. Following the prescription of proposition 1, we can sum equation (22) over the low and middle income classes and over all three classes. The corresponding aggregated summer-winter usage ratios are 0.808 and 0.846, respectively. For $r > 0.846$, the low-income group, the low-income together with the middle-income group, and all groups of consumers aggregated together gain.[10] Thus, by proposition 1, for any feasible r greater than 0.846 there is a set of price changes in that ratio whose effects on consumers would be desirable in the view of any SDM whose preferences satisfy axioms 1–3.

Of course, for $1.03 > r > 0.846$, a move toward peak-load pricing that would leave profit constant would social-welfare-dominate but would not Pareto-dominate the status quo, because the middle- and high-income groups would lose. However, for such a policy, their losses would be smaller than the gains to the low-income households, and the move would be desirable under axiom 3. Table 2.1 displays these gains and losses for $r = 0.846$, scaled by setting $s = \$0.01$.

To illustrate the discussion of the preceding section, we note that for $0.846 > r > 0.51$ the peak-load pricing policy decreases the aggregate real income of electricity consumers and fails to social-welfare-dominate the status quo. Yet, such changes benefit the low-income group and may be desirable to some SDMs who satisfy axioms 1–3. In contrast, for $r < 0.51$, the price changes are social-welfare-dominated by the status quo. The analysis suggests that if such a policy was carried out under stable production costs, the SDM was either misinformed or deliberately ignoring consumers' interests.

Welfare-Optimal Pricing of Long-Distance Telephone Services

The next policy we evaluate is a set of price changes in the direction that yields the best local improvement in aggregate welfare, given that the net revenue[11] from the studied group of services remains unchanged. The specific example involves 1973 long-distance telephone prices in the United States.

Our work with this example began with a pilot study of the 1973 price structure of direct-distance-dialed (DDD) telephone services (Willig and Bailey 1977b). The study sought to determine whether these prices satisfied first-order conditions for welfare optimization under the constraint that net revenues be held at the then-current level.

The relevant first-order conditions with equal welfare weights for all consumers, no external effects, and no cross-elasticities are given by the inverse elasticity rule:

$$\alpha_i \equiv \frac{P_i - MC_i}{P_i} \times e_i = \alpha, \qquad \text{for all } i, \tag{24}$$

where e_i, P_i, and MC_i are the elasticity, price, and marginal cost of service i, respectively. The α_i are Ramsey numbers.[12] The Ramsey rule states that, from service to service, the percentage deviation of price from marginal

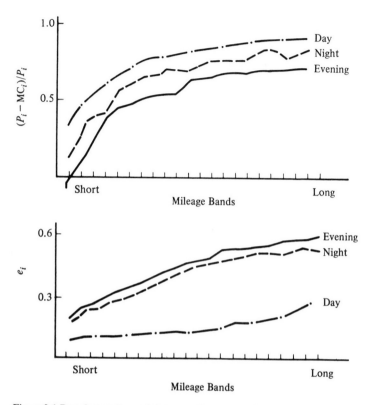

Figure 2.1 Rough experimental data on price, marginal cost, and elasticity for 1973 DDD services.

cost times the price elasticity of demand should be constant. The more unresponsive the demand for a product to changes in its price, the less welfare is lost if that price is increased, and so the larger the optimal deviation between price and marginal cost. Thus, the overhead expenses for services produced with economies of scale are best covered with revenues from the more inelastic of the services.

The two components of the inverse elasticity formula are displayed in figure 2.1 for day, evening, and night/weekend calls for each of 21 mileage bands (short-haul to long-haul). The price variable is the revenue from a call of average duration. The price elasticity and marginal cost for each distance and time-of-day element of the DDD schedule are calculated from rough, experimental pre-1973 data,[13] on which we performed a number of interpolations.

It is readily seen that day calls had the largest relative markup of price

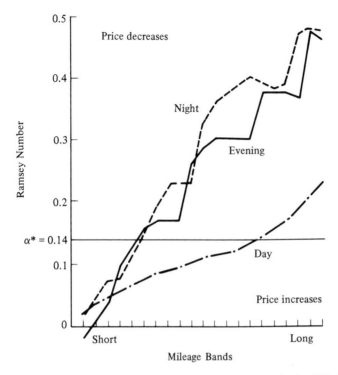

Figure 2.2 Critical Ramsey numbers for direct-distance dialing in 1973, determined from experimental data by the economic-gradient method with the Euclidean metric.

over marginal cost for any given mileage band, and the lowest elasticities. Inversely, evening calls had the lowest relative deviation of price from marginal cost and the highest elasticities. These qualitative relationships are in accord with equation (24). However, across mileage bands, the long-haul calls had both the highest relative markup of price over marginal cost and the highest elasticities. These qualitative directions violate the dictum of equation (24).

Figure 2.2 shows a plot of Ramsey numbers calculated from the experimental data for the DDD services. It is evident that these data suggest that the 1973 prices of day, evening, and night/weekend telephone services classified by length of haul do not satisfy equation (24), as the Ramsey numbers do not all coincide. Instead there is a systematic bias, with low Ramsey numbers in short mileage bands and large Ramsey numbers in the longer mileage bands, and with larger Ramsey numbers for evening and night calls than for day calls for almost all of the mileage bands.

To calculate candidate Ramsey-optimal prices, we made assumptions

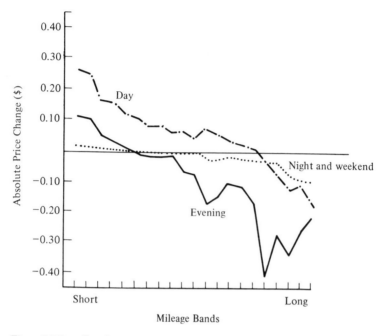

Figure 2.3 Best directions of price change, with greatest price change equal to 100 percent (based on experimental data).

about the functional forms for demands and costs. In particular, we supposed that the marginal cost of a unit of any service remains unchanged throughout the relevant range, and that demands either were linear or had constant elasticity. Though we had no assurance that these functional forms spanned the likely cases, we felt they might yield information concerning the closeness of the 1973 prices to those that would have been optimal at that time. Unfortunately, we found that these assumptions about demand and cost curves led to calculated price increases in the shortest mileage bands of day calls that were so large in percentage terms that they undermined the credibility of our assumptions for the range of price changes indicated. We did, however, calculate the size of the welfare improvement under these assumptions, and found that the change in total welfare was small when viewed as a percentage of the total consumers' surplus from, or the total consumers' expenditures on, these services.

To circumvent the difficulties in determining global functional forms for demands and costs, we applied the economic-gradient method (Willig and Bailey 1977a). This method determines the feasible direction of price change that is locally optimal from data on demands, costs, elasticities, and marginal costs at the current point of operation. It also requires the specification of a metric to measure the sizes of sets of price changes.

Figure 2.2 displays the critical Ramsey number, α^*, determined by the economic-gradient method with the Euclidean metric. The best feasible direction entails decreases in the prices of services with Ramsey numbers above the critical line, and inversely. Figure 2.3 shows the price changes that result from a specific move in the locally best direction,[14] a move that is normalized to make the largest percentage change in a single price equal to 100 percent. All short-haul prices increase, long-haul prices decrease, night/weekend prices remain relatively unchanged, day prices generally rise, and evening prices generally fall. The largest percentage change is in the price of the shortest-distance day calls.

Welfare analysis showed that, while not substantial, the rate of change in total consumers' surplus with respect to the size of price changes in this best local direction was significantly positive. Our initial conjecture about the income-distribution consequences of these price changes was that they would produce regressive transfers of real income. We supposed this because it seemed to us that richer households would place a higher proportion of their calls on the long-haul routes. However, the data did not confirm this conjecture.

Figure 2.4 displays data from AT&T's Market Research Information System (MRIS) on relative usage patterns of the lowest income class and a middle-income group. Surprisingly, the patterns are very similar, and thus it appears on the basis of this evidence that pricing of these services might be distributionally neutral. Table 2.2 summarizes usage patterns by time of day for all the income groups. It is clear that the richer households placed a larger proportion of their calls during the day rate period and a smaller proportion during the night/weekend rate period. Consequently,

Table 2.2 Distribution of telephone traffic by income class and rate period: 1973 MRIS data for long-distance service.

Income Class	Percentage of Calls		
	Days	Evenings	Nights, Weekends
<$3,000	23.10	45.59	31.31
$3,000–$4,999	23.93	45.40	30.66
$5,000–$7,499	23.84	46.47	29.69
$7,500–$9,999	26.90	45.05	28.05
$10,000–$14,999	26.84	46.86	26.31
$15,000–$19,999	29.33	46.97	23.70
$20,000–$29,999	29.87	45.44	24.69
⩾$30,000	32.20	46.07	21.73

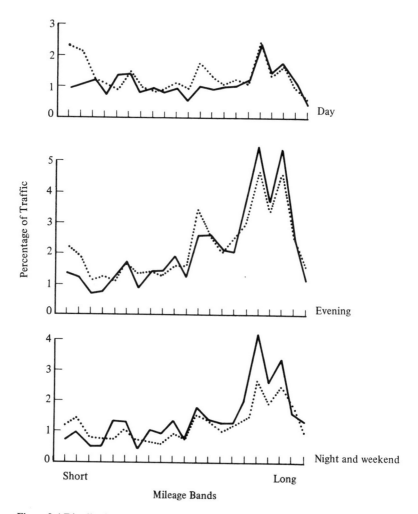

Figure 2.4 Distribution of telephone traffic by income class, mileage band, and time of day. Solid line represents <$3,000 income class; dotted line represents $10,000–$14,999 class.

a pricing policy that would increase the off-peak discount for nights and weekends would yield relatively larger benefits to poorer households.

Making use of the MRIS data on demand patterns by income class, we applied the method suggested by Theorem 3 to price changes in the locally best direction. By construction, this direction is feasible in that it maintains the status-quo level of net revenues. Also, local movement of prices in this optimal direction is guaranteed to increase total surplus. Thus, the first two conditions of theorem 3 are satisfied. To check the third, we defined the benefits to be the relative price decreases times initial quantities, and the costs to be the relative price increases times initial quantities. Table 2.3 summarizes the resulting benefit-cost ratios for the sample households. The differences in the rate-period-specific ratios among income classes reflect the differing distributions of calls among mileage bands. Surprisingly, these ratios show that the very poorest households place a greater proportion of their calls on the longest routes and a smaller proportion on the shortest routes than do other households. This pattern is most pronounced during the discounted evening and night/weekend rate periods.

All classes suffer from the increases in day rates and benefit from the general increase in the offpeak discounts. The total benefit-cost ratios generally decrease with income, owing to the fact (documented in table 2.2) that poorer consumers place a smaller fraction of their calls during the day rate period, which bears the brunt of the price increases. Most striking, however, is the result that all the total benefit-cost ratios substantially exceed 1. This suggests that the policy of changing prices in the locally best direction results in a significant Pareto improvement for residential consumers by income class.

There is an apparent contradiction between this finding and our earlier observation that the total net benefits from large price changes to a calculated Ramsey optimum were not substantial. This contradiction can be resolved by recognizing that the data underlying the Ramsey analysis include both business and residential calls. Although we do not have explicit information on relative proportions of business and residential calls over the various mileage and time-of-day categories, we do know that business calls are concentrated during the day. Thus, the substantial price increases for this category of calls probably mean that the business class as a whole will lose from the policy. As these losses are passed on to consumers in the form of increased product prices or declines in the values of securities, much of the immediate welfare gain to consumers will be dissipated.

Table 2.3 Benefits and costs of price changes in the locally best direction for social welfare: 1973 MRIS data for long-distance telephone service.

Income	Benefit/Cost Ratio			
	Days	Evenings	Nights, Weekends	Total
< $3,000	0.45	23	40	5.2
$3,000–$4,999	0.39	14	24	3.8
$5,000–$7,499	0.45	13	23	3.9
$7,500–$9,999	0.21	12	27	3.1
$10,000–$14,999	0.30	14	25	3.3
$15,000–$19,999	0.25	14	23	2.7
$20,000–$29,999	0.33	14	30	3.3
≥ $30,000	0.42	13	23	3.0

It seems plausible, moreover, that these losses will fall more heavily on richer households than on poor ones. To the extent that business outlays for telephone calls are overhead costs rather than marginal costs, and to the extent that consumer-goods prices move with marginal rather than with average costs, the losses in business telephone consumers' surplus will decrease profits rather than be passed through to households in the form of higher consumer-goods prices. Such declines in profit would undoubtedly affect richer individuals more than proportionately.

If this were the case, then the income-class-specific benefit-cost ratios resulting from the full effects of the price changes would be smaller than those shown in table 2.3, but it is plausible that they would be declining with income. Further, the aggregate net benefits would be positive by the construction of the price changes. Then, theorem 3 would enable us to infer from our crude data and assumptions that there existed a set of regulated price movements in the locally best direction that social-welfare-dominated the then-current status quo.

Conclusion

We have presented a variety of necessary and sufficient conditions for social-welfare dominance of regulatory policies—conditions that can be tested by means of market data. In our study of electricity pricing, we showed that the entire gamut of policy conclusions could be spanned by varying the relative levels of winter and summer prices. In the study of long-distance-telephone pricing we showed that, contrary to our expectations, a move in the locally best direction might have satisfied the monotonicity requirement of theorem 3 and might thus have been social-welfare-dominant. Our discussion of these specific pricing policies has served to demonstrate the workability of our new approach, and to highlight the usefulness of the concept of social-welfare dominance.

It gives us pleasure to thank Jim McCabe for his critical contributions, Glenn Loury for many stimulating conversations on this subject, and W. J. Baumol and R. Schmalensee for their helpful editorial suggestions.

Notes

1. This approach was taken most recently by Broadway (1976).

2. Katzner 1970 gives a clear treatment and the original references.

3. This approach to normative analysis of pricing is due to Feldstein (1972b).

4. The choice of these axioms was inspired by the Rothschild-Stiglitz (1973) analysis of nominal income inequality. Their axioms are extended here to carefully defined measures of real incomes. Yet more general versions of the axioms are studied in Willig and McCabe 1977.

5. Here, for convenience, we assume that ψ and W are differentiable. The development in Willig and McCabe 1977 dispenses with this assumption.

6. These possibilities are analogous to the case of a risk-averse investor who seeks securities with returns that are negatively correlated with the returns on his portfolio. Such an investor will gladly give up some aggregate mean return in order to reduce the risk of his total holdings.

7. This scalar constraint can be easily replaced, as is shown below, by a vector of constraints.

8. We are grateful to R. Schmalensee for pointing out that the case of ties in real income requires special treatment.

9. This illustration is far simpler than the policies being studied in a number of current electricity-pricing experiments (see, for example, CPUCA 1977 and Manning et al. 1976), but the principles developed here can be readily adapted to more complex cases.

10. These numerical results are sensitive to the numbers of households in each income class. For example, had there been 5 low-income, 72 middle-income, and 11 high-income households, the policy for which $r = 1$ would have been beneficial in the aggregate but would have failed to social-welfare-dominate the status quo.

11. Net revenue = total revenue − (sum of marginal costs × quantities).

12. These are named for Frank Ramsey, who first derived this rule in the context of optimal taxation. See Baumol and Bradford 1970 for a discussion of the rule and its history.

13. Consequently, the elasticities and marginal costs do not reflect post-1973 price levels, production technologies, and potentially competitive market structures. Further, to facilitate this pilot study, we assume that there are zero cross-elasticities among the studied categories of calls, that changes in the prices under consideration do not affect the net revenues from other categories of calls, and that the durations of calls do not change endogenously. Without these somewhat unrealistic assumptions, the conditions for Ramsey optimality are more complicated than equation (24).

14. Of course, the calculated locally best feasible direction depends crucially on the use of the inverse elasticity rule and on the magnitudes assigned to its variables. Thus, the quantitative and qualitative price movements displayed in figure 2.3 have no more validity than do the underlying data and the assumptions detailed in n.13.

References

Atkinson, A. B. 1970. "On the Measurement of Inequality." *Journal of Economic Theory* XX: 244–263.

Baumol, W. J., and Bradford, D. F. 1970. "Optimal Departures from Marginal Cost Pricing." *American Economic Review* 60: 265–283.

Broadway, R. 1976. "Integrating Equity and Efficiency in Applied Welfare Economics." *Quarterly Journal of Economics* 90: 541–556.

Connecticut Public Utilities Control Authority (CPUCA). 1977. Connecticut Peak Load Pricing Test.

Debreu, G. 1960. "Topological Methods in Cardinal Utility Theory." In K. J. Arrow et al. (eds.), *Mathematical Methods in the Social Sciences* (Stanford University Press).

Feldstein, M. S. 1972a. "Distributional Equity and the Optimal Structure of Public Prices." *American Economic Review* 62: 32–36.

————. 1972b. "Equity and Efficiency in Public Sector Pricing: The Optimal Two-Part Tariff." *Quarterly Journal of Economics* 86: 175–187.

Hurwicz, L., and Uzawa, H. 1971. "On the Integrability of Demand Functions." In J. S. Chipman et al. (ed.), *Preferences, Utility, and Demand* (New York: Harcourt Brace).

Katzner, D. 1970. *Static Demand Theory*. New York: Macmillan.

Leontief, W. W. 1947. "Introduction to a Theory of the Internal Structure of Functional Relationships." *Econometrica* XX: 361–373.

McCabe, J., and Willig, R. D. 1977. Consumer Surplus and the Effect of Relative Price Changes on the Distribution of Real Income. Manuscript.

Mangasarian, O. L. 1969. *Nonlinear Programming*. New York: McGraw-Hill.

Manning, W. Jr., Mitchell, B. M., and Acton, J. 1976. Design of the Los Angeles Peak-Load Pricing Experiment for Electricity. Rand Corp. report R-1955-DWP.

Mitchell, B. M., and Acton, J. 1977. Peak-Load Pricing in Selected European Electric Utilities. Rand Corp. report R-2031-DWF.

Peltzman, S. 1976. "Toward a More General Theory of Regulation." *Journal of Law and Economics* 19: 211.

Roth, W. E. 1976. "Micro-Data Measurement of Residential Rate Restructuring." *Public Utilities Fortnightly*, January 15, pp. 28–34.

Rothschild, M., and Stiglitz, J. 1973. "Some Further Results on the Measurement of Inequality." *Journal of Economic Theory* 8: 188–204.

Samuelson, P. A. 1963. *Foundations of Economic Analysis*. Cambridge, Mass.: Harvard University Press.

Stigler, G. 1971. "The Economic Theory of Regulation." *Bell Journal of Economics and Management Science* 2: 3–21.

Willig, R. D. 1973. Consumer's Surplus: A Rigorous Cookbook. Technical report 98, Institute for Mathematical Studies in the Social Sciences, Stanford University.

————. 1976. "Consumer's Surplus Without Apology." *American Economic Review* 66: 589–597.

————. 1981. "Social Welfare Dominance." *American Economic Review* 71.

Willig, R. D., and Bailey, E. E. 1979. "The Economic Gradient Method." *American Economic Review* 69: 96–101.

———. 1977b. "Ramsey-Optimal Pricing of Long Distance Telephone Services." In J. T. Wenders (ed.), *Pricing in Regulated Industries: Theory and Application.* Mountain States Telephone and Telegraph Co.

Willig, R. D., and McCabe, J. 1977. Social Welfare Dominance. Manuscript.

Comment

Alvin K. Klevorick

Students of public regulation have developed a number of competing theories about the interactions between regulated firms and regulatory agencies and about the social effects of those interactions. The paper I am to discuss represents an output of regulator/regulatee cooperation that differs in kind from the outputs discussed by most of those theories. (Admittedly, though, the interaction that generated this paper does not fit the typical situation considered in these theories, since the regulator from the CAB does not regulate Bell Labs!) Willig and Bailey have produced an interesting, carefully done piece of theoretical and applied work on an important subject.

The authors present new methodological tools for taking income-distribution concerns into account in regulatory policymaking. They also provide pilot applications of these new "social welfare dominance" methods to regulatory policymaking. The illustrative applications are interesting in and of themselves, and also indicate how the theoretical methods developed in the first part of the article might be put to use. At the same time, the electricity and telephone pricing examples serve to highlight several basic problems facing any attempt to apply the theoretical development in deciding real issues. I shall discuss two of these problems of implementation and then turn to some questions about the theoretical results themselves.

First, two of the axioms that underlie the social-welfare-dominance relation—axiom A2 (anonymity) and axiom A3 (which I shall call "regressive-transfer aversion")—are stated in the form "At prices $\mathbf{p}^0$, the social decisionmaker. . . ." However, the prices $\mathbf{p}^0$ are not defined. These prices constitute the basis for computing real income. In the seasonal electricity pricing example, Willig and Bailey use the then-current set of prices as the base for real incomes. Though they do not say so explicitly, I take it they also use the then-current set of prices as $\mathbf{p}^0$ in the long-distance-telephone pricing example. At only one point in the paper is there a caveat about these base prices: In discussing theorem 1, which provides necessary and sufficient conditions for one policy to social-welfare-dominate another, the authors note that the partial sum of the aggregated surpluses of the poorest k consumers is independent of

p^0 "if the identities of the relevant consumers are independent of p^0." But why should those identities be independent of p^0?

If the ranking of consumers by real income does depend on the base prices, we face a substantial (even if traditional) index-number problem. It would seem to be a serious problem for a methodology put forth to treat income-distribution concerns that its conclusions are sensitive to the choice of base prices p^0. Application of the tools presented in the Willig-Bailey paper could indicate that one policy social-welfare-dominates a second under one set of base prices but that the second policy social welfare dominates the first under an alternative set of base prices. What criterion are we to use in choosing the base prices?

A second difficulty an analyst faces in applying the paper's theoretical results to actual policy issues derives from the level at which the theoretical development proceeds. The tests for social-welfare dominance presented in the paper's theorems and propositions are stated in terms of real-income changes (and benefit-cost ratios) of individual consumers. Bailey and Willig realize, however, that in practical analysis considerations of data availability will generally require that consumers be grouped into a manageable number of income classes; indeed, they use such classes in their pilot applications. This involves considering as identical the welfare weights of all consumers within a class and applying the paper's theoretical results across classes rather than across consumers. But then a finding that one policy social-welfare-dominates a second may well depend on the income classes one chooses to use or is forced to use because of data limitations. At a minimum, some sensitivity analysis of any policy conclusion should be performed to see whether alternative partitionings of consumers into income classes yield different conclusions. If grouping consumers differently does change the ranking of policies according to the social-welfare-dominance criterion, what policy conclusion should we draw? How are we to choose the "correct" income-class partition?

Let us turn now to the authors' interpretation of their basic result (theorem 1) and, specifically, to condition (15), which it imposes on the real-income changes of the k poorest consumers. Willig and Bailey suggest that their condition incorporates the Rawlsian dictum that the poorest member of society be made better off. If we identify Rawls's view with his difference principle or a maximin social-welfare strategy, then in a pairwise comparison of policies a Rawlsian would prefer the policy that improved the lot of the worst-off person. (Philosophers would object to such a narrow view of Rawls's theory of justice.) Hence, for pairwise comparisons, the authors' interpretation is strictly correct. But, in the context of choosing one policy from a set of many alternatives, there is a difficulty with viewing the authors' condition as incorporating Rawls's dictum: From the set of all feasible policies, someone following Rawls's maximin principle would choose that course which *maximized* the well-being of the worst-off person. And that policy need not be a social-welfare-dominating one; it need not satisfy the conditions in the authors' theorem 1. This, in fact, provides an illustration of the point Willig and Bailey make when they present "positive and normative views" of their theorems and approach. They write: "Suppose an analyst observes that an SDM has effected a policy move that has resulted in real-income changes ... that fail to satisfy equations (15) and (16)[the conditions of their fundamental theorem]. The move can certainly not be logically criticized on those grounds, even by believers in axioms 1–3. It is possible that the chosen policy was optimal for the SDM's particular preferences, and that those preferences satisfy the axioms."

Since we have mentioned Rawls's maximin criterion, it is worth noting that Willig and Bailey are subject to a question (with an implied criticism) which has frequently been directed at Rawls. It concerns the lexicographic nature of their conditions. How large would the gains of the best-off $n - k$ people in the society have to be before one would be willing to tolerate a very small loss (an ε loss) in the well-being of the lowest-placed k individuals? To put this another way, is there no conceivable ratio of benefits to costs for society as a whole that would induce one to accept an ε loss in the partial sum of real-income changes for some group of low-ranking consumers, where the ranking is, as throughout, by real income? Perhaps the answer is that there is no such total benefit-cost ratio that one would accept. But surely this question merits reflection, for if such an overall benefit-cost ratio does exist, we should have some doubts about how readily we can accept the Willig-Bailey axioms.

More generally, the article implicitly raises, but does not address, one fundamental question. The analysis proceeds on the basis of an axiom that sounds weak but is, in fact, quite strong (in the sense that it does a lot of work in generating the results): axiom 3, which stipulates that the social decisionmaker displays "regressive-transfer aversion." It states: "At prices $\mathbf{p}^0$, the SDM does not find desirable any transfer of income from a nominally poorer to a richer consumer." But the supposition that the SDM has this view must be based on some conception on his part of what the just distribution of income is and how the distribution at prices $\mathbf{p}^0$ compares with that just distribution. The paper provides us with no underlying theory of the justice of the income distribution. To ask that it provide one is, to be sure, to give the authors a large order to fill. But without an appeal to some theory (be it an existing one or a new one) of what ought to be, and how this compares with what is at any time, it is difficult to evaluate how compelling the Willig-Bailey axioms are. And, as Willig and Bailey recognize, any policy interest their results have must ultimately depend on how compelling one finds the axioms that lead to those results.

One should also ask whether the methodology presented in this paper is, in fact, well suited for application to piecemeal regulatory policy actions, or whether it is not better suited for evaluating *complete* social structures and states of the world. A decision chosen because it is social-welfare-dominating will generate a new set of nominal incomes and a new set of prices p^0, which will, in turn, serve as the basis for the next piecemeal policy decision. The result of all these piecemeal policy steps need not social-welfare-dominate the position from which we begin. Alternatively, consider independent policy decisions being made simultaneously by different regulatory agencies, none of which takes into account the changes any of the others is making. The fact that each agency chooses a policy that social-welfare-dominates the status quo does not guarantee that the sum total of these policy choices will social-welfare-dominate the starting position.

While I think that both the implementation issues and the broader questions I have raised about the Willig-Bailey analysis need attention before their results can have substantial impact on policy decisions, the authors have given us a very stimulating and thought-provoking paper.

Comment

Richard Schmalensee

In this very interesting and well-written paper, Willig and Bailey propose, defend, and apply a general test for the desirability of economic policies that takes into account both the magnitude of net benefits and their incidence. Their basic approach follows that used by Atkinson, by Rothschild and Stiglitz, and by others in analysis of income-inequality measures. (Thus, what is called "social-welfare dominance" here has been called "Lorenz dominance" by Dasgupta, Sen, and Starrett.)

Willig and Bailey consider a class of social-welfare functions that are nondecreasing and symmetric in real incomes and have the property that regressive transfers do not increase welfare. (It follows from work by Rothschild and Stiglitz that this latter condition is implied by quasiconcavity of the welfare function, but it does not imply quasiconcavity.) They show that in a society with n individuals, if a proposed policy would lead to a new income distribution in which the total of the lowest k incomes exceeds the same total in the existing distribution, for all k between 1 and n, all social-welfare functions in this class would be increased by adoption of the policy. The policy (or the income distribution to which it gives rise) is said to dominate the status quo. If all these sums would be lower with the policy in effect than in the status quo, all welfare functions in their class would be lowered by adoption of the policy, and the status quo dominates. If some sums are higher and some are lower, neither situation dominates, and the desirability of the policy cannot be determined without more information about the welfare function.

The stochastic dominance literature, to which this approach is intimately formally related, suggests a simple illustration of this test. Suppose that incomes are initially normally distributed across individuals, with standard deviation σ_m. A policy is proposed that would yield a normal distribution of real net benefits across individuals, with mean $\bar{b}$, standard deviation σ_b, and correlation ρ_{mb} with initial incomes. Real incomes after adoption of the policy would then also be normal. It is easy to show that adotion of the proposed policy dominates the status quo in the Willig-Bailey sense if and only if (a) $\bar{b} > 0$ and (b) $\rho_{mb} \leq -\sigma_b/2\sigma_m$. If both these inequalities are reversed, the status quo dominates. Condition (a) always requires positive total net benefits. Condition (b) requires that inequality, as measured by the standard deviation of real incomes, not be increased. If all individuals receive $\bar{b} > 0$, condition (a) is satisfied, and both sides of the inequality in (b) are zero. If different individuals receive different benefits, so that σ_b is positive, benefits and initial income must be negatively correlated if the policy is to dominate the status quo. Distaste for risk in the stochastic dominance literature is formally equivalent to distaste for inequality here.

Axiomatic welfare theory of the sort propounded in this paper is potentially useful only to the extent that the axioms chosen reflect widely held beliefs. If this is the case, it is at least conceivable that most policymakers could be persuaded to agree with the axioms, even if in advance of such persuasion their behavior violated those axioms. (The analogy with the axioms of expected utility theory is close but not exact, since, as Willig and Bailey note, actors in the political process may have selfish incentives to take actions that lower social welfare as they perceive it.)

From this perspective, axioms 2 and 3, though certainly as reasonable as most in the literature, seem less than totally compelling. Since Professor Klevorick examined axiom 3 at length, I will concentrate on axiom 2.

Suppose we are choosing between two proposed policies that affect only two people: person R, who has initial income of $20,000, and person P, who has initial income of $5,000. Policy 1 would give each $5,000 in net benefits, while policy 2 would lower R's real income by $10,000 and raise P's real income by $20,000. Since the two policies lead to the same *ex post* income distribution, axiom 2 says that the social decisionmaker must be indifferent between them. I would expect most policymakers to prefer policy 1, however, thereby exhibiting what might be called change aversion. In a real world where habits are not easily altered, there are costs to imposing large shocks on society, but axiom 2 assumes those costs away. Axiom 2 is compelling when one is evaluating hypothetical long-run equilibria; it is less so when one is considering the actual short-run impacts of proposed policies.

In order to apply the basic notions discussed above in a world of many commodities, in which prices change, one needs a definition of real income. As is well known, this concept has a unique meaning only under special assumptions; there is a classic index-number problem here. Willig and Bailey deal with this by choosing a single reference price vector, $\mathbf{p}^0$. If the actual price vector is $\mathbf{p}_1$, they define a household's real income as its money income plus the Hicksian equivalent variation associated with a price change from $\mathbf{p}^0$ to $\mathbf{p}_1$. In much of the paper, $\mathbf{p}^0$ is taken to be the actual initial price vector, so that net benefit from the price change becomes exactly the ordinary equivalent variation. As Willig has shown elsewhere, the choice of a reference price level and the choice between the equivalent and compensating variations do not matter much when policies with small income effects are considered. But if income effects are important enough that the Marshallian surplus approximation is questionable, these initial choices may affect the policy choices implied by the analysis. Willig and Bailey take a reasonable route around the index-number problem; they cannot eliminate it.

In the illustrative applications of their test, Willig and Bailey consider total net gains to all individuals originally in various income classes, rather than looking directly at distributions of individual incomes. That is, the operational version of the test requires that the net gain of the lowest income class be positive, that the total net gain of the lowest two income classes be positive, and so on. This provides only an approximate test, since policy may cause people to change income classes. To take an extreme example, consider a society composed only of individuals R and P, as described above. Suppose a policy would give \$17,000 to P and take \$16,000 from R. This passes the operational test as defined above; the gains to P are positive, and the gains to R and P together are positive. But since R is now the low-income individual, with an income of \$4,000, it is clear that the new income distribution does not dominate the old. For small changes, this sort of switching seems likely to be unimportant, and there is no obvious way to deal with it in applications in which individuals cannot be considered directly. But a problem does remain in principle when broad income classes are treated as individuals.

A few words on the potential applications of theorems 2 and 3 seem to be in order. These theorems state that if aggregate net benefits are positive, a sufficient condition for dominance (as defined above) is that there exist *some* division of net benefits received by each income class into gross benefits and costs such that the class-specific benefit-cost ratios decline with income. But this is only a sufficient condition, and the division of net benefits that does the trick need have no relation at all to the economic meanings of the terms "benefit" and "cost."

In a two-person society, suppose that a number of prices are changed on commodities consumed mainly by the poorer person, P. Suppose P receives \$10 in benefits from price reductions but loses \$9 from price increases. The richer person, R, gains \$2 from the price cuts but loses \$1 from price rises. The policy has produced a dominating income distribution, but the benefit-cost ratio is larger for the high-income R than for the low-income P. This is not a curiosum; in the last two rows of table 2.1, electricity pricing policies are presented that dominate the status quo but do not have declining benefit-cost ratios. Table 2.3 shows a telephone pricing policy with the same properties. If net benefits can be computed in any application, information can only be lost by converting the results to benefit-cost ratios. On the other hand, theorems 2 and 3 may be of considerable value in situations in which qualitative information is available but a complete quantitative analysis is impossible.

Willig and Bailey clearly feel that their dominance criterion can be used to improve actual regulatory policymaking. The pilot applications to electricity and telephone pricing that they present shed some light on the merit of this position. In testing for dominance, both studies employ data on residential customers only. Income classes, rather than individuals, are the focus of the analysis, and class-specific demand elasticities are unavailable. The key data give consumption of the commodities considered by income class at initial prices. Data sets of this sort can presumably be routinely constructed at moderate cost.

Using their proposition 1, Willig and Bailey show that these data can support interesting analyses of the direct effects of price changes on residential customers. The basic tool amounts to a first-order approximation to consumer surplus changes. Suppose that it is proposed to change a vector of prices from $\mathbf{p}$ to $\mathbf{p} + \Delta\mathbf{p}$. Let $\mathbf{X}_i$ be the vector of purchases of these commodities by individuals in income class i at prices $\mathbf{p}$. Then a first-order approximation to the net benefits received by class i is simply $B_i = -(\mathbf{X}_i)'(\Delta\mathbf{p})$. As the Willig-Bailey paper shows, if the B_i pass the fundamental test for dominance (and if it can be assumed that households do not switch income classes and that households with equal initial incomes satisfy the conditions of proposition 1), then there exists a positive constant, $\hat{t}$, such that the actual net benefits of a change from $\mathbf{p}$ to $\mathbf{p} + t(\Delta\mathbf{p})$ pass this same test as long as t is less than $\hat{t}$. There is no way to know if the original proposal passes this test (that is, to know if $\hat{t} \geq 1$) without income-class-specific demand elasticity information. Still, this sort of local analysis can make at least a strong *prima facie* case for or against proposed changes in prices paid by households.

However, in both pilot applications in the paper the proposed price changes would also affect business customers. The tools presented by Willig and Bailey do not help one to translate changes in firms' costs to changes in real incomes of households in different income classes. These latter changes, which may be important in many applications, must depend on households' various roles as input suppliers and output demanders, and on conditions in the directly and indirectly affected markets. It may seem plausible, for instance, that increased business telephone rates ultimately fall more heavily on rich households than on poor ones. But to demonstrate this quantitatively or even qualitatively in any particular case would require an elaborate and expensive general equilibrium analysis. Thus, while it is comparatively simple to analyze in a useful way the direct incidence of changes in prices that households pay, it is much harder to assess the total or ultimate incidence of price changes that also affect firms. It appears unlikely that the ultimate incidence of such changes could be considered on a routine basis by regulatory agencies or regulated firms unless new techniques of analysis are devised.

Difficulties of this same sort arise in principle even if one is concerned only with efficiency, of course. In a second-best world, with distortions elsewhere in the economy, precise measurement of the efficiency implications of any proposed price change becomes a very complex undertaking. But, efficiency analysis is greatly simplified if the rest of the economy is plausibly assumed to be approximately competitive. Simple pricing formulas, such as the Ramsey rule that Willig and Bailey employ, follow from this assumption. In analysis of incidence, however, the competitive assumption does not seem to have similar power. Without tractable methods for analyzing the ultimate incidence of price increases affecting firms, the value of the Willig-Bailey methodology to actual decision-makers is hard to judge.

Even if such methods are devised, problems arise when one considers the consequences of requiring a number of regulatory (or other policy-making) agencies to employ the Willig-Bailey tests. If a large number of agencies attempt to make progressive redistributions, their actions may have non-negligible effects on incentives to supply labor, to invest in skill acquisition, and to supply capital. As the optimal income tax literature has shown, incentive effects of this sort can substantially raise the optimal level of inequality. While such second-order indirect effects of regulatory policies might conceivably be well considered in especially creative academic analysis, regulatory agencies or regulated firms obviously could not do so on a routine basis. Further, as the paper notes, it is possible for two policies, neither of which dominates the status quo, to dominate it if imposed as a package. But individual agencies can only make packages that employ the instruments at their disposal. Suppose for the sake of argument that it is possible to apply the Willig-Bailey test correctly, and that regulators are instructed to adopt only dominant policies. Then two potential policies of the sort described above, in the hands of separate agencies, would likely fail to be adopted without much more coordination of decisionmaking than seems imaginable. On the other hand, if agencies are instructed only not to adopt dominated policies, a great deal of analytical effort (beyond that necessary to compute total net benefits) might be required per dominated policy detected. There is a case, I think, for centralizing responsibility for equity and decentralizing responsibility for efficiency.

The general message of this paper, that distributional effects deserve consideration in policymaking, is hard to quarrel with. Willig and Bailey propose an interesting and potentially usable test that considers such effects. I give them very high marks both for topic selection and for quality of output. Their tools permit one to assess the merit of changes in prices paid by households in a relatively convincing fashion. The value of their contribution would be greatly enhanced if similarly powerful tools were forged for analysis of changes in prices paid by firms.

3

Theory of Solvency Regulation in the Property and Casualty Insurance Industry

Patricia Munch
Dennis Smallwood

The objective of this article is to examine the case for solvency regulation of the property and casualty insurance industry and to examine the effects of regulation in its current form. The case for solvency regulation clearly derives from the difficulty of a policyholder in establishing the financial soundness of alternative firms. But policyholders are not the only parties concerned about the possibility of insolvency. A firm's owners also lose; in fact, they lose their equity completely, whereas policyholders and claimants may receive partial coverage. The insolvency risk is not determined exogenously, but is a byproduct of conscious choices taken to advance owner objectives. This study is motivated by the question: Under what conditions are the interests of owners sufficient to provide policyholders with an adequate level of protection?

Previous analyses have focused on two aspects of the problem: the intrinsic risks in writing insurance, and managerial incompetence or dishonesty. Analyses that focus on the intrinsic risks of the insurance business concentrate on the statistical properties of the loss distributions and on statistical-ruin problems. Taking the parameters of the loss distributions as given, such studies attempt to determine the level of surplus or reserves necessary to reduce the probability of insolvency to some small arbitrarily chosen level. The implicit (sometimes explicit) assumption is that insolvencies occur only because regulators have not applied the sophisticated mathematical and computational tools that are necessary to establish required capital requirements (see, for example, Hammond et al. 1978; Hofflander 1969). It is confidently hoped that improvements in regulatory skills can and should reduce or eliminate the insolvency problem.

Those who stress the importance of managerial incompetence or dishonesty (see McKinsey and Co. 1974) pin their hopes on more frequent examinations, and better trained auditors. In this case, there is an implicit assumption that a clear distinction exists between the behavior of firms that become insolvent and honest, well-managed firms. We ignore problems of fraud and dishonesty not because we deny their existence, but because they constitute a different problem that is amenable to a different type of analysis and regulatory response.[1]

We adopt the position that both the underlying risks of the insurance business and the behavior of management are important. We assume that managers will accept those risks that maximize the value of the firm to its owners. Thus, the underlying statistical properties of claims distributions and investment-returns distributions are relevant. But we reject the presumption that the risks accepted by the firm are exogenous. Rather, we assume that the risk of insolvency is selected by a management that is competent but is not motivated to avoid all risks, at any cost.

The article thus focuses on the choices of the firm that implicitly determine the probability of insolvency. An analysis of regulations to reduce the likelihood of insolvencies must consider how such regulations affect managerial decisions.

One-Period Model of an Insurance Firm

In this model, at the beginning of a given period the owners of a firm provide financial "capital" equal to K. The firm then sets a premium rate P and underwrites Q policyholders.[2] For simplicity, all claims and other costs are incurred at the end of the period. The ith policyholder imposes a cost C_i on the firm, which represents both the total claims cost for the ith policyholder (including both claims payments and "loss adjustment expenses") and the costs of writing and administering the policy. Thus, C_i has a positive, nonrandom component, but we shall nevertheless refer to C_i as the claims cost of the ith policyholder for convenience. Fixed, overhead insurer costs are ignored. Thus, total insurer costs, T, are

$$T = \sum_{i=1}^{Q} C_i \tag{1}$$

and we let $\bar{C}$ denote average realized claims cost per policyholder:

$$\bar{C} = T/Q = \left(\sum_{i=1}^{Q} C_i \right) \Big/ Q \tag{2}$$

so that $T = \bar{C}Q$.

Policyholders are assumed to have identical claims probability distributions and to impose equal nonrandom costs on the insurer. Thus, expected claims cost, denoted E_C, and the variance in claims cost, denoted σ_C, are equal for all policyholders:

$$E(C_i) = E(C_j) = E_C \qquad \text{for all } i,j, \tag{3}$$

$$\text{Var}(C_i) = \text{Var}(C_j) = \sigma_C = (S_C)^2 \qquad \text{for all } i,j. \tag{4}$$

Claims costs of different policyholders are not assumed to be independent random variables. The pairwise correlation coefficient for any two policyholders is assumed equal and is denoted by γ:

$$\text{Cov}[C_i, C_j] = \gamma\sigma_C \qquad \text{for all } i,j. \tag{5}$$

The assumption that claims costs of different policyholders are not independent implies that the variance per policyholder on "underwriting" does not necessarily approach zero as the number of policyholders increases, as is usually assumed. We demonstrate in appendix C (at the end of the article) that this aspect of the model can be interpreted as reflecting the firm's "uncertainty about the distribution of claims." That is, allowing $\gamma \neq 0$ widens the range of interpretation of the model to include the case where the firm is uncertain about the parameters of the claims distribution. While the firm may be expected to eventually infer the parameters of a stable claims distribution, uncertainty may persist if the claims environment is changing.

Since the firm obtains its capital and receives premiums at the beginning of a period, but does not pay claims until the end of the period, it must choose how to invest its funds during the period. We assume the investment environment of the capital asset pricing model (CAPM). Within that context, each investor chooses to divide his portfolio among a risk-free security and various risky securities.[3] But equilibrium within the securities market, which is attained after the price of each security has adjusted to equate supply and demand for that security, is shown to imply that each investor purchases the same combination of the available risky securities. In effect, in equilibrium each investor owns a share of the entire market.[4] Thus, investor differences are reflected only in the division of their portfolio between the "risk-free asset" and the "market asset," where the latter contains all of the risky securities in the proportion to their total market value.[5]

At the beginning of the period, the firm has total investible funds equal to $K + PQ$. Its second decision is to choose α, the proportion of these funds that will be invested in the risky ("market") asset, which earns a random rate of return R_m. The remaining proportion $(1 - \alpha)$ is placed in the risk-free asset, which earns a certain rate of return equal to R_f. At the end of the period, the firm's total realized assets then equal

$$(1 - \alpha)(K + PQ)(1 + R_f) + \alpha(K + PQ)(1 + R_m)$$
$$= [1 + (1 - \alpha)R_f + \alpha R_m](K + PQ), \tag{6}$$

where R_m is a random variable with expectation $E(R_m)$, variance denoted by σ_m, and standard deviation denoted by S_m.

Claims costs are not assumed to be necessarily independent of the return on the market asset.[6] We let $\sigma_{m,c}$ denote the covariance between the market rate of return and the claims cost of each policyholder, while ρ denotes the corresponding correlation coefficient:

$$\sigma_{m,c} = \text{Cov}[R_m, C_i] = \rho S_m S_c \qquad \text{for all } i. \tag{7}$$

In the usual model of the insurance firm, risk relates only to the randomness in claims, which are assumed to be independent across policyholders. Thus, the risk of insolvency becomes negligible as the number of policyholders becomes large, if the level of K per policyholder is held constant. In this model, uncertainty about the firm's investment returns is introduced, which does not become negligible as the firm increases in size. Furthermore, the correlation of claims costs across different policyholders —which can represent uncertainty about the probability distribution that applies to claims—means that the variability of the average claim does not necessarily become insignificant as the number of policyholders increases. Thus, the model encompasses three sources of insolvency risk: random claims variability, uncertainly about the parameters of the claims distribution, and variability of investment returns.

Maximizing the Market Value of an Insurance Firm

Let μ denote the difference between the total assets and total liabilities of the firm at the end of the period:

$$\mu = [1 + (1 - \alpha)R_f + \alpha R_m](K + PQ) - \left(\sum_{i=1}^{Q} C_i\right), \tag{8}$$

where K is the initial capital of the firm, PQ is total premium revenue, R_f and R_m are rates of return on the risk-free and the market assets, and C_i is claims costs for the ith policyholder. Taking limited liability into account, the net cash flow μ^+ is as follows:

$$\mu^+ = 0 \text{ if } \mu < 0$$
$$= \mu \text{ if } \mu \geq 0. \tag{9}$$

Under the CAPM, the market value of the ownership rights to μ^+, valued at the beginning of the period, is

$$V_+ = \left(\frac{1}{1 + R_f}\right)[E(\mu^+) - \theta\,\mathrm{Cov}(\mu^+, U)], \tag{10}$$

where U represents total cash flow in the entire securities market and θ is a parameter determined by general equilibrium in the market. The term involving the covariance of μ^+ and U represents the market-determined "penalty" for nondiversifiable risk.[7]

The ultimate problem is to analyze which combinations of K, P, Q, and α represent the firm's optimal choices with regard to market value, with limited liability taken into account. However, in the context of limited liability, the question of how to specify the demand relationship arises. Although the assumption of perfect knowledge by applicants is not an interesting context for examining solvency regulation, it would be useful to understand optimal firm behavior in that context.

Since Q, P, K, and α all affect the likelihood of insolvency, we can (conceptually) write demand as a function of these variables. Even beyond the complexity introduced by having Q appear on the right-hand side of the demand relationship $Q = D(Q, P, K, \alpha)$, this specification is too general to yield interesting results. Letting z represent the probability of insolvency, can we simply write $Q = D(P, z)$?

In fact, specifying demand as a function of only P and z neglects the possibility of partial claims recoveries. The condition $\mu < 0$ implies that claims cannot all be fully paid, but only in the extreme case in which total assets are zero at the end of the period will claims recoveries be zero. Thus, the theoretically justified perfect-knowledge assumption is that demand depends on the complete distributions of both final assets and claims. In addition to its complexity, such a specification severely stretches the perfect-knowledge assumption.[8]

Since policyholders are neither perfectly informed nor totally ignorant, the more relevant assumption would be that buyers are partially informed; but to analyze market equilibrium and the effects of regulation with such an assumption is extremely difficult.[9]

An alternative is to assume that applicants use reasonably simple rules, possibly involving proxies for financial solidity. But in that context, a new issue arises: In the context of buyers who use simple rules or proxies to estimate financial condition, firm value cannot be validly analyzed within a one-period model. The basis of firm value becomes fundamentally different. When applicants are assumed able to monitor all relevant parameters and infer their implications for claims outcomes, a firm has no opportunity to build intangible capital. Any firm can enter the market, set P, Q, K, and α, and sell to applicants who completely understand the significance of these choices. For the perfectly informed applicant, a firm's history—including whether it filed for bankruptcy in the previous period—is irrelevant.

Within any context other than perfect knowledge, demand will generally not be a function of only the current values of the parameters. In fact, it is quite reasonable for partially informed applicants, who realize that their inferences about financial condition are unreliable, to view proxies such as the age and size of the firm, and even its advertising budget,[10] as indicators of financial solidity of the firm.[11] But if two firms (in particular, an "old" firm and a "new" firm) that choose the same parameters nevertheless face different demand curves, a source of "goodwill" or "intangible capital" is created. Since a firm can be presumed to lose this intangible capital in the event of insolvency, a one-period model does not capture a crucial aspect of the problem. Since continuing access to the firm's demand curve creates this value, a multiperiod model is required.

We analyze a multiperiod model below, but we are forced to simply set α equal to zero. To gain some insight into the more general problem, we analyze the case of unlimited liability in the remainder of this section. Since policyholders are thus assured of total recovery of all claims, we may assume that demand is a function of only the premium rate, $Q = D(P)$.

The Case of Unlimited Liability
Under the assumptions that the firm's owners are subject to unlimited liability and that they have assets adequate to cover all possible claims, the net cash flow to owners at the end of the period is equal to μ, defined in equation (8), without regard to its sign. Demand is then a function only of the premium rate, $Q = D(P)$. Within this context, we can analyze the choices of Q and α that maximize market value. According to the CAPM, the market value of the ownership of μ is

$$V = \left(\frac{1}{1 + R_f}\right)[E(\mu) - \theta \operatorname{Cov}(\mu, U)]. \tag{11}$$

Total market cash flow U includes the additional cash flow generated by the insurance firm under consideration. However, the cash flows represented by the financial investment activity of the firm should obviously not be doubly counted when defining U. Thus, we decompose μ into two components:

$$\mu = \mu^* + \mu^{**}, \tag{12}$$

where

$$\mu^* = (1 + R_f)(K + PQ) - \left(\sum_{i=1}^{Q} C_i\right), \tag{13}$$

$$\mu^{**} = \alpha(R_m - R_f)(K + PQ). \tag{14}$$

Then μ^* can be considered as the additional cash flow generated by the firm,[12] while μ^{**} represents the net cash flow to the firm as a result of its investment in market securities. In other words, if we let M represent all other flows of funds in the securities market at the end of the period, we can write

$$U = M + \mu^*, \tag{15}$$

where μ^{**} is already included in M.

Thus, we can write

$$V = \left(\frac{1}{1 + R_f}\right)\{E(\mu) - \theta \operatorname{Cov}[\mu, U]\} \tag{16}$$

$$= \left(\frac{1}{1 + R_f}\right)\{E(\mu^* + \mu^{**}) - \theta \operatorname{Cov}[\mu^* + \mu^{**}, M + \mu^*]\}, \tag{17}$$

where M is independent of Q and α. Since $E(\cdot)$ and $\operatorname{COV}[\cdot]$ are linear, we can write

$$V = V^* + V^{**}, \tag{18}$$

where

$$V^* = \left(\frac{1}{1 + R_f}\right)\{E(\mu^*) - \theta \operatorname{Cov}[\mu^*, M + \mu^*]\}, \tag{19}$$

$$V^{**} = \left(\frac{1}{1 + R_f}\right)\{E(\mu^{**}) - \theta \operatorname{Cov}[\mu^{**}, M + \mu^*]\}. \tag{20}$$

The total value of the firm is thus the sum of V^* (which represents the value placed by the market on ownership right to the additional funds generated by the insurance firm) and V^{**} (the additional value generated by the investment activity of the firm).

For all Q and all α,

$$V^{**} = 0 \tag{21}$$

(this is proved in appendix A). Since V^* is independent of α, it follows that the market value of the insurance firm is independent of α, the proportion of investible funds placed in the market asset. The reason is that as the firm increases α, the increase in expected earnings is exactly counterbalanced by the penalty imposed by the market on nondiversifiable risk. Since an increase in expected return can be obtained only by increasing the covariance of μ with the market, the higher return on the investment portfolio is exactly offset by the premium demanded by equity owners for bearing additional risk.

Since V^{**} is identically zero and V^* is not a function of α, the value of the firm is maximized when V^* is maximized with respect to Q. Thus, we can write the market value of the insurance firm as

$$V = V^* = \left(\frac{1}{1 + R_f}\right)[E(\mu^*) - \theta \operatorname{Cov}(\mu^*, M + \mu^*)]. \tag{22}$$

In appendix A, we evaluate $E(\mu^*)$ and $\operatorname{Cov}(\mu^*, M + \mu^*)$ and show that

$$V = \left(\frac{1}{1 + R_f}\right)\{(1 + R_f)(K + PQ) - QE_C$$

$$- \theta[-QV_M\sigma_{m,C} + (1 + (Q - 1)\gamma)Q\sigma_C]\}, \tag{23}$$

where V_M represents the total market value of the ownership rights to M, all other end-of-period flows of funds in the market. Taking partials with respect to Q, the first-order condition for maximization of V is

$$(1 + R_f)\left(\frac{\partial PQ}{\partial Q}\right) = E_C + \theta[-V_M\sigma_{m,C} + (1 + (2Q - 1)\gamma)\sigma_C]. \tag{24}$$

We can more easily interpret this equation if we translate into different parameters. The general equilibrium within the securities market which is implied by the CAPM can be characterized in two ways. The first, already noted, is a condition relating the value of an asset to the expected value of its gross return μ and the covariance of the gross return with the total flow of funds in the market, U:

$$V = \left(\frac{1}{1 + R_f}\right)[E(\mu) - \theta \operatorname{Cov}(\mu, U)]. \tag{25}$$

Note that the market-determined parameter θ varies with the scale of the total market. An equivalent characterization of the asset market equilibrium can be written in terms of the rate of return on the jth asset, R_j, and the overall rate of return on the entire market, R_U. Equilibrium rates of return satisfy the equation

$$E(R_j) = R_f + \lambda \operatorname{Cov}[R_j, R_U]. \tag{26}$$

The parameter λ, sometimes termed the market risk premium, is equal to

$$\lambda = [E(R_U) - R_f]/\sigma_U, \tag{27}$$

where σ_U is the variance of R_U.[13] The relationship between θ and λ is

$$\lambda = \theta V_U, \tag{28}$$

where V_U refers to the total value of all market assets. Hence, we can rewrite the equilibrium condition as

$$(1 + R_f)\left(\frac{\partial PQ}{\partial Q}\right) = E_C - \lambda\sigma_{m,C}\left(\frac{V_m}{V_U}\right) + \lambda\left(\frac{[1 + (2Q - 1)\gamma]\sigma_C}{V_U}\right). \tag{29}$$

The third term on the right-hand side reflects the increase in total market variance due to the firm in question, and will be essentially zero for all but very large firms. Similarly, we can take $V_m/V_U \approx 1$, except where the firm represents a significant proportion of the total market.

Thus, we can summarize the conditions for maximization of the value of the insurance firm, except where the variability of the firm's returns represents a significant share of the total variance in the entire securities market, as follows:

$$\underset{\alpha,Q}{\text{maximize }} V \Rightarrow \left\{ \begin{array}{l} \alpha \text{ irrelevant} \\ (1 + R_f)\left(\dfrac{\partial PQ}{\partial Q}\right) = E_C - \lambda\sigma_{m,C} \end{array} \right\}, \tag{30}$$

where V is the market value of the insurance firm, Q is the number of policyholders it accepts at the premium rate P, α is the proportion of investible funds placed in the (risky) market asset, R_f is the rate of return on the risk-free asset, E_C is the expected claims costs per policyholder, λ is the market-determined risk premium, and $\sigma_{m,C}$ is the covariance between the market rate of return and claims costs.

Since $\partial PQ/\partial Q$ is the marginal revenue from adding a policyholder, equation (30) indicates simply that marginal revenue is equal to the discounted value of expected claims cost plus a risk premium which reflects the nondiversifiable component of claims costs. If we assume a competitive insurance market, we can set marginal revenue equal to the premium rate and interpret (30) as determining the competitive premium rate:

$$P = \frac{E_C - \lambda \sigma_{m,C}}{1 + R_f}. \tag{31}$$

Let us consider first the case where claims costs and the market are uncorrelated:

$$\rho = 0 \Rightarrow P = E_C/(1 + R_f). \tag{32}$$

Note that the competitive premium rate is equal to expected cost, per policyholder, discounted at the risk-free rate of return. The fact that the insurance firm can earn an expected rate of return higher than R_f by investing part of its portfolio in the market portfolio does not affect the competitive premium rate. The reason is that the higher return on the investment portfolio must be passed on to equity owners as a return for risk bearing. Exactly the same logic explains why the value of the firm is independent of α.

This equation sheds some interesting light on the long-standing debate over whether investment income should be included in formula for setting premium rates. In a recent hearing on rate setting in Massachusetts, the insurance commissioner argued that investment income should be included in the ratemaking formula. He argued that using the return on "the safest available asset, probably U.S. Treasury Securities, is the minimum standard for investment results in any year . . . . The investment results (of a company that invested only in risk-free bonds) provide a minimum standard for the investment results of real companies. They should on average over time be able to secure better investment returns than the hypothetical company." [14] Equation (31) indicates that even if higher investment returns are earned, they must be passed on to equity owners as a return for risk bearing. Therefore, a premium level set on the assumption of earning the minimum, risk-free rate of return should not be viewed as an upper bound on the level necessary to ensure a competitive rate of return to capital. On the other hand, the insurance firm also does not get a "premium" for bearing the variance related to claims fluctuations. With $\rho = 0$, claims variability is diversified away as the shares of the firm become a trivial fraction of each investor's portfolio.

With $\rho > 0$, the competitive premium rate is reduced below $E_C/(1 + R_f)$, because in that case underwriting income represents an asset with a return that is negatively correlated with the rest of the market. With $\rho > 0$, the insurance business is bad when the market is good, and vice versa; thus the market puts a premium on holding insurance stocks which drives P below E_C. With $\rho < 0$, the reverse applies and the competitive premium rate is above $E_C/(1 + R_f)$. But the effect of ρ on the competitive premium rate has nothing to do with the opportunities for internal portfolio diversification. It is relevant because of the external portfolio diversification opportunities of the firm's owners.

Multiperiod Model with Limited Liability

In the last section, we addressed the problem of how an insurance firm should choose α and Q so as to maximize its own market value. Since the firm's owners were implicitly assumed to face unlimited liability, the amount of invested capital was irrelevant; claimants were paid regardless of the level of K. With limited liability, K becomes a crucial determinant of the probability of insolvency, given the choices the firm makes with regard to other variables. K is therefore a crucial determinant of potential losses to both policyholders and shareholders. In this section we examine the firm's choice of K in the context of limited liability.

Consider first the situation in which applicants are aware of each firm's precise financial prospects. Then applicants will choose the level of safety they prefer, taking the cost of greater safety into account. Where policyholders are assumed to be capable of judging at zero cost the probability of insolvency and its consequences, there are thus no apparent benefits to regulation. Furthermore, an analysis of regulation for that context, whether the regulations are justified or not, would strike most as too unrealistic to be interesting.

In the opening section we discussed the difficulties of relaxing the perfect knowledge assumption. Rather than attempting to propose an "imperfect link" between the firm's choice of those parameters that affect its financial condition and the demand for its policies, we consider the case where demand for the firm's policies is unaffected by the firm's choice of K. This is one method of specifying an insurance-market environment in which applicants have great difficulty evaluating the financial condition and the nature of the risks accepted by insurance firms. It is also relevant to the case in which the policyholder is indifferent to financial condition, either because there is a guaranty fund to compensate the unpaid claimants of insolvent firms or because be purchased (only to qualify as a financially responsible person) insurance covering the liability claims of third parties.

Suppose we apply the assumption that demand for the firm's policies is independent of K in the one-period context. Since neither marginal revenue nor marginal cost is affected by K, the optimal choice for Q will be independent of K.[15] Within a one-period context with the demand curve given, the only function of K is to cover a greater proportion of claims if total claims turn out to exceed total end-of-period assets. Thus, within a one-period model, with limited liability and demand independent of K, the firm will choose to set K as low as possible. If we impose a constraint that K must be positive, we have a "one-cent insurance firm."

But in a multiperiod world, the insolvent firm loses the possibility of earning profits in future periods. The market value of the firm will generally be greater than its liquidation value at the beginning of the period, and, if the firm does not go bankrupt, it will be greater than residual funds at the end of the period. Owing to "goodwill" accumulated through previous service, to simple habit on the part of policyholders, to irrational belief in the solidity of the firm, or to any other phenomenon, the firm's owners possess a stock of intangible capital which is lost in the event of insolvency. We are able to capture this phenomenon by assuming that demand is independent of the firm's choice of K; the firm's intangible capital relates in our context to "access" to the assumed demand curve.[16]

By providing a large amount of paid-in capital K, the firm can protect its access to the market, and specifically its ability to exploit the demand function $Q(P)$. But the larger K is, the less advantage is limited liability if claims turn out to be disastrously high. Thus, in the context of a multiperiod model, the question becomes: Which of two forces is stronger— limited liability, which tends to reduce the optimal level of K to zero, or the desire to protect intangible capital, which is lost when insolvency occurs?

At the beginning of the period, the firm has paid-in capital K and access to the demand function $Q(P)$. Let V represent the market value of the firm at the beginning of the period. We assume that paid-in capital K is fully liquid at full value; thus, the liquidation value of the firm is K and it must be that $V \geq K$. The difference $V - K$ will be termed the intangible capital of the firm and denoted W. Thus,

$$V = K + W, \tag{33}$$

where V is the total value of the firm and W is its intangible capital.

At the end of the period, the firm has net assets of

$$\mu = [1 + \alpha R_m + (1 - \alpha)R_f](K + PQ) - \sum_{i=1}^{Q} C_i. \tag{34}$$

If $\mu \geq 0$, then the ongoing firm retains its intangible capital W but its tangible capital is now μ rather than K.

We assume that the firm is in a stationary environment. Thus, if $\mu \geq 0$, the firm continues to exist and is assumed to face the same demand curve and claims environment at the beginning of the next period. Furthermore, its owners are assumed to have the same investment environment.[17] If $\mu < 0$, the firm is insolvent, defaults on some proportion of its outstanding claims, and loses access to the market. Let us then consider alternative stationary policies, which can be defined thus: If $\mu > K$ at the end of the period, the owners withdraw profits of $\mu - K$; if $0 \leq \mu \leq K$, they provide additional capital of $K - \mu$.

After returning paid-in capital to the level K, the firm's choice environment is identical to that which existed at the beginning of the previous period. Thus, it is obvious that its optimal choices of Q and α will be unchanged from the previous period. Let $Q(K)$ and $\alpha(K)$ refer to the optimal choices for Q and α, given that the firm intends to always return paid-in capital to the level K as long as it remains solvent.

We can thus treat the firm as choosing from among alternative stationary policies $\{K, Q(K), \alpha(K)\}$.[18] Obviously the market value of the firm will depend on the stationary policy chosen, and we can write $V(K)$ to represent the market value of a firm that adheres to such a stationary policy, since K completely defines a stationary policy. With K allowed to vary, clearly $V(K)$ is not the variable that the firm's owners wish to maximize. In fact, the firm's owners will want to continue adding capital as long as the firm's market value increases by more than the addition. That is, the owner's wealth will be maximized if the firm chooses the policy that maximizes $V(K) - K$. If we continue to define "intangible capital" as the difference between the market value of the firm and its liquidation value, so that

$$V(K) = W(K) + K, \tag{35}$$

then the optimal policy is to choose the $\{K, Q(K), \alpha(K)\}$ combination that maximizes the intangible capital $W(K)$ of the firm.

We therefore analyze the nature of $W(K)$, which represents the intangible capital of a firm constrained to follow a stationary policy in which invested capital is always reset equal to K as long as $\mu \geq 0$. Let Y be the market value of the firm at the end of the period, after claims are paid but before capital is restored equal to K. If $\mu < 0$, the firm is insolvent and valueless. If $\mu \geq 0$, then the ongoing firm retains its intangible capital $W(K)$ but its tangible capital is μ rather than K. Thus,

$$Y = 0 \qquad\qquad \text{if } \mu < 0$$
$$= W(K) + \mu \qquad \text{if } \mu \geq 0. \tag{36}$$

Applying the capital asset pricing model,[19] we can evaluate $V(K)$:

$$V(K) = \left(\frac{1}{1 + R_f}\right)[E(Y) - \theta \operatorname{Cov}(Y,U)]. \tag{37}$$

The covariance term in (37) introduces great complexity, since Y is more likely to be zero if market returns are low. We have not been able to analyze the general case. In order to impose the restriction

$$\operatorname{Cov}(Y,U) = 0 \tag{38}$$

we must assume that claims and market returns are uncorrelated,

$$\rho = 0, \tag{39}$$

and that the firm does not invest in the risky "market security,"

$$\alpha = 0. \tag{40}$$

Either $\rho \neq 0$ or $\alpha \neq 0$ implies that $\operatorname{Cov}(Y,U) \neq 0$.
   With the assumptions $\rho = 0$ and $\alpha = 0$, we can write[20]

$$V(K) = W(K) + K = \left(\frac{1}{1 + R_f}\right)E(Y). \tag{41}$$

Let $\delta(K)$ represent the critical level for $\bar{C}$ (average realized claims), at which the firm becomes insolvent:

$$\delta(K) = (K + PQ)(1 + R_f)/Q, \tag{42}$$

so that $\mu < 0$ when $\bar{C} > \delta$. Then $Y = 0$ when $\bar{C} > \delta$, and we can write

$$E(Y) = E[\mu + W(K)|\bar{C} \leq \delta(K)]. \tag{43}$$

Let $f(\cdot)$ represent the probability density for $\bar{C}$:

$$\bar{C} \sim f(\bar{C}). \tag{44}$$

We can then write

$$E(Y) = \int_{-\infty}^{\delta} [W(K) + (K + PQ)(1 + R_f) - Q\bar{C}]f(\bar{C})d\bar{C}. \tag{45}$$

Let F_δ be the probability that the firm becomes insolvent during any single period:

$$F_\delta = \int_{\delta(K)}^{+\infty} f(\bar{C})d\bar{C}, \tag{46}$$

and let E_δ be expected claims costs, taking limited liability into account. That is, E_δ equals expected claims costs, conditional on $\mu \geq 0$:

$$E_\delta = \int_{-\infty}^{\delta(K)} \bar{C}f(\bar{C})d\bar{C}. \tag{47}$$

Combining these definitions with (45), we can write

$$V(K) = \frac{[W(K) + (K + PQ)(1 + R_f)](1 - F_\delta) - QE_\delta}{1 + R_f}. \tag{48}$$

Combining (41) and (48), we can solve for $W(K)$:

$$W(K) = \frac{PQ(1 + R_f)(1 - F_\delta) - K(1 + R_f)F_\delta - QE_\delta}{R_f + F_\delta}. \tag{49}$$

We now analyze the behavior of $W(K)$ as K varies.[21] First, $W(K)$ does not grow beyond bound. Since F_δ, the probability of insolvency, becomes zero as K grows while E_δ approaches E_C, it follows that[22]

$$W(\infty) = \frac{PQ(1 + R_f) - QE_C}{R_f} = \frac{(P(1 + R_f) - E_C)Q}{R_f}. \tag{50}$$

Clearly, $W(\infty)$ represents the profits of $P(1 + R_f) - E_C$ per policyholder which are earned with certainty each period when $K = \infty$.

We show in appendix B that if $W(K)$ has a positive slope for $K = K_1$, then it must have a positive slope for all K such that $K > K_1$, as long as the distribution of average claims falls within a wide class of distributions which include the range of plausible specifications.[23] It thus follows that $W(K)$ must follow one of the following four patterns:

Case 1
$W(K)$ decreases montonically toward $W(\infty)$.

Case 2
$W(K)$ decreases initially, then increases toward $W(\infty)$, with $W(0) > W(\infty)$.

Case 3
$W(K)$ decreases initially, then increases toward $W(\infty)$, with $W(0) < W(\infty)$.

Case 4

$W(K)$ increases monotonically toward $W(\infty)$.

We illustrate these four cases in figure 3.1.

Consider the firm that is free to set K at any level. This exhaustive list of cases indicates that an internal solution with $0 < K < \infty$ never exists. There are only two possibilities: When $W(0) > W(\infty)$, the firm will wish to put no capital into the firm; when $W(\infty) > W(0)$, intangible capital $W(K)$ can always be increased by adding more capital.[24]

This result is not surprising; it reflects the competing desires to take advantage of limited liability and to protect the intangible capital of the firm. If the value of access to the market is too small, then the lure of limited liability dominates. The optimal policy in that case is to continue in business only as long as total claims are "favorable" (that is, $\bar{C} < P(1 + R_f)$) and to "plan" to become insolvent in the first period in which total claims are "unfavorable." Although the firm may have intangible capital as a going concern, represented by $W(\infty)$, the value of guarding it is less than the potential value of taking advantage of limited liability.

When $W(\infty) > W(0)$, the optimal policy is to set $K = \infty$. If the value of access to the demand curve $Q(P)$ is sufficiently great, then the addition of capital, by increasing the expected longevity of the firm, increases the market value of the firm by more than the value of the added capital. But as the firm's owners supply more capital, the probability of insolvency continues to fall and becomes negligible. As capital is added, the firm looks more and more like an infinitely safe financial intermediary. The "cost" of adding capital continues to fall. Within the assumptions of the model, the value of the firm continues to increase by more than the value of the added capital, and thus there is no finite solution for K.[25]

The absurdity of the "solution" $K = \infty$ reflects the limited realism of the model. Various real-world considerations imply that the supply price of capital to be added to firm reserves would eventually rise. The risk of embezzlement, other fiducial risks, and the desire of investors to diversify across different investment managers, would all act in that direction. But the principle remains: The insurance firm with an incentive to add capital and to drive the risk of insolvency to a low level can then continue to add to reserves at a very low cost and thereby drive that risk to a negligible value. Thus, when we refer to the "solution" $K = \infty$, we refer to a situation in which capital has been added until these problems of agency responsibility dominate. If the "fiducial responsibility" risks are not great, as would be expected for trusted managers, we can conclude that a "realistic"

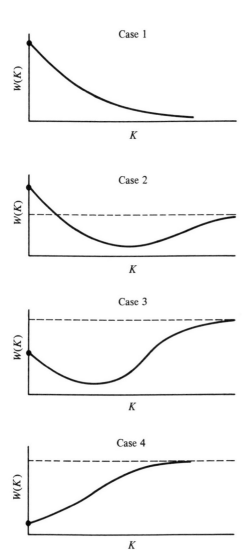

Figure 3.1 Four possible shapes for $W(K)$.

Table 3.1 Illustrative values of ξ and the corresponding threshold for R_f.

ξ	$R_f = \psi(\xi)$
0.000	0.000
0.025	0.032
0.039	0.050
0.050	0.064
0.075	0.097
0.077	0.100
0.100	0.131
0.114	0.150
0.149	0.200
0.150	0.201
0.200	0.274
0.250	0.350
0.300	0.430
0.400	0.598
0.500	0.780

solution for this case is characterized by a value for K large enough that the probability of insolvency is negligible.

The ratio of $W(\infty)$ to $W(0)$, thus, is a crucial determinant of firm behavior with respect to K. We have been unable to obtain any perfectly general results, but we have derived an interesting result for the case in which average claims are assumed to be normally distributed.[26] Thus, we now assume that $\bar{C}$ is normally distributed with mean E_C and standard deviation $\bar{S}$:[27]

$$\bar{C} \sim N(E_C, \bar{S}_C).$$ (51)

Let us express the premium rate, inflated at the risk-free rate of return, in terms of E_C and $\bar{S}_C$:

$$P(1 + R_f) = E_C + \xi \cdot \bar{S}_C.$$ (52)

Thus, if $\xi = 0.10$, the inflated premium rate is 10 percent of one standard deviation above the mean of the distribution of average claims.

We show in appendix B that the relationship between $W(0)$ and $W(\infty)$ depends only on ξ and R_f; specifically,

$$W(0) > W(\infty) \quad \text{for } R_f > \psi(\xi),$$

$$W(\infty) > W(0) \quad \text{for } R_f < \psi(\xi),$$

Table 3.2 Critical levels for $[P(1 + R_f) - E_C]/S_C$.

R	Q		
	100	1,000	10,000
With $\delta = 0$:			
0.05	0.0039	0.0012	0.0004
0.10	0.0077	0.0024	0.0008
0.15	0.0114	0.0036	0.0011
0.20	0.0149	0.0047	0.0015
With $\delta = 0.10$:			
0.05	0.0129	0.0124	0.0124
0.10	0.0254	0.0245	0.0244
0.15	0.0375	0.0361	0.0359
0.20	0.0493	0.0474	0.0472

where ψ is a function which relates to the normal distribution.[28] Over the interesting range, $\psi(\xi)$ is between 25 and 50 percent greater than ξ. Illustrative values of $\psi(\xi)$ are shown in table 3.1. For $\xi = 0.10$, $\psi(\xi) = 0.131$. Thus, if the inflated premium $P(1 + R_f)$ is 10 percent of $\bar{S}_C$ above E_C, then the critical value for R_f is 0.131. With $R_f < 0.131$, the firm will want to place an infinite amount of capital in the firm, but if $R_f > 0.131$ the firm will want to withdraw all of its capital. Conversely, with $R_f = 0.20$, the critical value for is ξ is 0.149.

Since ξ refers to the margin between the inflated premium rate and a standard deviation of the average claims distribution, it appears clear from table 3.1 that only a narrow margin is necessary for the firm to protect its market access, for firms of even moderate size. In table 3.2, for instance, we translate the implied margins into units in S_C rather than in $\bar{S}_C$. Thus we compute the critical level for $[P(1 + R_f) - E_C]/S_C$ above which the firm will want to set $K = \infty$, where S_C is a standard deviation for the claims distribution of each policyholder, rather than for the average claims distribution.

With $\delta = 0$, the critical margin between $P(1 + R_f)$ and E_C is much less than 1 percent of a standard deviation, unless the firm is very small or the risk-free rate of return is very high.[29] Even with 100 policyholders and $R_f = 0.20$, the critical level is only 1.5 percent of a standard deviation.

If we allow the claims of different policyholders to be correlated, however, the critical margin increases significantly and the effect of firm size is virtually eliminated. As noted above, the case of $\gamma \neq 0$ can be interpreted as reflecting uncertainty about the location of the claims distribution. Table 3.2 also shows the margins with $\gamma = 0.10$.[30] The margins then range from 1 percent to 5 percent and are affected only slightly as Q ranges from 100 to 10,000 policyholders.

With the product $Q\delta$ is even moderately large (>200), we can use the following excellent approximation for the critical level ξ:

$$[P(1 + R_f) - E_C]/S_C \approx \xi\sqrt{\delta}. \tag{53}$$

Thus, even when δ approaches 1 the critical margin does not exceed ξ. When $R_f = 0.20$, the critical margin thus does not exceed 0.149, regardless of the level of δ and the source of the variation in the average claims distribution.

Regulating Minimum Capital

We now consider the effect of regulating the level of paid-in capital. Suppose the firm is constrained by a requirement that $K \geq \bar{K}$. The effect will depend on the behavior of $W(K)$. In figure 3.2 we add a constraint on K to the four cases we have identified. For case 3 and case 4, in which $W(\infty) > W(0)$ and the unconstrained firm will choose $K = \infty$, the constraint is clearly not binding and the regulation will have no effect.

With case 1, in which $W(K)$ is monotonically decreasing, the regulated firm will clearly choose $K = \bar{K}$, the constraint will be binding, and the firm will choose to keep only as much capital as required by regulation.

Case 2 provides an interesting possibility. With $K = \bar{K}_1$, such that $W(\bar{K}_1) > W(\infty)$, the firm will choose to set $K = \bar{K}_1$, and the constraint will be binding, just as with case 1. But suppose that $K = \bar{K}_2$, for which $W(\bar{K}_2) < W(\infty)$. In this case the optimal policy for the firm which is required to have $K \geq \bar{K}_2$ is $K = \infty$. Although the unconstrained firm would choose to set $K = 0$, the constrained firm would choose $K = \infty$.

It is thus of interest to determine when the different cases occur. Although we have not found a simple characterization of the parameter combinations that produce the four cases, calculations of $W(K)$ for a wide range of parameter values show a consistent and plausible pattern. Cases 1, 2, 3, and 4 occur in that order as ξ is increased from $\xi = 0$, with the other parameters held constant. Thus, if the claims distribution and the interest rate R_f are held constant, the nature of $W(K)$ is successively represented by cases 1, 2, 3, and 4 as the inflated premium $P(1 + R_f)$ is increased from expected claims cost E_C to larger values. Because Q is being held constant, these calculations implicitly refer to a shifting demand curve, or, in a competitive market, to an increasing competitive premium rate.

We demonstrate in appendix B that $W(K)/Q$ is completely determined by the parameters E_C, $\bar{S}_C$, R_f, ξ, and s, where

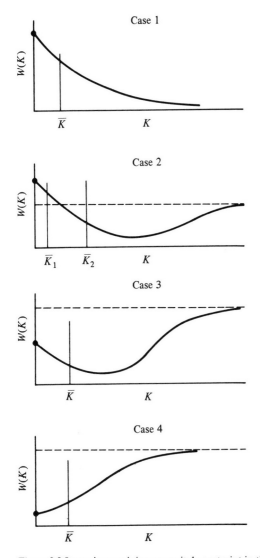

Figure 3.2 Imposing a minimum-capital constraint in the four cases.

$s = K/PQ.$

Figure 3.3 shows $W(K)/Q$ for values of s ranging from 0 to 0.20, with the other parameters fixed at illustrative values. For this set of parameters, the four cases occur as follows:

Case 1 $\xi = 0$
Case 2 $\xi = 0.025, 0.050, 0.075$
Case 3 $\xi = 0.100, 0.150, 0.200$
Case 4 $\xi = 0.50$ (not shown on figure).

Over the range of parameters for which $W(K)/Q$ was calculated,[31] the same sequence for the four cases was followed consistently;[32] however, we have no proof that it will hold for every parameter combination.

Insurer Behavior: A Partial Integration

In the preceding section we analyzed the firm's optimal policy with respect to K, treating its choices of the premium (P) and the number of policy-holders (Q) as given. We found that the firm's behavior with respect to invested capital depends on the relationship among the premium rate, the average claims distribution, and the risk-free rate of return. Suppose the inflated premium rate is expressed in units that refer to the number of standard deviations by which $P(1 + R_f)$ lies above the mean of the claims distribution. That is, let ξ be defined such that

$$P(1 + R_f) = E_C + \xi \cdot \bar{S}_C, \tag{54}$$

where E_C and $\bar{S}_C$ are the mean and the standard deviation of the distribution of average claims costs. We find that if

$$\psi(\xi) < R_f \tag{55}$$

then the unregulated firm will choose to set $K = 0$, but if

$$\psi(\xi) > R_f \tag{56}$$

the firm will choose to set $K = \infty$, where $\psi(\cdot)$ is a function derived from the density function of the normal distribution.[33] Although the "solution" $K = \infty$ is not literally acceptable, this case appears to be validly interpreted as a solution for which the probability of insolvency is reduced to a negligible value and can be treated as essentially zero.

   These results refer to the optimal choice for K with P and Q given, with investment opportunities assumed irrelevant,[34] and with the demand

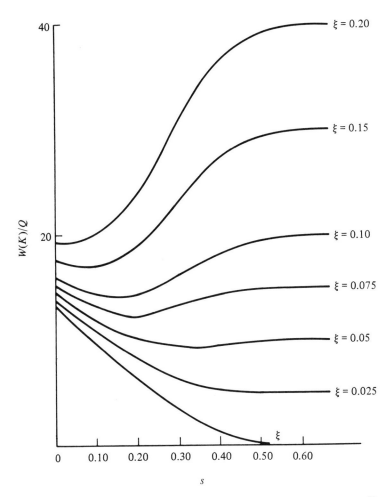

Figure 3.3 $W(K)/Q$ as a function of s for different values of ξ, with $E_C = 100$, $\bar{S}_C = 20$, and $R_f = 0.10$.

relationship $P(Q)$ assumed independent of K. The issue arises: Which combinations represent joint optima, under these conditions, when the firm simultaneously maximizes with regard to P, Q, and K?

Let $W(P,Q,K)$ represent the net, or intangible, value of the firm.[35] The fundamental relationship

$$\underset{P,Q,K}{\text{maximum}}\ W(P,Q,K) = \underset{P,Q}{\text{maximum}}\ \{\underset{K}{\text{maximum}}\ W(P,Q,K)\} \qquad (57)$$

holds generally. However, as demonstrated in the preceding section, the problem

$$\underset{K}{\text{maximize}}\ W(P,Q,K) \qquad (58)$$

results in a solution of either $K = 0$ or $K = \infty$ for all possible P and Q. Thus, if we obtain solutions, subject to the constraint represented by the demand relationship, for the two problems

$$\underset{P,Q}{\text{maximize}}\ W(P,Q,0) \qquad (59)$$

$$\underset{P,Q}{\text{maximize}}\ W(P,Q,\infty), \qquad (60)$$

we can, in theory, find all joint equilibria by finding solutions that are mutually consistent. That is, suppose we can find triples P^*, Q^*, K^* such that K^* is optimal, given P^* and Q^*, while P^* and Q^* are optimal, given K^*. Such a combination represents a joint equilibrium and a local optimum.[36] The global joint optimum must be one of these local joint optima.

But the analysis for problem (60) has been done. When the firm sets $K = \infty$, limited liability obviously becomes irrelevant. Thus, the analysis of the first section ("One-Period Model ..."), restricted to the case of $\alpha = 0$ and $\rho = 0$, applies. The optimal values for P and Q derived in that section are independent of the value assumed for K; this follows from the implicit assumption of unlimited liability. Clearly, if we now assume that K is sufficiently large that limited liability is irrelevant, the same solution results.

Under the restriction $\rho = 0$, and thus $\sigma_{m,c} = 0$, the optimal solution obtained in the first section is simply the premium and policies-written combination for which marginal revenue equals discounted expected claims cost:

$$MR = \left(\frac{1}{1 + R_f}\right)E_C. \qquad (61)$$

Let P^* and Q^* represent the values that satisfy (61). Further, let ξ^* denote the corresponding value for ξ:

$$P^*(1 + R_f) = E_C + \xi^* \cdot \bar{S}_C. \tag{62}$$

Then there are two cases to consider. Suppose first that, for this combination,

$$\psi(\xi^*) > R_f. \tag{63}$$

Then it is clear that the combination $[P^*, Q^*, K = \infty]$ represents a local joint optimum. The choices P^* and Q^* imply that $K = \infty$ is optimal, while $K = \infty$ implies that P^* and Q^* are optimal. In this case the probability of insolvency is negligible and policyholders effectively enjoy complete protection.

Now suppose instead that

$$\psi(\xi^*) < R_f, \tag{64}$$

so that, with P^* and Q^* given, the firm would choose $K = 0$. It does not follow that the combination $[P^*, Q^*, K = 0]$ is a local optimum, since the optimality of P^* and Q^* presumes unlimited liability. With $K = 0$, the optimal choices for P and Q obviously must reflect limited liability. Although we have not made a complete analysis of P^{**} and Q^{**}, the optimal choices with $K = 0$, it must be true that

$$\psi(\xi^{**}) < R_f, \tag{65}$$

where ξ^{**} corresponds to P^{**}.[37] Thus, in the case for which $\psi(\xi^*) < R_f$, we know that some P^{**} and Q^{**} exist such that the combination

$$[P^{**}, Q^{**}, K = 0]$$

represents a global optimum for the simultaneous determination of all three variables. Policyholders face a risk of insolvency. There is no bound on the probability of insolvency, at least with the assumptions given. A demand curve and a claims cost distribution could be defined for which the firm would choose a probability of insolvency arbitrarily close to unity.

For the case in which $\psi(\xi^*) > R_f$, if does not necessarily follow that the combination

$$[P^*, Q^*, K = \infty]$$

is a global optimum, even though it is a local optimum. It may be that a combination exists with $K = 0$ which dominates it. In essence, the firm

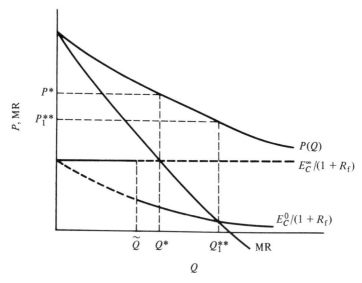

Figure 3.4 Equilibrium with $Q^* > \tilde{Q}$.

has a choice of operating with the marginal-cost curve E_C with assured survival, or of operating with a lower marginal-cost curve by setting $K = 0$. Of course, by choosing the lower marginal-cost curve, it accepts a lower probability of survival each period. Whether the local optimum represented by P^*, with $K = \infty$, or the local optimum represented by P^{**}, with $K = 0$, represents a higher level for intangible capital depends on the precise nature of the demand curve.

The different cases can be clarified diagrammatically. Limited liability effectively reduces marginal expected policyholder costs, with the effect on marginal cost becoming greater as Q increases and the probability of insolvency grows.[38] In figure 3.4 we depict marginal expected policy-holder cost with $K = 0$, labeling it E_C^0, while using E_C^∞ to label "full" expected marginal cost,[39] corresponding to $K = \infty$. We let $\tilde{Q}$ correspond to $\tilde{\xi}$ such that

$$\psi(\tilde{\xi}) = R_f, \tag{66}$$

so that the firm will choose to set $K = \infty$ if $Q < \tilde{Q}$, and will choose to set $K = 0$ if $Q > \tilde{Q}$.[40] Thus, the expected-marginal-cost curve E_C^∞ applies for $Q < \tilde{Q}$, while E_C^0 applies for $Q > \tilde{Q}$.

The case in which $Q^* > \tilde{Q}$, and thus $\psi(\xi^*) < R_f$, is illustrated in figure 3.4. It is clear that the solution for the one-period problem corresponds to the point at which marginal revenue equals $E_C^0/(1 + R_f)$. We

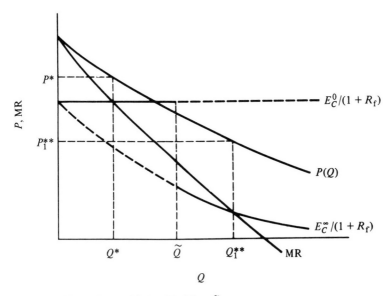

Figure 3.5 Alternative equilibria with $Q^* < \tilde{Q}$.

use Q_1^{**} and P_1^{**} to label the one-period solution. Note that P_1^{**} could be less than E_C^{∞}; in the case of limited liability, the firm could choose to write policies below "full" expected costs.

But within a multiperiod context, the value of survival becomes relevant. Decreasing P and increasing Q both decrease the probability of survival. If P^{**} denotes the optimal premium for the multiperiod case with $K = 0$, it is clear that P^{**} will be greater than P_1^{**}.[41]

Figure 3.5 illustrates the case for which $Q^* < \tilde{Q}$ and $\psi(\xi^*) > R_f$. The two possible one-period equilibria are indicated, and it is clear that the global optimum will depend on the elasticity of the demand curve at prices below P^*. The relevant comparison, of course, is between $[P^*, Q^*, K = \infty]$ and $[P^{**}, Q^{**}, K = 0]$. If the demand curve is sufficiently elastic, the profits expected to be made by increasing Q, setting $K = 0$, and taking eventual advantage of limited liability dominate the value of assured survival.

A global equilibrium with regard to the simultaneous choice of P, Q, and K can thus be characterized by three possible cases. If $\psi(\xi^*) < R_f$, it follows that the firm will choose to set $K = 0$ if it has complete discretion. It is possible that P may be chosen to be below $E_C(1 + R_f)$. Policyholders face a risk of insolvency which, at least given our assumptions, may be arbitrarily high. If a guaranty fund protects claimholders, then the deficits are shifted to the industry as a whole.

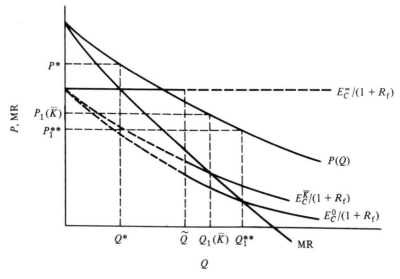

Figure 3.6 Equilibrium with $Q^* < \tilde{Q}$ and $K \geqslant \bar{K}$.

If $\psi(\xi^*) > R_f$, then two cases are possible. It may be that P^* and Q^*, as defined by (61) are optimal along with $K = \infty$. But if the demand curve is sufficiently elastic below P^*, the firm may attain a still higher market value by setting $K = 0$ and adjusting its premium and number of policies written. We can prove that the choice for P will be below P^* and that the policies written will be greater than Q^*.

Regulation and Minimum Required Capital

We can now consider the effect of regulating minimum K when P, Q, and K are simultaneously chosen to maximize the net market value of the firm. Obviously, in the case in which the optimal strategy for the firm (in the unregulated context) is to set $K = \infty$, imposing the requirement $K \geq \bar{K}$ has no effect. Within the context of our assumptions, the costs of regulation are entirely administrative and enforcement costs. Costs of inefficiency that arise as firms adapt to regulations do not occur.

As we have demonstrated, the only alternative case is that in which the unregulated firm would choose a combination $[P^{**}, Q^{**}, K=0]$. We saw above that when the constraint $K \geq \bar{K}$ is introduced, with P and Q held constant, the firm may choose to set $K = \bar{K}$ or may choose to set $K = \infty$. When P and Q are allowed to vary, these same cases are possible.

Imposing a minimum capital requirement rotates the expected-marginal-cost curve toward E_C^∞. Figure 3.6 illustrates, for one value of $\bar{K}$, the case in which the unregulated firm would choose $[P^{**},Q^{**},K=0]$ even though $\psi(\xi^*) > R_f$. For the one-period solution, the regulated firm clearly might choose either $[P^*,Q^*,K=\infty]$ or the combination $[\bar{P},\bar{Q},K=\bar{K}]$. Obviously, the same possibilities exist for the multiperiod case.

It is also clear that, for $\bar{K}$ large enough, the firm will choose $[P^*,Q^*, K=\infty]$. However, for the case in which $\psi(\xi^*) < R_f$, the firm will never choose to switch over to $K = \infty$.

Thus, we can characterize the effects of regulation in terms of the two basic cases. For $\psi(\xi^*) < R_f$, the unregulated firm will choose to set $K = 0$. The regulated firm, which is required to set $K > \bar{K}$, will choose to set $K = \bar{K}$. Furthermore, it will also respond by setting a higher premium rate P and reducing the number of policies written. Thus, for a firm that would choose to "exploit" limited liability, the imposition of a minimum capital requirement reduces the level of risk accepted, in addition to providing a cushion for those policies written.

For $\psi(\xi^*) > R_f$, there are two possibilities. The unregulated firm may choose to set $K = \infty$. The unregulated firm would voluntarily choose to be "infinitely safe," and regulations are neither necessary nor relevant. The other possibility is that the unregulated firm would choose a combination $[P^{**},Q^{**},K=0]$. If a small minimum capital requirement is imposed, the firm will react as above: by setting $K = \bar{K}$, raising the premium rate, and reducing Q. However, for a sufficiently high $\bar{K}$, the firm will make a discontinuous jump to the combination $[P^*,Q^*,K=\infty]$. Thus, minimum capital requirements can generate "infinitely safe" firms in some cases. But "infinitely safe" firms also may exist in the absence of regulation, as a result of the desire to protect access to a profitable market.

Solvency Regulation: Repairing a Deficit
One aspect of the analysis requires clarification. We have assumed, in the analysis of the case of limited liability, that the firm is faced with the following possibilities: If total funds μ at the end of the period exceed total claims, the firm pays all claims, repairs capital to its beginning level, and begins the next period; if total claims exceed total funds, then all remaining funds are used to pay claims and the firm is then declared insolvent.

This set of assumptions is consistent with the power of state insurance commissioners to liquidate any firm whose capital and surplus falls below the required level. But one important possibility is left out: the possibility that the firm's owners will be given the opportunity to "resurrect" the firm by adding capital at the end of the period. Clearly, "resurrection" may or may not be in the interests of the owners, depending on just how large the deficit is.

Owners cannot be forced to repair a deficit, given limited liability. If they are always allowed to repair a deficit, then the optimal strategy with regard to invested capital, within this model, is obvious. With demand totally insensitive to K, the firm will always choose to set $K = \bar{K}$. The only function of "excess" capital in that context is to pay a greater proportion of claims in the event that claims are sufficiently high, in some period when it is not worthwhile to salvage the firm.

This situation presents the regulator with a dilemma. The regulator will always want to allow the owners to salvage the firm, *ex post*, if he ignores the effect on future incentives. But if he always allows owners to salvage when they wish, the incentive to provide the firm with more than the minimum required capital disappears. On the other hand, the owners are more likely to want to salvage the firm if they know they can choose whether to salvage in the future. The firm is worth more if its owners have a right to salvage.

Where other aspects of the cost of capital are ignored, as we have done here, the answer seems clear. Since in our context the cost of capital relates only to the uncertainty about claims variations, and becomes negligible as the probability of insolvency becomes small, the regulator should provide the incentive to set $K = \infty$. But these other aspects of the supply of capital impinge not only on the costs of existing and established firms, but also on the difficulty of entry and on the startup costs of new and young firms. The effects of solvency regulation seem to be clearest with respect to the total supply of firms in the industry, rather than with respect to insolvency rates (Munch and Smallwood 1980). Thus, one should be cautious in drawing policy conclusions from the analysis.

Summary and Conclusions

We first examine optimal firm choices in the context of unlimited liability. We find that α, the proportion of initial funds invested in the risky asset, does not affect the market value of the firm. Under the assumptions of the CAPM, the insurance firm's owners are indifferent with regard to the investment behavior of the insurance firm. Although the firm's expected rate of return will be higher if it invests in the risky asset, the securities market requires a compensating premium to the extent that the additional risk is nondiversifiable.

The optimal choice for P also reflects the extent to which investors can diversify away the variance in the firm's cash flow. The optimal P and Q are defined by

$$(1 + R_f)\text{MR} = E_C - \lambda\sigma_{m,C}. \qquad (67)$$

That is, inflated[42] marginal revenue is equal to expected policyholder cost plus a term representing compensation for nondiversifiable risk. For a competitive market, we can interpret equation (67) as defining the competitive premium rate. Thus, investment opportunties are relevant to the level of competitive premiums, but the link involves the external investment opportunities of investors and will operate through the cost of capital to the firm. The fact that the insurance firm can invest its capital and reserve funds in assets which earn an expected return above R_f is irrelevant to the optimal choice of P and Q (for a firm with market power) and to the premium level in a competitive market.

It is important to note that the indifference of owners to the firm's investment behavior is not based on an assumption of investor risk neutrality. Within the CAPM, the community of investors are assumed to be risk-averse, and they can be assumed to be risk-averse to an arbitrarily high degree. The point is that their own portfolio diversification renders the investment behavior of the firm irrelevant.

These conclusions may be considered unrealistic, but it is important to recognize the nature of the phenomenon that must be modeled to make the analysis significantly more realistic. Three assumptions implicit in the CAPM drive these conclusions. The first is that securities trading does not involve transactions costs, in the sense that ownership may be transferred without cost. The second is that all potential investors share common information about the distribution of returns to all firms. The third is that the returns of each firm are given, and implicitly that the behavior of managers is thus also given and unaffected by changes in ownership. Let us call these the problems of *ownership transfer*, *information*, and *agency*, respectively.

Although the costs of ownership transfer clearly affect the small investor, it seems implausible that the market value of firms would be highly sensitive to such costs in a world in which the information and agency problems did not exist. The existence of large traders and financial intermediation would tend to eliminate its effect for all but very small firms. Thus, to improve significantly on the CAPM analysis of market value, particularly for the case of closely held firms we must address the information and agency problems.

The agency problem relates to the classic issues involving incentives and control when management is divorced from ownership. One might presume that managers will want to minimize the possibility of insolvency, but this depends on the nature of their remuneration and on their risk aversion.

With regard to information, managers may well have a better understanding of the relationships among claims costs, returns on securities, and the regulations specific to the forms in which reserves must be held. Thus, the external portfolio management of owners may not be perfectly substitutable for internal portfolio management, and the firm's investment behavior may not be irrelevant to market value.

If the problems of agency and information were explicitly modeled, the analytical results would quite likely be modified somewhat, particularly for the closely held firm. But we still believe them to be first-order solutions that are fundamentally correct.

Analysis of a firm's optimal choices in the context of limited liability presents a fundamental problem: How should demand for the firm's product be specified, given the possibility of insolvency? Since the case of perfect knowledge is uninteresting, the problem becomes one of specifying the response of partially informed buyers. But there is no obvious and convincing method for specifying the relationship between the firm's choices and the judgments that partially informed prospective policyholders make about the solidity of the firm.

Rather than analyze some arbitrary specification of the link between demand and the firm's choice for these variables, we analyze the case in which demand is sensitive to only the premium rate. For the case in which policyholders are protected by a guaranty fund providing claims coverage when the insurer becomes insolvent, this seems the appropriate assumption in any case. Where no guaranty fund exists, it is still useful to understand the nature of firm behavior when demand is completely insensitive.

Even with demand taken as a function of only the premium rate, an analysis of the joint determination of K, α, P, and Q in the context of limited liability is complex, primarily because a one-period model is no longer adequate. When buyers are less than perfectly informed, their behavior and beliefs represent sources of intangible capital that is lost when insolvency occurs. In our model, the firm's intangible capital relates to access to the demand curve $Q(P)$, which the firm is assumed to lose when insolvency occurs.

Under a multiperiod model, market value is determined by the distribution of returns and by the probability of survival each period. In order to keep the analysis tractable, we impose the restrictions $\alpha = 0$ and

$\rho = 0$. Thus, the role of investment behavior is assumed away.[43] For the case of limited liability, we consider only the firm's choices for K, P, and Q.

The optimal choice for K (and thus the probability of survival) is initially analyzed with a given distribution of returns (with P and Q fixed). Market value is determined for alternative stationary policies in which the owners reestablish K at a specific level each period as long as the firm survives. The level of intangible capital, or market-value net of K, is demonstrated to be a U-shaped function that monotonically approaches an asymptote as K grows. This shape reflects two competing forces: a high level for K ensures survival, whereas a low level allows the firm to exploit limited liability in the event of large claims.

The optimal policy is thus found to consist of two extremes: The firm should choose to set $K = 0$ or $K = \infty$, depending on its profitability and on the rate of interest. Specifically, let ξ be the number of standard deviations of the distribution of average claims cost by which the inflated premium rate lies above expected average claims cost:

$$P(1 + R_f) = E_C + \xi \bar{S}_C. \tag{68}$$

The optimal choice for K can then be characterized as follows:

$$K = 0 \Leftrightarrow \psi(\xi) < R_f,$$
$$K = \infty \Leftrightarrow \psi(\xi) > R_f, \tag{69}$$

where $\psi(\cdot)$ is a function that relates to the normal distribution.[44] Though the "solution" $K = \infty$ cannot be accepted literally, it is based on a real effect. As the firm adds capital and the probability of insolvency becomes negligible, it essentially acts as a financial intermediary. The cost of holding additional capital becomes correspondingly negligible, or at least no greater than for other non-risk-bearing intermediaries. The policyholders, of a firm that chooses $K = \infty$ receive complete protection against insolvency.

In considering joint equilibria with respect to K, P, and Q, we let P^* and Q^* represent the solutions corresponding to unlimited liability. Since $\rho = 0$ by assumption, P^* and Q^* are the solutions to

$$MR = E_C/(1 + R_f) \tag{70}$$

and we let ξ^* denote the corresponding value for ξ:

$$P^*(1 + R_f) = E_C + \xi^* \bar{S}_C. \tag{71}$$

There are three cases to consider:

Case 1 $\psi(\xi^*) < R_f$.

Case 2 $\psi(\xi^*) > R_f$, and the unregulated firm will choose to set $K = \infty$.

Case 3 $\psi(\xi^*) > R_f$, and the unregulated firm will choose to set $K = 0$.

In case 1 the unregulated firm will choose to set $K = 0$ and will choose a corresponding P^{**} and Q^{**}. With the requirement $K \geq \bar{K}$ imposed on it, the firm will be led to set $K = \bar{K}$, raise its premium, and lower the number of policies written. As $\bar{K}$ is increased the probability of insolvency continues to fall, but it remains positive.

In case 2 regulation is obviously unnecessary. The unregulated firm chooses to be perfectly safe. Although monitoring costs exist, imposing a minimum capital requirement does not create costs of adjustment. In particular, imposing the requirement has no effect on P and Q.

In case 3 the firm behaves as in case 1 for low $\bar{K}$, but at a certain level for $\bar{K}$ the firm responds discountinuously and switches over to $K = \infty$. Sufficiently high minimum capital requirements will induce the firm to forsake the advantage of limited liability and add capital to the point where it is essentially perfectly safe.

These results suggest a schizophrenic regulatory environment. At least within the context of an insensitive demand curve, some firms are led to pursue an ultrasafe strategy. In that case solvency regulation, in the form of minimum levels for K, is unnecessary. But the results also imply that such regulation is costless, at least in the sense that it would not alter firm behavior, and thus inefficiencies will not arise as the firm adapts. For firms that would choose to set $K = 0$, regulatory constraints on minimum K will obviously have an effect. In some cases a firm that would choose $K = 0$ in the absence of regulation will choose to set $K = \infty$ when required to set $K \geq \bar{K}$!

What do the results imply for regulatory policy? Just as the results are somewhat paradoxical, so the implications may depend on how one views the different conclusions we derive.

"Completely safe" firms may arise naturally in a context in which applicants have only primitive notions of how to discriminate among firms, and use simple rules to try to attain safety. Not only are astute applicants not needed for safe firms to arise; indeed, it is the existence of applicants who rely on simple rules that creates the intangible capital that encourages the firm to protect its existence.

Thus, one can argue that regulation may not be needed in exactly the situation where it appears most clearly justified: where applicants are largely oblivious of the details of firms' financial structures and rely on simple proxies to provide them with safety. Suppose applicants generally divide firms into old or established firms and new or unknown firms. If applicants treat "old" firms as "safe" and are willing to pay a premium for safety, this creates the intangible capital that leads the firm to want to protect its position and to set $K = \infty$. The belief that old firms are safe becomes self-fulfilling.

If there a sufficient supply of firms viewed as old, the premiums of old firms will still be driven down to a competitive level but the competitive level will reflect the full costs of effectively unlimited liability. Those applicants who want safety can buy safety, and the market will provide it. Those applicants who are willing to rely on their own judgment and who may be willing to accept some nontrivial risk of insolvency are free to go to new or unknown firms. As long as all applicants understand that they have a choice of buying from an old firm or of relying on their own evaluations of the safety of a new firm, the case for regulation seems to degenerate to ensuring the protection of applicants who put more faith in their ability to judge firms than is warranted. Solvency regulation, in this view, protects not the naive but the arrogant.

But this conclusion assumes that the market position of each of the old firms is sufficiently profitable to protect by setting $K = \infty$. If the profitability of an old firm is too low, to the point where the incentives of limited liability come to dominate the value of protecting its position, then those applicants who are willing to pay for safety will be unwittingly exploited.

What conditions might lead to the profitability of old firms dropping to the point where it is not worthwhile to protect the intangible capital inherent in the perception that the firm is old and reliable? It is important to note that the threat of excess capacity is essentially absent; the amount of specific physical capital in the insurance industry is negligible. Marginal and average costs vary little, and firms can contract from an level of extended "production" with few problems. Indeed, the ease with which insurance firms can contract has produced some of the dissatisfaction with the insurance market's performance in recent years.

Clearly, rate regulation is one possibility. Forcing rates below long-run full cost levels could eliminate the desire to protect one's market access. Indeed, firms have been required, against their desires, to stay in some insurance markets in some states. The leverage—for better or ill—exists because these have been multiline firms for which the insurance line at issue represents only a proportion of their business, and because only one or a few states were exploiting this leverage.

Similarly, while technical change and structural innovation can disrupt the position of "old" firms, the insurance product is basically fixed, although methods of packaging and selling the product undergo significant changes. But methods differ considerably across different lines—particularly between personal and commercial lines—and structural changes have tended to affect old, established firms in only one or a few lines at any time.

Thus, to the extent that "old" firms, which sell (at least in part) to those who seek essentially complete safety, are highly diversified across different lines, the likelihood that conditions in different lines would simultaneously deteriorate to the point where an insolvency would dominate the selective exit from some markets seems very low.[45] Obviously, if several state regulators were to keep rates below full-cost levels in several lines this conclusion would be in jeopardy.

Another factor that destroys this line of argument is the existence of guaranty funds, which reimburse those who have claims against insolvent firms. If applicants are aware of guaranty funds and believe they provide perfect protection against a partial claim recovery, all reason for concern with their insurer's financial condition disappears. Indeed, applicants will not simply be indifferent between firms with different financial policies; those firms that set $K = 0$ will be able to sell at a lower premium than those setting $K = \infty$. In both cases policyholders will have complete protection. The existence of a perfect guaranty fund allows policyholders to share in the benefits of limited liability without incurring any of the costs.

It would seem that the existence of a perfect[46] and understood guaranty fund should destroy an insurance market. Each firm would choose $K = 0$. Applicants would choose the lowest premium available. Thus, as applicants were added, their full expected costs would be added to the industry's expected costs but not to the firms underwriting them. As firms became insolvent the liabilities of surviving firms would grow, and presumably the expected costs of new entrants would increase as the unpaid liabilities grew. A type of externality would exist, in that a firm would impose expected costs on its competitors as it wrote more applicants.

The inevitable result seems clearly pathological. As firms become insolvent, their liabilities are spread over existing firms in proportion to market share. It seems possible that a point would be quickly reached at which new entrants would wait until all surviving firms had gone under. Thus, the existence of a guaranty fund creates the need for financial regulation. However, it should be noted that financial regulation only modifies the problem created when applicants have no incentive to avoid financially risky firms. According to the model we have analyzed, firms will choose to set $K = \bar{K}$, the probability of insolvency will be positive, and the "externalities" problem will still exist.

Although the existence of a guaranty fund destroys the rationale for protecting a firm's existence which we have modeled here, other factors also generate intangible capital. All firms incur startup costs and fixed costs in becoming established. Furthermore, writing an individual policy has fixed costs which are recouped only as the policyholder continues to renew. Thus, being an established firm has value even if applicants are indifferent to all firm attributes except premium rate. A sufficiently large capital requirement will produce the case where the value of survival dominates the advantages of limited liability, and firms will choose to become perfectly safe in the face of financial regulations.

Thus, the combination of a guaranty fund and financial regulations may produce a viable insurance market in which policyholders have perfect protection against insolvency. However, this result may have substantial costs, particularly as it affects the vigor of competition in the market. Firms which service those willing to trade off premium costs against the risk of partial claims recovery are eliminated. If all firms were equally efficient and if competition among "old" firms were vigorous, this cost would seem likely to be slight. The lower premium offered by some firms, such as in cases 2 and 3 above, would be lower only because limited liability lowers expected costs. For a risk-averse individual who buys insurance to provide compensation in the event of some catastrophe, it seems evident that a lower premium would not be attractive if the cost saving related to some probability of a partial or zero claim payment.

Suppose, however, that competition among "old" firms is not as vigorous as it could be, and that in a world of perfect ability to judge firms' financial conditions premiums would be lower. Suppose further that old firms do not always innovate quickly as new insurance needs appear. Then some individuals, while risk-averse, will want to buy insurance from new firms—either because they have confidence in their ability to judge financial condition and have faith in certain new and unestablished firms, or because they have unusual insurance needs to which the established firms are not responding and are willing to accept some probability of insolvency in order to obtain a product more suited to their needs. Both situations appear to have existed in recent years.

In this case, the effect of financial regulations on entry and on the vigor of competition in the industry must be considered. As we show elsewhere (Munch and Smallwood 1980), the effects of solvency regulation seem to be clearest with respect to the total supply of firms in the industry rather than with respect to insolvency rates. As discussed in that paper, financial regulations offer opportunities for abuse by a regulator who accepts the position that competition in the industry should be stifled.

The danger that financial regulations may protect policyholders from competition rather than from unrecognized risks is particularly clear in commercial lines. When firms find it difficult to join and form their own insurance pools to cover product liability, or when groups of professionals cannot establish new facilities for providing malpractice coverage, there is obviously a question as to who benefits from the regulations. The necessity for financial regulations across all lines to ensure solvency, and the existence of guaranty funds, should be evaluated critically.

Appendix A

Let M be total market flows at the end of the period in the absence of the insurance firm in question. The value V_M of ownership of rights to M is

$$V_M = \frac{E(M) - \theta \, \text{Cov}(M,M)}{1 + R_f} = \frac{E(M) - \theta \, \text{Var}(M)}{1 + R_f}$$

according to the capital asset pricing model. We can treat the introduction of the firm in two steps. First, the additional cash flow represented by the additional firm:

$$\mu^* = (1 + R_f)(K + PQ) - \sum_{i=1}^{Q} C_i$$

is added to total end-of-period market flows:

$$U = M + \mu^*.$$

The value of θ and all asset values must adjust, and we have

$$V_U = \frac{E(U) - \theta^* \, \text{Cov}(U,U)}{1 + R_f}$$

since an infinite supply of a risk-free asset with rate of return R_f is assumed. Thus, for a specific cash flow D_j, we have

$$V_{D_j} = \frac{E(D_j) - \theta^* \operatorname{Cov}(D_j, U)}{1 + R_f}.$$

The insurance firm now invests a proportion α of its funds in a balanced portfolio which represents the total market (including the firm in question). The net end-of-period cash flow arising from the investment is

$$\mu^{**} = \alpha(R_U - R_f)(K + PQ),$$

where $V_U(1 + R_U) = U$ by definition. Let d denote the fraction of the total market which the firm has purchased. Thus, we have

$$\alpha(K + PQ) = dV_U$$

at the beginning of the period, and

$$\alpha(1 + R_U)(K + PQ) = dU$$

at the end. Therefore,

$$\mu^{**} = \alpha(1 + R_U)(K + PQ) - \alpha(1 + R_f)(K + PQ)$$
$$= dU - d(1 + R_f)V_U,$$

so that

$$E(\mu^{**}) = dE(U) - d(1 + R_f)V_U,$$

$$\operatorname{Cov}(\mu^{**}, U) = \operatorname{Cov}(dU, U) = d\operatorname{Cov}(U, U).$$

Hence,

$$V^{**} = \frac{dE(U) - d(1 + R_f)V_U - \theta^* d\operatorname{Cov}(U, U)}{1 + R_f}$$

$$= d\left[\left(\frac{E(U) - \theta^* \operatorname{Cov}(U, U)}{1 + R_f}\right) - V_U\right]$$

$$= 0.$$

To compute V^*, the market value of the rights to μ^*, we use

$$E(\mu^*) = (1 + R_f)(K + PQ) - QE_C.$$

Since $(1 + R_f)(K + PQ)$ is constant, it follows that

$$\text{Cov}(\mu^*, M + \mu^*) = \text{Cov}\left(-\sum_{i=1}^{Q} C_i, M - \sum_{i=1}^{Q} C_i\right)$$

$$= -\sum_{i=1}^{q} \text{Cov}(C_i, M) + \text{Var}\left(\sum_{i=1}^{Q} C_i\right)$$

$$= -QV_M\sigma_{m,c} + Q\sigma_C + Q(Q-1)\gamma\sigma_C$$

because

$$\text{Cov}(C_i, M) = \text{Cov}(C_i, (1 + R_m)V_M)$$

$$= V_M\text{Cov}(C_i, R_m).$$

Appendix B

In the third section we derived

$$W(K) = \frac{(1 + R_f)[PQ(1 - F_\delta) - KF_\delta] - QE_\delta}{R_f + F_\delta}.$$

From the definitions of $\delta(K)$, F_δ, and E_δ, it follows that

$$\frac{d}{dK}F_\delta = -\frac{f(\delta)}{Q},$$

$$\frac{d}{dK}E_\delta = \frac{\delta f(\delta)}{Q},$$

since only K is treated as variable in that section. If we multiply both sides above by $R_f + F_\delta$ and differentiating with respect to K, it follows that

$$\frac{dW(K)}{dK} = \left(\frac{1}{R_f + F_\delta}\right)\left[\left(\frac{W(K)}{Q}\right)f(\delta) - (1 + R_f)F_\delta\right]$$

$$= A(K)\left[\left(\frac{1}{1 + R_f}\right)\left(\frac{W(K)}{Q}\right) - \frac{F_\delta}{f(\delta)}\right],$$

where

$$A(K) = \left(\frac{1 + R_f}{R_f + F_\delta}\right)f(\delta)$$

is a function of K that is always positive, if $f(\delta) > 0$ for all K.

For an average claim distribution that is a normal distribution, or approximately normal, the ratio $F_\delta/f(\delta)$ is monotonically decreasing. The class of distributions for which this ratio is monotonically decreasing are known as the increasing-failure-rate distributions in the literature of statistical reliability theory. These distributions, which include the gamma $G_{\lambda,\alpha}$ distributions with $\alpha > 1$, the truncated normal distribution, and the χ^2 distributions, provide approximately normal distributions which are non-negative and have thick upper tails, and are therefore appealing as a claims distribution for a firm with a finite number of policyholders. Thus, our results certainly do not depend on less appealing aspects of assuming a normal distribution.

Suppose that, at $K = K_1$, $W(K)$ has a positive slope. Then, since $W(K)/Q$ is growing while $F_\delta/f(\delta)$ is falling, the slope will continue to be positive for $K_2 > K_1$. Thus, it follows that

$$\left.\frac{dW}{dK}\right|_{K=K_1} > 0 \Rightarrow \left.\frac{dW}{dK}\right|_{K=K_2} > 0 \qquad \text{for } K_2 > K_1.$$

We now indicate how $W(K)/Q$ can be written in terms of standardized parameters, assuming that average claims $\bar{C}$ have a normal distribution

$$C \sim N(E_C, (\bar{S}_C)^2),$$

so

$$t = (\bar{C} - E_C)/\bar{S}_C \sim N(0,1).$$

For the normal distribution, we have

$$E_\delta = E_C(1 - \Gamma(Z)) - \bar{S}_C(\phi(Z)).$$

With the definition of $\delta(K)$, we have

$$W(K) = \frac{(1 + R_f)[PQ(1 - F_\delta) - KF_\delta] - QE_\delta}{R_f + F_\delta}$$

$$= \frac{(1 + R_f)PQ - \delta \cdot F_\delta \cdot Q - QE_\delta}{R_f + F_\delta},$$

so

$$\frac{W(K)}{Q} = \frac{(1 + R_f)P - \delta \cdot F_\delta - E_\delta}{R_f + F_\delta}.$$

Since

$$P(1 + R_f) = E_C + \xi \cdot \bar{S}_C,$$

we can use the expressions for E_C, $\bar{S}_C$, and $\delta(K)$ to obtain

$$\frac{W(K)}{Q} = \frac{[\xi - Z\,\Gamma(Z) + \phi(Z)]\bar{S}_C}{R_f + \Gamma(Z)}.$$

Since $Z(0) = \xi$, we have

$$\frac{W(0)}{Q} = \frac{[\xi - \xi\Gamma(\xi) + \phi(\xi)]\bar{S}_C}{R_f + \Gamma(\xi)}.$$

As K approaches infinity, $Z(K)$ also approaches infinity while $Z\Gamma(Z)$ and $\phi(Z)$ approach zero, so

$$\frac{W(\infty)}{Q} = \frac{\xi\bar{S}_C}{R_f},$$

from which it follows that

$$W(\infty) > W(0) \qquad \text{if } R_f < \xi\Gamma(\xi)/[\phi(\xi) - \xi\Gamma(\xi)].$$

Let Z correspond to $\delta(K)$, the value of average claims below which the firm is insolvent:

$$Z(K) = [\delta(K) - E_C]/\bar{S}_C.$$

If we let $\phi(\cdot)$ represent the density function for the standard normal, it follows that

$$f(\bar{C}) = \phi(t)/\bar{S}_C$$

and

$$dC = (\bar{S}_C)dt,$$

so

$$
\begin{aligned}
F_\delta &= \int_{\delta(K)}^{+\infty} f(\bar{C})d\bar{C} \\
&= \int_{[\delta(K) - E_C]/\bar{S}_C}^{+\infty} \phi(t)dt \\
&= \int_{Z(K)}^{+\infty} \phi(t)dt \\
&= \Gamma(Z),
\end{aligned}
$$

where $1 - \Gamma(Z)$ is the cumulative distribution function of a standard normal random variable. Similarly, integrating E_δ by parts leads to

$$E_\delta = \int_{-\infty}^{\delta(K)} \bar{C} f(\bar{C}) d\bar{C}$$

$$= E_C(1 - F_\delta) + (\bar{S}_C) \int_{-\infty}^{Z} t\,\phi(t)dt.$$

Because[47]

$$\int_{-\infty}^{Z} t\,\phi(t)dt = -\phi(Z),$$

we have

$$E_\delta = E_C(1 - F_\delta) - \bar{S}_C\phi(Z).$$

Last, we show that $P^{**} > P_1^{**}$, where P^{**} and P_1^{**} are the multiperiod and one-period solutions, respectively, for the case in which P and Q are allowed to vary, with K fixed at zero. Differentiating W with respect to Q produces

$$(R_f + F_\delta)\left(\frac{\partial W}{\partial Q}\right) + \left(\frac{\partial F_\delta}{\partial Q}\right)W = \left(\frac{\partial(PQ)}{\partial Q}\right)(1 + R_f)(1 - F_\delta) - E_\delta,$$

because

$$\left(\frac{\partial E_\delta}{\partial Q}\right) = -P(1 + R_f)\left(\frac{\partial F_\delta}{\partial Q}\right).$$

Since P^{**} occurs at a point at which

$$\frac{\partial W}{\partial Q} = 0$$

and since $W > 0$ and

$$\frac{\partial F_\delta}{\partial Q} > 0,$$

it follows that P^{**} occurs at a point where

$$(1 + R_f)\left(\frac{\partial(PQ)}{\partial Q}\right) > \frac{E_\delta}{1 - F_\delta} > E_\delta$$

and thus that $P^{**} > P_1^{**}$, if marginal revenue is monotonically decreasing.

Appendix C

Let $C_1,\ldots,C_Q$ be identically distributed with a common mean μ_C. We conceptualize a model in which μ_C is first determined randomly, which then defines the joint distribution of the C_j. Let E_μ refer to expectations taken with respect to the distribution that produces μ_C, let $E_{C/\mu}$ refer to the conditional expectations of the C_j given μ_C, and let E refer to the unconditional expectations which reflect the combined stochastic processes. Then μ_C has first moment

$$E_\mu(\mu_C) = \bar{\mu}_C$$

and second moment

$$\mathrm{Var}_\mu(\mu_C) = v^2,$$

while the conditional moments of the C_j are

$$E_{C/\mu}(C_j/\mu_C) = \mu_C,$$

$$\mathrm{Var}_{C/\mu}(C_j/\mu_C) = \sigma_C,$$

$$\mathrm{Cov}_{C/\mu}(C_i,C_j/\mu_C) = \gamma\sigma_C,$$

$$\mathrm{Cov}_{C/\mu}(C_i,R_\mathrm{m}/\mu_C) = \rho S_\mathrm{m} S_C.$$

Our purpose is to compute the unconditional moments, which show that we can make the model implicitly reflect "uncertainly about μ_C" by appropriately specifying the assumed parameters. The mean μ_C is assumed to be distributed independently of both the C_j and R_M. Letting * denote unconditional moments, we have

$$\mu_C^* = E(C_j)$$

$$= E_{C/\mu}\{E_\mu(C_i)\}$$

$$= E_\mu\{E_{C/\mu}(C_i)\}$$

$$= E_\mu(\mu_C)$$

$$= \bar{\mu}_C,$$

$$\sigma_C^* = E[(C_i - \bar{\mu}_C)^2]$$

$$= E[(C_i - \mu_C + \mu_C - \bar{\mu}_C)^2]$$

$$= E_\mu\{E_{C/\mu}[(C_i - \mu_C)^2 + 2(C_i - \mu_C)(\mu_C - \bar{\mu}_C) + (\mu_C - \bar{\mu}_C)^2]^2\}$$

$$= E_\mu[\sigma_C + (\mu_C - \bar{\mu}_C)^2]$$

$$= \sigma_C + E_\mu[(\mu_C - \bar{\mu}_C)^2]$$

$$= \sigma_C + v^2.$$

It similarly follows that

$$Cov^*(C_i, C_j) = Cov(C_i, C_j) + v^2,$$

$$Cov^*(C_i, R_m) = Cov(C_i, R_m).$$

Thus, we can write

$$\mu_C^* = \bar{\mu}_C,$$

$$\sigma_C^* = \sigma_C + v^2,$$

$$Cov^*(C_i, C_j) = \delta^* \sigma_C^* = Cov(C_i, C_j) + v^2 = \delta\sigma_C + v^2,$$

$$Cov^*(C_i, R_m) = S_C^* S_m \rho^* = Cov(C_i, R_m) = S_C S_m \rho.$$

Therefore,

$$\delta^* = \frac{\delta\sigma_C + v^2}{\sigma_C^*}$$

$$= \frac{\delta\sigma_C + v^2}{\sigma_C + v^2}$$

$$= \delta\left(\frac{\sigma_C}{\sigma_C^*}\right) + \left(\frac{v^2}{\sigma_C^*}\right)$$

$$= \delta\left(\frac{\sigma_C}{\sigma_C + v^2}\right) + 1\left(\frac{v^2}{\sigma_C + v^2}\right),$$

while

$$S_C^* S_m \rho^* = S_C S_m \rho,$$

$$\rho^* = \left(\frac{S_C}{S_C^*}\right)\rho.$$

Thus, if there is uncertainty about the true mean, the effect on the relevant moments is that the claims variance σ_C is increased ($\sigma_C^* > \sigma_C$) by an amount equal to the variance of the uncertain mean, and the pairwise correlation of claims is increased ($\delta^* > \delta$; note that δ^* is a weighted average of δ and 1), while the correlation between each claim and the market rate of return is decreased in absolute value ($|\rho^*| < |\rho|$, since $S_C^* > S_C$).

In particular, note that claims may be uncorrelated, given the mean ($\delta = 0$), but that uncertainty about the mean of the claims distribution ($v^2 > 0$) implies that the overall correlation among claims is positive ($\delta^* > 0$ if $\delta = 0$) and is then equal to the ratio of the variance of the mean to the total unconditional variance.

Notes

1. The McKinsey study of 101 insolvencies of life companies and 129 insolvencies of property-liability companies found dishonesty to be the primary cause of insolvency much more frequently for life companies (77 percent) than for property-liability companies (34 percent). The principal cause (59 percent) of property-liability insolvencies has been underwriting losses.

2. The firm is not able to distinguish between better and poorer risks in the relevant population, and thus there is no active policyholder selection.

3. The "riskless asset" may represent bonds with essentially zero default risk, such as government bonds. The impossibility of hedging perfectly against inflation is ignored.

4. This conclusion depends on the assumption of zero transactions costs in the securities market. We comment on the relevance of the CAPM framework below.

5. Throughout the analysis we ignore the effect of the firm in question on the distribution of R_m. However, we do not ignore its impact on total flows of funds in the market at the end of the period, as will be clear below.

6. The correlation between the market asset and claims costs can reflect various phenomena, such as the effect of unanticipated inflation on both claims and the market asset. Similarly, it is widely believed that OPEC price increases affected both the stock market and gasoline consumption and thus automobile insurance claims.

7. That is, to the extent that variations in μ^+ are correlated with U, they cannot be effectively "diversified away" as all investors devote an insignificant proportion of their portfolios to the ownership of this firm.

8. Note that assumed knowledge must include parameters which reflect the firm's uncertainty about the location of the claims distribution.

9. Furthermore, the results depend critically on assumptions made about the nature of the partial ignorance, about the awareness of buyers of their limitations and their response to it, and about the behavior of firms in such a context and their ability or willingness to exploit buyer behavior.

10. If the returns from advertising are not entirely exhausted in the current period, a firm that advertises extensively can be assumed not to expect immediate dissolution, *ceteris paribus*.

11. Indeed, we show below that such behavior tends to be self-fulfilling: To the extent that demand is insensitive to current choices, firms will have the incentive to become very safe.

12. The capital asset pricing model implicitly presumes an infinitely elastic supply of the risk-free security; our inclusion of K as a cash flow thus has no effect on the conclusions.

Treating μ^* as a new flow into the market assumes that the writings of other insurance firms remain unchanged as the firm in question changes its premium rate.

13. The parameter λ is often defined alternatively as $[E(R_U) - R_f]/S_U$, with a corresponding adjustment in the equilibrium equation.

14. "Rate of Return & Profit Provision in Automobile Insurance," State Rating Bureau, Division of Insurance.

15. Assuming that the firm chooses to stay in business; we discuss this possibility briefly below.

16. Also involved is the implicit assumption that after insolvency the firm cannot be resurrected and write policies according to the given demand curve.

17. Of course, the firm's past experience will affect the investment environment of its owners by changing their wealth; we ignore this effect.

18. It is clear that the overall optimal policy for the firm is a stationary policy.

19. The CAPM is essentially a one-period model. However, it can be applied by noting that Y represents the net cash flow of an owner who sells his interest in the firm at the end of the period, after claims have occurred but before paid-in capital has been restored.

20. Equation (41) could alternatively be obtained by assuming that all investors are risk-neutral. However, the CAPM conclusions are obtained on the assumption that investors are risk-averse, to an unspecified degree. Equation (41) follows not from risk-neutrality, but rather from the assumption that investors can costlessly diversify their own portfolios.

21. In analyzing the behavior of $W(K)$, we treat Q as fixed, ignoring the dependence of $Q(K)$. This assumption is relaxed in the fourth section.

22. The product $K \cdot F_\delta$ approaches zero for any distribution.

23. This conclusion can be derived for the increasing failure rate distributions, which include both the truncated normal and other approximately normal distributions that are non-negative and have thick upper tails, and are thus appealing as assumed claims distributions for a firm with a finite number of policyholders.

24. For simplicity of exposition, we ignore the case $W(0) = W(\infty)$, in which the firm is perfectly indifferent between $K = 0$ and $K = \infty$.

25. Of course, the change in $V(K) - K$ becomes trivially small as K becomes large.

26. The distribution of $\bar{C}$ must approach a normal distribution as Q increases, by the central limit theorem.

27. In terms of the previously defined parameters, $(\bar{S}_C)^2 = [1 + (Q - 1)\gamma](S_C)^2/Q$.

28. $\psi(\xi) = \xi Z(\xi)/[\phi(\xi) - \xi Z(\xi)]$, where $\phi(\xi)$ is the density function of the standard normal distribution and $Z(\xi)$ is the probability that a standard normal random variable is greater than ξ.

29. R_f represents the real risk-free rate of return.

30. The case $\gamma = 0.10$ can be interpreted as a claims environment in which 10 percent of the total variance in the distribution of individual policyholder claims is attributable to uncertainty about the location of the distribution (that is, uncertainty about the location of the mean) and 90 percent represents the variation of claims about the true mean.

31. The range includes $E_C = 100.0$; $\bar{S}_C = 20.0, 30.0$; $R_f = 0.03, 0.06, 0.10, 0.15, 0.20$; $\xi = 0, 0.025, 0.050, 0.075, 0.10, 0.15, 0.20, 0.50, 1.0, 2.0$; $b = 0, 0.05, 0.10, 0.15, \ldots, 0.95, 1.0$.

32. However, the specific values of ξ for which the different cases appear vary.

33. Although Q (the number of policyholders), does not appear explicitly, it affects $\bar{S}_C$.

34. That is, it was assumed both that $\alpha = 0$ and that $\rho = 0$; these assumptions continue to be maintained in this section.

35. As in the third section, the firm's owners clearly will not wish to maximize total market value $V(P,Q,K)$ with K variable, but net market value $W(P,Q,K) = V(P,Q,K) - K$.

36. It may be that if P, Q, and K are allowed to vary simultaneously, a still better position could be found. The combination $[P,Q,K]$ that represents the best possible simultaneous choice of all three variables is the global optimum.

37. The combination $[P^{**},Q^{**},K=0]$ dominates $[P^*,Q^*,K=0]$ (because P^{**} and Q^{**} are optimal with $K = 0$), which dominates $[P^*,C^*,K=\infty]$ (because $\psi(\xi^*) < R_f$), which dominates $[P^{**},Q^{**},K=\infty]$ (because P^* and Q^* are optimal with $K = \infty$). Thus, if $[P^{**},Q^{**},K=\infty]$ dominated $[P^{**},Q^{**},K=0]$, one would have a mutually inconsistent chain, as in an Escher drawing.

38. Marginal expected policyholder cost is the mean of the claims cost distribution that has been truncated at the point at which insolvency occurs. As Q is increased, the truncation point falls.

39. Thus, E_C^∞ corresponds to E_C.

40. One can prove that ξ falls monotonically as Q increases over the relevant range. Multiplication of equation (54) by Q, differentiation with respect to Q, and manipulation leads to

$$\frac{\partial \xi}{\partial Q} = \frac{(1 + R_f)MR - E_C}{S_C\sqrt{Q}} - \frac{\xi}{2Q}$$

for the case $\gamma = 0$. It is simple to then show that monotonicity continues to hold for $\gamma > 0$.

41. Proof that $P^{**} > P_1^{**}$ is given in appendix B. However, it is not obvious that P^{**} will be lower than P^*. Intuitively, it seems that the influence of limited liability, which reduced the optimal premium rate, should dominate the influence of the survival motive; after all, we are considering the case where, at the premium rate P^*, the firm chooses to set $K = 0$. But we have no proof for this conjecture.

42. (Because premiums are received at the beginning of the period while claims are paid at the end.)

43. Given the assumption $\rho = 0$, the CAPM equation for market value collapses down to the sum of discounted expected net profits, adjusted for the probabilities of survival. As above, this result is not based on an assumption that investors are risk-neutral, but rather reflects their opportunities for portfolio diversification.

44. The conclusions that the optimal K is either $K = 0$ or $K = \infty$ is obtained by assuming that average claims costs follow an increasing risk probability distribution, which includes both the normal and related distributions that span the range of plausible distributions. The characterization (69) assumes that the distribution of average claims costs is normal.

45. Geico is highly specialized to automobile insurance.

46. As opposed to a fund that provides only partial compensation, or provides compensation with a significant lag, or with significant associated hassle.

47. We thank Gus Haggstrom for pointing this out.

References

Hammond, J. D., Shapiro, Arnold F., and Shilling, Ned. 1978. Regulation of Insurer Solidity through Capital and Surplus Requirements. Technical report, Department of Insurance, Pennsylvania State University.

Hofflander, Alfred E. 1969. "Minimum Capital and Surplus Requirements for Multiple Line Insurance Companies: A New Approach." In S. L. Kimball and H. S. Denenberg (eds.), *Insurance, Government, and Social Policy* (Homewood, Ill.: Irwin).

Jensen, Michael C. 1972. "Capital Markets: Theory and Evidence." *Bell Journal of Economics and Management Science* 3: 357–398.

Joskow, Paul. 1973. "Cartels, Competition, and Regulation in the Property/Liability Insurance Industry. *Bell Journal of Economics and Management Science* 4: 375–427.

Mayerson, Allen L. 1969. "Ensuring the Solvency of Property and Liability Insurance Companies." In S. L. Kimball and H. S. Denenberg (eds.), *Insurance, Government, and Social Policy* (Homewood, Ill.: Irwin).

McKinsey and Co., Inc. 1974. Strengthening the Surveillance System. Report to National Association of Insurance Commissioners.

Munch, P., and Smallwood, D. 1980. "Solvency Regulation in the Property/Casualty Insurance Industry: Empirical Evidence." *Bell Journal of Economics* 11: 261–279.

National Association of Insurance Commissioners. 1974. Monitoring Competition. Report.

Olson, Douglas, G. 1970. Insolvencies among Automobile Insurers. Report to U.S. Department of Transportation.

Scott, J. H., Jr. 1976. "A Theory of Optimal Capital Structure." *Bell Journal of Economics* 7: 33–54.

Comment

Howard Kunreuther

In this interesting and stimulating paper Munch and Smallwood raise the following question: Does solvency regulation of the casualty insurance industry produce sufficient benefits in the form of consumer and owner protection to justify the operating and monitoring costs of such a system?

The authors appropriately note that consumers may be imperfectly informed about the financial stability of different companies. Two empirical studies support their point by shedding additional light on the imperfect information consumers have been obtaining on insurance. J. D. Cummins et al. ("Consumer Attitudes Toward Auto and Homeowners Insurance," Wharton School Department of Insurance report) found in a field survey of 2,462 individuals who purchased automobile and/or homeowners coverage that few compared the policy terms from different companies before making their purchase decision. Similar behavior was found by Kunreuther et al. (*Disaster Insurance Protection: Public Policy Lessons* [New York: Wiley-Interscience, 1978]) in a field survey of 3,000 homeowners residing in flood- and earthquake-prone areas. This study revealed that most homeowners were either unaware of terms in their policies or had misinformation on such relevant data as premiums and deductibles. If consumers are reluctant to collect data on these characteristics, which directly affect them, it is unlikely that they have information on the financial quality of the company. The latter information would require detailed reading of balance sheets and perhaps inside information on recent company performance and strategy.

The above empirical findings raise a question of whether the capital assets pricing model (CAPM) is an appropriate model for describing an insurance firm's behavior. If companies know that consumers have limited interest in collecting detailed information on insurance and hence have imperfect data on policy terms, then their behavior and marketing strategies are likely to differ from actions they would take if they assumed that consumers collected detailed information and expected them to try to maximize utility. There is no way to answer specifically the question of what assumptions firms are making about consumer behavior unless we undertake more detailed empirical analyses. However, on a theoretical plane it should be possible to investigate a firm's profit-maximizing behavior by postulating that the consumer has limited and imperfect information on characteristics of the insurance market.

The interesting work Munch and Smallwood have undertaken on the CAPM can be used as a starting point for determining whether alternative models produce significantly different results in insurance companies' behavior. In particular, one should then be able to discover whether different assumptions about consumer behavior will affect the actions of firms in a way that influences bankruptcy possibilities.

Let me turn now to the model Munch and Smallwood investigate. To make their multiperiod analysis tractable from a mathematical point of view, the authors make the following simplified assumptions regarding consumer and firm behavior:

• that consumers are indifferent to the financial condition of the firm, either because they have imperfect information, because they are protected through a guaranty fund, or because they buy insurance solely to satisfy responsibility requirements; and

• that firms do not invest in risky market securities.

As a result of these assumptions, a firm should choose to set its financial capital (K) equal to either 0 or ∞. The choice of either extreme is determined by the relative advantages of minimizing the liability should the firm go bankrupt $(K = 0)$ and of reducing the probability of bankruptcy to a negligible level $(K = \infty)$. The reason for this dichotomous policy is that the firm, if it exists, faces the same demand curve and claims policy as in the previous period.

To make the model more realistic and interesting, Munch and Smallwood might want to view consumer demand as a function of both the premium and the perceived financial stability of the firm as represented by K. One way to do this in the spirit of their analysis is to divide consumers into old customers (who continue to purchase a policy from the firm with which they started, independent of its financial stability) and new customers (who may be sensitive to the financial condition of firms in making their choice, but can misperceive this information). In each period, a fraction of old customers leave the market and another fraction of new customers enter. In this case the firm will have to concern itself with the impact that K has on demand so that the optimal value may be somewhere between 0 and ∞. This paper discusses a special case of this more general model: New customers do not exist, so demand is solely a function of the premium (P).

The performance of several other regulatory systems, aside from minimum capital requirements, could be investigated by the authors in the context of the broader model proposed above. They might want to investigate the performance of a policy where K is a function of the number of policyholders (Q). Such a policy may be more desirable than specification of a fixed K if the variance of the claims distribution, and hence the probability of bankruptcy, were assumed to change with Q.

Another alternative the authors might want to investigate would be to have the regulatory commissioner specify a minimum level of capital, K, below which a firm would have to undertake special steps to avoid bankruptcy. These could include raising additional capital from outside sources or reducing the number of policyholders in future periods (for example, by not renewing all policies). Under such a system, K serves the same function as safety stock in inventory systems where the firm faces uncertain future demand. The minimum capital requirement would then directly affect the future probability of bankruptcy by forcing the firm to pay special attention to factors that affect it directly.

As Munch and Smallwood indicated in an earlier version of this paper, a variant of this system is in operation in some states which require a minimum capital requirement (K) and an additional surplus requirement (S). Once a firm's assets fall below $K + S$, it is forced to take special steps such as adding to reserves. By developing a theoretical analysis of this problem, Munch and Smallwood could address the implications of such a system for firm behavior and insolvency probabilities. Admittedly there are monitoring problems associated with measuring surplus, as the authors pointed out, and these costs would have to be included in an evaluation of such a regulatory policy. A more detailed discussion can be found in A. L. Mayerson's "Ensuring the Solvency of Property and Liability Insurance Companies," in *Insurance, Government and Social Policy*, ed. S. L. Kimball and H. S. Denenberg (Homewood, Ill.: Irwin, 1969).

In an earlier version of this paper, the authors provided empirical evidence on insolvencies which indicates that failures are more common among firms writing automobile insurance than engaging in commercial lines. On the basis of this evidence the authors conclude that these data are consistent with the hypothesis that insolvencies may be caused by poorly informed purchasers of auto coverage.

Empirical evidence from a study by D. Olson (*Insolvencies Among Automobile Insurers* [Washington, D.C.: U.S. Government Printing Office, 1970]) suggests a different interpretation of why insolvencies have occurred in the automobile insurance market. In recent years many states have instituted financial responsibility laws and/or have required automobile insurance as a condition for a license. (A financial responsibility law requires a driver who has caused an accident to show proof of ability to pay the loss, either through an insurance policy or by posting bond.) These structural changes naturally expanded the demand for insurance. During this same period many leading companies felt that automobile rates were inadequate, and hence were reluctant to renew existing policies let alone to extend market coverage to new customers. This gap between supply and demand led many new firms to enter the automobile insurance market. Olson cites detailed empirical evidence indicating that most auto-insurer insolvencies were due to "intentional management ineptness bordering on fraudulent behavior rather than on impersonal market forces" (p. 43). If newly formed companies were intentionally engaging in such behavior, they would be more likely to enter states where there was no minimum capital requirement.

Another factor that may have caused insolvencies in the automobile market is the difficulty firms may have had in determining risks on which their premiums were based. Olson indicates that expenses for automobile claims are not restricted to a single year, because individuals may be able to collect today on injuries from accidents that occurred in past years. Hence, premiums may not be easily determined by looking at the past claims distribution. The problem of setting economically variable rates is exacerbated by state regulatory agencies which restrict proposed rate increases by companies.

The difficulty firms have in estimating future losses provides an additional reason for instituting minimum capital requirements. If firms are unable to determine the mean and variance of their future claims from past data, then their decisions on optimal premiums and policyholders may be based on incorrect information. Minimum capital requirements may then serve the useful function of encouraging the entry of larger firms, which may be in a better position than smaller companies to absorb unexpected losses.

The authors may also want to investigate the impact of a requirement proposed by P. Joskow ("Cartels, Competition, and Regulation in the Property/Liability Insurance Industry," *Bell Journal of Economics* 4: 275–326) that all firms be required to carry complete insurance against bankruptcy, with rates varying directly with their premium/capital ratio. Such a requirement should reinforce minimum capital requirements in protecting firms and consumers against their own actions based on imperfect information.

The Munch-Smallwood paper is an interesting first step in addressing policy questions related to the impact of financial regulation on insolvency. Before one advocates specific recommendations, further work should be undertaken to relate the decision processes of consumers and firms to the institutional arrangements currently in force. Such research may then lead to more definitive answers to the general question about the desirability of regulation posed at the beginning of the paper.

Comment

Michael P. Lynch

Regulations that are designed to "insure" insurance-company solvency may have an important impact on the entire insurance industry, yet they have received very little attention from economists from either a theoretical or an empirical point of view. Munch and Smallwood provide a welcome first step toward a theory of the economics of solvency regulation by asking why an unregulated market will not automatically produce the efficient level of solvency and by proposing a model to answer this question. Their model is designed to apply to the casualty-and-property segment of the insurance industry, but it is worth noting that solvency regulation figures prominently in the $30-billion-a-year life insurance business. For example, a well-known textbook (D. McGill, *Life Insurance*, revised edition [Homewood, Ill.: Irwin, 1976]) states the following (p. 776):

The primary purpose of state insurance regulation is to maintain the solvency and financial soundness of the companies providing insurance protection. In states having large domestic insurers the amount of effort expended in the supervision of the insurers' affairs exceeds that involved in all other kinds of supervisory work combined.

This emphasis on solvency regulation exists despite the rarity of insolvencies among life insurance companies and the even greater rarity of consumers being hurt by insolvency. (Equity Funding was a case of defrauding stockholders, not policyholders.)

Solvency regulations that include minimum capital or surplus requirements, restrictions on portfolio composition, reserve requirements, and asset-valuation requirements may have an important impact on the level and structure of life insurance prices. Indeed, these regulations may be an important cause of the poor rate of return on the savings element offered by life insurance relative to banks, savings and loan associations, and other financial intermediaries. Though it is difficult to find consumers who have been hurt by firms becoming insolvent, it is not at all difficult to find consumers who have paid higher than necessary amounts for their insurance coverage from highly solvent firms. These considerations suggest that there is a tradeoff between increased solvency and increased prices and that, at least in life insurance, the optimal insolvency rate may be higher than the one currently observed.

Another problem worth exploring is the reasons for the regulations in the first place. Who demanded them? Consumers? Reformers? The industry itself? The first two seem unlikely. I will suggest that the industry itself demanded these regulations, and that the benefits derived are subtle and cannot be measured in terms of reduced insolvencies.

Let me turn now to the theoretical analysis in the Munch-Smallwood article. As a first step in analyzing the costs and benefits of regulation, the authors quite appropriately ask how the probability of insolvency would be determined in an unregulated market. The owners of an insurance company, as well as its policyholders, have an interest in the company's solvency. Under some circumstances, at least, there may be no need for solvency regulation, since the owners will have the proper incentives to choose the "optimal" probability of solvency. The capital assets pricing model (CAPM), at first glance, appears to provide an attractive framework for analyzing this problem. It seems as though this model can be used to solve for the amount of paid-in capital; the number of policies to be sold; and the proportion of the firm's assets to be invested in risky assets rather than in the (elusive) riskless asset, which maximize the market value of the firm. Since solvency regulations commonly specify some minimum paid-in capital and impose restrictions on how much of a company's assets may be invested in certain "risky" assets, the CAPM seems to provide a convenient framework for the analysis. I believe that, in this case, appearences are deceptive.

The CAPM is a theory of how a given set of risk-averse investors value a given set of risky earning streams. It assumes that investors have full information on the probability distributions of these risky earnings streams and that they can and will bear unlimited liability for them. It is basically a theory of the demand for risky assets. Equilibrium prices are obtained by assuming that there is a fixed supply of risky assets, which must be held. The model is not useful for the problem at hand, for the following reasons:

• It focuses on the behavior of the investors in an insurance company, whereas the focus should be on the policyholders. It is the possibility that the insurance company may not pay valid claims, and the impact of this possibility on the demand for its product, that makes insurance-company insolvency special. As Munch and Smallwood point out, the unlimited-liability assumption rules out the problem of insolvency from the policyholders' point of view. They attempt to drop this assumption, but at the cost of assuming that investors are risk-neutral and that policyholders are indifferent to the level of paid-in capital. These assumptions appear to me to rule out any meaningful analysis of policyholder concern about insolvency.

• Contrary to appearances, the basic CAPM does not have any interesting implications for the optimal level of paid-in capital or the optimal mix of risky and riskless assets. The model determines a value for each asset. The current value of K dollars is simply K dollars. The current value of each insurance policy, the random variable $P - C_i$, is the discounted value (at the riskless rate of return) of the expected difference between the premium and the claim cost minus the market price of risk times the undiversifiable risk between the policy and the total set of risky assets (including the policy itself). The market value of the "company" is simply the sum of the value of its assets. The value of the "firm" appears to be independent of the particular owners' choice of α, just as the value of the CAPM "firm" is independent of the owner's choice of a debt-equity ratio (the famous proposition 1 of F. Modigliani and M. Miller, "The Cost of Capital, Corporation Finance, and the Theory of Investment," *American Economic Review* XLVIII [1958]: 261–297; for a proof that this proposition holds in the CAPM see J. Lintner, "The Valuation of Risk Assets and the Selection of Risky Investments in Stock Portfolios and Capital Budgets," *Review of Economics and Statistics* XLVII [1965]: 13–37). The risk preferences of the initial owners influence the value of the firm only insofar as they influence the market price of risk. In equilibrium, all investors who hold any risky assets at all hold some risky insurance assets. That is, all risky investors are "owners" of the insurance firm.

• As far as determining the optimal number of policyholders, the Munch-Smallwood analysis is at least incomplete and perhaps mistaken. Every time a new policy is underwritten, a new random variable is added on the supply side of the market. This requires that a new equilibrium set of values be determined. This may result in a change in the equilibrium value of the "market price of risk" and a change in the total value of the universe of risky assets in the market. Munch and Smallwood implicitly assume that the market price of risk is independent of the number of policies written. Were this so, then the market value of each new policy would be the same as each old policy, at least in the special case where the insurance claim variables are assumed to be independent of all other risky assets in the market. If it was worthwhile to write one policy, then it would be worthwhile to write an indefinite number of policies; that is, the market value of the firm would increase without limit as the number of policyholders increased.

• As may be obvious from the above, I do not think the model has "interesting implications" concerning the proper treatment of investment income for insurance ratemaking purposes. The complexities of the investment income problem arise more from the difficulty of determining how much of the income derives from policyholders' capital rather than investors' capital than from determining the proper risk-adjusted rate of return for stockholders.

The CAPM does not seem to provide a useful framework for the analysis of insurance company solvency. I shall sketch an alternative model that may prove helpful. I start from the assumption that it is not the problem of the investors that makes an insurance company's possible insolvency special—indeed the problem doesn't arise for a large portion of the business which is sold through mutual companies. It is the effect of the possibility of insolvency on the policyholder that makes insurance company insolvency special and has led to the special regulations. The belief in the mind of a potential policyholder that the company may fail fundamentally alters the product that the company is trying to sell; that is, the fear of insolvency may greatly change the demand for the product.

Let us take the simplest case. A risk-averse individual is subject to a loss of C with probability p. He can purchase a full-coverage insurance policy for a premium kpC, where $k > 1$ and represents the "loading" in the policy. The figure portrays how this individual can be made better off so long as he can obtain an insurance policy with a loading between 1 and k^*, where the latter depends on his degree of risk aversion.

The situation changes radically if the consumer believes there is some probability s that the firm will be unable to pay off on a claim. The consumer can no longer pay a small amount to rid himself of large uncertain loss. He is still subject to the uncertain large loss, and, in addition, to the certain small premium payment. Graphically (see figure), this means that he trades a point on one line segment (such as I) for another point on another segment (for example, III) instead of trading a risky situation (I) for a riskless situation (II). This means that, for any given loading, the insurance is worth less to the individual than in the no-insolvency case, and for any given k makes it more likely that he will actually be made worse off if he buys the policy.

Suppose, as seems likely, that the consumers cannot judge the level of s very well, nor can they compare one company's chance of insolvency to that of another. The thing that is easy to compare is the premium that each company will charge to assume the risk. With other things equal, the lower the "loading" the greater the probability of insolvency. If consumers cannot distinguish one company from another in terms of solvency, and so choose their policies on the basis of premium alone, then the insolvency-prone companies will drive out the more solid

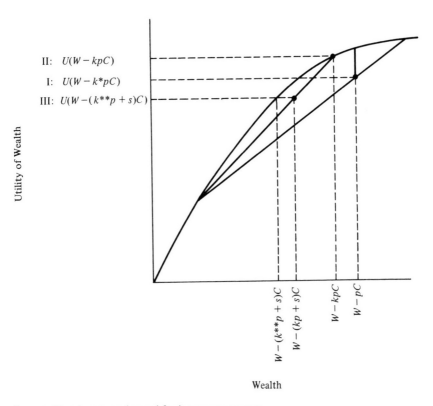

II: $U(W - kpC)$

I: $U(W - k*pC)$

III: $U(W - (k**p + s)C)$

Utility of Wealth

$W - (k**p + s)C$

$W - (kp + s)C$

$W - kpC$

$W - pC$

Wealth

Impact of insolvency on demand for insurance coverage.

companies. Of course, as consumers learn that there is a significant chance of insolvency they will simply stop buying insurance policies. Thus, the end result is the destruction of the entire market. This story is similar, if not identical, to George Akerlof's "market for lemons" ("The Market for Lemons: Quality, Uncertainty, and the Market Mechanism," *Quarterly Journal of Economics* LXXIV [1970]: 488–500).

From this point of view, the benefits of solvency regulation cannot be measured merely in terms of reduced insolvency rates. The main benefits are in the increased size of the market which is made possible by the policyholders' belief that insolvencies either won't occur or that, if they do, the policyholders will not be hurt.

I have not made a detailed study of the history of life-insurance solvency regulations, but what little I know of it is consistent with the "lemon" theory of insolvency regulation. In the 1840s the life insurance industry began to grow very rapidly with the successful introduction of the "mutual" policy and the beginnings of the agency system (see J. O.

Stalson, *Marketing Life Insurance: Its History in America*, revised edition [Homewood, Ill.: Irwin, 1969], pp. 217–236 and 292–326). Success attracted new entrants, some of whom began to offer "dividends" (paid in scrip, not cash) amounting to 70–80 percent of the annual premium. Agents for company A would suggest that company B was offering dividends far in excess of what they could really pay. The claims gained credence when some companies failed in the 1850s. As Stalson puts it (p. 226),

The suspicion of all companies which these competitive assaults on individual companies engendered, however, unquestionably did every company more harm that it did any individual agent or company good.

It was about this same time (the early 1850s) that the states began to impose minimum capital requirements on life insurance companies and the first reserve-valuation laws were passed.

If the "lemon" theory of solvency regulation has much truth in it then it will be very difficult to assess regulation's benefits. One would have to estimate what the size of the market would have been in the absence of regulation. I doubt that this can be done, though it may be worthwhile to see whether differences in solvency regulations among the states result in any detectable differences in the size of their markets. But I don't think the interesting policy questions concern whether or not solvency regulations should be eliminated. Neither industry nor consumers appear to be pushing for their removal. Rather, I think the interesting policy questions concern whether the methods that have been adopted to achieve a given probability of insolvency are low-cost ways of doing so, and how one would go about deciding on an appropriate insolvency rate.

The first question, the relationship between paid-in capital (K), the premium "loading" (k), and the probability of insolvency or "ruin" (S), has been the subject of a great number of theoretical articles under the general title of "collective risk theory," and a much smaller number of empirical studies. (For a general review of these see Seal, *Stochastic Theory of Risk Business* [New York: Wiley, 1969], chapters 4 and 5, and K. Borch, *The Mathematical Theory of Insurance* [Lexington, Mass.: Lexington Books, 1974], parts III and IV.) The theoretical literature provides, under some simplifying assumptions, some fairly tractable closed-form analytical expressions for the function $s = g(k, K)$.

Some insight may be gained into the second question, the appropriate level for an insolvency rate, by exploring further the simple example I gave to illustrate the workings of the lemon principle. The rational regulator (a species at least as rare as the rational economic man) might reason as follows: For any given insolvency rate (s), I can use the technique illustrated in the figure to compute the "certainty equivalent" level of wealth for each policyholder. I can change s by requiring companies to change the "loading" they built into their rates or by changing the minimum capital requirement. What "loading" and minimum capital requirement should I require, if I want to maximize the sum of the policyholder's wealth certainty equivalents? The answer to this question could be found by solving the following maximization problem:

$$\text{Max}_{k,K} \sum_{i=1}^{n} \left[U(W_i - P)(1 - s) + U(W_i - P - C)(s) \right],$$

where

$s = g(k, K)$ and $P = f(k, K)$.

In solving this problem, the regulator could look explicitly at the tradeoff between increasing solvency and decreasing the premium. Note that the expected utility hypothesis is being used for a "normative," rational policy purpose, rather than for a "positive" purpose, such as to predict the way people actually behave.

Summary

I have suggested

• that solvency regulations in the life insurance industry deserve at least as much attention as those in the property and casualty lines,
• that Munch and Smallwood should look to Akerlof's "market for lemons" for a theoretical framework, rather than to the CAPM, and
• that the focus for policy research should be on the tradeoff between lower premium rates and lower insolvency rates, rather than on whether there should be any solvency regulations at all.

The views expressed in this comment are solely those of the author and do not necessarily represent those of the FTC or any of its other staff members.

4

Regulation, Barriers to Exit, and the Investment Behavior of Railroads

Richard C. Levin

Evidence abounds that the railroad industry is in decline. Since World War II industry profits have remained chronically low, lower than those of any manufacturing industry in the United States.[1] In the past decade there have been eight bankruptcies of class I railroads. Although measured productivity gains have been relatively high, there is good reason to believe that conventional productivity measures are biased upward in the case of railroads.[2] More important is the widespread feeling that railroad productivity performance has been especially poor relative to latent technological opportunities. In addition, there are persistent complaints from customers of the railroads about poor service and maintenance.

For the past two decades most economists have presumed that the major source of troubles for the railroads has been the regulation of freight rates by the Interstate Commerce Commission. The familiar story, given emphasis in the work of Meyer et al. (1959) and retold most recently by Moore (1975), is that the persistence of value of service pricing—a legacy of an earlier era of railroad monopoly—induced the shift of high-valued manufactured traffic from rail to truck, reducing the volume of railroad traffic and weighting its composition heavily toward less remunerative traffic in agricalatural and mineral products. Rate deregulation, it was held, in addition to eliminating the dead-weight loss from misallocation, would restore the financial viability of the railroads via increased volume. This conventional wisdom has been challenged by more recent econometric studies (Boyer 1977; Levin 1978) which suggest that the direct allocative effects of rate deregulation are likely to be minimal. The low estimated price elasticity for rail transport implies that both the welfare gains and the traffic shifts attendant upon deregulation would be small.

This recent work on rate regulation suggests that the major causes of the railroad problem may be elsewhere. The most plausible candidate, which occupies a parallel (if not so widely emphasized) strand in the literature on transport economics, is the burden of excess capacity. The problem here, long recognized by farsighted railroad executives such as John Barriger (1956), is that the existing railroad network was designed and built in response to the technological imperatives and locational patterns of the nineteenth-century economy. The advent of alternative technologies (trucking and intermodal) and dramatic shifts in the location of industry and the consuming population have rendered much of the existing rail plant obsolete, despite traffic growth on other portions of the rail network.

The longevity of railroad capital alone would be sufficient to create subnormal profits under such conditions, but the problem has been exacerbated by regulatory control over the exit of capital. Apart from the recent abandonments authorized by congressional action in the restructuring of the northeast rail system, line abandonments require the approval of the Interstate Commerce Commission. Past abandonment proceedings have been lengthy and expensive, and the probability of success before the ICC, though difficult to assess from available data, may be sufficiently low to deter substantially the efforts of railroad firms to rationalize their operations.

The problem of excess capacity is exacerbated by rate regulation as well as by abandonment regulation. The issue here more closely parallels an aspect of airline rate regulation than the problems usually discussed in the rail-rate-regulation literature. One of the oldest principles of ICC rate regulation is that shipments of comparable goods over comparable distances should be comparably priced.[3] Since the cost of providing rail service over low-density lines is substantially higher than over high-density lines, application of this principle has entailed cross-subsidization of low-density traffic by high-density traffic. It is possible that some low-density lines would remain viable if rates were allowed to rise to cover the variable costs of providing service, although in a great many cases remunerative rail rates would surely induce a shift to alternative modes.

The combination of barriers to exit and cross-subsidization has adverse static and dynamic consequences. Statically, the requirement that firms operate low-density lines (LDLs) lowers industry profits at existing prices and alters the distribution of profits and losses across firms; to the extent that LDL traffic could be carried intermodally or by alternative modes at costs below rail costs, pure waste or productive inefficiency is induced. Moreover, cross-subsidization entails a dead-weight loss from misallocation of resources between high- and low-density rail lines, which is unmeasured by conventional welfare-loss calculations based on the average discrepancy of rates from marginal costs within commodity groups and/or distance blocks. Dynamically, the formation of new road capital on the viable portions of the rail network is constrained, thus retarding the diffusion of superior technology embodied in capital goods, such as centralized traffic control, automated switching yards, continuous welded rail, and improved signaling equipment. New investment is retarded through two distinct mechanisms. First, to offset the losses on LDLs, rates on HDLs exceed marginal cost, which restricts output and consequently reduces the desired stock of capital on viable portions of the rail network. Second, the lower profitability and associated higher risks of bankruptcy entailed by exit barriers raise the cost of capital to railroad firms and thus reduce investment.

The object of this investigation is to assess the available evidence for the existence and magnitude of these effects. The economic literature on excess rail capacity has focused heretofore on two aspects of the problem: measuring the extent of excess capacity and estimating the social cost (in the sense of productive rather than allocative inefficiency) of operating the rail network at suboptimal traffic density. This study will present new evidence that bears on the first point, but the static social costs will be measured only partially and indirectly. Instead, the focus here will be upon the consequences of abandonment regulation and cross-subsidization for the profitability, and especially the investment behavior, of firms in the railroad industry. While the redistributive consequences of regulation across railroad firms will be emphasized, the distributive effects of rail abandonments on shippers and local communities (a serious and important issue) will not be discussed.

The Simple Economics of Rail Freight Density

In prior attempts to measure the extent of excess line capacity, Friedlaender (1971) and Keeler (1974, 1976) estimated short- and long-run rail cost functions from data supplied by rail firms. Despite important differences in methodology and functional specification, these authors reached broadly similar conclusions. Both found that the actual cost of operating at existing traffic levels substantially exceeds the cost of providing the same level of service along the long-run cost envelope. In light of the methods employed by these authors, the latter statement is equivalent to a finding of excess line capacity, since each author identifies miles of track as the fixed factor of production in the short run. Keeler finds that minimum cost provision of rail service at 1969 levels would have required only 20–25 percent of the existing miles of road.

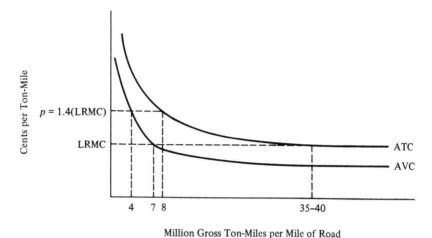

Figure 4.1 Unit total costs, operating costs, and traffic density.

In other words, if all lines operated at efficient levels of traffic density, 75–80 percent of rail route mileage would have been redundant.[4]

Harris (1977) focused directly on the relation of unit rail costs and traffic density, and despite a different specification of the cost function his findings are virtually identical to those of Keeler.[5] Figure 4.1 is a schematic picture of the relation of unit costs and traffic density.[6] Unit costs decline sharply with density, but they become constant once density reaches approximately 35–40 million annual gross ton-miles per mile of road.[7] This represents the level of minimum efficient density, and (roughly speaking) one can think of this as the capacity of a single track between two points, the fundamental indivisibility in the rail cost structure. Higher traffic density can be served at approximately constant cost by adding segments of parallel track and signaling devices. This picture of economies to traffic density is consistent with the findings of Borts (1960), Friedlaender (1971), Keeler (1974), and Caves and Christensen (1976) that the long-run production function for railroad services is linearly homogeneous.[8]

By plotting average rail rates on figure 4.1 it is possible to estimate the break-even level of traffic density.[9] For Harris's cost function (evaluated at the mean average length of haul for firms in his sample) the break-even density was 7.93 million gross ton-miles per mile of road in 1973. Keeler's cost function yields an estimate of break-even density of 8.12 million gross ton-miles per mile of road. Since rates do not vary with traffic density in principle (though they may vary slightly in practice), with commodity type and length of haul held constant, it seems reasonable to infer that profits on traffic carried over lines with density in excess of roughly 10 million gross ton-miles per mile of road subsidize losses on traffic carried on lower-density lines. This proposition will be put to a crude test in the next section.

The observation that rail rates do not cover average total cost on a particular rail line does not necessarily make that line a candidate for abandonment. A firm will presumably offer service if rates cover average variable cost. Economists unfamiliar with railroad costs are inclined to wonder why this criterion would not be satisfied, since they assume that decreasing unit costs of rail service are associated strictly with the fixed cost of road and track, which is sunk. But, as figure 4.1 illustrates, unit operating costs decline sharply with traffic density. Decreasing average variable costs are thought to be primarily attributable to two factors: the fact that low traffic density necessitates shorter trains, which in conjunction with locomotive requirements and especially labor requirements implies higher unit operating cost; and the fact that maintenance costs are largely independent of traffic density. Harris's estimate of average operating costs suggests that, at actual 1973 rates, lines with traffic density below 4.15 million gross ton-miles per mile of road fail to earn revenues in excess of variable cost. If rates were permitted to fall to long-run marginal cost, many lines which cover variable cost at inefficient prices would become candidates for abandonment, at least from the point of a view of a private, profit-maximizing enterprise. Figure 4.1 shows that efficient prices (actual prices divided by 1.4) would cover operating costs where traffic density exceeds 7.03 million gross ton-miles per mile of road. This figure is close to the level of break-even density at existing rates.

New Evidence on the Extent of Excess Capacity

Until recently, econometric work on the excess-capacity problem has been limited to the use of cross-sectional firm data, in which the only indicator of a firm's freight density characteristics is the quotient of its total output and its route mileage. A considerably more detailed picture can now be obtained from data collected by the Department of Transportation in a study mandated by the Railroad Revitalization and Regulatory Reform Act of 1976. The DOT data classify each line segment in the U.S. rail network by the density of its traffic in 1975.[10] Although the DOT is unwilling to release exact density information by line segment, it does place each segment within one of six density categories.[11] When combined with data from the Federal Railroad Administration's network model, the line-segment-density data permit a tabulation of the distribution of each railroad's route mileage by density class. The exact traffic density for each line segment is unknown, but a good approximation to the distribution of each railroad's output by density class may be calculated on the assumption that each line segment has a traffic density equal to the cell mean. Table 4.1 presents this information for class I railroads in 1975.

The percentage of each railroad's route mileage and output in the lowest three density categories are reported in the LDL columns of table 4.1. These density categories account for all segments below 10 million gross ton-miles per mile of road, and correspond closely to the break-even level of density implicit in the estimates of Keeler and Harris. Ten million gross ton-miles per mile of road is also the closest approximation, though perhaps a modest overstatement, of the density level below which efficient rail rates would fail to cover variable costs. These LDLs account for nearly two-thirds of the route mileage of class I railroads yet they carry only 18 percent of the traffic. Only five of the sixty railroads tabulated have less than 20 percent of their route mileage in LDLs; twelve railroads have networks consisting entirely of LDLs. Three of these twelve are bankrupt, and none of the rest are in good financial health.

The HDL columns of table 4.1 report the share of each railroad's mileage and output in the highest of the six DOT density categories. These line segments, which operate at approximately minimum efficient density, represent only 10.9 percent of class I railroad mileage, yet they carry over one-third of the nation's freight. It is remarkable that thirty-two class I railroads have no HDL segments in their networks, and only one (the small but highly profitable Richmond, Fredericksburg, and Potomac) has a system composed entirely of HDLs.

It follows by combining the information reported in columns 4 and 6 that the remaining 25.9 percent of the nation's rail network operates at traffic densities that are remunerative at existing rates but would not be profitable if rates fell to the level of long-run marginal cost. These lines of intermediate density carry nearly half (48.2 percent) of the nation's freight.

Low-Density Lines and Profitability

Before examining the impact of barriers to abandonment and cross-subsidization on railroad investment behavior, it seems worthwhile to

Table 4.1 Line density of Class I railroads, 1975.

	Route Miles Classified	Gross Ton-Miles (Millions)	Mean Density, GTM/MR	LDL Miles/Route Miles	LDL Output ÷ GTM	HDL Miles/Route Miles	HDL Output ÷ GTM
Ann Arbor[a]	342.0	171.00	0.500	1.000	1.000	0.000	0.000
Atchison, Topeka & Santa Fe	12,209.1	156,948.30	12.855	0.576	0.119	0.203	0.553
Baltimore & Ohio	4,732.8	63,531.72	13.424	0.515	0.143	0.179	0.467
Bangor & Aroostook	503.0	2,144.00	4.262	0.950	0.708	0.000	0.000
Bessemer & Lake Erie	170.0	3,597.00	21.159	0.247	0.041	0.171	0.282
Boston & Maine	1,098.5	8,653.35	7.877	0.751	0.208	0.000	0.000
Burlington Northern	20,859.1	204,218.80	9.790	0.651	0.162	0.081	0.289
Canadian Pacific Lines in Maine	305.1	3,480.50	11.393	0.350	0.145	0.000	0.000
Central Railroad of New Jersey[a]	252.4	328.70	1.302	1.000	1.000	0.000	0.000
Central Vermont	363.0	1,779.50	4.902	1.000	1.000	0.000	0.000
Chesapeake & Ohio	4,158.1	53,346.29	12.829	0.637	0.167	0.209	0.570
Chicago & Eastern Illinois[b]	384.5	5,017.50	13.049	0.429	0.095	0.044	0.119
Chicago & Northwestern	9,567.4	64,979.22	6.792	0.791	0.281	0.055	0.282
Chicago, Milwaukee, St. Paul & Pacific	8,889.5	52,894.02	5.950	0.772	0.371	0.002	0.014
Chicago, Rock Island & Pacific	6,220.6	46,218.29	7.430	0.719	0.369	0.001	0.005
Clinchfield	289.0	6,171.00	21.353	0.076	0.011	0.000	0.000
Colorado & Southern	586.4	3,709.50	6.326	1.000	1.000	0.000	0.000
Delaware & Hudson	624.1	8,261.55	13.238	0.479	0.178	0.000	0.000
Denver & Rio Grande Western	1,740.2	21,287.00	12.223	0.496	0.154	0.000	0.000
Detroit & Toledo Shore	61.6	924.00	15.000	0.000	0.000	0.000	0.000
Detroit, Toledo & Ironton	343.8	3,515.50	10.225	0.573	0.232	0.000	0.000
Duluth, Mesabe & Iron Range	319.0	4,004.50	12.553	0.564	0.115	0.197	0.551

Table 4.1 (continued)

	Route Miles Classified	Gross Ton-Miles (Millions)	Mean Density, GTM/MR	LDL Miles/ Route Miles	LDL Output ÷ GTM	HDL Miles/ Route Miles	HDL Output ÷ GTM
Duluth, Winnepeg & Pacific	78.0	1,170.00	15.000	0.000	0.000	0.000	0.000
Elgin, Joliet & Eastern	178.4	1,784.00	10.000	0.583	0.226	0.000	0.000
Erie Lackawanna[a]	2,261.2	15,488.14	6.850	0.713	0.215	0.000	0.000
Florida East Coast	512.6	5,856.50	11.425	0.283	0.058	0.000	0.000
Fort Worth & Denver	1,094.4	5,476.00	5.004	1.000	1.000	0.000	0.000
Georgia, Lessee Organization	309.0	2,759.00	8.929	0.586	0.304	0.000	0.000
Grand Trunk Western	892.7	9,314.90	10.435	0.586	0.123	0.000	0.000
Green Bay & Western[c]	253.0	759.00	3.000	1.000	1.000	0.000	0.000
Illinois Central Gulf	8,919.1	77,861.38	8.730	0.736	0.349	0.040	0.162
Illinois Terminal	167.0	830.00	4.970	1.000	1.000	0.000	0.000
Kansas City Southern	1,442.9	14,331.20	9.932	0.565	0.293	0.000	0.000
Lehigh Valley[a]	632.0	3,499.25	5.537	0.835	0.483	0.016	0.100
Long Island	298.5	759.00	1.358	1.000	1.000	0.000	0.000
Louisville & Nashville	5,995.5	84,604.00	14.111	0.491	0.111	0.147	0.364
Maine Central	757.0	2,853.75	3.770	0.998	0.987	0.000	0.000
Missouri-Illinois[c]	120.0	345.0	2.875	1.000	1.000	0.000	0.000
Missouri-Kansas-Texas	1,797.7	16,402.04	9.124	0.587	0.237	0.013	0.049
Missouri Pacific	7,536.8	78,752.00	10.449	0.611	0.193	0.071	0.237
Norfolk & Western	6,665.4	93,045.88	13.960	0.522	0.126	0.176	0.441
Norfolk Southern	860.0	2,841.75	3.304	1.000	1.000	0.000	0.000
Northwestern Pacific	305.0	1,421.00	4.659	1.000	1.000	0.000	0.000
Penn Central[a]	14,716.0	174,329.30	11.846	0.647	0.158	0.171	0.505

Pennsylvania-Reading Seashore[a]	295.6	406.30	1.374	1.000	1.000	0.000	0.000
Pittsburgh & Lake Erie	177.2	4,705.00	26.552	0.011	0.000	0.524	0.690
Reading[a]	931.0	6,853.70	7.362	0.786	0.153	0.096	0.454
Richmond, Fredericksburg & Potomac	122.5	4,287.50	35.000	0.000	0.000	1.000	1.000
St. Louis–San Francisco	4,480.5	40,518.79	9.043	0.630	0.194	0.000	0.000
St. Louis–Southwestern	1,198.6	22,934.00	19.134	0.388	0.055	0.359	0.656
Seaboard Coast Line	8,716.3	100,022.30	11.475	0.534	0.152	0.081	0.247
Soo Line	4,158.3	27,148.94	6.529	0.759	0.323	0.000	0.000
Southern Pacific	10,551.4	169,603.10	16.074	0.486	0.084	0.300	0.653
Southern[d]	9,334.0	105,501.50	11.303	0.607	0.174	0.075	0.233
Texas-Mexican	177.0	1,893.50	10.698	0.322	0.049	0.000	0.000
Texas & Pacific[b]	1,789.6	21,086.00	11.783	0.536	0.166	0.050	0.149
Toledo, Peoria & Western	271.0	2,021.00	7.458	0.849	0.696	0.000	0.000
Union Pacific	8,356.5	114,870.40	13.746	0.587	0.116	0.250	0.636
Western Maryland	427.1	3,454.50	8.088	0.679	0.255	0.035	0.152
Western Pacific	1,046.1	18,669.50	17.847	0.215	0.057	0.179	0.351
Totals	181,844.1	1,953,640.1	10.743	0.632	0.180	0.109	0.338

a. Merged into Conrail in 1976.
b. Merged into Missouri Pacific in 1976.
c. Class II railroads in 1975; subsequently class I.

d. Includes density data on four Southern Railway subsidaries: Alabama Great Southern; Central of Georgia; Cincinnati, New Orleans & Texas; and Georgia Southern & Florida.

attempt to gauge the impact of these regulatory policies on profitability. If output prices for comparable commodities do not differ substantially across firms, and if the commodity mix of traffic and other factors determining revenues and costs are accounted for, one would expect that the share of a railroad's traffic carried on LDLs would be an important determinant of interfirm differences in profitability. Indeed, the results of estimating a cross-section profit equation may be used to provide an indirect test of the hypothesis that LDLs are cross-subsidized.

Estimating cross-section profit functions is a tricky business. Many of the well-known pitfalls stemming from systematic differences in the tax treatment, capital structure, riskiness, or accounting practices across industries are not relevant when the firms compared are in the same industry and are governed by a common set of accounting rules. Nevertheless, specification of a profit equation is rendered quite difficult by the presence of a large number of highly collinear variables that affect the revenue or cost structure of railroad firms. The results reported in table 4.2 should therefore be regarded as merely suggestive, since the parameter estimates are somewhat sensitive to which variables are in-

Table 4.2 Regression results: railroad profitability in 1975. The dependent variable is the Rate of return on total assets (= [net income plus net interest payments ÷ the book value of assets] × 100). Sample mean = 3.59.

Independent Variables	Estimated Coefficient	Standard Error
Constant	10.9226	9.8984
PCTLDL[a]	−0.3551[b]	0.1771
PCTLDL^2 × 100	0.2521[b]	0.1341
Mean[c]	0.0827	1.0082
Mean^2	−0.0253	0.0321
PCTAG[d]	−0.2759[b]	0.1439
PCTMIN[e]	−0.0399	0.0311
ALH[f]	0.5345	0.5000
EFF[g]	6.9817	7.2815

Note: Number of observations = 31; R^2 = 0.4209
a. Percentage of traffic carried on LDLs = (Output on LDLs ÷ Total output) × 100.
b. Significant at the 0.05 level.
c. Mean = Mean density of firm's network = Gross ton-miles ÷ Route miles.
d. Percentage of agricultural traffic = (Revenue tons of agricultural commodities ÷ Total revenue tons) × 100.
e. Percentage of mineral traffic = (Revenue tons of mineral commodities ÷ Total revenue tons) × 100.
f. Average length of haul, in hundreds of miles.
g. Revenue ton-miles ÷ Gross ton-miles.

cluded in or omitted from the equation. The pattern of signs and significance, however, is less sensitive to the specification.[12]

The explanatory variable of major interest is the percentage of traffic carried on low-density lines (PCTLDL), where low-density lines are those segments below the approximate break-even density of 10 million gross ton-miles per mile of road. While this variable is significant at the 10 percent level when entered linearly, its significance increases when a squared term is added to account for a nonlinearity which is readily apparent from a simple plot of profit rate against PCTLDL. The sign on the squared term is somewhat surprising, since the shape of the average cost curve suggests the opposite sign. Nevertheless, it is clear that the combined effect of the light density line terms is to reduce the level of profits.

The mean density of the firm's network is included in order to explain the cost structure more fully. One expects that, given the LDL percentage, higher average density will be associated with higher profits, at least over some range. Collinearity between mean density and PCTLDL is less severe than one might expect (the simple correlation is 0.61), but the coefficients on mean and mean^2 are insignificantly different from zero despite having the expected signs.[13]

Since both rates and costs depend on commodity type, measures of each firm's commodity mix are included. PCTAG is the share of agricultural and forest products in a firm's total freight tonnage. Since rates on agricultural products are distinctly lower than on manufactured products (the omitted variable), the negative sign conforms to expectations. There is no clear expectation regarding the effect on profitability of mineral products; while rates are lower than on manufactures, high-volume operation (especially on coal traffic) suggests lower costs as well. A similar ambiguity is involved with average length of haul. Rates and unit costs clearly both decline with increases in ALH, and it is widely believed the net effect on profit is positive. The expected sign results in each estimated specification, but the variable is never significant.

Regional dummy variables were consistently insignificant in a wide variety of specifications, despite the expectation that firms operating in the eastern region—with its higher costs and allegedly unfavorable rate divisions—would prove less profitable than those in the west and south. The regional dummies are excluded here because of their high collinearity with ALH and the commodity-mix variables. The final included variable, EFF, is meant to be a measure of efficient equipment utilization, the ratio of revenue ton-miles to gross ton-miles. It has the expected sign, but it is statistically insignificant.

The estimated parameters of the profit function may be used to predict the impact of abandoning low-density lines. The first column of table 4.3 reports the predicted rate of return in 1975 given the existing route structure of each firm in the sample. The second column indicates the predicted rate of return when PCTLDL is set equal to zero. The effect is dramatic. The average rate of return would rise from 3.88 percent to 8.85 percent, with eleven firms earning returns in excess of 10 percent. In dollar terms, returns to capital of the thirty-one railroads would increase by $1.4 billion. This figure almost certainly overstates the avoidable losses recoverable by abandonment. The exercise reported in table 4.3 involves predicting the profitability of each firm on the assumption that its route structure contains no LDLs. It is implicitly assumed in performing this calculation that firms will save the full cost of LDL service, but abandonment will in fact only permit firms to save operating costs. It is not possible to ascertain the precise magnitude of capital costs associated with LDLs, but Harris's figures suggest they are unlikely to be more than one-third of total costs. Thus, each firm's predicted gains should be scaled down by about one-third, and a more plausible estimate of the profit increase resulting from abandonment would be just under $1 billion for the thirty-one sample firms. Since the sample firms own about two-thirds of the industry's capital stock, an extrapolation of this estimate to the industry as a whole yield a predicted increase in profits of $1.4 billion. However, private gains of this magnitude would not be fully realized by abandonment if rates on high-density traffic fell towards marginal costs through intensified competition or regulatory action. The profit increases predicted here implicitly assume that rates would remain constant.

Despite the crudeness of the estimated equation, it seems reasonable to conclude that the low-density lines are a significant drain on railroad profitability. The evidence discussed thus far clearly supports the hypothesis that high-density lines are more profitable. To determine whether LDLs are in fact cross-subsidized, predicted values of the rate of return were calculated on the assumption that PCTLDL = 1. Under these circumstances, twenty-four of the thirty-one sample firms would earn negative rates on return on total capital, which indieates that revenues would fail to cover variable costs (that is, net income before interest charges would be negative). All but two of the remaining firms, while covering variable costs, would nevertheless fail to recover fixed costs.

Table 4.3 Effect of low-density-line abandonment on profitability.

	Predicted 1975 Rate of Return With LDLs	Predicted 1975 Rate of Return Without LDLs	Predicted Increase in Profits (in millions)
Alabama Great Southern	5.82	11.24	$ 9.21
Atchison, Topeka & Santa Fe	3.17	7.04	87.02
Baltimore & Ohio	4.39	8.96	63.86
Burlington Northern	3.84	8.92	163.16
Central of Georgia	4.69	10.11	13.01
Cheasapeake & Ohio	4.62	9.85	73.80
Chicago & Eastern Illinois	5.54	8.68	4.53
Chicago & Northwestern	1.86	9.84	35.68
Chicago, Rock Island & Pacific	−2.51	7.16	42.29
Clinchfield	1.89	2.27	0.30
Cincinnati, New Orleans & Texas	3.14	8.56	10.60
Colorado & Southern	4.81	15.11	15.60
Delaware & Hudson	4.52	10.04	5.44
Detroit & Toledo Shore	5.94	5.94	0.00
Duluth, Mesabe & Iron Range	5.94	9.69	4.18
Illinois Central Gulf	0.62	9.94	121.16
Illinois Terminal	3.21	13.51	4.06
Kansas City Southern	2.74	10.98	20.67
Louisville & Nashville	4.76	8.39	48.59
Maine Central	2.49	12.99	8.28
Missouri-Kansas-Texas	1.69	8.69	14.01
Missouri Pacific	3.00	8.92	80.95
Norfolk & Western	4.46	8.53	99.31
St. Louis–San Francisco	4.59	10.53	31.62
Seaboard Coast Line	5.34	10.16	91.21
Soo Line	2.76	11.60	28.65
Southern Pacific	5.20	8.00	83.33
Southern	4.83	10.24	114.36
Texas & Pacific	2.50	7.70	16.47
Union Pacific	3.31	7.09	93.11
Western Maryland	2.33	9.75	14.48
31 firms	3.88	8.85	$1,398.94

These results seem to support overwhelmingly the hypothesis that LDLs are unprofitable, and to support strongly the presence of cross-subsidization in the strict sense.

A Model of Railroad Investment Behavior

To estimate the effects of regulatory constraint on railroad investment behavior, I shall work within the general framework of the neoclassical model of investment developed by Dale Jorgenson (1965, 1967, and others too numerous to mention).[14] Though the Jorgenson model has been subjected to several well-known criticisms,[15] it has proved serviceable in a variety of applications and it seems a reasonable starting point. The novelty in the present application of the neoclassical investment model is the attempt to take proper account of the institutional peculiarities of the railroad industry. To do so requires specific incorporation of the regulatory constraint on prices and of the requirement to maintain service on low-density lines. Moreover, investment in rolling stock should be separated from investment in road and structures, since both the cost of funds and the impact of regulatory constraints are different for these two types of capital.

The results of prior attempts to estimate neoclassical investment functions from railroad data have been poor, possibly because of a failure to take account of these special characteristics. Jorgenson and Handel (1971) estimated a railroad investment function from time-series industry data. They incorporate price regulation but assumed that prices are set equal to marginal cost. They failed to disaggregate road and equipment investment, and did not take account of abandonment regulation and cross-subsidization. Jorgenson and Handel seemed reasonably satisfied with their results, but they failed to observe that the magnitude of the theoretically unjustified constant term in their estimated equation strongly suggests specification error. In the only other attempt to estimate a neoclassical investment function with railroad data that I know of, Swanson (1968) disaggregated road and equipment investment. However, he failed to include any type of regulatory constraint. He claimed only mixed success for his time-series estimates on individual firms.

The newly available DOT data on line-segment density and the convenient separation of road and equipment accounts required by the ICC make possible the estimation of a model that accounts for the special features of railroad investment behavior. Using 10 million gross ton-miles per mile of road as the dividing point, and denoting high- and low-density lines by the subscripts 1 and 2 respectively, we can write the objective function for a firm that seeks to maximize the present discounted value of its stream of revenues minus expenditures as

$$\text{Max} \int_0^\infty e^{-rt}[p(Q_1 + Q_2) - w(L_1 + L_2) - q(I_1 + I_2) - s(J_1 + J_2)]dt,$$

(1)

where Q, L, I, and J denote output, labor, gross road investment, and gross equipment investment respectively; p, w, q, and s are the prices associated with output, labor, road investment goods, and equipment investment goods respectively; and r is the discount rate. All variables are functions of time, but this notation is suppressed. (The objective function already incorporates one aspect of regulatory behavior: Output prices are constrained to be equal on high- and low-density lines. Factor prices, of course, do not depend upon the use to which the factors are put.)

The regulated railroad firm maximizes equation (1) subject to a set of constraints. First, output on high- and low-density lines is constrained by the production functions

$$F_1(L_1,K_1,E_1) - Q_1 = 0,$$
$$F_2(L_2,K_2,E_2) - Q_2 = 0,$$

(2)

where K and E denote road capital and rolling stock, respectively.[16]

Rate regulation takes the form of requiring the firm to serve all shippers at the regulated price. Since each railroad firm faces downward-sloping demand curves for high- and low-density output in the absence of regulation, we can think of p, a parameter set by the ICC, as determining the levels of output along the demand curves.[17] Thus, the firm's constraint may be written in terms of output as

$$\bar{Q}_1 - Q_1 = 0,$$
$$\bar{Q}_2 - Q_2 = 0.$$

(3)

This form of writing the regulatory constraint makes clear that two of the most widely noted objections to the neoclassical investment model are irrelevant to the present formulation. First, since the firm is constrained by demand, it is unnecessary to assume that the production function is strictly convex. Second, the fact that output is indeed exogenous here disarms the criticism that output and investment are determined simultaneously.

A third set of constraints are the growth equations for equipment capital, in which the change in the capital stock must be equal to gross investment minus depreciation:

$$\dot{E}_1 - J_1 + \theta E_1 = 0,$$
$$\dot{E}_2 - J_2 + \theta E_2 = 0,$$

(4)

where θ is assumed to be the proportional rate of depreciation of the stock of equipment capital.

Finally, abandonment regulation enters in conjunction with the growth constraints on road capital. It is assumed that the exit of road capital is constrained. That is, $\dot{K}_1$ and $\dot{K}_2$ are constrained to be greater than or equal to zero. If it is further assumed that exit barriers are a binding constraint only on low-density lines, then $\dot{K}_2 = 0$. Thus, the growth equations for road capital may be written as

$$\dot{K}_1 - I_1 + \delta K_1 = 0,$$
$$- I_2 + \delta K_2 = 0,$$

(5)

where δ is the proportional rate of depreciation on road capital.

The constraints (5), as written, imply that road capital on low-density lines must be replaced as it depreciates. This seems unduly stringent. It is perhaps more reasonable to assume that barriers to exit are interpreted as a requirement that gross investment be non-negative. In other words, the rate of net disinvestment is constrained by the rate of depreciation. If exit barriers in this sense are a binding constraint for low-density lines, the growth equations for road capital become

$$\dot{K}_1 - I_1 + \delta K_1 = 0,$$
$$\dot{K}_2 + \delta K_2 = 0.$$

(5')

The form of our data makes it possible to estimate with some confidence the model with the constraints (5) imposed, but the alternative specification involving (5') requires certain *ad hoc* assumptions, which will be discussed below. Both versions of the model were estimated.

If we tie together the firm's objective function, (1), with its set of constraints, (2)–(5), the Lagrangian expression for a maximum of the firm's present value may be written as

$$\int_0^\infty \{e^{-rt}[p(Q_1 + Q_2) - w(L_1 + L_2) - q(I_1 + I_2) - s(J_1 + J_2)]$$

$$+ \lambda_1[F_1(L_1,K_1,E_1) - Q_1] + \lambda_2[F_2(L_2,K_2,E_2) - Q_2]$$

$$+ e^{-rt}\pi_1(\bar{Q}_1 - Q_1) + e^{-rt}\pi_2(\bar{Q}_2 - Q_2)$$

$$+ \phi_1(\dot{K}_1 - I_1 + \delta K_1) + \phi_2(-I_2 + \delta K_2)$$

$$+ \psi_1(\dot{E}_1 - J_1 + \theta E_1) + \psi_2(\dot{E}_2 - J_2 + \theta E_2)\}dt$$

$$= \int_0^\infty f(t)dt. \tag{6}$$

The Euler necessary conditions for a maximum of present value subject to the eight constraints involve ten pairs of equations ($i = 1,2$ for all pairs):

$$\frac{\partial f}{\partial Q_i} = e^{-rt}p - \lambda_i - e^{-rt}\pi_i = 0, \tag{7a}$$

$$\frac{\partial f}{\partial L_i} = -e^{-rt}w + \lambda_i\frac{\partial F_i}{\partial L_i} = 0, \tag{7b}$$

$$\frac{\partial f}{\partial I_i} = -e^{-rt}q - \phi_i = 0, \tag{7c}$$

$$\frac{\partial f}{\partial J_i} = -e^{-rt}s - \psi_i = 0, \tag{7d}$$

$$\frac{\partial f}{\partial K_1} - \frac{d}{dt}\frac{\partial f}{\partial \dot{K}_1} = \lambda_1\frac{\partial F_1}{\partial K_1} + \phi_1\delta - \frac{d}{dt}\phi_1 = 0,$$

$$\frac{\partial f}{\partial K_2} - \frac{d}{dt}\frac{\partial f}{\partial \dot{K}_2} = \lambda_2\frac{\partial F_2}{\partial K_2} + \phi_2\delta = 0, \tag{7e}$$

$$\frac{\partial f}{\partial E_i} - \frac{d}{dt}\frac{\partial f}{\partial \dot{E}_i} = \lambda_i\frac{\partial F_i}{\partial E_i} + \psi_i\theta - \frac{d}{dt}\psi_i = 0, \tag{7f}$$

$$\frac{\partial f}{\partial \lambda_i} = F_i(L_i,K_i,E_i) - Q_i = 0, \tag{7g}$$

$$\frac{\partial f}{\partial \pi_i} = e^{-rt}(\bar{Q}_i - Q_i) = 0, \tag{7h}$$

$$\frac{\partial f}{\partial \phi_1} = \dot{K}_1 - I_1 + \delta K_1 = 0,$$

$$\frac{\partial f}{\partial \phi_2} = -I_2 + \delta K_2 = 0, \tag{7i}$$

$$\frac{\partial f}{\partial \psi_i} = \dot{E}_i - J_i + \theta E_i = 0. \tag{7j}$$

To interpret these first-order conditions, note that the π_i, the Lagrange multipliers associated with the regulatory constraint on output, may be regarded as the profit on a marginal unit of output, price minus marginal cost. Thus, we may presume that π_1 is greater than zero, reflecting the excess of price over marginal cost on high-density lines, while π_2 is less than zero, reflecting the unprofitability of low-density traffic. This interpretation leads to the natural conclusion that the shadow prices of output (λ_1 and λ_2), which from (7a) are equal to $e^{-rt}(p - \pi_i)$, may be understood as the discounted marginal cost of high- and low-density output, respectively.

The marginal-productivity conditions for the services of road capital may be derived from (7e) with appropriate substitutions from (7a) and (7c):

$$\frac{\partial F_1}{\partial K_1} = \frac{q(\delta + r - \dot{q}/q)}{p - \pi_1}, \tag{8a}$$

$$\frac{\partial F_2}{\partial K_2} = \frac{q\delta}{p - \pi_2}. \tag{8b}$$

The right-hand sides of these expressions may be understood as the ratio of the shadow price of capital services to the shadow price of output. The numerator of the right-hand side of (8a) may be modified to take account of the effects of the corporate income tax, as shown by Hall and Jorgenson (1967). Under these circumstances, we can write the marginal productivity condition for high density road capital as

$$\frac{\partial F_1}{\partial K_1} = \frac{c}{p - \pi_1}, \tag{8a'}$$

where

$$c = (1 - k)q \left[\left(\frac{1 - uv}{1 - u} \right)\delta + \left(\frac{1 - uw}{1 - u} \right)r - \left(\frac{1 - ux}{1 - u} \right)\frac{\dot{q}}{q} \right].$$

The parameters k, u, v, w, and x reflect aspects of the corporate tax structure: k is the investment tax credit, u is the rate of corporate income tax, v is the proportion of economic depreciation charged against income for tax purposes, w is the proportion of the total cost of capital charged against income, and x is the proportion of capital gains charged against income.

The marginal-productivity condition for road capital on low-density lines differs from (8a) as a consequence of the exit constraint. The implicit service price of low-density road capital is just its nominal depreciation $q\delta$, since the exit constraint renders the opportunity cost component of the service price effectively zero.

The marginal-productivity conditions for equipment capital may similarly be derived from (7f), with substitutions from (7a) and (7d) yielding

$$\frac{\partial F_i}{\partial E_i} = \frac{s(\theta + r - \dot{s}/s)}{p - \pi_i}, \qquad i = 1, 2. \tag{9}$$

As above, (9) may be modified to take account of the corporate income tax as follows:

$$\frac{\partial F_i}{\partial E_i} = \frac{d}{p - \pi_i}, \tag{9'}$$

where

$$d = (1 - k)s\left[\left(\frac{1 - uv}{1 - u}\right)\theta + \left(\frac{1 - uw}{1 - u}\right)r - \left(\frac{1 - ux}{1 - u}\right)\frac{\dot{s}}{s}\right].$$

The marginal-productivity conditions (8a') and (9') may be solved for the firm's desired stock of high-density road capital, K_1^*, and desired equipment capital, E_1^* and E_2^*. The desired level of road capital on low-density lines, however, is irrelevant to the firm's investment decision, since the exit constraint requires that $\dot{K}_2 = 0$ in the version of the model incorporating constraint (5). When the alternative constraint (5') is in force, $I_2 = 0$ as long as the actual level of capital, K_2, exceeds its desired level, K_2^*. I assume that this is true on light-density lines over the time horizon under study.

To derive expressions for K_1^*, E_1^*, and E_2^*, assume that the production functions for high- and low-density lines have the identical Cobb-Douglas form:

$$Q_i = L_i^{1-\alpha-\beta} K_i^\alpha E_i^\beta, \qquad i = 1, 2. \tag{10}$$

The marginal-productivity conditions may now be solved for the levels of desired capital:

$$K_1^* = \alpha \frac{(p - \pi_1)Q_1}{c}, \tag{11a}$$

$$E_1^* = \beta\frac{(p - \pi_1)Q_1}{d},$$

(11b)

$$E_2^* = \beta\frac{(p - \pi_2)Q_2}{d}.$$

(11c)

The Jorgenson investment model has two components: Expenditure on replacement investment is assumed to be a constant proportion of the capital stock, and net investment expenditure at time t is a distributed lag of changes in desired capital. In the present application, when regulation requires the replacement of capital on low-density lines, replacement investment for road capital at time t is simply[18]

$$R_t = (\delta K_1)_t + (\delta K_2)_t = \delta K_t.$$

(12)

If all road capital is replaced and net investment in low-density-road capital is assumed to be zero, the firm's net investment in all road capital, N_t, is a distributed lag of changes in the desired level of high-density-road capital:

$$N_t = I_t - R_t = \mu_0(\Delta K_1^*)_t + \mu_1(\Delta K_1^*)_{t-1} + \cdots + \mu_n(\Delta K_1^*)_{t-n},$$

(13)

where $\mu_0, \mu_1, \ldots, \mu_n$ is a sequence of non-negative numbers which sum to unity.[19] The expression for net investment in equipment corresponds, except that the distributed lag is expressed in terms of changes in the desired level of all equipment, $\Delta E_1^* + \Delta E_2^* = \Delta E^*$.

Jorgenson derives his analog of equation (13) from the assumption that the firm places new orders each period such that its present capital stock plus outstanding orders equals its current level of desired capital. The parameters μ_i thus represent the distribution of delivery times—the fraction μ_0 of new orders arrive in the current period, μ_1 in the next period, and so forth.[20]

To complete the model, Jorgenson assumes that the sequence $\mu_0, \ldots, \mu_n$ has a rational generating function. Then the model (13) can be written as a rational distributed lag function in net investment and changes in desired capital:

$$\omega_0 N_t + \omega_1 N_{t-1} + \cdots + \omega_m N_{t-m} = \gamma_0(\Delta K_1^*)_t + \gamma_1(\Delta K_1^*)_{t-1} + \cdots$$

$$+ \gamma_k(\Delta K_1^*)_{t-k}.$$

(14)

The restrictions that the μ_i be non-negative and sum to unity imply a set of constraints on the ω_i and γ_i, which are thoroughly discussed in Jorgenson 1966. Without loss of generality, ω_0 may be set equal to unity. Recalling that $N_t = I_t - \delta K_t$ and limiting the order of the ω_i sequence to 3 and that of the γ_i sequence to 2,[21] we write the model in its final form:

$$I_t = \gamma_0(\Delta K_1^*)_t + \gamma_1(\Delta K_1^*)_{t-1} - \omega_1 N_{t-1} - \omega_2 N_{t-2} + \delta K_t. \tag{15}$$

Our principal interest is in estimating the parameters of the road-investment equation (15) and using them to predict the impact of LDL abandonment on capital formation on the viable portions of the rail network. Rolling stock is obviously less critically affected by the regulatory constraint on abandonment, but examination of the marginal-productivity conditions (11) shows that cross-subsidization does affect the desired stock of equipment capital. We therefore also estimate an equation for gross equipment investment, J_t, as a function of current and lagged changes in desired capital, $(\Delta E^*)_t$ and $(\Delta E^*)_{t-1}$; lagged net investment, M_{t-1}; and the stock of capital, E_t:[22]

$$J_t = \gamma_0'(\Delta E^*)_t + \gamma_1'(\Delta E^*)_{t-1} - \omega_1' M_{t-1} + \theta E_t. \tag{16}$$

Estimating the Model of Railroad Investment Behavior

The parameters of equations (15) and (16) describing road and equipment investment were estimated on a cross-section sample of annual data on thirty-two class I railroads for the year 1975.[23] Estimation of the model required data on road and equipment capital stocks, gross and net investment, and desired capital. In constructing capital stocks for each firm, book values of net road and equipment capital as of January 1, 1969 were taken as benchmarks. Gross road and gross equipment investment series for each firm taken from *Moody's Transportation Manual* were expressed in real terms using appropriate price deflators.[24] From the benchmark capital stocks and real-gross-investment figures, real capital stocks and real net investment in both road and equipment for each year from 1969 to 1975 were calculated annual depreciation rates of 0.04691 for road capital and 0.06907 for equipment. These depreciation rates were estimated from Department of Commerce (1974) time series on industry aggregates of fixed railroad structures and railroad equipment.[25]

Desired capital stocks can be known only up to a multiplicative constant, since the output elasticities of each type of capital, α and β, are unknown *a priori*. Recall from (11) that the expressions for desired capital are

$$K^* = K_1^* = \alpha \frac{(p - \pi_1)Q_1}{c}, \tag{17a}$$

$$E^* = E_1^* + E_2^* = \beta\left(\frac{(p - \pi_1)Q_1}{d} + \frac{(p - \pi_2)Q_2}{d}\right). \tag{17b}$$

Since α and β are unknown, the model is actually estimated with changes in K^*/α and E^*/β as independent variables. Thus, instead of using equations (15) and (16) as written, the empirical procedure is to estimate

$$I_t = \gamma_0\alpha\left(\Delta\frac{(p - \pi_1)Q_1}{c}\right)_t + \gamma_1\alpha\left(\Delta\frac{(p - \pi_1)Q_1}{c}\right)_{t-1}$$

$$- \omega_1 N_{t-1} - \omega_2 N_{t-2} + \delta K_t \tag{18}$$

and

$$J_t = \gamma_0'\beta\left[\Delta\left(\frac{(p' - \pi_1)Q_1}{d} + \frac{(p - \pi_2)Q_2}{d}\right)\right]_t$$

$$+ \gamma_1'\beta\left[\Delta\left(\frac{(p - \pi_1)Q_1}{d} + \frac{(p - \pi_2)Q_2}{d}\right)\right]_{t-1}$$

$$- \omega_1' M_{t-1} + \theta E_t. \tag{19}$$

As Jorgenson (1966) showed, consistent estimates of production function parameters may be obtained by application of the formulas $\alpha = \Sigma\gamma_i\alpha/\Sigma\omega_i$ and $\beta = \Sigma\gamma_i'\beta/\Sigma\omega_i'$.

To measure K^*/α and E^*/β we can use the previously noted empirical finding of Keeler (1976) and Friedlaender (1971) that the ratio of price to marginal cost on high-density lines is 1.4. Since $p - \pi$ may be interpreted as marginal cost, it follows that $p - \pi_1 = 0.71p$. Since we know from the DOT density data the percentage of each firm's output carried on lines above break-even density we can measure $(p - \pi_1)Q_1$ by the product of 0.71, the firm's freight revenue, and the share of its output carried on lines with density greater than 10 million gross ton-miles per mile of road. For the equipment equation we need to know $p - \pi_2$ as well. On the somewhat dubious assumption that price is set such that profits on high-density lines equal losses on low-density lines for the rail system as a whole, $p - \pi_2 = 2.32$.

The prices of capital services are calculated by Jorgenson's standard procedure of assuming that capital gains are regarded by firms as transitory. We thus assume that the capital service prices for road and equipment are

$$c = (1 - k)q\left[\left(\frac{1 - uv}{1 - u}\right)\delta + \left(\frac{1 - uw}{1 - u}\right)r\right], \tag{20}$$

$$d = (1 - k)s\left[\left(\frac{1 - uv'}{1 - u}\right)\theta + \left(\frac{1 - uw}{1 - u}\right)r'\right].\qquad(21)$$

Values of c and d were computed for each firm using the depreciation rates and investment goods prices already discussed and the statutory rates of corporate income tax and investment tax credit. The parameter v, the proportion of economic depreciation charged against incomes, was calculated separately for road and equipment from each firm's income statement as reported in Moody's. The parameter w, the ratio of interest payments to the total dollar cost of capital, could not be computed separately for road and equipment since interest payments are not disaggregated in the income statements.

An important part of the story is that the cost of capital differs for road and equipment. Thus, r is measured using the weighted average yield of the firm's outstanding general purpose bonds (such as mortgage issues and income debentures), and r' is measured using the weighted average yield of the firm's outstanding equipment trust certificates.[26]

One final complication must be discussed before empirical results can be presented: In the railroad industry, direct investment represents only one means of adjusting a firm's capital stock toward its desired level. The firm may also adjust its stock of rented capital. Whereas leased or rented road capital is only a small fraction of the total capital stock, rented equipment represents a considerable fraction of rolling stock. By dividing rental payments reported on income statements by the appropriate service price of capital, we can impute the stocks of rented equipment and rented road capital. Annual changes in the stock of rented capital (ΔKR and ΔER) are added to the dependent variable (and to lagged net investment) in the estimation of equations (18) and (19).

The empirical model of investment behavior is completed by assuming that equations (18) and (19) each contain an additive error term. If the error term is distributed identically and independently over observations and independently of the changes in desired capital stock, and if the estimated equation represents a stable difference equation in net investment, then the ordinary least-squares estimator is best, asymptotically normal, and also asymptotically efficient if the constraints implied by the non-negativity of the sequence $[\mu_i]$ are satisfied. In the present instance, estimating the model on a cross-section of firms suggests that the assumption of identically distributed errors is unwarranted. When the residuals of the ordinary least-squares estimates are ranked by firm size (as measured by freight revenue), the hypothesis of homoscedasticity was decisively

Table 4.4 Regression results: Investment in road and structures in 1975. The dependent variable is gross investment plus change in rented capital. All variables are measured in thousands of 1969 dollars.

Independent Variables	Estimated Coefficients (Standard Errors in Parentheses)	
	Ordinary Least-Squares	Weighted Least-Squares
$(\Delta K^*/\alpha)_{1975}$	0.00946[a] (0.00195)	0.00873[a] (0.00256)
$(\Delta K^*/\alpha)_{1974}$	−0.00109 (0.00354)	0.00080 (0.00351)
$(N + \Delta KR)_{1974}$	0.45936[a] (0.06676)	0.39983[a] (0.07683)
$(N + \Delta KR)_{1973}$	0.17230[b] (.08740)	0.17213[b] (0.08895)
K_{1975}	0.03256[a] (0.00256)	0.03153[a] (0.00314)
No. of observations	32	32
$\bar{R}^2$	0.9384	—
F	82.26	33.86

a. Significant at the 0.01 level.
b. Significant at the 0.05 level.

rejected by nonparametric Goldfeld-Quandt tests on each of the reported specifications. Glejser-type regressions of the residuals on various transformations of revenue consistently suggested weighting the investment regressions by the square root of revenue.

Ordinary and weighted least-squares (OLS and WLS) estimates of the parameters of the road investment equation are presented in table 4.4. It is obvious by inspection that weighting has very little effect on the parameter estimates. It is also reassuring that the estimated parameters satisfy all the inequality constraints required to ensure the non-negativity of each element in the sequence of delivery lag coefficients. Moreover, the stability of the difference equation in net investment and changes in desired capital is ensured.[27]

The parameters of the gross investment equation can be used to calculate α, the elasticity of output with respect to road capital, and the sequence $[\mu_i]$ describing the form of the lagged response of net investment to changes in desired capital. The OLS and WLS estimates of α are 0.0227 and 0.0223 respectively. Though there is no reason (given the divergence of actual and desired capital stocks as well as the output price distortion) for the estimated value of α to approximate the empirically observed share of payments to road capital in the value of output, estimates in the range of 2 percent do seem distinctly low.[28]

Table 4.5 Form of the lagged response of net road investment.

Lag	Parameter	OLS Estimate	WLS Estimate
Current year	μ_0	0.4165	0.3921
1 year	μ_1	0.1432	0.1926
2 years	μ_2	0.1375	0.1444
3 years	μ_3	0.0878	0.0909
4 years	μ_4	0.0640	0.0612
5 years	μ_5	0.0445	0.0401
6 years	μ_6	0.0315	0.0266
Remainder	$\sum\limits_{i=7}^{\infty} \mu_i$	0.0750	0.0521

The sequence of lag coefficients computed from OLS and WLS estimates is reported in table 4.5. Each element μ_i may be interpreted as the proportionate response of net investment to changes in the level of desired capital i periods earlier. In Jorgenson's view, these coefficients reflect the structure of delivery lags; μ_i may also be interpreted as the proportion of orders placed today that will arrive i periods hence. Hall (1977), however, notes that the latter interpretation is not necessary to justify the former; net investment response may reflect a combination of delivery lags and the placement of orders based on expected future levels of desired capital. In any case, the relatively rapid response of investment to changes in desired capital, wherein nearly 60 percent of the total response is effected within one year, seems quite consistent with Healy's (1954) detailed institutional description of the railroad investment process.

Since the estimated parameters of our road investment equation are to be used to predict the impact of altered regulatory policy, it is especially important to check the estimates for sensitivity to specification error. One simple check is the addition of an intercept term to the model. Since the constant term has no theoretical justification, we should be wary of an intercept estimate significantly different from zero, and we should be troubled to find the other parameters significantly altered. In fact we find that the addition of an intercept term produces no significant alternation in the estimated parameters, nor is the constant itself significantly different from zero.

Another check is to examine the estimated coefficient on the capital stock term. If the model of replacement investment is correctly specified, the estimated coefficient $\hat{\delta}$ should not differ significantly from the rate of depreciation used in calculating the capital stock. In this case, however, both the OLS and WLS estimates of the replacement rate are significantly below the depreciation rate of 0.04691. This finding is not surprising in light of our initial skepticism about the assumption that the entire stock of road capital on low-density lines is replaced.

An alternative view of replacement investment is that only capital on high-density lines is replaced, while capital on LDLs is allowed to depreciate. By imposing the constraint (5'), that gross investment on LDLs is zero, an alternative investment equation may be estimated involving the current value of K_1 (high-density-road capital) on the right-hand side. The difficulty in estimating this form of the model is that K_1 is unknown. The DOT line-segment data permit the computation of high-density-route mileage and output, but the stock of capital associated with high-density lines is not known directly. An upper bound may be placed on K_1 by assuming that the proportion of each firm's road capital invested in high-density lines (K_1/K) equals the proportion of its output carried on HDLs (Q_1/Q). Similarly, it seems plausible that the share of HDLs in each firm's route mileage represents a lower bound on K_1/K.[29]

The alternative investment model was estimated using each of these proxy measures for the high-density capital stock. The results were somewhat surprising in that none of the coefficients reported in table 4.4. was significantly altered. The estimated replacement rate remained 0.031, still significantly below the rate of depreciation used in computing the capital stock. These results suggest either that the assumed rate of depreciation is too high or that there is not full replacement of depreciated capital even on high-density lines. To check the sensitivity of the results to the assumed 0.04691 rate of depreciation, the alternative capital stock series was calculated using 0.031 as the rate of depreciation. The model was then reestimated using each of the alternative assumptions about replacement investment. Even in this form, the estimated replacement rate was consistently below the assumed depreciation rate, but once again none of the other parameters of the model differed significantly from the estimates reported in table 4.4. This failure to adequately model replacement investment is troubling, but the stability of the remaining coefficients across alternative specifications is reassuring in that it suggests that using these parameters in predicting the response to changes in regulatory policy is not unreasonable.

A final check on the validity of my specification was to estimate the model with additional terms reflecting changes in desired capital on low-density lines. In other words, this alternative specification assumes that there is no constraint on exit. If the model is correct in assuming that

Table 4.6 Regression results: Investment in equipment in 1975. The dependent variable is gross investment plus change in rented capital. All variables are measured in thousands of 1969 dollars.

| | Estimated Coefficients (Standard Errors in Parentheses) | | | |
| | Unconstrained estimates | | Constrained estimates | |
Independent Variables	OLS	WLS	OLS	WLS
$(\Delta E^*/\beta)_{1975}$	0.02271[a] (0.00763)	0.01843[a] (0.00956)	0.02370	0.01963
$(\Delta E^*/\beta)_{1974}$	-0.02124 (0.01289)	-0.01464 (0.01425)	-0.01011	-0.00965
$(M + \Delta ER)_{1974}$	0.46116[a] (0.08861)	0.51140[a] (0.09733)	0.42638	0.49164
E_{1975}	0.06766[a] (0.00713)	0.07635[a] (0.00979)	0.07153	0.07841
No. of observation	32	32	32	32
$\bar{R}$	0.8483	—	—	—
F	39.13	25.81	—	—

a. Significant at the 0.01 level.

only changes in desired capital on high-density lines affect output, then the parameter estimates reported in table 4.4 should be unaffected, while the coefficients on the added terms should be insignificantly different from zero. This is precisely what happens in the WLS case. In the OLS case the only exception is that $(\Delta K_2^*)_t$ has a significant coefficient with the incorrect (negative) sign.

While our primary interest attaches to road investment, the parameters of the equipment investment function were also estimated by both ordinary and weighted least-squares methods. The estimates, which are presented in the "unconstrained estimates" columns of table 4.6, fail to satisfy one of the inequality constraints necessary to ensure the non-negativity of the distributed lag coefficients $[\mu_i]$. In particular, the constraint $\gamma_1' > \gamma_0' \omega_1'$ is violated. Imposition of this nonlinear constraint with equality required an iterative estimation procedure to produce the maximum likelihood estimates reported in the "constrained estimates" columns of table 4.6.[30] The constrained estimates are quite similar to the unconstrained estimates. The hypothesis that replacement investment is proportional to the current capital stock appears to be supported here, since the estimated $\hat{\theta}$ in the OLS and WLS equations is not significantly different from the 0.06907 rate of depreciation used in calculating the capital stock.

One implication of imposing the constraint $\gamma_1' = \gamma_0' \omega_1'$ is that the underlying sequence of distributed lag coefficients takes the form of

$[1, 0, \ldots, 0]$. In other words, the results suggest that equipment investment adjusts fully to changes in desired capital within one year. The data provide further support for this claim. If the rational distributed lag structure is replaced by a more straightforward regression of gross investment on the current capital stock and on current and lagged changes in desired capital, only the coefficients associated with current values of independent variables are statistically significant. The finding of full adjustment within one year is not entirely implausible, since the dependent variable includes changes in the stock of rented equipment. While the delivery lag for new rolling stock sometimes exceeds one year, there is an active rental market. On the other hand, the unusual lag structure found here may be an artifact of using data from 1975, a slack year for equipment investment.

Impact of Abandonment of Low-Density Lines on Railroad Investment

There are two distinct mechanisms by which abandonment of LDLs may stimulate the formation of new capital on the economically viable high-density portions of the rail network. First, since abandonment would eliminate the need for cross-subsidization, rates on HDLs could be permitted to fall toward marginal cost. The lower rates would attract additional traffic and thus raise the level of desired capital.[31] Second, LDL abandonment may lower the cost of capital to rail firms by improving long-run profitability and reducing the risk of bankruptcy. The lower cost of funds would bring forth new capital formation.

These two mechanisms can be seen in the context of the algebraic expression for the firm's desired capital stock:

$$K^* = \frac{\alpha(p - \pi_1)Q_1}{c}.$$

The former mechanism operates through the numerator of this expression. With constant returns to scale on HDLs $p - \pi_1$ (which equals marginal cost) remains constant as both p and π_1 fall, but the fall in p induces an increase in Q_1, which depends on the elasticity of demand. The latter mechanism operates primarily through the denominator as a fall in the cost of capital, r, reduces c, the service price of capital, and thus increases K^*.[32] For convenience we will refer to the former mechanism as the *price effect* of abandonment, and to the latter mechanism as the *capital cost effect*.

To predict the magnitude of the price effect on new road investment, we need to know the extent to which prices will fall on HDLs and the elasticity of rail demand. In fact, the magnitude of the price effect on investment is simply proportional to the product of $\Delta p/p$ and the elasticity of demand. Given the divergence of price and marginal cost estimated by Friedlaender and Keeler (which suggests that $\Delta p/p$ would be approximately 0.3), and given the recent demand estimates of Boyer and Levin (which suggest that average demand elasticities are about 0.3 or 0.4), it seems reasonable to expect that LDL abandonment would produce an increase in output (and hence in the desired HDL capital stock) of approximately 10 percent. Under alternative assumptions about demand elasticity and price response, the predicted change in the capital stock would vary proportionately.

Predicting the magnitude of the effect of capital cost on new investment is a more complicated matter. It remains to establish the point that barriers to the abandonment of LDLs do in fact raise the cost of capital to railroad firms. To do so, it is necessary to formulate and test a simple model of the determinants of the cost of capital. The parameters of the capital-cost equation may then be used to predict the effect of LDL abandonment on capital cost, and the predicted capital cost may then be fed into the investment equation in order to predict the short- and long-run investment response.

My argument about the cost of capital concerns the perceived riskiness of various railroad securities and the associated costs of bankruptcy. Equipment trust certificates are perceived as virtually riskless assets, presumably because rolling stock is easily disposed of in the event of bankruptcy. General-purpose bonds secured by road capital or simply by future income are considerably more risky, since the liquidation value of fixed railroad property is usually well below its going-concern value and since the length and outcome of railroad bankruptcy proceedings are highly uncertain. If this argument is correct, then those factors that raise the probability of railroad bankruptcy ought to increase the cost of raising funds to finance road investment through corporate bonds but have negligible effect on the cost of funds for investment in new equipment.

In a strikingly successful attempt to predict railroad bankruptcies using discriminant analysis,[33] Altman (1973) found measures of long-run profitability and current solvency to be the most important determinants of the probability of bankruptcy. His results motivated the specification of the equations reported in table 4.7, where the percentage of low-density lines in a firm's network (PCTLDL) is used as a proxy for long-run profitability and the ratio of net income before fixed charges to fixed

Table 4.7 Regression results: Cost of railroad capital in 1975.

Independent Variables	Estimated Coefficients (Standard Errors in Parentheses)	
	Bonds[a]	Certificates[b]
Constant	9.4218[c] (0.2414)	9.0010[c] (0.1939)
PCTLDL (= Output on LDLs ÷ Total output) × 100	0.0289[c] (0.0158)	0.0138 (0.0127)
PCTLDL^2 × 100	0.0226[d] (0.0148)	0.0141 (0.0119)
Assets (in hundred million \$)	−0.0083 (0.0117)	−0.0229[c] (0.0094)
Coverage LE 1 (Net income before fixed charges ÷ Fixed charges, if ≤ 1; zero otherwise)	−0.1967[c] (0.0456)	−0.0065 (0.0366)
Coverage GT 1 (Net income before fixed charges ÷ Fixed charges, if > 1; zero otherwise)	−0.0005 (0.0005)	0.0000 (0.0004)
No. of observations	44	44
R^2	0.4699	0.1690

a. In this column the dependent variable is weighted average yield on outstanding long-term corporate bonds. Sample mean = 9.8529.
b. The dependent variable is weighted average yield on outstanding equipment trust certificates. Sample mean = 9.0072.
c. Significant at the 0.05 level.
d. Significant at the 0.01 level.

charges is employed as a measure of solvency. Separate coefficients were estimated for high and low values of the solvency measure, since it was felt that investors would be more responsive to changes in the coverage ratio when a firm was showing losses than otherwise. A firm-size measure was added to the equation to explore the possibility that smaller firms have somewhat greater difficulty in marketing their securities. Finally, the PCTLDL term is squared to account for a nonlinearity that was apparent in a simple plot of the data.

The results seem strongly supportive of my hypotheses. The percentage of low-density lines in a firm's network, which appears from the cross-section profit estimates to be the most important determinant of long-run profitability, has a significant positive impact on the cost of capital to finance road investment. Solvency, another important indicator of the probability of bankruptcy, has a strong impact over the range where firms are failing to cover fixed charges. As expected, neither the density nor the solvency measure has a significant impact on the cost of equipment capital. Firm size, however, does have a small but significant role

in reducing the cost of equipment capital. The presence of LDLs significantly raises a firm's cost of road capital, but the magnitude of the effect
is rather small. If firms of equal size and solvency are compared, the cost
of capital for a firm with 50 percent of its output carried on LDLs will be
less than one percentage point (0.88 percent) higher than that for a firm
with no LDLs at all.[34]

Table 4.8 shows the predicted effect of LDL abandonment on the cost
of road capital for each of the thirty-two firms in the investment sample.
The first column shows the fitted value of each firm's corporate bond
rate, given its current route structure. The second column indicates the
predicted bond rate if PCTLDL were set equal to zero. The final column
multiplies the reduction in the bond rate by each firm's stock of road
capital to obtain its implicit capital cost savings from abandonment. The
average reduction in the bond rate is a little under half a percentage
point, but there is good reason to believe this an understatement of the
impact of abandonment. Since abandonment would improve cash flow,
the coverage ratio would improve, producing a further decrease in the
bond rate for those firms currently unable to meet fixed charges out of
current income.

The ultimate effect of LDL abandonment on investment in road capital
is reported in table 4.9. The predictions are based on the WLS estimates
of the parameters of the investment equation, and the OLS predictions
are virtually identical. The short-run-price, capital-cost, and combined
effects reported in the first three columns represent the first-year impact
on investment on the remaining portions of the rail network in the event
of LDL abandonment. The final three columns show the long-run response, which is 2.5 times as great if the lags implied by the investment
equation are taken into account. The estimates are of course sensitive to
the assumption of a 10 percent increase in output, and as noted the full
extent of the capital cost effect is likely to be larger than that reported.

The firms in the sample own approximately two-thirds of the road-
capital stock in the industry. If they are assumed to be representative, the
predicted $106 million in new capital formation produced by LDL aban-
donment should be inflated to approximately $160 million for the industry
as a whole. This represents about one-third of the average annual level
of gross road investment undertaken by class I railroads in the United
States over the past decade. By this standard, $160 million would seem
a hefty influx of new investment. On the other hand, it represents only
a little more than 1 percent of the existing stock of road capital, and it is
considerably less, for example, than estimates of the cost of upgrading the

Table 4.8 Effect of LDL abandonment on cost of capital.

	Predicted 1975 Bond Rate		Predicted Cost Savings (in millions $)
	With LDL	Without LDL	
Alabama Great Southern	9.84	9.41	0.74
Atchison, Topeka & Santa Fe	9.54	9.23	7.01
Baltimore & Ohio	9.67	9.30	5.13
Burlington Northern	9.56	9.15	13.08
Central of Georgia	9.83	9.40	1.04
Chesapeake & Ohio	9.72	9.30	5.92
Chicago & Eastern Illinois	9.66	9.41	0.37
Chicago & Northwestern	9.96	9.33	2.83
Chicago, Rock Island & Pacific	12.58	11.82	3.31
Cincinnati, New Orleans & Texas	9.84	9.40	0.85
Colorado & Southern	10.04	9.41	0.95
Delaware & Hudson	9.84	9.40	0.44
Detroit & Toledo Shore	9.42	9.42	0.00
Detroit, Toledo & Ironton	11.71	11.17	0.46
Elgin, Joliet & Eastern	9.93	9.39	0.64
Fort Worth & Denver	10.04	9.41	0.47
Grand Trunk Western	10.08	9.75	0.56
Kansas City Southern	10.05	9.40	1.63
Louisville & Nashville	9.60	9.31	3.91
Maine Central	10.06	9.41	0.51
Missouri Pacific	9.78	9.30	6.47
Norfolk & Western	9.55	9.22	7.99
Pittsburgh & Lake Erie	9.40	9.40	0.00
St. Louis–San Francisco	9.85	9.38	2.53
St. Louis–Southwestern	9.53	9.38	0.78
Seaboard Coast Line	9.65	9.26	7.32
Soo Line	10.09	9.39	2.26
Southern Pacific	9.40	9.17	6.73
Southern	9.68	9.24	9.16
Texas & Pacific	9.81	9.39	1.32
Union Pacific	9.52	9.22	7.50
Western Maryland	9.99	9.40	1.15
32 firms	9.91	9.49	103.07

roadbed and track along the Boston-Washington corridor to a standard
sufficient to accommodate current best-practice technology in high-speed
passenger transport.

Summary and Conclusions

The evidence presented herein lends considerable support to the
hypothesis that the burden of excess capacity is a primary source of the
unprofitability and the sluggish performance of the U.S. railroad industry.
Analysis of recently compiled DOT line-segment data revealed that
nearly two-thirds of the nation's class I railroad mileage is below or
barely above the break-even level of traffic density at current rail rates,
and a substantial fraction of these lines fail to produce revenues sufficient
to cover variable costs. Interfirm profitability differences were found to
depend upon the proportion of low-density lines in a firm's network, and
our profitability model provided strong support for the hypothesis that
losses on low-density lines are cross-subsidized by profits on lines of
higher density. It was predicted that abandonment of uneconomic lines
would increase railroad industry profits by at least $1.4 billion (in 1975
dollars). Although clearly of the same order of magnitude, this figure is
somewhat smaller than the savings from abandonment predicted with
the cost function estimated by Friedlaender (1971) and Keeler (1974).

The dynamic impact of the burden of excess capacity is somewhat less
dramatic but nevertheless significant. Investment in roadway and structures was found to be explained well by a model of investment behavior
that specifically incorporated cross-subsidization and a constraint on the
exit of LDL capital. The cost of capital used to finance road investment,
in contrast to the cost of funds raised with equipment trust certificates,
was found to depend on the extent of excess line capacity. LDL abandonment, by lowering the cost of capital and by permitting lower rates
on the remaining rail network, would bring forth approximately $160
million in new capital formation, presumably enhancing the growth of
productivity since many of the opportunities for technical change in
railroad operations are embodied in capital goods. Nevertheless, the $160
million capital shortfall produced by regulatory constraint on exit and
cross-subsidization may appear small in contrast to the static losses from
excess capacity.

Thus, my results generally support the view that low-density lines
constitute a serious impediment to the attainment of static and dynamic
efficiency in the railroad industry. The potential improvement in railroad

Table 4.9 Effect of LDL abandonment on new investment in road and structures, 1975. (Figures in millions of 1975 dollars.)

	Short-Run Response to Lower Price	Short-Run Response to Lower Capital Cost	Total Short-Run Increase in Investment	Cumulative Response to Lower Prices	Cumulative Response to Lower Capital Cost	Total Cumulative Increase in Investment
Alabama Great Southern	0.14	0.04	0.18	0.34	0.11	0.47
Atchison, Topeka & Santa Fe	2.50	0.59	3.15	6.38	1.50	8.04
Baltimore & Ohio	1.34	0.33	1.71	3.42	0.85	4.36
Burlington Northern	2.94	0.84	3.87	7.50	2.16	9.88
Central of Georgia	0.33	0.10	0.44	0.84	0.25	1.12
Chesapeake & Ohio	1.24	0.36	1.64	3.16	0.94	4.19
Chicago & Eastern Illinois	0.13	0.02	0.15	0.32	0.05	0.38
Chicago & Northwestern	1.64	0.78	2.50	4.18	1.98	6.37
Chicago, Rock Island & Pacific	0.73	0.30	1.06	1.86	0.76	2.70
Cincinnati, New Orleans & Texas	0.21	0.07	0.28	0.53	0.18	0.72
Colorado & Southern	0.00	0.00	0.00	0.00	0.00	0.00
Delaware & Hudson	0.19	0.06	0.25	0.48	0.15	0.65
Detroit & Toledo Shore	0.03	0.00	0.03	0.07	0.00	0.07
Detroit, Toledo & Ironton	0.16	0.07	0.23	0.42	0.17	0.60
Elgin, Joliet & Eastern	0.30	0.12	0.44	0.77	0.30	1.10
Fort Worth & Denver	0.00	0.00	0.00	0.00	0.00	0.00
Grand Trunk Western	0.49	0.11	0.61	1.23	0.27	1.56
Kansas City Southern	0.43	0.20	0.65	1.10	0.51	1.66
Louisville & Nashville	2.40	0.48	2.93	6.13	1.21	7.47
Maine Central	0.00	0.00	0.00	0.01	0.00	0.01
Missouri Pacific	1.25	0.39	1.67	3.18	0.99	4.27
Norfolk & Western	2.35	0.56	2.97	6.00	1.42	7.57

Pittsburgh & Lake Erie	0.22	0.00	0.22	0.56	0.00	0.56
St. Louis–San Francisco	1.01	0.32	1.36	2.57	0.83	3.48
St. Louis–Southwestern	0.54	0.06	0.60	1.38	0.14	1.54
Seaboard Coast Line	2.54	0.68	3.29	6.47	1.74	8.39
Soo Line	0.26	0.13	0.40	0.67	0.31	1.02
Southern Pacific	3.01	0.47	3.53	7.66	1.20	8.99
Southern	1.19	0.36	1.59	3.03	0.93	4.05
Texas & Pacific	0.32	0.09	0.42	0.81	0.22	1.06
Union Pacific	4.32	0.96	5.37	11.01	2.43	13.69
Western Maryland	0.13	0.06	0.19	0.34	0.14	0.50
32 firms	32.34	8.55	41.76	82.48	21.76	106.46

performance strongly recommends lifting the exit constraints on private, for-profit railroad firms. If for reasons of distributional equity some form of subsidy to affected shippers and local communities is desired, a variety of solutions appears less costly than requiring railroad firms to pay to the subsidy out of their meager profits. The Railroad Revitalization and Regulatory Reform Act of 1976 has already lain groundwork to facilitate the purchase of abandoned lines by state and/or local government with generous federal subsidies. While this form of subsidization may be superior to requiring cross-subsidization it would behoove legislators and rail planners to recognize that subsidizing an inefficient transport mode (low-density rail movements) is in many (perhaps most) cases distinctly inferior on efficiency grounds to scrapping the line and subsidizing shippers all or part of the difference between truck or intermodal rates and rail rates.

One puzzle remains to be explained. Given the burden imposed on railroads by low-density lines, one might expect that there would be persistent efforts to abandon large portions of the rail network, and that such efforts would be repeatedly rebuffed by the Interstate Commerce Commission. Instead, over the past decade an average of considerably less than 1 percent per year of the nation's route mileage has been proposed for abandonment (aside from the petitions of firms already in bankruptcy). Moreover, from 1968 through 1976, 97.5 percent of the abandonment petitions acted upon by the ICC were approved, with the denials involving only 3.1 percent of the route mileage proposed for abandonment.[36] On first consideration these figures suggest that regulatory barriers to exit are minimal, and that the railroad themselves are to blame for the persistence of excess capacity.

The incentives for managers to maintain the size of their firms may partially explain the reluctance of railroads to seek abandonment. This explanation has some plausibility for firms composed entirely or in very large part of low-density lines, where abandonment would actually threaten the jobs of top management; it is a less compelling explanation for the behavior of the roughly thirty firms that carry most of the nation's rail freight. Despite the possible importance of managerial incentives to keep LDLs in operation, there are several reasons for supposing that regulatory barriers to exit are considerably more formidable than the data on abandonment petitions suggest.

First, abandonment proceedings are lengthy and costly, especially when the petition to abandon is contested by shippers, local communities, labor unions, and state governments. In a detailed study, Sloss et al. (1974)

found that 63 percent of all abandonment petitions filed between January 1968 and December 1970 were approved within six months, 78 percent within one year, and 96.5 percent within two years. The picture is quite different, however, when one considers contested cases in which the decision of the hearing officer or administrative law judge was appealed to the Finance Division of the Commission. Of the contested cases between 1970 and 1976, 56.5 percent required more than two years from initial filing to final decision and 34.8 percent required more than three years; only 21.7 percent were resolved within one year, and the average time from filing to resolution was 28.7 months.[37] Second, in the face of strong opposition to abandonment, the probability of a successful petition diminishes. Of the 23 cases carried to final appeal between 1970 and 1976, four petitions were wholly denied and two others denied in part. Third, for a period after 1971 the ICC held that opponents of abandonment bear the burden of proof in cases where it is clearly established that the annual volume of rail traffic is less than 34 carloads per mile. Virtually all proposed abandonments in recent years have met this standard, but the 34-carload standard covers only about 10–15 percent of the nation's remaining route mileage—perhaps no more than one-quarter of the total route mileage that would be uneconomic at rates equal to long-run marginal cost. Finally, in recent years only firms in or near bankruptcy have attempted to abandon large portions of their route network, which is not surprising in view of the ICC's explicit position that the weakness of a carrier's overall financial position weights in its favor in abandonment cases. These attempts, especially that of the Penn Central to abandon one-quarter of its total mileage, leave little doubt that railroad firms are aware of the unprofitability of low-density lines. Nevertheless, bankruptcy only improves the probability of success before the ICC; massive abandonment in the northeast ultimately required legislation.

The foregoing considerations suggest that railroad firms are willing to undertake the costly and time-consuming process of piecemeal abandonment only when the probability of success is high. In view of the costs of litigation (recently increased by the court-imposed requirement that environmental impact be considered in each abandonment case), the incentive to abandon for a still-solvent firm is probably small unless the 34-carload standard is satisfied and opposition is expected to be minimal. The barriers to abandonment are also doubtless increased by the piecemeal nature of the process. The ICC decides cases on a line-by-line basis, and the potential savings from abandoning a given 10- or 20-mile branch line may appear small when weighed against the fixed costs of litigation and the uncertainty of opposition. Yet the benefits from abandoning the sum of many small line segments may be substantial.[38] A simplified regulatory procedure, or, better still, freedom of exit accompanied by transitional subsidies to ease adverse distributional impact, would be likely to improve the performance of the railroad industry significantly. The 4-R Act, in its attempt to speed and simplify the regulatory process when abandonment proposals meet no opposition and in its recognition that direct subsidy is superior to cross-subsidy, has taken at least a few small steps in the right direction.

I am indebted to Daniel Richards for able assistance in research, to Martin Baily for numerous conversations on the theory of investment, and to David Coppock, Theodore Keeler, Paul MacAvoy, Richard Nelson, Sharon Oster, Merton J. Peck, Sidney Winter, and the conference discussants for helpful suggestions. This research was supported by grants from the Alfred P. Sloan Foundation and the Eno Foundation.

Notes

1. Source: First National City Bank *Monthly Letter* (various issues).

2. A strong argument in support of this position is put forth in the report of the Task Force on Railroad Productivity (1973).

3. The issue that has received most attention in the controversy over rate regulation is that shipments of different commodities over comparable distances are not priced comparably despite comparable costs.

4. Friedlaender concludes that 26 percent of rail route mileage was redundant in 1961–1963. Her lower estimate may be in part a consequence of her use of an earlier sample period, but one suspects it is primarily attributable to methodological peculiarities. As Nelson (1971) pointed out, Friedlaender's estimate of the extent of excess capacity in the rail system as a whole is rendered somewhat suspect by her implausible finding that eastern railroads such as the Pennsylvania, the New York Central, Central of New Jersey, Lehigh Valley, and the Maine Central had a deficiency rather than an excess of line capacity in 1961–1963.

5. Friedlaender does not report sufficient information to permit derivation of the relation between unit cost and density implied by her cost and production function estimates.

6. Throughout this article density is measured by gross ton-miles per mile of road. This measure is distinctly inferior to revenue ton-miles per mile of road, since gross ton-miles includes the weight of engines and freight cars. The use of gross ton-miles was unavoidable since it was the measure used in the DOT line-segment data on traffic density discussed below.

7. Strictly, Keeler's average-cost curve becomes flat, but Harris's asymptotically approaches a lower bound at a level that is approximately equal to the flat range of Keeler's function.

8. As Harris aptly notes, there is considerable confusion in the literature between economies of scale and economies of density. Economies of scale are present when—allowing for variation in all inputs, including route mileage—increased output leads to falling unit costs. Economies of density are present when unit costs fall as output increases, with route mileage held constant.

9. Friedlaender and Keeler are in precise agreement about the relation between actual average rail rates and estimated long-run marginal costs (that is, average costs at efficient density). Friedlaender found that the ratio of estimated long-run marginal costs in long-run equilibrium to observed average costs was 0.736 in 1969. If this ratio has remained constant over recent years, it follows that the ratio of observed rates to long-run marginal cost has varied within the range 1.385–1.423 since 1969. Keeler (1976) found the ratio to be 1.42 in 1969.

10. The data are reported in tabular form in *Final Standards, Classification and Designation of Lines of Class I Railroads in the United States*, Volume II. A computer tape containing this information and others indicating the mileage of each line segment were supplied to the author by the Federal Railroad Administration.

11. The density categories are as follow:

Density Class	Gross Ton-Miles per Mile of Road
1	0–1
2	1–5
3	5–10
4	10–20
5	20–30
6	> 30

12. Data on the first four independent variables listed in table 4.2 are derived from the DOT line-segment density data presented in table 4.1. Data on the dependent variable and the remaining independent variables were taken from *Moody's Transportation Manual 1976*. The eastern firms under the temporary jurisdiction of the U.S. Railway Association were excluded from the sample, and a number of other firms had to be excluded on grounds of insufficient data.

13. When mean and mean^2 are dropped from the regression, the significance of the PCTLDL terms drops to the 0.10 level but the estimated parameters are virtually unchanged.

14. One might reasonably wonder why an economist trained and employed at Yale would choose to employ a neoclassical investment function instead of the Keynes-Tobin alternative. Rest assured that I am most impressed by the suitability of the so-called "q" theory for my purposes, and indeed I had intented to compare the performance of the two theories when they are modified to take account of the special characteristics of the railroad industry. Unfortunately, the data requirements of the q theory (especially the need to measure the market value of each firm's securities) proved insurmountable, since the equity of many railroads is held either by other railroads or by diversified holding companies.

15. See, for example, Tobin 1967, Gould 1969, and Brainard 1977.

16. The independence of the production functions for output on high- and low-density lines is assumed primarily to simplify analysis. While it is not difficult to imagine interdependence in production, it is not entirely clear how it should be modeled.

17. It should perhaps be noted that, while time notation is supressed, each firm's demand curves may be shifting over time, and the regulated price may also vary over time.

18. When constraint (5′) operates, replacement is simply proportional to the stock of high-density-road capital, not to the entire stock of road capital; that is, $R'_t = (\delta K_1)_t$.

19. Under the alternative constraint (5′), depreciation on low-density-road capital, $(\delta K_2)_t$, must be subtracted from the right-hand side of (13).

20. I cannot resist commenting on certain defects of the Jorgenson model. The assumed behavior is peculiarly myopic. The firm acts as if it is entirely ignorant of delivery lags; it is always adjusting its stock of outstanding *orders* to its current level of desired capital. But if the firm knew anything about delivery lags, even probabilistically, one might expect it to place its orders such that expected deliveries this period (if some orders are filled immediately) or next period (if that is the minimum delivery lag), plus the actual capital stock, would equal the actual or expected level of desired capital. Such a formulation leads to an estimating equation quite similar to Jorgenson's, but with a different interpretation of the parameters. A second peculiarity is that delivery lags exist only on new investment, not on replaced capital.

21. Jorgenson (1966) showed that the sequence $[\mu_i]$ may be approximated to any desired degree of accuracy with a finite number of parameters, ω_i and γ_i. No clear criterion has been established to determine the preferred number of terms in each sequence of parameters. I followed Jorgenson's procedure of experimenting with a wide variety of specifications and choosing that which minimized the adjusted standard error of the regression. Very little seems to have been lost by limiting the sequences ω_i and γ_i to three and two terms respectively; in none of the tested specifications were any higher-order terms statistically significant.

22. In the model of equipment investment the sequence ω_i is limited to two terms ($\omega_0 = 1$ and ω_1) by application of the criterion discussed in note 21.

23. Of the 58 class I line haul railroads in 1975, I excluded the eight bankrupt northeastern roads involved in reorganization on the grounds that the assumed profit-maximizing behavior was implausible. Auto-Train and the Long Island Railroad were also excluded on grounds of noncomparability with ordinary freight-hauling railroads. Sixteen other firms were excluded on grounds of deficient data.

24. The equipment series was deflated by the wholesale price index for railroad equipment. There is no comparable WPI deflator for railroad structures, although the ICC developed an index for road investment that runs from 1914 to 1966. The ICC index has not been updated, but it turns out to be extraordinarily highly correlated ($r = 0.993$) in the period prior to 1966 with the index of purchased materials and supplies (excluding fuel) developed by the Association of American Railroads. The AAR index was therefore used as a deflator for road investment.

25. The Commerce Department series on capital stocks and annual depreciation was constructed using a modified perpetual-inventory method, assuming a distribution of service lifetimes based on IRS Bulletin F estimates, an initial benchmark, and an industry series on gross investment. The Commerce Department annual depreciation figures were regressed on the current capital stock, assuming second-order serial correlation. Experimentation showed that estimated proportionate depreciation rates since World War II were significantly higher than before World War II, so that the rates used in this study were derived from regressions run over the period 1947–1972.

26. Computing the cost of capital was a laborious task. Price data reported by Moody's for many general-purpose bond issues allowed yields to be computed directly. Price data were often unavailable for some of a firm's rated bond issues; in such cases Moody's average yield on railroad bonds of identical rating was used as a proxy. Unrated bond issues were ignored, but they were always a small share of outstanding debt. The directly computed or imputed yield of each issue was then weighted by its share of the firm's outstanding general-purpose debt, and the firm's cost of road capital was obtained by summing over all outstanding rated issues.

For equipment obligations, price data were unavailable. It was therefore necessary to impute the Moody's average yield for the appropriate rating category to each outstanding equipment trust certificate, and compute a weighted average yield for each firm. For some of the few firms in the sample that had no equipment trust certificates, Moody's reported data on the terms of conditional sales agreements which permitted assignment of the firm to a Moody's rating class. A small number of the firms had either no reported equipment obligations or no general-purpose bonds. For these firms, the missing cost of capital was imputed by assuming that the firm's differential between equipment and road capital costs were equivalent to the mean differential of firms issuing both types of obligations.

27. The constraints on γ_i and ω_i, as well as the stability condition, are given in Jorgenson 1966.

28. Implausibly low estimates of output elasticity have been reported in every one of Jorgenson's papers on investment behavior. Jorgenson and Stephenson 1967 suggests that measurement error may be responsible, but there is no reason to believe that measurement error would lead to a clear direction of bias. To my knowledge, no convincing explanation has yet been offered for the apparent downward bias of the output elasticity.

29. In other words, I am asserting that $M_1/M < K_1/K < Q_1/Q$. This seems plausible since one clearly expects K_1/M_1 (capital per route mile on HDLs) to exceed capital per mile on LDLs, because improvements are more likely to have been made on these portions of the route system. On the other hand, the capital-output ratio on HDLs will be lower than that on LDLs if there is excess capacity on LDLs.

30. Constrained estimates were obtained as follows. The initial regression equation is of the form

$$J_t = \gamma_0'\beta(\Delta E^*/\beta)_t + \gamma_1'\beta(\Delta E^*/\beta)_{t-1} - \omega_1' M_{t-1} + \theta E_t + \varepsilon_t.$$

Imposing the constraint $\gamma_1' = \gamma_0'\omega_1'$ and rearranging terms yields

$$J_t - \gamma_0'\beta(\Delta E^*/\beta)_t = \omega_1'[\gamma_0'\beta(\Delta E^*/\beta)_{t-1} - M_{t-1}] + \theta E_t + \varepsilon_t.$$

For any chosen value of $\gamma_0'\beta$, ω_1' and θ may thus be estimated by least squares. The value of $\gamma_0'\beta$ that minimizes the sum of squared residuals produces maximum-likelihood estimates of the parameters given the constraint $\gamma_1' = \gamma_0'\omega_1'$.

31. One objection to this line of argument is that the traffic gains from lower rates might be more than offset by the loss of HDL traffic that originated on LDLs. While it is undoubtedly true that some (perhaps a large portion) of LDL traffic is fed on to higher-density routes, it is easy to exaggerate the importance of LDLs as "feeder" lines. In a study of LDLs outside the northeast, Matzzie et al. (1977) showed that 55 percent of carloads originating on LDLs contained agricultural products. Since these products are typically transported by truck to a nearby rail terminal, it is unlikely this traffic would be lost to the railroads if the trucks were required to go a bit farther to a rail line of efficient density. Indeed, intermodal transport is probably the least costly alternative for most of the other commodities originating on LDLs. Moreover, a significant fraction of the potential losses of feeder traffic is likely to be prevented by state or local takeover of branch lines or by subsidy to private short-line operators. In sum, the traffic losses on the remainder of the rail network resulting from LDL abandonment are likely to be small.

32. A reduction in the cost of capital also reduces long-run marginal cost $(p - \pi_1)$, partially offsetting the effect of the declining denominator. It is easily shown that the decrease in the numerator is exactly α times the decrease in the denominator, and since $\alpha < 1$ (in this case it is about 0.02), an increase in K^* is ensured.

33. On the basis of research completed in 1971, Altman proposed ten class I railroads as "probable bankrupts." Five of the ten—Ann Arbor, Erie Lackawanna, Milwaukee, Reading, and Rock Island—subsequently filed bankruptcy petitions. Several of the remaining five are still on or near the brink.

34. Several alternatives to the model estimated in table 4.7 were tested. When a direct measure of current profitability, the rate of return on total assets, was added to the first equation, it was insignificant and PCTLDL remained significant. When the rate of return was substituted for PCTLDL, it was statistically significant at the 0.10 level, but the R^2 dropped substantially. I interpret these results as supporting the rather plausible view that PCTLDL is a better indicator of long-run expected profitability than current level of profits.

35. The cost-of-capital equations were estimated from a larger sample than the investment equations, because capital cost data were available for some firms that reported insufficient investment, depreciation, or tax data to be used in the investment sample.

36. Abandonment data are taken from ICC *Annual Reports* (1969–1976). The percentages cited omit from consideration the roughly 20 percent of petitions filed that were dismissed without decision over the same period. Dismissals are usually based on technical grounds unrelated to the merits of the case.

37. These figures were computed from a survey of all abandonment decisions taken by the full commission or its finance division as reported in the ICC *Reports* (volumes 338–346). I am indebted to Alice P. White for assistance in compiling these data.

38. This line of argument places considerable emphasis on litigation costs. While there is no solid evidence on the magnitude of these costs, one Conrail official reported that the costs in terms of legal fees and especially in terms of the diversion of corporate personnel were indeed substantial. In particular, contested cases involve considerable diversion of effort by top management to the appeasement of politicians and community and shipper groups. These direct and indirect costs probably measure in the tens of thousands of dollars for a relatively minor case. To see that this is not a trivial impediment to seeking abandonment, consider that the average abandonment petition over the past decade involved a line segment of 17 miles. If litigation costs of such petitions were $50,000–$100,000, the cost of piecemeal abandonment all LDLs in the system in 17-mile segments would be $350 million–$700 million.

References

Altman, E. I. 1973. "Predicting Railroad Bankruptcies in America." *Bell Journal of Economics and Management Science* 4: 184–211.

Barriger, J. W. 1956. *Super Railroads for a Dynamic American Economy.* New York: Simmons-Boardman.

Borts, G. H. 1960. "The Estimation of Rail Cost Functions." *Econometrica* 28: 108–131.

Boyer, K. D. "Minimum Rate Regulation, Modal Split Sensitivities, and the Railroad Problem." *Journal of Political Economy* 85: 493–512.

Brainard, W. C. "Comment on Hall." *Brookings Papers on Economic Activity* 1: 112–117.

Caves, D. W., and Christensen, L. R. 1976. Modeling the Structure of Production in the U.S. Railroad Industry. Paper presented at meeting of Econometric Society, September 1976.

Department of Commerce, Bureau of Economic Analysis. 1974. *Fixed Nonresidential Business Capital in the United States, 1925–1973.* Springfield, Va.: National Technical Information Service.

Department of Transportation. 1977. *Final Standards, Classification, and Designation of Lines of Class I Railroads in the United States,* vol. II. Washington, D.C.: Government Printing Office.

First National City Bank. 1947–1977. *Economic Letter.* Various issues.

Friedlaender, A. F. 1971. "The Social Costs of Regulating the Railroads." *American Economic Review* 61: 226–234.

Gould, J. P. 1969. "The Use of Endogenous Variables in Dynamic Models of Investment." *Quarterly Journal of Economics* 83: 580–599.

Hall, R. E. 1977. "Investment, Interest Rates, and the Effects of Stabilization Policies." *Brookings Papers on Economic Activity* 1: 61–103.

Hall, R. E., and Jorgenson, D. W. 1967. "Tax Policy and Investment Behavior." *American Economic Review* 57: 391–414.

Harris, R. G. 1977. "Economics of Traffic Density in the Rail Freight Industry." *Bell Journal of Economics* 8: 556–564.

Healy, K. T. 1954. "Regularization of Capital Investment in Railroads." In M.G. de Chazeau (ed.), *Regularization of Business Investment*. Princeton, N.J.: Princeton University Press.

Interstate Commerce Commission. 1970–1977. *Annual Reports*, 1969–1976. Washington, D.C.: Government Printing Office.

———. 1969–1977. *Reports*, vol. 333–348. Washington, D.C.: Government Printing Office.

———. No date. Schedule of Annual Indices for Carriers by Railroad, 1914 through 1966. Unpublished.

Jorgenson, D. W. 1965. "Anticipations and Investment Behavior." In J. S. Duesenberry et al. (eds.), *The Brookings Quarterly Econometric Model of the United States*. Chicago: Rand-McNally.

———. 1966. "Rational Distributed Lag Functions." *Econometrica* 34: 135–149.

———. 1967. "The Theory of Investment Behavior." In R. Ferber (ed.), *Determinants of Investment Behavior*. New York: National Bureau of Economic Research.

Jorgenson, D. W., and Stephenson, J. A. 1967. "Investment Behavior in U.S. Manufacturing, 1947–1960." *Econometrica* 35: 169–220.

Jorgenson, D. W., and Handel, S. S. 1971. "Investment Behavior in U.S. Regulated Industries." *Bell Journal of Economics and Management Science* 2: 213–264.

Keeler, T. E. 1974. "Railroad Costs, Returns to Scale, and Excess Capacity." *Review of Economics and Statistics* 56: 201–208.

———. 1976. On the Economic Impact of Railroad Freight Regulation. Working paper, University of California, Berkeley.

Levin, R. C. 1978. "Allocation in Surface Freight Transportation: Does Rate Regulation Matter?" *Bell Journal of Economics* 9: 18–45.

Matzzie, D. E., Weinblatt, H. B., Harman, J., and Jones, J. R. 1977. Light Density Railroad Line Abandonment: Scaling the Problem. Paper presented at the Annual Meeting of the Transportation Research Board.

Meyer, J. R., Peck, M. J., Stenason, J., and Zwick, C. 1959. *The Economics of Competition in the Transportation Industry*. Cambridge, Mass.: Harvard University Press.

Moody's Investor Service. 1969–1976. *Moody's Transportation Manual*. New York.

Moore, T. G. 1975. "Deregulating Surface Freight Transportation." In A. Phillips (ed.), *Promoting Competition in Regulated Markets*. Washington, D.C.: Brookings Institution.

Nelson, J. R. 1971. "Comment on Friedlaender, et al." *American Economic Review* 61: 239–241.

Sloss, J., Humphrey, T. J., and Krutter, F. N. 1975. *An Analysis and Evaluation of Past*

Experience in Rationalizing Railroad Networks. Springfield, Va.: National Technical Information Service.

Swanson, J. A. 1968. Railroad Investment Demand, 1948–1965: A Neoclassical Model. Ph.D. diss., University of Wisconsin.

Task Force on Railroad Productivity. 1973. *Improving Railroad Productivity.* Washington, D.C.: National Commission on.Productivity and Council of Economic Advisers.

Tobin, J. 1967. "Comment on Crockett-Friend and Jorgenson." In R. Ferber (ed.), *Determinants of Investment Behavior.* New York: National Bureau of Economic Research.

Comment

John J. McGowan

According to Levin's analysis, eliminating regulatory impediments to abandonment of low-density lines might increase railroad profits by about $1.4 billion per year. He suggests that, after such abandonment, rates on high-density lines would fall toward marginal cost because those rates would no longer need to generate the sufficient revenues to subsidize the low-density lines. Lower rates would lead to an increase in output and the desired stock of capital on high-density lines, and, in addition, abandonment would reduce the supply price of capital to railroads. The combined effect of lower rates and lower capital cost would lead to an increase in investment (in the long run) of about 106 million 1975 dollars per year for the railroads in his sample.

Despite the high quality of Levin's economic analysis and econometric work, I remain troubled by some of his conclusions. To begin with, if the railroads really could increase profits by $1.4 billion per year, thus more than doubling their rate of return on total investment, I wonder why they are not actively pursuing abandonment to the fullest extent. Levin's explanation is that the transaction cost of pursuing abandonment proceedings at the ICC and the low probability of success therein reduce the expected return from pursuing abandonment to almost zero. He also suggests that management, in its own interest, may attach some utility to size itself and so does not pursue increased profitability through abandonment with the vigor that profit maximization might imply. He may be right about management's tendency to pursue objectives other than maximum profit, but if so should he not reconsider the theoretical basis of the investment equations he estimates? He may also be right about the expected returns from undertaking abandonment proceedings, but I find his arguments far from persuasive.

First of all, although litigation is expensive, $1.4 billion will buy an awful lot of it. Hearsay suggests that the services of first-rate law firms can be purchased at rates approximating $100 per person-hour. If expenses run at approximately 25 percent of professional services billings, $1.4 billion would buy more than 5,000 person-years of high-quality legal services. Even allowing for some expert economic testimony, the potential annual savings would clearly purchase a massive litigation effort. Of course, this is an oversimplified analysis. One must consider the probability of success in estimating what legal effort is warranted by the estimated savings of $1.4 billion per year. However, one must also consider that the probability of success may be an increasing function of the legal effort, and also that the present value of the savings from abandonment is the relevant benefit measure, not the annual savings. Perhaps more important, one should consider the technology for achieving abandonment approval. Levin's discussion assumes that abandonment must be pursued within the existing ICC procedures for achieving it, and that legal expenses are incurred in that context. However, if the benefits through abandonment are as large as he estimates, would not firms explore alternative technologies for achieving abandonment, such as bypassing ICC procedures through promotion of superseding legislation?

If Levin's explanation for railroads' lack of vigor in pursuing abandonments is faulty, is there any reason to suspect that his estimates are overly optimistic? I am not enough of a railroad buff to offer solid evidence on this score, but one possibility is that Levin's approach assumes that profits on high-density lines would be unaffected by abandoning low-density lines. It seems at least conceivable that, by abandoning low-density lines, railroads would lose business over high-density lines to the competing intra- or intermodal competitors, who would then originate or terminate some shipments.

Levin suggests that his $1.4 billion figure may be an overestimate because regulators might take back some of the increased profits by forcing rate reductions on the high-density lines. Casual inspection of the data presented by Levin suggests that this might not be a likely explanation for the failure of railroads to pursue abandonments more vigorously. Table 4.3 indicates that after abandonment of low-density lines the firms in his sample would have an average rate of return on assets of 8.85 percent, while according to table 4.8 the cost of capital for firms in his sample after low-density-line abandonment would have a cost of capital on the average of 9.49 percent. Since it seems unlikely that regulation would force rate reductions when the rate of return on assets is below the cost of capital, it does not seem from Levin's data that, on average, the fear of regulation-enforced rate reductions reduces the prospective benefits from abandoning low-density lines. Closer inspection of tables 4.3 and 4.8 indicates that twenty-six railroads appear in both tables. For thirteen of them, the rate of return after abandoning low-density lines as shown in table 4.3 would still be below their cost of capital after abandoning low-density lines, which appears in table 4.8.

(They are the following: Atcheson, Topeka & Santa Fe; Baltimore & Ohio; Burlington Northern; Chicago & East Illinois; Chicago, Rock Island & Pacific; Cincinnati, New Orleans & Texas; Detroit & Toledo Shore; Louisville & Nashville; Missouri Pacific; Norfolk & Western; Southern Pacific; Texas & Pacific; and Union Pacific.) According to the last column of table 4.3, these railroads account for $793 million of Levin's estimated $1.4 billion of the increased profits due to low-density-line abandonment. Accepting Levin's overall estimate, it appears that railroad profits could be increased by about at least $800 million through abandonment of low-density lines.

Would there in fact be any incentive for the abandoning railroads to increase investment on their high-density lines? In general, Levin estimates that investment will increase both because rates will fall and because the cost of capital will fall as a result of abandonment of low-density lines. However, if we recall that the thirteen railroads that account for the $800 million increase in profit due to abandonment would, even after abandonment, be earning rates of return on capital lower than their costs of capital, I fail to see why they would have any incentive to reduce prices. Thus, I do not believe that the approximately $55 million cumulative increase in annual investment that Levin estimates would be undertaken by these railroads because of lower prices would ever materialize. In sum, it appears that even if we accept Levin's estimate of the potential for increasing profits through abandonment of low-density lines, the effect of abandonment on investment would be somewhat less than one-half of the approximately $106 million per year he estimates in the long run.

Comment

Almarin Phillips

Professor Levin has provided a stimulating and provocative paper. His attack on the conventional wisdom regarding the source of railroad problems is, indeed, quite persuasive. The argument moves smoothly among facts, theory, and econometrics—so smoothly that just a few critical comments seem in order.

It is not clear, as Levin implies in his discussion and assumes explicitly in equation (1) of his model, that value-of-service pricing, price discrimination, and cross-subsidization are so bad. One would suppose that, in general, the low-density lines have higher demand elasticities than do the high-density lines. It is quite clear that few railroads are currently pressing on a rate-of-return constraint. This brings into question the impact of the "principle" that "shipments of comparable goods over comparable distances should be comparably priced."

If one takes at all seriously the theory of Ramsey-type pricing, there are reasons to suspect that this nondiscrimination regulatory constraint is, along with abandonment, an important source of railroads' problems. In the context of general second-best theory—and with some important limitations involving externalities, cross-elasticities, and a defined set of goods whose prices are regulated—W. J. Baumol and D. P. Bradford have shown that an inverse elasticity rule applies ("Optimal Departures from Marginal Cost Pricing," *American Economic Review* 60 [1970]: 265–283; see also Baumol, "Quasi-Optimality: The Welfare Price of a Nondiscriminatory Price System," in *Pricing in Regulated Industries: Theory and Application*, ed. J. T. Wenders [Denver: Mountain States Telephone and Telegraph Co., 1977]). Until the rate-of-return constraint is satisfied, outputs of the several goods—in this case, transportation of goods among origin and destination pairs—should be reduced proportionately from their respective price-equals-marginal-cost ($P = MC$) points. Prices charged would then vary inversely with demand elasticities. If (as seems to be the case with railroads) the return constraint does not become binding up to the point of profit maximization, we are left with a second-best welfare condition with marginal cost equal to marginal revenue ($MC = MR$) across the goods in question.

Hesitation in the practical application of this theory is obviously necessary, but so is hesitation in pursuing a free abandonment policy when nondiscriminatory pricing is an operational constraint. Whether it is called cross-subsidization or not, there may be genuine welfare reasons for charging different rates for the same goods over comparable distances.

If this is correct, Levin's conclusions about the differences in investment with and without abandonment are questionable. Ramsey-type price discrimination—keeping those lines where $P \geq MC$, even though there is a bookkeeping loss—would improve carrier rates of return and foster the desired capital investment. Lines which might be abandoned with a full and complete linear pricing system might not be abandoned with linear pricing by commodity within origin and destination pairs but price discrimination by commodity across origin and destination pairs.

A related issue concerns sequential abandonments of LDLs and their system effects. If a line between A and B is abandoned, it will reduce traffic between A and $C, D, \ldots$ Similarly, it will reduce traffic between B and $C, D, \ldots$ Thus, the first abandonment increases the likelihood that, say, a line between A and C, or A and D, or B and C, or B and D, or indirectly between C and D, etc., will qualify for abandonment in the future. It is an interdependent network system, no single component of which can be judged in isolation. With interdependence, the condition that $P \geq MC$ on each line is no longer necessary for profit maximization, constrained or unconstrained.

None of these comments suggest that Levin's basic conclusion, that excess capacity is a primary source of unprofitability, is wholly erroneous. They do suggest that care should be exercised before fully free abandonment is encouraged. The carriers may, in fact, not have pursued persistent efforts for abandonment for just these reasons, rather than those Levin somewhat tortuously proposes. Managers may recognize varying elasticities and the interdependence of their systems. Rather than pressing for wholesale abandonments, they might rationally seek instead to relieve their problems through more discriminatory (and, perhaps, more welfare-inducing) pricing structures. Neither the theory nor the econometrics of the paper covers these alternatives.

5

The Political Economy of Federal Regulatory Activity: The Case of Water-Pollution Controls

Robert A. Leone
John E. Jackson

Increasingly, policymakers have resorted to regulation of private corporate activity as a means of achieving socially desirable ends (Schultze 1977; Leone 1977). Despite this growth in regulation, there has been little investigation of the dynamic political process by which regulations are formulated and implemented. There has also been little systematic analysis of the dynamic economic process of regulatory compliance.

Several aspects of the regulatory approach to public problem solving merit investigation. Perhaps the most obvious question is whether regulations achieve desired ends. It is certainly possible for Congress to mandate certain goals and to establish bureaucratic machinery to promulgate the necessary rules; yet these two acts alone do not guarantee attainment of the stated objectives. We leave examination of this most basic question to others who are already so engaged.[1]

To address these questions we present a model of policy-development processes and industry-response processes. At the core of this model are the economic costs and benefits created by regulation and their distribution among firms and regions. Analysts customarily measure total benefits and a limited set of aggregate total costs estimated by comparing the equilibrium prices and outputs predicted with the static economic model.[2] Our model provides for the important role that distributional effects and industry dynamics play in determining regulatory impacts. Distributional effects are required because, among other things, they create many pressures on the political organizations that develop and administer policies. The dynamic analysis is motivated by the hypothesis that the constraints and difficulties firms encounter in the short run in attempting to adjust to specific regulations have important aggregate and distributional implications. These short-run effects relate to the availability of capital and the ease with which different firms can adjust their capital stock and their manufacturing and marketing strategies to new conditions.

Economic Impacts of Regulation

Our analysis begins with costs. The costs of regulation are more difficult to define and more uncertain than those of other public activities. In public-works projects, for example, the principal cost uncertainties are organizational (such as unforeseen delays and unanticipated obstacles to construction) and economic (inflation), and are largely exogenous to decisions about the project itself. Costs of most business regulations also are subject to organizational and external economic uncertainties. But, in addition, these costs depend on factors internal to the regulated industry (such as the rate and direction of technological change), on the existence of capacity pressures within an industry, and on differences in costs between new and existing facilities. Costs also are sensitive to uncertainties created by the regulatory process itself: How much time will be left for compliance? Are standards likely to change? Will enforcement be uniform and equitable? Stated differently, the definition of costs for a public-works project is basically an engineering and managerial exercise; the identification of costs associated with a business regulation is primarily an exercise in dynamic economic and political analysis, with all the attendant difficulties and uncertainties this implies. This distinction is intended to stress the variety of methodological approaches that may be required to analyze regulatory policies.

When not seen from an engineering perspective, costs usually are viewed from the standpoint of the competitive-market model and associated static equilibrium. Viewed this way, regulations prohibit certain production processes, require additional capital and operating expenditures, and increase some factor prices, thus shifting the long-run supply curve within an industry upward. This method is deficient in two important ways: It only estimates aggregate costs, and it ignores all short-run and dynamic adjustment problems.

Distribution of Economic Impacts

The focus on total costs obscures some very important characteristics of regulatory costs. From the standpoint of aggregate efficiency, comparisons of total costs and estimated benefits may be an appropriate decision criterion. However, decisionmakers' objectives are not solely focused on this criterion. Hidden within any specific set of aggregate costs are highly variable consequences for different plants within a firm, for firms within an industry (and among industries, for that matter), and for regions of the country. These distributional effects may run counter to other policy

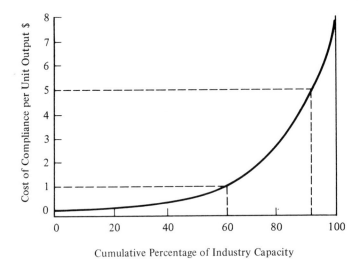

Figure 5.1 Compliance-cost curve.

objectives, such as antitrust goals or regional development concerns. At the same time, the firms and regions most affected presumably will work to influence policy choice. Thus, any eventual policies will not be based simply on aggregate efficiency effects, but will reflect accommodation to political pressures created by distributional effects.[3]

Estimating the distributional impacts of national policies is particularly difficult. For a variety of reasons, the incidence of compliance costs within an industry and among regions need not be uniform. Plant-to-plant differences in costs may be quite large, depending on the nature of regulations, the ages and values of existing capital stocks, and the constraints placed on manufacturing processes by regulations.

However, if the cost structure of each plant in an industry were known, we could measure disaggregated effects of regulatory policies from shifts in the cost curve of each plant brought about by new regulations; and if individual plants were then arrayed in descending order according to their average unit costs, an industry cost curve could be generated.

Figure 5.1 shows the distribution of industry costs due to a hypothetical regulation that results when the compliance costs of individual plants are arrayed in descending order. The vertical axis represents the unit cost of compliance, the horizontal industry capacity. For this hypothetical regulation, 60 percent of the industry (in terms of capacity) can comply with a unit cost increase of $1 or less, while for 10 percent of capacity compliance increases costs by more than $5 per unit of output.

The importance of figure 5.1 is that it can be used to determine which plants will be hardest hit by proposed regulations and which actually may benefit. If an aggregate economic analysis at the industry level yields an overall price increase of $2, close to 75 percent of industry capacity will receive revenue increases that exceed their compliance costs. For the remaining proportion of the industry capacity, represented by the rightmost portion of the curve, the regulations entail an economic loss.

Identifying where individual plants fall on the cost curve is an important component of our impact analysis. Even if the aggregate costs are less than the aggregate benefits, the incidence of costs on certain plants may conflict with other policy objectives, raising questions of whether a program should be implemented. For example, various national policies encourage competition in manufacturing industries and try to prevent the economic decline of various regions. Yet if heavily impacted plants are those of smaller producers or are concentrated in a specific region, the effects of proposed regulations may be to increase concentration in an industry or to exacerbate regional economic disparities. These possible deleterious effects ought to be identified and considered prior to the promulgation of regulations. Other governmental tools may make it possible to overcome such unwanted side effects, but they are seldom used when regulations are taking effect and are altering the structures of industries and the regional distribution of jobs and income.

Short-Run Economic Impacts
Accurate assessment of intraindustry and interregional impacts requires understanding how individual plants may respond to proposed standards, in both the short and the long run. Thus, we try to model how regulatory constraints affect representative plants and how effects on individual plants are distributed among firms and regions. This requires identification of the age and other attributes of the capital stock of various plants, their specific production processes, and their existing effluent control measures. It becomes critical to specify required production changes and capital investments for various plants. These conditions determine both short- and long-run consequences for the industry. New plants may have compliance costs substantially different from those of older plants.

Identification of short-run distributional effects becomes very important when considering alternative regulatory policies. Firms and regions that see themselves suffering from promulgated regulations—even if only

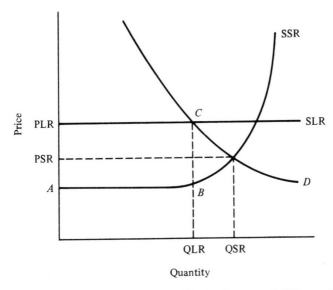

Figure 5.2 Short-run and long-run equilibrium. D: demand. SSR: supply, short-run (based on ascending average variable costs). SLR: supply, long-run (based on total economic costs, including return on investment). QLR, QSR: equilibrium quantity, long-run and short-run respectively. PLR, PSR: equilibrium price, long-run and short-run respectively.

temporarily—are likely to mount campaigns aimed at altering the regulations, weakening their enforcement, or simply preventing further regulation. Conversely, firms and regions benefiting from regulations, either because they receive benefits at relatively low cost or because they gain financially, can be expected to oppose changes in regulations.

Our model is expanded to consider short-run effects as well as distributional impacts. In figure 5.2 we depict a demand curve (D), a short-run supply curve (SSR), and a long-run supply curve (SLR). For the moment, assume that D does not change over time. SSR is an upward-sloping curve which, as described, arrays individual plants in an industry according to ascending average variable costs.

SLR is drawn as a horizontal line, representing the underlying assumption that in the long run an effectively unlimited supply of new capacity can be brought on line at the average total cost (including a return to capital) of the lowest-cost source of new capacity.

Understanding the relationship between SSR and SLR is critical to determining the impact on industry of a government regulation. As drawn in figure 5.2, new capacity is relatively costly. We could just as easily

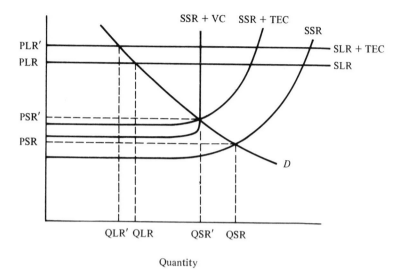

Figure 5.3 Short-run and long-run equilibrium with added costs of regulation (case 1;
PSR′ < PLR′). TEC: total economic costs of regulation (including return on investment).
VC: variable costs of regulation. All variables with prime are the after-regulation
equivalents of the unprimed variables. See figure 5.2 for definitions of other abbreviations.

have depicted new capacity as relatively inexpensive—owing, perhaps,
to scale advantages, technical change, or factor substitution. The point,
of course, is that the actual relationship between SLR and SSR is an
empirical question.

Furthermore, the path the industry follows from SSR to SLR depends
on a number of factors, perhaps the most significant of which is the
economic longevity of existing facilities. Thus, as drawn in figure 5.2,
the long-run equilibrium quantity QLR is less than the short-run equilibrium quantity QSR. The time path of adjustment from QSR to QLR
depends on how rapidly the existing capacity is retired.

If the highest variable cost capacity is retired first, then at some
intermediate point in time the supply curve will be marked by the points
ABC and the long-run price and output levels will have been reached.
As more old facilities are retired the supply curve will continue to shift
from ABC to SLR, but in so doing it will merely dissipate the quasirents
of existing facilities without influencing price and output levels.[4]

In figure 5.3 government regulation is imposed on this situation, and
its costs shift both the short- and long-run supply curves upward. Consider
first the impact on the short-run curve. The curve labeled SSR + TEC
reflects the old short-run supply curve plus the total economic costs

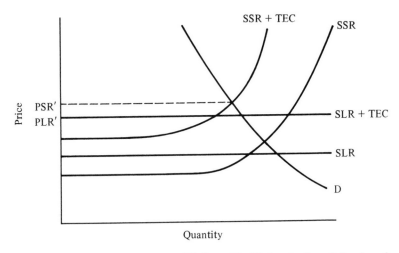

Figure 5.4 Short-run and long-run equilibrium with added costs of regulation (case 2; PSR' > PLR').

(including a return on investment) of the government regulation. No rational firm in a fully informed and perfectly competitive market will comply with a regulation unless it can expect to recover the full costs of compliance. This cost recovery need not imply price increases equal to cost increases, however. As part of this recovery, the profit-maximizing firm will count contributions to sunk costs of all prior investments, which it would have to forgo if it did not comply. This new curve is a combination of variable and total economic costs. The maximum capacity a rational firm will bring into compliance will be QSR.

Once compliance investment decisions have been made, short-run behavior will be predicated on an industry's variable cost structure. The curve marked SSR + VC in figure 5.3 is such a curve, for it reflects the old short-run supply curve, the variable costs of government regulation, and the capacity constraint implied by QSR. This short-run curve is now vertical at the desired quantity level, because government regulations force firms to rationalize the industry's capital stock.

A similar vertical shift in SLR is due to added costs of regulation for new facilities. Again, depending on the rate of retirement of old capacity, there is a time path of adjustment from PSR', OSR' to PLR', OLR'.

Nothing in this logic just described requires PLR' to be greater than PSR'. Indeed, if the costs of retrofitting existing capacity are high and the incremental costs of compliance in new facilities are low, it is quite possible for PSR' to exceed PLR' (see figure 5.4.)

Obviously, government regulation, by shifting long-run supply costs, will influence the total size of an industry; as depicted, however, it will not influence profit margins of new plants. However, returns (or quasi-rents) to existing plants will be materially affected by both the height of any vertical shift in the supply curve and the time path of adjustment to the new long-run equilibrium. Furthermore, the economically critical factor is not the average vertical shift, but the shift that occurs at the relevant margin. This may be more or less than the average. For example, if any industry's high-cost producers also have relatively high compliance costs, then the marginal cost of compliance will exceed average costs and new quasirents will be created by regulation. If compliance costs of marginal facilities are low, then regulation will dissipate some quasirents. (In both cases, some quasirents are terminated as the industry contracts.) Whether the net impact on rents is positive or negative is an empirical question we will address below in the context of tissue manufacturing.

It should be clear that to calculate impacts of regulations we must consider short-run effects, and not merely show differences in long-run costs, prices, and outputs. To obtain a better estimate of regulatory costs, the observed time stream of these cost and price increases needs to be discounted.

The above discussion was predicated on the assumption of constant demand. More realistically, demand is likely to shift over time. In some instances, this shift will be upward (as income grows, for example); in other instances, the shift will be to downward (as when lower-cost foreign supplies become available). The addition of a dynamic element to demand only reinforces our conclusion on the importance to impact analysis of the time path an industry follows in adjusting to government regulation.

In this same vein, any movement from a short-run to a long-run equilibrium requires investment, the timing of which can significantly influence the costs of compliance. For example, Leone et al. (1975) concluded that the annualized price per ton customers would pay as a result of the Federal Water Pollution Control Act Amendments of 1972 could be as low as $2.45 per ton if expenditures for pollution-control devices did not necessitate deferral of investments in production capacity. In contrast, if investments in new capacity were deferred on a dollar-for-dollar basis to allow for financing of pollution control devices, the annualized price per ton could be as high as $14.20. Under both assumptions, the estimated long-run (15–20 years) price per ton was virtually the same, as would be expected.[5]

Furthermore, short-run costs may have substantial impacts in the long run because they may seriously affect the competitive structure of an industry. If high short-run costs fall disproportionately on the smaller, more marginal plants and firms within an industry, these firms may not be able to stay in business. The result would be a more oligopolistic industry by the time the "long run" was attained. If this is the case, then long-run market conditions will be different from those described by the competitive-market equilibrium discussed above.

There is one further important reason for considering these short-run distributional effects: Members of the public at large, as well as various interest groups, may substantially alter their support for intended policy objectives if they do not perceive the costs initially or if they feel they are bearing a disproportionate share of the costs. People may favor improving water quality and support legislation promising to do so when costs of the program are as vague and hidden as they are in the environmental area; they may also change their positions radically once costs are perceived.

In her insightful article, Dorfman (1975) estimates the total economic costs of air and water pollution-control programs passed in the 1970s and shows that the near-term costs are substantially greater than the long-run costs. She further suggests that the vast majority of these costs are in the form of higher industry costs, which will be passed on to consumers. We think it is fair to speculate that these costs may not have been accurately perceived and fully discussed when the legislation was passed and may have turned out to be far greater than what the public is willing to pay for improved environmental quality. Once these costs begin to be perceived, which will occur as regulations are written and enforced, political support for these programs may erode. Our model of policy development must take such changing forces into account.

We have briefly outlined the model necessary to define and measure economic impacts of proposed regulations on an industry. The remainder of this paper applies the model to development of the 1972 amendments to the Federal Water Pollution Control Act and subsequent rulemaking by the EPA for the pulp and paper industry. We hope to demonstrate how the model is estimated in practice, to indicate the magnitudes of quasirents being created and dissipated by the EPA, and to show where and how costs and rents influence regulatory policy.

Economic Impacts and Congressional Consideration of Water-Pollution Regulations

The 1972 amendments to the Federal Water Pollution Control Act represent a major turning point in the public approach to water-pollution control. Previous legislation required state enforcement of policies based on local water quality. There was a general feeling that this approach had not been effective because each state had a considerable incentive to protect its economic base and thus not to set or enforce strong standards. The 1972 amendments decreed that policy would now be based on uniform effluent standards defined and enforced by the federal Environmental Protection Agency, regardless of the quality of the receiving water or local economic impacts. The act, as passed over a presidential veto, established 1985 as the date for "ending all discharge of pollutants" (EDOP) and set interim standards for 1977 based on "best practicable technology" (BPT) and for 1983 based on "best available technology" (BAT). Not only are the costs of attaining these standards large; they are anything but uniform in their economic impact on different regions and on competitors within an industry.

The passage of this legislation provides important clues about possible reasons for continued use of the regulatory approach to solve important social problems. Prior to passage, there had been growing concern among the American people about environmental problems. Opinion polls record that between 1965 and 1970 the proportion of persons who said water pollution was a "serious" or "very serious" problem rose from 35 percent to 74 percent (Erskine 1972).

Numerous politicians tried to capitalize on this concern by proposing new legislation. The most notable was Senator Edmund Muskie (D, Maine), who was preparing for his expected presidential campaign of 1972 (Ingram 1979). Muskie was chairman of the Air and Water Subcommittee of the Senate Public Works Committee, and thus had a major role in drafting the original version of the 1972 amendments. Muskie had been stung by accusations from Ralph Nader's organization that he was weak on water-quality policy. He responded by promoting a bill embodying the regulatory approach with strong effluent standards. The full Senate Public Works Committee unanimously (16–0) reported the Muskie bill without questioning the regulatory approach or the likely economic consequences. The Senate passed the bill unanimously (86–0) five days later, essentially unchanged.

The Senate's biggest concern appeared to be the expenditures the federal government ultimately might incur. The committee supplemental report (filed by five Republicans) and two of the three floor roll-call votes concerned provisions in the bill providing federal grants to local governments for constructing water-treatment facilities. (The other vote was on a proposal to allow the Small Business Administration to establish a subsidized loan program for small businesses finding it hard to raise necessary capital to install pollution-control devices.) The only alternative to the regulatory scheme was a proposal from Senator William Proxmire (D, Wisconsin) to include an effluent-tax system. This proposal was debated briefly and then rejected on a voice vote.

In the House of Representatives, the Public Works Committee considered the bill in early 1972 and reported its version in March 1972. There were several marked differences between the Senate and the House Committee versions. The most important was that the House would establish as goals rather than as mandatory the zero discharge standard for 1985 and the BAT requirement for 1981 (later amended in conference to 1983). The House version also required a study by the National Academy of Sciences on the environmental, technological, economic, and social feasibility of meeting the 1981 and 1985 goals prior to the mandating of their implementation.[6] Thus, the House Public Works Committee expressed concern over the uncertainty of economic impacts and sought to delay implementation until further study. However, it did not question the regulatory approach or the ultimate objectives. In dissenting reports, Democrats Bella Abzug and Charles Rangel of New York supported a set of modifications, known as the Reuss-Dingell Clean Water Package, and proposed several amendments of their own. These proposals would have reinstituted the Senate language mandating the 1981 and 1985 policies and added other strengthening requirements. A minority report filed by Republicans Roger Zion (Indiana) and John Terry (New York) expressed concern about the long-run economic impacts of the regulations and requested more information on potential price increases, employment impacts, balance-of-trade effects, and budget commitments. They did not propose any specific alterations to the committee version, however. House floor debate focused largely on the stronger Reuss-Dingell amendments, which were defeated, and the municipal-treatment grant program. The final version, passed by the House on a 380–14 vote, was very close to the version reported by the House committee. The final version of the bill, as reported by the conference committee and passed over President Richard M. Nixon's veto, kept the EDOP goals, but mandated implementation of BAT standards in 1983.

What role did potential costs and economic impacts play in the passage of these 1972 amendments? There was, of course, the expected conflict between industry, labor, and environmentalist groups over the proposed regulations. Presumably those individuals who would bear a small proportion of the costs and who value environmental quality would be more likely to support the legislation and to expect their representatives to do likewise. Beyond that, our model suggests that some firms and regions will be more disadvantaged than others; some may end up better off, depending upon their location on the compliance-cost curve in figure 5.1. We would then expect to find differences in positions taken by different firms in their testimony before congressional committees, in the behavior of various representatives, in industry and regional presentations and comments to the regulatory agency, and in firms' participation in lawsuits filed over the promulgated regulations, depending upon relative economic impacts. Our concern is how influential these various political activities may be in policy processes.

Perhaps the most conspicuous arena for these political considerations is the House of Representatives, which is organized on a regional basis and comprises legislators closely tied to district concerns. It would be surprising if the expected or most obviously perceived distributional impacts of proposed policies were not influential in the congressional decision process. Thus, by examining regional distributions of costs and benefits one ought to be able to explain, at least in part, the behavior of the House in establishing the regulatory policy.

We have already commented that total costs of the 1972 Water Pollution Control Amendments apparently were not considered in the development and passage of the legislation. However, some of the direct cost and employment effects were sufficiently large and concentrated to have influenced congressional decisions. Other things being equal, such as local pressures for environmental programs, it would be expected that representatives from districts with large concentrations of potentially impacted businesses would be more likely to oppose stronger versions of the bill than representatives from districts likely to suffer little adverse economic impact.

The amendments offered and voted on in the House of Representatives provide an opportunity to examine how these direct regional consequences influenced the legislation. Table 5.1 shows the six (of nine) recorded floor votes taken in the House, which we will analyze.[7] The amendments are ordered in terms of increasing regulatory strength, and presumably in severity of impacts on industry. For example, passage of the Abzug and

Table 5.1 House votes on the 1972 Water Pollution Control Amendments.

Included in Analysis	Location of Amendment Relative to Vote for Passage[a]
Passage of the bill. Passed 380–14.	0.00
McDonald (R, Michigan). Amendment to exempt industries from paying capital costs on federally funded municipal waste treatment plants which they use, in addition to paying user charges for maintenance, operation, and expansion. Rejected 66–337. A Nay vote was considered to be in support of the act.	0.56 (0.12)
W. Ford (D, Michigan). Amendment to guarantee public hearings in EPA investigations of employee firings or layoffs resulting from effluent limitations or orders under the act. Adopted 275–117.	1.52 (0.15)
Reuss (D, Wisconsin). Amendment to require adoption of toxic-pollutant standards and effluent limitations before EPA could transfer permit programs over to the states, and to give EPA permit-by-permit veto power over state programs; amendment would also have eliminated a provision in the bill giving immunity until 1976 to polluters who applied for discharge permits. Rejected 154–251.	2.72 (0.17)
Reuss (D, Wisconsin). Amendment to require industries to use the "best available" water pollution control technology by 1981. Rejected 140–249.	3.04 (0.17)
Abzug (D, New York). Amendment to require impact statements under the National Environmental Policy Act of 1969 for all activities covered by the bill. Rejected 125–268.	3.50 (0.18)

a. For an explanation of the entries in this column see the discussion in the text.

Reuss amendments would have produced a much stronger bill with more severe impacts on manufacturing firms. Conversely, the McDonald amendment was designed to limit impacts on firms by exempting them from capital costs of new municipal waste-treatment plants.

We have categorized legislators who voted according to which amendments they supported or opposed to obtain a measure of support for the legislation. For example, someone voting against all amendments and the bill itself was placed in the first category, while someone who just voted for the bill is put in the second category, and so on. Representatives who voted for all amendments fall into the seventh, or highest, category.[8] The distribution of representatives by respective categories is given in table 5.2. Fifteen representatives did not cast enough votes to be located on the scale and are omitted from further analysis. The scale has a fairly broad distribution, with only some bunching at the upper end. Thus,

Table 5.2 Distribution of representatives voting, by category.

	Category[a]							
	7	6	5	4	3	2	1	Total
No. of representatives	105	42	28	126	89	20	10	420

a. In most instances, the number of categories is equivalent to the number of votes a representative cast for pollution control. A representative who cast a vote for a more stringent amendment, but against a less stringent one, was assigned to a category that would maximize the coefficient of reproducibility.

Table 5.3 Model of House voting on the 1972 Water Pollution Control Act Amendments. Dependent variable: Scale category from table 5.2.

Independent Variables		Coefficient[a]	Standard Error
Constant		4.82	1.64
Demand	Region:		
	Border[b]	−0.78	0.22
	South[c]	−0.81	0.28
	Upper Midwest[d]	0.45	0.23
	Lower Midwest[e]	−0.46	0.21
	Upper West[f]	0.30	0.35
	Lower West[g]	−0.31	0.22
	Population density (log)	0.10	0.04
	Median house value × % owner	0.01	0.21
	Median rent × % renter	0.62	0.54
	Median age in district (population over 25)	0.06	0.02
	% suburban	0.38	0.26
Northern Democrats		1.08	0.15
Southern Democrats		0.66	0.28
Age of congressman (log)		−1.48	0.32
Cost[h]	Primary metals	0.24	0.18
	Mining	−0.02	0.32
	Petroleum extraction	−0.53	0.24
	Paper production	−0.18	0.19
	Paper production × cost/ton	−0.003	0.03

a. These coefficients and the coefficients reported in table 5.1 were estimated using n-chotomous multivariate probit techniques.
b. Maryland, West Virginia, Kentucky, Tennessee, Missouri, Oklahoma.
c. Virginia, North Carolina, South Carolina, Georgia, Florida, Alabama, Mississippi, Louisiana, Arkansas, Texas.
d. Michigan, Wisconsin, Minnesota, North Dakota, South Dakota.
e. Indiana, Illinois, Iowa, Nebraska, Kansas.
f. Montana, Idaho, Oregon, Washington, Alaska, Wyoming.
g. Utah, Colorado, New Mexico, Arizona, Nevada, California, Hawaii.
h. The primary metals, mining and petroleum extraction variables are dummy variables equal to 1 if the industry is important to the district's economy (as reported by the Almanac of American Politics). Paper production is tons of capacity from *Lockwood's Directory of the Pulp and Paper Industry*. The cost/ton data are derived from Leone et al. 1975.

it should provide a good measure of the positions of most legislators on the issue of water-pollution-control regulations.

The next step is to relate these positions to demands for environmental quality and to the economic impacts in each district. We focus on the pulp and paper industry, and we want to know specifically if the likelihood of a representative's supporting strong environmental legislation decreases if there are pulp or paper mills in the district, and if this support is further reduced if likely compliance costs for district mills would increase.

The model and the statistical method used to explain House voting on the 1972 amendments are described elsewhere (Jackson and Leone 1978), but we can easily summarize its contents and results. The major determinants of a representative's position on the legislation are hypothesized to be the district's demand for environmental cleanup, the likely economic consequences for the district, and the representative's party affiliation and personal preferences. The precise variables used in the analysis, their estimated effects on legislators' positions, and the standard errors of the coefficients are shown in table 5.3.[9]

The statistical method provides an estimate of relative location, or spacing, of votes used to constitute our scale of support for stronger water pollution regulation. The numbers in table 5.1 are these estimated locations, with the vote for passage arbitrarily defined as zero to locate the scale. (The parenthetical numbers are standard errors of estimated locations.) The three amendments in the Clean Water Package are located close together, while the largest distances are between these amendments and the Ford amendment, and between the Ford amendment and the two weakest votes. The magnitudes of distances between votes aid in interpreting coefficients in the underlying model. For example, it would take a difference of at least 1.2 in estimated positions of two representatives to bridge the gap between the Ford amendment and the first Reuss amendment.

The specification of demand variables is based on a model of people's willingness to pay (in dollars) for environmental cleanup, as estimated with data from a 1969 Harris survey (Jackson 1979). This model shows that willingness to pay is strongly related to a person's region and place of residence, age, family size, education, and income.[10] Unfortunately, data on income and education levels of congressional-district residents is not available for 1972.[11] We hope that inclusion of housing-stock variables serves as a proxy for these characteristics. The population-density variable is included to represent estimated willingness-to-pay differences between rural and metropolitan areas. Coefficients on these variables are consistent with the demand model. Only a district's median voter age did not perform as expected. This may be explained by the small variation in this variable and by the fact that what variation exists is largely attributable to the location of large military bases, with their younger nonresident populations. We thus conclude that representatives' positions were related to the environmental demands of their constituents.

The party-affiliation variables are self-explanatory. Northern Democrats exhibited much stronger support for the legislation than did Republicans, with the support of southern Democrats somewhere in between. The results are consistent with the pressure President Nixon put on the House to weaken the bill. The age of legislators is used to proxy their own preferences, and this has the expected sign: Younger representatives show preferences for more stringent regulations.

In addition to economic impacts associated with the pulp and paper industry, we make a crude attempt to include the presence in districts of other industries likely to be adversely affected by the regulations. The *Almanac of American Politics* (Barone et al. 1972) gives a brief summary of the industrial base of each district, compiled from the 1970 census. The variables, primary metal, mining, and petroleum extraction, are simply dummy variables based on whether the almanac mentioned the appropriate economic activity. As such, they may not be completely reliable, particularly for metropolitan areas where census data are not available on a congressional-district level. The authors of the almanac admitted that for these districts the description is based largely on characteristics of the entire metropolitan area. This difficulty may help explain the wrong sign on the primary metal variable, since many steel mills are located in metropolitan areas. It may also be the case that water quality is lower in such districts and the legislator was voting for cleanup in spite of economic effects.

Local compliance costs for the pulp and paper industry are our particular concern here. The importance of this industry to a district is measured by production capacity in thousands of tons per day of mills in the district. Cost data, in dollars per ton to meet 1983 BAT standards, are from the National Commission on Water Quality (NCWQ) study. The NCWQ model used for estimating these costs is the predecessor to the industry model described elsewhere in this paper. Our hypothesis is that the greater the estimated cost of complying with the 1983 standards, the greater the adverse economic impact on a district—in terms of both personal income and employment—and the less likely a representative was to support stronger versions of the 1972 amendments.[12]

There are two alternative hypotheses about the expected signs on the two pulp and paper variables. A naive hypothesis is that paper companies (and, presumably, representatives from districts with economies based on pulp and paper) are sensitive to any regulation that may raise their costs and reduce output and profits. Particularly, given uncertainty about how regulations might be written and enforced, firms may simply be wary of the unknown and oppose any government regulation. If this is the case, we would expect congressional voting to be sensitive to the amount of pulp and paper production in a district, but relatively insensitive to costs, which were only determined after the EPA began to define industry categories and establish effluent standards. The hypothesis based on more sophisticated behavior is that firms are aware not just of their own expected pollution-control costs, but how these costs compare with those of competing firms. With this knowledge, firms estimate their expected change in net worth, not just cost increases. This calculation is based on the shape of the compliance-cost curve of figure 5.1. According to this analysis, firms in the left-hand portion of the curve potentially stand to have increases in net worth because expected price increases resulting from a shift in the aggregate supply curve may exceed their compliance costs, resulting in increased profit margins. Sophisticated firms in the left portion of the curve may actually gain economically from imposition of pollution standards and might be expected to support the legislation. A large negative coefficient on the cost multiplied by the production variable and a positive (or at least a zero) coefficient on the production variable would support this hypothesis.

The estimates do not support the more sophisticated model of firm behavior, but indicate that representatives from districts with pulp and paper mills were less likely to support the legislation. Although the standard error of each coefficient is large, the null hypothesis that pulp and paper presence and costs have no effect (that is, that both coefficients equal zero) can be rejected at the 0.01 level. The χ^2 value for this hypothesis is 10.0 with 2 degrees of freedom. (If the production capacity multiplied by cost per ton variable is deleted, the coefficient of production capacity is -0.20, with a standard error of 0.06.)

Overall, voting was not sensitive to estimated compliance costs. For a district with the maximum capacity (6,500 tons per day), the predicted effect on congressional voting of a $10 per ton cost difference (the maximum difference among districts) is only -0.20.[13] For smaller cost differences or for districts with less capacity, expected voting differences will be even smaller.

In contrast, the mere presence within a district of 6,500 tons of daily pulp and paper production capacity at the average compliance cost of $6 per ton affects a representative's vote by -1.30.[14] Each 1,000-ton decrease in capacity increases the expected support for pollution-control regulations by 0.20 at the average compliance cost of $6 per ton. The significance of these magnitudes can be ascertained by consulting table 5.1 for differences in locations of votes.

We conclude from these results that congressional voting on the 1972 amendments was sensitive to potential direct economic effects on a district, but in a rather unsophisticated manner. Representatives did not seem to be pressing a possible economic advantage to their region by supporting legislation that would give local mills a competitive advantage; they simply opposed regulations affecting local industry.

An obvious rationale for the relative unimportance of variations in compliance costs in explaining congressional voting is that intraindustry impacts were not known at the time the legislation was considered. The development of a regulatory policy is largely defined by the stream of administrative decisions made by the regulatory agency once the legislation is passed. In the case of the 1972 Water Pollution Control Act Amendments, the bill simply specified that industry had to satisfy effluent standards consistent with the BPT by 1977 and the BAT by 1983 for given industries and industry subcategories. It was left to EPA to define the subcategories, to specify what constituted BPT and BAT standards for various industries and subcategories, and to establish the norms. Only when the EPA begins this process are firms able to predict how they will be affected. Without these predictions, one might expect a strong, general opposition to the concept of being regulated (possibly in anticipation of adverse economic consequences), with no variation in opposition in response to variations in economic impacts.

Administrative Rulemaking and Regulatory Impacts

The fact that distributional consequences within an industry (and thus between regions) are not defined until rulemaking regulatory processes begin has strong implications for the effect of distributional impacts on policy processes. The regulating agency (in this case the EPA) determines these impacts, which implies that the agency and not the Congress becomes the focus for the political forces they generate. The question now to be asked is: How, and to what extent, are an administrative or regulatory agency's rulemaking and enforcing decisions affected by pressures related to the economic consequences of their decisions? A brief glimpse at this process, and at possible influences of economic effects, is obtained by noting that the EPA published three different versions of BPT and BAT standards for a large section of the pulp and paper industry. These different versions and solicitation of industry and public comments are part of the required rulemaking procedure. Subsequent alterations of the standards and industry categorizations provide clear evidence of accommodation to various pressures from segments of the industry and from environmentalists.

Investigation of the question posed in the preceding paragraph and analysis of different standards proposed by the EPA require that we estimate for a segment of the pulp and paper industry the detailed model described in the first section of this paper. This is done for the tissue portion of the industry.

In estimating impacts of regulations, first it is necessary to identify the distribution of costs the tissue industry will confront in meeting the regulations. That is, we must estimate the compliance-cost curve (figure 5.1). Second, these costs must be translated into price effects and microlevel impacts. The specific procedures used to calculate the costs the tissue industry will incur in complying with mandated water-pollution reductions and associated total costs of manufacture are described elsewhere (Leone 1980). Here, we merely note that these costs are estimated on a plant-by-plant basis. This is done by taking cost levels estimated for "representative" or hypothetical mills and regressing them on various mill characteristics. The resulting equations permitted estimation of costs for sixty-four existing mills in the industry.[15]

In calculating pollution-control costs, we assume that each plant will minimize the discounted present value (with an interest rate of 15 percent) of compliance costs for the anticipated sequence of 1977, 1983 and 1985 standards, and that all in-process or end-of-pipe changes that reduce pollution loads and yield a 15 percent return will be made. Occasionally, this assumption may not be valid. For example, the 1985 standards are merely a "goal" in the 1972 act. If they are not enforced, then on a present-value basis a company may take a different course of action to meet the 1983 standards. Furthermore, we ignore issues of regulatory uncertainly; that is, we assume that standards are known and will be strictly enforced.

The principal benefit of this microlevel cost orientation is that it permits simulating the distributional consequences of regulation which we argued are so important to understanding the political economics of business regulation.

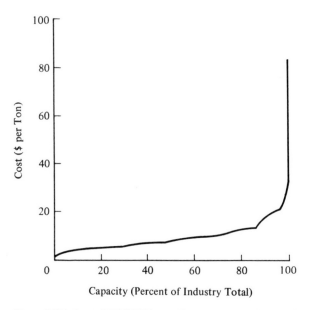

Figure 5.5 Estimated 1977 BPT compliance-cost curve (economic-cost basis).

The estimated compliance-cost curve for the tissue portion of the pulp and paper industry for 1977 BPT effluent control levels is shown in figure 5.5. The BPT costs range from $1.85 to $82.82 per ton.[16] About 80 percent of capacity has unit costs of $12.34 per ton or less. The average economic cost for the tissue industry is $9.41 per ton.

Figure 5.6 is identical in construction to figure 5.5, but shows various definitions of total manufacturing costs estimated in 1974 prices.[17] The middle curve reports total costs of production on an accounting cost basis before the act; thus, it excludes all water-pollution-control costs associated with the act except those with a rate of return of 15 percent on the required investment. The range of production costs is substantial: from $556 to $693 per ton. The weighted average cost of $613 per ton is exceeded by thirty-five of the sixty-four mills in our sample, which indicates that the lower-cost mills are predominantly the larger ones.

Although it cannot directly be discerned by comparing figures 5.5 and 5.6, it is worth noting that there is no obvious correlation between a mill's BPT compliance costs and its total manufacturing costs. It is not the case, for example, that mills with high production costs necessarily have high BPT compliance costs. Accordingly, to understand the economic consequences of BPT regulations it is not sufficient to examine

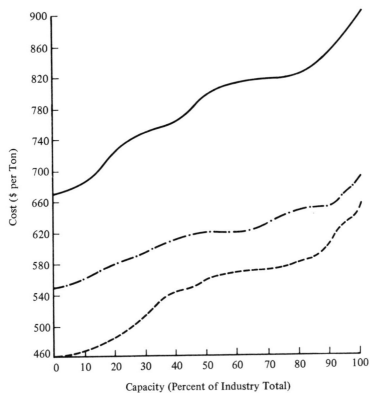

Figure 5.6 Various definitions of total cost of production for the tissue industry. Solid line: economic-cost basis, BAT. Dash-dot line: accounting-cost basis, before the act. Dotted line: variable-cost basis, before the act.

the distribution of BPT costs alone; it also is necessary to examine the underlying distribution of manufacturing costs.

Because the accounting cost numbers in figure 5.6 represent total costs, they are not relevant to short-run decisionmaking. Thus, we also report in figure 5.6 our estimates of the variable costs of production without effluent controls. These figures reflect costs observed in the second quarter of 1974. At that time, the capacity-utilization rate in the tissue industry was approximately 94 percent and a typical price for tissue was $638 per ton (Arthur D. Little, Inc., 1974). In view of the extensive possibilities for error in our cost-estimation procedures, these observed price and utilization levels are quite consistent with the numbers shown in figure 5.6. Indeed, at a 94 percent utilization rate, figure 5.6 implies a price of $627 per ton; at a price of $638, figure 5.6 forecasts a utilization rate of 97 percent. These predictions are very close to the observed values.

Table 5.4 The tissue industry's costs of production with BPT controls in place (1974 prices, accounting-cost basis), by mill.

Mill Total Cost with BPT Controls ($ per Ton)	Percentile Ranking of Mill with BPT Controls	Mill Capacity (Tons per Day)	Identification No. of Mill	Percentile Ranking of Mill with No Controls
559.33	7	648	2	7
560.35	10	204	4	10
574.93	12	208	42	13
581.00	17	453	50	18
582.35	18	104	57	11
587.87	21	272	49	21
589.46	22	68	16	22
591.57	31	816	1	31
601.99	32	29	11	32
604.12	33	116	38	35
604.35	35	181	55	34
613.89	37	133	44	41
614.18	39	172	20	37
614.66	39	37	30	39
614.78	41	140	10	39
618.14	43	181	43	43
619.31	43	36	12	47
619.68	47	362	53	47
620.06	48	45	8	48
621.85	49	90	63	49
623.04	49	18	58	48
623.51	50	72	7	60
623.91	59	816	47	58
624.51	60	54	27	59
627.04	60	45	3	68
629.37	61	36	22	66
630.00	65	408	51	64
631.20	66	72	61	66
633.06	66	45	33	65
633.82	67	40	31	67
633.87	67	31	46	69
634.19	68	54	9	67
635.47	69	58	15	68
636.29	69	58	32	70
638.28	70	108	5	74
639.71	71	27	36	69
641.22	71	36	37	71
641.78	72	72	59	73
642.74	72	7	41	47
643.39	72	22	48	69
643.39	73	22	62	70
643.45	73	22	34	74
645.06	73	31	21	71
645.67	73	18	26	71
646.81	75	145	52	77

Table 5.4 (continued)

Mill Total Cost with BPT Controls ($ per Ton)	Percentile Ranking of Mill with BPT Controls	Mill Capacity (Tons per Day)	Identification No. of Mill	Percentile Ranking of Mill with No Controls
648.31	75	22	24	71
649.09	77	155	64	76
649.18	77	22	35	72
651.70	85	725	54	90
653.69	87	136	14	82
653.96	90	222	17	80
654.43	90	12	28	72
656.93	90	7	25	43
659.37	91	126	29	91
662.81	92	108	39	92
668.03	93	90	19	94
670.67	94	22	23	93
670.71	94	68	18	93
673.19	95	48	60	96
678.01	96	93	45	96
680.93	98	167	6	98
684.09	99	67	13	99
692.88	100	77	56	100
697.34	100	36	40	100

Deviations may be attributed to two phenomena. First, most assuredly, is the rudimentary nature of our costing procedures. Second, we incorporated all profitable internal and external process changes into the costs shown in figure 5.6. In practice, not all mills in 1974 had yet adopted these cost-saving measures; furthermore, the fact that savings manifest themselves principally in lower variable costs partially explains our understatement of price at the observed utilization rate.[18]

Total manufacturing costs in 1977 with BPT pollution controls in place are shown in table 5.4, which shows the same kind of information presented graphically in preceding figures. The second column shows the percentile ranking of each mill after BPT controls; the rightmost column shows the same ranking without controls. A comparison of these two columns indicates some interesting competitive consequences of BPT regulations. For example, without controls mill 25 ranks at the 43rd percentile of industry costs; with BPT controls it ranks at the 90th percentile. The economic circumstances of mill 25 are almost surely politically sensitive, given its dramatic shift in relative competitive position after imposition of BPT effluent controls.

For most mills, relative shifts in competitive advantage are far less dramatic than the shift experienced by mill 25. For example, twenty-six mills are relatively worse off after BPT controls; that is, they have percentile rankings higher after BPT than before. Only fifteen of these mills have shifts of two percentile points or more. However, the largest shifts occur at the high-cost end of the spectrum, precisely where they are most important from the standpoint of economic survival. Note, for example, that in addition to mill 25, mills 28, 17, 14, 35, and 24 all have relatively major shifts at the high-cost end of the spectrum.

Seventeen mills have improvements in their relative total-cost position after BPT; eleven of these shift by two or more points. Thus, overall, forty-three of sixty-four mills in our sample experience a relative shift in competitive advantage that is due to BPT effluent controls.

These relative cost shifts have two distinguishable, but related, impacts on the economics of an individual plant. The first effect is obvious: The higher a plant's relative costs, the lower any quasirents it might earn. Thus, relative cost shifts due to regulations create and dissipate quasirents earned by producers. There is a second impact, however, which is distinguishable from the first. The lower a plant's percentile cost ranking, the less vulnerable it is to changes in an industry's overall economic conditions. Thus, a plant that shifts to a lower ranking because of regulation may be able to sustain a higher rate of capacity utilization than its disadvantaged competitors.[19] In sum, a favorable shift in the cost ranking of an individual plant both increases the plant's margins and reduces the likelihood that its full capacity will be underutilized.

Alternative abatement standards imply different mill costs and quasirent distributions. The EPA's water-pollution-control effort in moving from BPT to BAT and then to EDOP can create or destroy competitive advantages. We suggest that one dimension of competitive advantage is a plant's costs relative to its competition. These shifts in competitive advantage are summarized in table 5.5 for tissue producers at mandated water-pollution-abatement levels. If nothing else, this table quickly demonstrates the likely complexity of political forces set in motion by water-pollution controls. As noted earlier, of sixty-four mills in our sample, seventeen are in a relatively better cost position after BPT standards are in place. For only two or three of these mills is the improvement at all substantial. In contrast, twenty-six mills experience a relative loss of competitive advantage. For about half a dozen, the deterioration is substantial. In other words, gains and losses are not symmetrical in absolute magnitude. Primarily, this is because some very small facilities experience significant deterioration in their relative positions, but, being small in aggregate, their losses do not result in large gains for other mills.

Table 5.5 Percentile ranking of mills in the tissue industry.

Identification No. of Mill	No Controls	BPT	BAT	EDOP	BAT Replacement
1	31	31	31	31	21
2	7	7	7	10	7
3	68	60	60	60	66
4	10	10	10	2	18
5	74	70	70	67	29
6	98	98	99	98	62
7	60	50	59	48	85
8	48	48	48	41	83
9	67	68	67	68	93
10	39	41	39	40	81
11	32	32	32	35	62
12	47	43	43	59	84
13	99	99	97	99	45
14	82	87	87	85	64
15	68	69	69	68	94
16	22	22	22	13	46
17	80	90	90	88	54
18	93	94	94	94	45
19	94	93	93	93	60
20	37	39	41	39	88
21	71	73	73	86	98
22	66	61	61	67	91
23	93	94	94	95	99
24	71	75	75	90	99
25	43	90	90	100	100
26	71	73	75	91	99
27	59	60	60	58	86
28	72	90	90	95	100
29	91	91	91	90	90
30	39	39	37	41	82
31	67	67	68	70	92
32	70	69	69	69	93
33	65	66	66	70	95
34	74	73	73	70	96
35	72	77	76	91	99
36	69	71	71	74	97
37	71	71	71	74	97
38	35	33	35	33	78
39	92	92	92	92	96
40	100	100	100	100	100
41	47	72	73	99	99
42	13	12	12	12	12
43	43	43	43	43	48
44	41	37	37	37	23
45	96	96	96	96	59
46	69	67	67	71	94
47	58	59	58	57	75
48	69	72	72	89	90

Table 5.5 (continued)

Identification No. of Mill	No Controls	BPT	BAT	EDOP	BAT Replacement
49	21	21	16	16	51
50	18	17	21	22	20
51	64	65	66	65	42
52	77	75	75	73	89
53	47	47	47	47	59
54	90	85	85	84	37
55	34	35	34	35	66
56	100	100	100	100	76
57	11	18	13	17	83
58	48	49	49	67	89
59	73	72	72	72	87
60	96	95	95	94	97
61	66	66	61	65	92
62	70	73	72	89	90
63	49	49	49	59	86
64	76	77	77	76	44

Note: These are total accounting costs except the right most column, which reflects replacement costs on an economic basis.

Given that BPT standards are in place, a move to BAT standards yields very few changes in relative competitive position. Indeed, only five mills experience an absolute change of ranking of three or more percentile points. Thus, it appears that BAT standards principally affect the height but not the shape of the industry's effluent-control-cost curve. Under such circumstances, it would be expected that the industry would be able to sustain a fairly unified political position against BAT standards. EDOP standards, however, produce relatively large shifts in competitive advantage within the industry.

Whenever the politics of pollution controls are discussed, the issue of plant closings invariably receives a great deal of attention. Our analysis yields some interesting insights on the closure question.

On an economic basis, management will choose to close a facility rather than invest in pollution-abatement equipment if it cannot expect to earn an adequate return on its pollution-control expenditures. Thus, if the anticipated product price is less than the sum of variable costs of manufacturing plus economic costs of pollution control, a facility will be closed. Examined in this way, the estimated price increase due to BAT controls is about $4 per ton. Alternatively, if it is believed that investors cannot make perfect decisions and precisely estimate the desired level of industry capital stock, the price for tissue can be determined after firms have complied with BAT standards by examining variable costs of production with BAT standards in place.[20] At a 94 percent capacity utilization rate, variable costs with BAT are $3 higher than variable costs without effluent controls. The discrepancy of $1 per ton from the two different methods is well within our estimate of error. Since $3 or $4 would constitute a price increase of less than 0.5 percent and since tissue demand is relatively price-inelastic, we ignored any quantity effects.[21]

If producers correctly forecast a $3 price increase and make their pollution-control-compliance decisions on that basis, five of the sixty-four facilities in our sample will close. (These five represent less than 4 percent of total capacity; hence, their closing would not influence our estimate of the BAT price.)

Of these five closure candidates, only one was among the fifteen highest-cost facilities when measured on the basis of unit costs of abatement. In other words, the cost of regulatory compliance is a poor predictor of plant closings. Indeed, three of the five closure candidates had BAT costs less than the industry average, and two of these had costs less than half the industry average.

In contrast, all five closure candidates were among the top ten most costly plants when ranked on a variable-cost basis. It would be "correct" to conclude—as most closure impact studies do—that these facilities would have closed anyway, since they are the highest-cost facilities in the industry. Furthermore, they represent less than five percent of industry capacity and thus could reasonably be expected to constitute the 5–6 percent of capacity one would expect to retire in any given year or two simply by the process of normal economic depreciation. However, their demise is clearly accelerated by pollution-control regulations (how much is difficult to say in the absence of a dynamic model of industry investment).

If it is assumed that these plants close two years earlier than they would have otherwise, the capital losses associated with plant closings can be calculated. Variable costs per ton prior to pollution controls for our closure candidates are reported in table 5.6. Note that four of the five already had average variable costs that exceeded the preabatement price of $638 per ton. Thus, they were already operating, if at all, on the thinnest of margins. Indeed, in the aggregate these five facilities would need to forgo a $5 per ton contribution (price minus variable cost) on their entire output (which is highly unlikely) for the capital loss (present value at 10 percent) due to pollution controls to equal $1 million.

This analysis merely illustrates that important capital losses due to pollution controls are not found in the closing plants. Consider mill 3.

Table 5.6 Variable costs per ton (1974 prices) for mill closure candidates, with no controls.

Identification No. of Mill	
59	$634
52	640
60	643
23	655
40	692

It will not close because of pollution controls. However, prior to imposition of controls it had total costs of $625 per ton, and thus was earning an accounting profit of $13 per ton. Mill 3 has a capacity of 45 tons per day; it is a high-cost mill, with a life expectancy of, say, ten years. With BAT controls, its revenue rises by $3 per ton; however, its economic costs of BAT compliance rise by about $8 (they are relatively high because capital must be recovered in 10 years). Thus, its profit rate drops to $8 per ton—a loss of $5 per ton. The capitalized value of this $5 per ton loss for ten years at fifteen percent is about $400,000.

In fact, only two mills, representing less than 2 percent of industry capacity, have economic costs of BAT compliance that are less than the $3 per ton price increase. Recall from table 5.5 that BAT raises the curve in figure 5.4 for all firms but does not alter the ranking significantly. Thus, the remaining fifty-seven mills which can economically justify compliance do so only by taking a reduction in the economic returns they were earning prior to pollution controls. The capital losses associated with all these changes in rents swamp the capital losses due to plant closures; the potential capital loss for mill 1 alone is $13 million.

An aggregate industry estimate of potential capital losses associated with dissipated quasirents can be calculated as follows: The average economic cost per ton with BAT (after plant closures) is $11.82; the added revenue is $3. The capitalized value of the resulting $8.82-per-ton loss for ten years at 15 percent is $130 million. Thus, effluent-control regulations have the potential of dissipating large quasirents. These losses do not affect the marginal decisions of managers of existing facilities, but they certainly do influence the overall profitability of this industry.

The political entanglements created by these potential losses raise intriguing questions of public policy. In effect, our analysis suggests that a major economic consequence of water-pollution controls may be better measured by the resulting redistribution of wealth than by the price and quantity effects that receive so much attention.

These capital losses have been described as "potential" because thus far we have ignored any dynamic consequences of effluent controls. We now turn to issues of economics of new mills so as better to understand these dynamic impacts and the long-run price and profit effects. Figure 5.6 reported the total economic costs of replacing existing facilities in the tissue industry, assuming that these mills comply with BAT standards. A similar calculation of replacement costs prior to controls shows virtually no change in the rankings of the lowest-cost mills. Thus, BAT regulations do not seriously affect the overall geographic and technological thrust of the tissue industry. However, BAT controls do add $10–15 per ton to the price required to justify investment in this industry—approximately a 2 percent increase in total costs.

This seemingly small change actually is quite important to the dynamic performance of the tissue industry. New mills are high-cost producers; thus, this added 2 percent would not merely dissipate a quasirent that otherwise would have been earned by new producers, but would influence the marginal economics of this industry. By influencing marginal economics, it would significantly impact the quasirents of existing producers —indeed, it would likely raise their quasirents in the long run by the total $10–$15-per-ton economic-cost differential. In other words, because new facilities are high-cost, existing producers would recoup the quasirents they appear to have lost in our earlier comparative static analysis.

Compare the situation in the tissue industry in 1974 (before controls) with that in 1984 (post-BAT). Presumably, in this period 20–25 percent of existing capacity would have been retired owing to physical depreciation. The marginal producers, therefore, would all have new facilities. This would necessitate a return on the margin of total economic costs, and hence prices would be set on this basis. As shown in figure 5.3, all existing capacity would have to operate at virtually 100 percent utilization for this to occur. In these circumstances prices would have to be at least $679 per ton, the break-even cost of the lowest-cost source of new capacity shown in figure 5.6. Of course, new facilities would also have high cost in the absence of controls.

Thus, our scenario is the same for 1984 without controls, except that the break-even price is only $669 per ton—the lowest cost source of new capacity in the absence of controls. Consequently, the long-run effects of BAT controls do not make the industry any more or less sensitive to the business cycle, because the marginal producers are the new producers in either case. However, BAT controls would create a $10 price umbrella over the rest of the industry, wiping out their potential losses in quasirents due to controls and extending the economic life of old plants. Thus, viewed in long-run perspective, BAT controls are likely to reduce plant closures and increase profits for existing producers. The higher prices dictated by this process contract the overall size of the industry, but this manifests itself in fewer new plants rather than in lower profits for the existing ones.

Fewer new plants implies lost economic opportunities for regions that would have housed new plants and gains for regions that find their old plants more profitable. Since the price elasticity of demand is low and the price increases due to controls are small, the impact of pollution controls on total capacity need not be very great; the total capacity of the tissue industry declines only 0.5 percent. The second effect is quite substantial, however; the price umbrella of $10 per ton significantly increases profits of existing plants. The existence of quasirents may justify some life-extending investments. Increases in quasirents due to BAT controls would create still greater incentives for such investments.

The preceding discussion illustrates the complexities of analyzing the political economy of business regulation. Three methodological conclusions emerge. First, to determine the impacts of costs associated with regulatory policies, it is essential to understand the nature of the underlying costs of production upon which they will be superimposed. High costs of compliance cannot simply be equated with negative economic impacts. Second, we observed that regulations can create and dissipate quasirents of important magnitudes, but to appreciate the true impacts of shifts in competitive advantage it is essential to consider costs of production associated with marginal sources of capacity in an industry. Third, any final assessment of net impacts on industry of alterations in quasirents requires a careful analysis of the timing of these changes. We have suggested that losses in early years are likely to be offset by gains in later years; whether the net result is capital losses or capital gains to individual competitors depends critically on time streams of cost and price increases.

Regulations create and dissipate quasirents, which undoubtedly accounts for much of the political maneuvering of economic actors faced with regulation. We examine this hypothesis by analyzing various standards proposed by the EPA. When the EPA established compliance requirements for 1977, it did so in three steps. In 1975 the agency proposed a set of standards. The industry commented on these, and the EPA subsequently revised them in 1976. These standards were again revised before

Table 5.7 Proposed effluent standards in three tissue-industry subcategories.

| | Influent Load^a (Pounds per Ton) | | Pounds Removed per Ton | | | | | |
| | | | 1975 Proposal | | 1976 Proposal | | 1977 Proposal | |
	BOD^b	TSS^b	BOD	TSS	BOD	TSS	BOD	TSS
Bleached kraft	80	100	12.7 (84%)	20.6 (79%)	13.9 (83%)	30.2 (70%)	14.2 (82%)	25.8 (74%)
Deinking	65	220	14.0 (79%)	25.3 (89%)	18.9 (71%)	28.4 (87%)	18.8 (71%)	25.9 (88%)
Nonintegrated tissue	30	75	8.4 (72%)	8.5 (89%)	8.5 (72%)	11.8 (84%)	8.5 (72%)	11.8 (84%)

a. Raw loads are based on representative mills.
b. Biological oxygen demand (BOD) and total suspended solids (TSS) are two important measures of water pollution in the tissue industry.

they became final in 1977. Changes for three typical subcategories of the tissue industry are reported in table 5.7.

Note that the standards were not always made less stringent in subsequent rounds. In two of these subcategories, standards for total suspended solids (TSS) were more stringent in 1977 than those proposed in 1976. For the most part, however, these tighter standards were not more costly; that is, the relationship between waste treatment and cost is not a monotonic continuous function. With a given removal method, it may be possible to raise standards without raising costs. For example, primary waste treatment might effectively remove 30 percent of all biological oxygen demand in a plant's waste stream. A standard that requires 25 percent removal has no higher cost than one that requires 20 percent removal under these circumstances.

The net effect of EPA's three efforts was to relax standards and lower the overall height of the compliance-cost curve. However, it is necessary to consider the shape of the compliance-cost curve as well as its height, for it is alterations in shape that determine changes in quasirents due to pollution controls. The flatter the compliance-cost curve, the smaller the additional rents.

It seems reasonable to hypothesize that the EPA, as a political agency, seeks to flatten the compliance-cost curve and thus avoid creating or dissipating substantial competitive advantages as a result of its pollution-control activities. Indeed, in conversation with a representative of a pulp and paper industry trade association, we were told that the lobbying objective of that association was to "flatten our curve."

It is difficult to test the hypothesis that the EPA tries to flatten the curve, because of the nature of effluent-control technology and the

Table 5.8 Cost changes (per ton) due to changes in proposed standards.

Subcategory	Compliance Cost, 1975 Proposed Standard	Change in Cost, 1976 vs. 1975 Proposed Standard	Change in Cost, 1977 vs. 1976 Proposed Standard
Bleached kraft:			
Low cost	$ 1.52	− $0.03	0
Average cost	6.74	− 0.08	0
High cost	21.04	− 0.25	0
Deinking mills:			
Low cost	$ 3.39	− 0.27	0
Average cost	7.38	− 0.32	+ $0.30
High cost	27.68	− 1.52	+ 0.30
Nonintegrated mills:			
Low cost	$ 1.21	− 0.11	0
Average cost	5.72	− 0.49	0
High cost	69.44	− 5.90	0

available data. As a rule of thumb, a particular treatment system is thought to remove a given percentage of raw waste; for example, primary treatment typically removes 30 percent of the raw-load biological oxygen demand (BOD). Though we have no information on actual raw loads for individual plants, we have been advised to assume that loads are constant among plants using similar technology.[22] With such an assumption, a given change in standard is a constant percentage change in required treatment for all competitors and shifts the compliance-cost curve a constant percentage distance at all points. This necessarily flattens the curve. However, tissue manufacturers fall into several subcategories, so the EPA can further alter the shape of the compliance-cost curve for this industry as a whole by differentially changing standards for each subcategory. This strategy would produce the flattening we predict with our "equal pain" hypothesis; however, this flattening, if observed, would not be a consequence of the way the data are constructed.

Percentage changes in compliance costs associated with the subsequent rounds of effluent standards for tissue manufacturers in three subcategories are shown in table 5.8. Note that the subcategory with the lowest average cost (nonintegrated tissue) experienced the greatest reduction in costs with subsequent versions of the BPT standards. However, this category's low average cost masks its very high maximum cost. Bleached kraft, with the lowest maximum compliance cost, experienced the least reduction in its average costs in subsequent rounds.

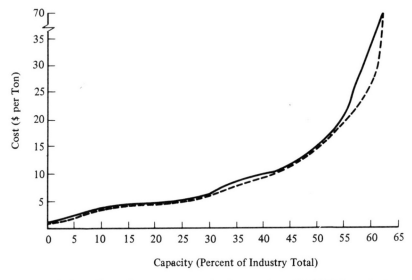

Figure 5.7 Estimated compliance-cost curves for three versions of 1977 BPT standards. Solid line: 1975 version. Dashed line: 1976–1977 versions (the two curves are virtually indistinguishable).

Within each subcategory, the low-cost tissue producers experienced the greatest percentage but lowest absolute cost reductions. Thus, flattening of the MCC curve is observed because higher-cost producers receive the largest absolute decreases in costs.

Cost-versus-capacity results for tissue manufacturers are shown in figure 5.7. Between 1975 and 1976 (the two rounds that matter most) the low-cost plants experienced an $0.11-per-ton reduction in costs, versus $5.93 per ton for the high-cost mills. The average dropped by $0.23 per ton. In interpreting the impacts of these cost reductions, it is important to note that rents earned are determined by two components: a producer's own costs and those of the industry's marginal producers.

For comparison with the earlier discussion, assume that this industry operates at 94 percent of capacity. The absolute decrease in costs at the relevant margin due to the less stringent 1976 standard is between $0.20 and $0.50 per ton, as determined by the shift in total production costs that results from the shift in compliance costs shown in figure 5.7. Because this is the relevant margin for determining prices, we predict a price drop of that magnitude. Our low-cost producer has a cost savings of about $0.11 per ton with the less stringent standards, while high-cost producers save up to $6.00 per ton; the average decrease is $0.23 per ton.

Table 5.9 Differences in cost and waste loads associated with standards announced in 1975 versus those announced in 1977.

Subcategory	Change in Average Cost per Ton	Change in Pollution (Pounds per Ton)	Cost per Pound[a]
Bleached kraft	−$0.08	+1.2[b]	$0.067
Deinking mills	− 0.30	+4.9[b]	0.065
Nonintegrated	− 0.49	+3.3[c]	0.148

a. Without knowing how the EPA "trades off" BOD versus TSS, we cannot compare the numbers for nonintegrated mills with those for the other subcategories.
b. For this subcategory, the binding constraint is the BOD standard; lower costs yield higher levels of BOD in the subcategory's effluent.
c. For this subcategory, the binding constraint is the suspended-solids standard; lower costs yield higher levels of TSS in the subcategory's effluent.

Thus, the EPA appears to have reduced the average cost of pollution abatement and the price of tissue to consumers by roughly comparable amounts. Furthermore, it appears that the reduction in standards yields distributional impacts consistent with the equal-pain principle. Low-cost producers receive cost decreases less than the price decrease ($0.11 per ton versus $0.20–$0.50 per ton); high-cost producers' cost decreases exceed the price decrease ($5.93 per ton versus $0.20–$0.50 per ton). For the average producer, costs and prices decrease by comparable amounts.

One could argue, of course, that the distributional consequences of the EPA's actions are incidental to its efforts to develop a rational environmental policy. Indeed, a policy that maximized environmental quality would equate cost—on the margin—across sources of pollution. (Strictly, the equation should be between incremental benefits and incremental costs. A proper assessment of this tradeoff would require geographic and other details.)

Differences in cost and waste loads associated with changes in standards can be observed in table 5.9. The evidence for the bleached kraft and deinking subcategories suggests that the EPA values BOD, on the margin, at about 6.5–6.7 cents per pound and that the leveling of the compliance-cost curve may be a result of the EPA's efforts to achieve an efficient environmental policy. Unfortunately for our purposes, the observed flattening of the tissue industry's compliance-cost curve is largely the consequence of changes in standards for nonintegrated producers. For these facilities, however, TSS is the constraining pollutant, and the rates at which the EPA "trades off" TSS for BOD are not known. Thus, we cannot now conclude whether the observed flattening of the compliance-cost curve is attributable to the EPA's response to an equity (equal pain) or an efficiency (equal marginal cost) criterion.[23]

Evaluating Regulation as a Social-Policy Tool

The model developed earlier in this article and its application to water-pollution controls in the pulp and paper industry provide several important insights into the use of business regulation to achieve selected public goals. These insights concern both how the effects of proposed regulations are modeled and how effectively public institutions consider these effects in formulating policy.

Perhaps the principal insight is that one must model industry on a disaggregated basis and in a dynamic context in order to measure the economic impacts of proposed regulations. This conclusion holds even if one is interested only in aggregate costs of regulations. Shifts in industry supply curves resulting from regulations are a function of the relationship between marginal costs imposed on individual plants by regulations and plants' existing cost structure. If the highest marginal control costs fall predominantly on the lowest-cost producers, the shift in the aggregate industry supply curve and the ultimate consumer burden will be relatively small. If the highest marginal control costs are incurred by the otherwise highest-cost producers, the resulting shift in the aggregate supply curve and changes in market prices could be quite large. Given the heterogeneous nature of the cost structures of firms in an industry, we conclude that virtually the only way to obtain information on an industry's "relevant margins" is with a highly disaggregated model such as the one developed here for the tissue segment of the pulp and paper industry.

Our efforts also reveal that the model should be dynamic as well as disaggregated. Many of the consequences of regulation surface as firms try to adjust their capital stock and rationalize operations to the new, regulated circumstances. These short-run costs are important both in determining the total cost of imposing regulations and in affecting the structure of the industry. For example, if short-run effects fall predominantly on small, marginal producers, the results might be the demise of these marginal producers (regardless of whether they could have been viable in the long run), large short-run price increases, and a more oligopolistic industry. Use of aggregate, static models and sole reliance on engineering-cost calculations of the capital and operating costs of regulatory compliance will miss these important effects entirely.

The model also points out the sensitivity of overall economic impacts to the administrative decisions of regulatory agencies. This is demonstrated by our analysis of the EPA's development of regulations for the tissue industry, where even relatively small changes in regulatory standards or definitions have large distributional impacts. The 1–3 percent reduction in BPT standards proposed by the EPA in 1976 relative to those proposed in 1975 constitutes a small reduction in overall pollution control. The analysis also implies that the aggregate cost savings to consumers is small; prices dropped by 0.03–0.07 percent ($0.20–$0.50 per ton on a base of $638 per ton). However, the redistribution of potential profits among firms is quite large.

From a policy-formation perspective it is important that administrative decisions are made by regulatory agencies well after Congress has made the decision to adopt a regulatory approach and legislated requirements to set standards. Because of this "decoupling" of legislative and administrative processes, it is extremely difficult for information about economic costs and their incidence to influence the initial decisions about the regulatory process. We feel that, because of the difficulty of predicting economic costs and the late timing of the decisions most relevant to costs, the choice to proceed with regulations and the decisions about their stringency are made without adequate attention to economic impacts.

The disincentives for adequate consideration of costs are compounded by the largely private nature of production and pollution-control costs. Most public activities require specific authorization and appropriation of public funds. Particularly with the present budget process, Congress is required explicitly to consider the costs of specific programs with respect to those of other programs, increased taxes, or larger deficits. These same procedures do not apply to most regulatory policies, however, because most costs of these programs never appear in government budgets. Dorfman (1975) estimated that in the long run only about 25 percent of the total abatement costs of air and water pollution-control programs passed in the early 1970s will be borne by the public sector. Since this includes state and local funds as well as federal, we may presume that Congress has passed legislation for which it must account for only a small proportion of the abatement costs. In light of this "off the balance sheet" financing and the absence of accountability, one may expect Congress to grant easy passage to privately expensive programs, particularly if they have attractive benefits.

Our findings are consistent with this hypothesis. Indeed, Congress was clearly under pressure from the public and from environmental interest groups "to do something about the environment" in 1972. We contend that the difficulty in predicting or even observing regulatory costs and the fact that many of these costs are not publicly funded help explain why Congress gave them so little consideration. In retrospect, it is rather striking to note that virtually all the Senate deliberations and important parts of the House debate concerned the size of the federally funded municipal-waste-treatment grant program, although it made up only a small fraction of total program costs. Although some representatives did try to raise questions about potential impacts of the regulations, and the House even considered a delay in mandating the 1985 and 1983 standards pending a National Academy of Sciences study on feasibility and impacts, these cautions were rejected. We pose an obvious question: If Congress were politically responsible for funding the full impact of its water-pollution program, would the legislation have passed both houses by so wide a margin?

A related difficulty concerns the timing of important decisions in the regulatory process and its consequences for rational social policymaking. We have already noted that the EPA's administrative decisions are important determinants of overall policy. It would be expected that potential impacts, such as those documented here, would influence both the legislative and administrative development of regulatory policy. Unfortunately, information on such impacts is not known to the Congress, and is not readily calculable, during the legislative process. Furthermore, the only institution potentially able to take these impacts into account (the EPA), like most administrative or regulatory agencies, is not structured to respond properly. In the first place, the EPA has little choice but to implement regulations mandated by the Congress. The agency cannot explicitly, and probably cannot even implicitly, decide that costs exceed possible benefits—either in the aggregate or even in local situations—and weaken the standards. Secondly, most administrative agencies will be lobbied and pressured by groups motivated by distributional impacts. But it is not clear that many agencies are institutionally structured to respond explicitly and rationally to such pressures. Thus, agency decisions undoubtedly reflect responses to "politically" motivated pressures, but we can have little confidence that these are socially appropriate responses for which an agency can or should be held accountable.

A final problem with the regulatory approach—and, in our view, the biggest weakness of our model—relates to uncertainty. A large array of complex and poorly understood factors influence the final regulations and their impacts. They range from the dynamic market structure of an industry, and its rate of technological change, to the narrow bureaucratic behavior of a regulatory agency. The effects of these and many other elements on promulgated standards are virtually impossible to predict, for policymakers, regulators, or businesses. It should be stressed that these uncertainties are not simply the conventional absence of information about the probability of various exogenously determined stochastic outcomes. Much uncertainty of regulatory effects is endogenous to the process. Incremental decisions of each participant, public and private, at each step in the development and promulgation of regulations, alter market structures and condition the subsequent behavior of individual firms and political actors. Given the magnitudes of the microlevel impacts of even small administrative decisions, we would expect that the endogenous character of uncertainty would significantly affect decisionmaking processes.

The length and complexity of the theoretical empirical exercise we have described in this paper should, by itself, be evidence for one of our principal conclusions: If it is easy for legislators to pass regulations, it is far from easy to accommodate adequately the complex and indirect effects of these regulations in the policymaking process. This suggests to us the need for caution in adopting regulatory prescriptions for social ills.

The Economic Development Administration provided the principal financial support for this research. Resources for the Future provided additional support. We are grateful to Professors Robert Dorfman, Malcolm Getz, John Meyer, and Roger Schmenner for their critical comments during the progress of this research. We are indebted to Gene Flood for his efforts to satisfy our constantly expanding data requirements.

Notes

1. See, for example, Kneese and Schultze 1975; Jacoby and Steinbruner 1973; National Academy of Sciences 1974. These studies examine policies intended to improve environmental quality, but reflect a continuing focus of analysts on the wider problems of controlling externalities through government regulation. A more general "Study of Federal Regulation" is now being prepared by the Committee on Government Affairs of the U.S. Senate. Much of the literature on regulation now focuses on issues of regulatory reform. This volume itself is a product of such a focus. See also Domestic Council Review Group on Regulatory Reform 1977 and any issue of *Regulation*, a magazine published by the American Enterprise Institute of Washington, D.C. Theoretical analysis of regulatory reform proposals fill the pages of the *Bell Journal*. Indeed, articles on regulatory reform are too numerous to mention. For a concise discussion of general principles, see Edley 1977.

2. National Academy of Science 1974 illustrates the complexities of this type of study. For a more disaggregated treatment of similar issues see Harrison 1975.

3. See Buchanan and Tullock 1975 for a discussion of some distributional consequences of different forms of regulation.

4. In our terminology, quasirents equal the difference between price and economic costs for new facilities, and the difference between price and variable costs for existing facilities.

5. The present value of $2.45/ton-year at a 10 percent discount rate is $24.50. The $24.50 rate is the present value of the time stream of the annually varying price increases actually forecast in Leone et al. 1975.

6. In other differences, the House version authorized an additional $4 billion for construction of local treatment plants, limited the EPA's control over state permit programs, restricted the ability of environmental groups to sue industry and the federal government over implementation of the act, and created an Environmental Financing Agency to help local governments pay their share of treatment-plant construction costs.

7. The other three all contain references to issues unrelated to the regulation of water quality, such as the authority of the Appropriations Committee, which make them poor indicators of the position of representatives on the issue of effluent standards.

8. For readers familiar with Guttman scales, this scale has a coefficient of reproducibility of 0.96 and a minimal marginal reproducibility of 0.77. These terms indicate that 96 percent of all votes cast fit the pattern (anything over 90 percent is considered a good scale) and that 77 percent could be correctly predicted by assuming that all representatives voted with the majority on each roll call.

9. The estimation procedure recognizes that the voting variable is a set of ordinal categories based on voting patterns described in tables 5.1 and 5.2. We do not know where each amendment is located on some underlying proregulation dimension, and we have grouped together representatives who may have different true positions but whose positions fall between the same two amendments. These problems make the dependent variable an interval measure of support for the regulations and thus inappropriate for ordinary least-squares regression. The estimation procedure used in this case is the n-chotomous extension of the multivariate probit model, which estimates both the location of the amendments and the parameters of the underlying relationship with the explanatory variables that make the observed grouping of legislators most likely. For a complete discussion, see Zavoina and McKelvey 1975.

10. The estimated equation is $\log$(Willingness to pay) $= -0.78 - 0.62 \times$ South $+ 0.04 \times$ Midwest $+ 0.19 \times$ West $+ 0.34 \times$ Suburb $- 0.11 \times$ Town $- 0.58 \times$ Rural $- 0.33 \times \log$(Family size) $- 0.53 \times \log$(Age) $+ 1.51 \times \log$(Education) $+ 0.99 \times \log$(Income).

11. Demographic data on congressional districts are available for the session beginning in 1973. Unfortunately, the massive redistricting demanded by the courts after the 1970 census significantly altered most districts' composition, making the 1973 data useless for analyzing votes in 1972.

12. Our own analysis shows that this is too simplistic a representation of a complex reality. For example, eleven of thirteen tissue-paper manufacturers in New England suffered a deterioration of relative competitive advantage due to the 1977 standards, but twelve of the thirteen actually reap a competitive advantage when the standards are tightened to the 1983 level. See Meyer and Leone 1978.

13. $-0.003 \times \$10/\text{ton} \times [(6,500 \text{ tons/day})/10^3] = -0.20.$

14. $(-0.18 - 0.003 \times 6 \text{ \$/ton}) \times [(6,500 \text{ tons/day})/10^3] = -1.30.$

15. These 64 mills have a total capacity, by our estimate, of 2.9 million metric tons of tissue per year. Lockwood's estimate of "practical maximum capacity" is 4.0 million tons per year. The difference stems, first, from problems associated with identification of the capacity of a single product in multiproduct operations, and, second and more important, from the lack of publicly available information on the capacity of several important mills in this industry. The magnitude of this difference is disturbing, but, practically and conceptually, our results do not appear sensitive to this discrepancy.

16. These are total economic costs; that is, they include a 15 percent return on investment.

17. These are total accounting costs; that is, they include depreciation and other fixed charges but exclude a return on investment.

18. A third explanation is that this industry does not operate according to strictly competitive principles. Our cost estimates are not sufficiently accurate to permit us to make a judgment on this point.

19. Astute managers may make capital investment decisions in a regulated environment on the basis of this effect. See Greening and Leone 1977. As significant regulations (particularly, price controls of one form or another) become more pervasive, this may be an increasingly common managerial practice.

20. Variable costs of manufacturing plus variable costs of BAT. In other words, economic costs of BAT determine whether a mill will or will not comply; but once this decision is made, prices will be set on the basis of variable costs alone.

21. Arthur D. Little, Inc. (1977) estimated the price elasticity of demand for tissue to be −0.45.

22. This was the advice of Ivan Metzger of Belmar, N.J., water and waste-water program management consultant to this and numerous other projects.

23. For a more detailed discussion of administrative reactions to the competitive effects described here, see Koch and Leone 1979.

References

American Paper Institute. 1974. *Monthly Statistical Summary*, November.

Arthur D. Little, Inc. 1977. *Economic Impacts of Pulp and Paper Industry Compliance with Environmental Regulations*. Cambridge, Mass.

Barone, Michael, Ujifusa, Grant, and Matthews, Douglas. 1972. *Almanac of American Politics*. Boston: Gambit.

Buchanan, James, and Tullock, Gordon. 1975. "Polluters' profits and Political Response: Direct Controls versus Taxes." *American Economic Review* 65: 139–147.

Dorfman, Nancy, and Snow, Arthur. 1975. "Who Will Pay for Pollution Control? The Distribution by Income of the Burden of the National Environmental Protection Program, 1972–1980." *National Tax Journal* 28: 101–115.

Edley, Christopher. 1977. Toward a Framework for Analysis of Regulatory Reform. Mimeographed. Harvard University.

Erskine, Hazel. 1972. "The Polls: Pollution and its Cost." *Public Opinion Quarterly* 36: 120–135.

Greening, T., and Leone, R. A. 1977. Energy Corporation of Louisana (A) and (B). Cases 9-678-054 and 9-687-055. Intercollegiate Case Clearing House, Boston.

Harrison, David. 1976. *Who Pays for Clean Air?* Cambridge, Mass.: Ballinger.

Ingram, Helen. 1979. "The Political Rationality of Innovation: The Clean Air Amendment of 1970." In Ann F. Friedlaender (ed.), *Approaches to Controlling Air Pollution*. Cambridge, Mass.: MIT Press.

Jackson, J. 1979. Measuring the Demand for Environmental Quality with Survey Data. Working paper, Center for Political Studies, University of Michigan, Ann Arbor.

Jacoby, Henry D., and Steinbruner, John. 1973. *Clearing the Air*. Cambridge, Mass.: Ballinger.

Kneese, Allen V., and Schultze, Charles L. 1975. *Pollution, Prices and Public Policy*. Washington, D.C.: Brookings Institution.

Koch, C. J., and Leone, R. A. 1979. "The Clean Water Act: Unexpected Impacts on Industry." *Harvard Environmental Law Review* 3: 84–111.

Leone, R. A. 1977. "The Real Costs of Regulation." *Harvard Business Review*, November–December: 57–66.

———. 1978. Derivation of Production Costs for Tissue Producers. Working paper, Harvard Graduate School of Business Administration.

Leone, R. A., Startz, R., and Farber, M. 1975. The Economic Impact of the 1972 Amendments to the Federal Water Pollution Control Act on the Pulp and Paper Industry: A Report to the National Commission of Water Quality by the National Bureau of Economic Research. National Technical Information Service report PB-248801.

Meyer, J. R., and Leone, R. A. 1978. "The New England States and their Future: Some Implications of a Changing Industrial Environment." *American Economic Review* 68: 110–115.

National Academy of Sciences. 1974. The Costs and Benefits of Automobile Emission Control, Vol. 4. Prepared for Senate Committee on Public Works.

Schultze, Charles L. 1977. "The Public Use of the Private Interest." *Harper's*, May: 43–62.

United States Domestic Council Review Group on Regulatory Reform. 1977. The Challenge of Regulatory Reform. Report to the President.

Zavoina, William, and McKelvey, Richard. 1975. "A Statistical Model for the Analysis of Ordinal Level Dependent Variables." *Journal of Mathematical Sociology* 4: 103–120.

Comment

Allen V. Kneese

I am extremely impressed with the research reported in this paper. General statements about indirect effects of pollution-control regulations and about the distribution of costs and benefits among firms, regions, and individuals are to be found in the literature, but this paper represents the most far-reaching attempt at quantification of these effects and of linking the results to the political processes involved in implementation that I have seen. The authors' research has yielded some important insights. For example, I blush to admit that it had never occurred to me that some (or, as the authors show, perhaps many) firms in an industry could actually benefit from pollution regulation. This is an important finding that, again as the authors show, may yield important insights into both the legislation and the implementation of pollution-control policy.

Editor's note: At the conference, Professor Kneese provided a brief legislative history of various water-pollution-control amendments. For a full discussion see Kneese and Schultze 1975 (listed in references above).

Comment

Richard Zeckhauser

Contemporary theories of government regulation are distressingly incomplete. Rarely are their assumptions or conclusions put to rigorous test. In many ways this is understandable. At least in the federal sphere, a single agency is generally responsible for dealing with a particular problem; we have no opportunity to make judicious comparisons among different regulatory approaches. Variation occurs only over time, with too many factors changing simultaneously to permit strong conclusions. Many of the most important variables elude quantification.

When solid data are not available, it becomes all the more important to pull together every shard of information. This is not easy to do in the area of regulation. An understanding of political science, empirical analysis, economic model building, and business behavior would be required for an effective "assembly job." This is what Leone, a business administration professor with a background in economics, and Jackson, a quantitatively oriented professor of political science, have attempted in this article, which explores the links between political decisions on regulation and their anticipated economic consequences. That their success is limited does not diminish their accomplishment.

This is an ambitious and unconventional article, ranging widely from theoretical models to empirical analyses, from legislative to administrative behavior, from the purely economic to the predominantly political, from broad economic magnitudes to data on individual mills. Some exercises are more successful than others.

The authors are to be applauded, for instance, for undertaking statistical work to explain congressional voting patterns on environmental legislation. The data, however, do not fully support their conclusion that "congressional voting on the 1972 amendments was sensitive to the potential direct economic effects on a district." Only one of the five variables they employ to represent economic activity affected results in a statistically significant manner. Two had values not worth distinguishing from zero. Of the remaining two, which are about equal in significance, one had a sign contrary to prediction. Hardly an impressive record.

Leone and Jackson then go on to a more sophisticated model, which if validated would be a considerable contribution. The notion is that firms may be primarily concerned with the way environmental impositions will affect their position within their industry, rather than with the effect on the industry in general. Through a more sophisticated investigation, a firm may determine that a proposed regulation would hurt it less than others and would thus represent a source of competitive advantage. In this case, the congressional representatives of relatively advantaged firms might be more receptive to the proposed legislation. This hypothesis should appeal particularly to economic determinists and regulatory cynics. It goes one step beyond the common refrain that once regulation is imposed, the surviving members of the industry are likely to welcome its continuance. Leone and Jackson suggest that firms will make an *a priori* assessment of whether proposed regulatory measures will hurt or help them relative to their competitors. The observed voting patterns do not validate this hypothesis. It is not clear, however, whether firms do not make such assessments or whether congressmen do not vote according to the interests of firms within their districts.

Indeed, the sad news is that the variables that are most significant statistically are the very ones we would have suspected were important had we never heard of economics: geographic region and party affiliation. (There is so much collinearity between "South" and Southern Democrat" that it is hard to know what to make of the interaction between region and party.) One other variable is significant: the age of the representative. Leone and Jackson merely conclude that "younger representatives show preferences for more stringent regulations than older ones." Perhaps age is just the correlate here, and the real factor is recency of election. If the electorate is becoming more sensitive to the environment, and if incumbents have some tendency to adhere to their former views, then the newly elected, who are likely to be younger, are also likely to be more environment-minded. Alternatively, a long incumbency may merely provide concentrated political interests (in this case, it would be those opposed to environmental programs) greater opportunity to exert their pressures.

Leone and Jackson have constructed an interesting independent variable for their vote-prediction model, basically a count of how many proenvironment issues a congressman has favored. Such constructed variables, when there is a natural spectrum but not a natural scale, may have unusual properties—particularly when there is a clustering at one extreme, as there was here with the proenvironment group. The use of variables of this sort demands caution in testing hypotheses or drawing any other statistical conclusions. To avoid misinterpretation, the authors should have said a bit more about their estimation techniques.

In the last portion of their article, Leone and Jackson delve into specific data on the tissue industry. They go down to the level of individual mills to judge differential cost impacts and differential effects in terms of quasirents (and in some cases viability itself) in the face of EPA effluent standards. These standards were proposed in 1975, revised in 1976 in response to industry comment, and revised once again when they became final in 1977. By exploring how the EPA responded to the predicted effects of its impositions on the distribution of quasirents, the authors hope to shed light on administrative decisionmaking in general. Their central hypothesis is that political pressure would lead the EPA to design its standards to pursue what might be perceived as equity objectives as opposed to those of efficiency (equal marginal cost of cleanup across firms). Equity, as always, is an ambiguous concept. At the very least, however, it would seem to connote that some firms should not be driven out of business while others suffer mildly or even benefit. That is the interpretation it is given here. Unfortunately, insufficient data prevent the authors from testing this hypothesis.

In formulating this hypothesis, Leone and Jackson are in accord with much contemporary thinking about the formulation of government policy. In response to both political pressure and appeals to equity, government agencies and actors (legislative, administrative, and executive) are thought to avoid solutions that would impose large costs on an identified group of parties. In future studies, perhaps of other industries, it seems likely that the authors could bear out their models and conjectures.

The chief weakness of this article is that it conveys little useful factual knowledge. To some extent this may be due to inadequate data. Some of the major hypotheses, however, may remain unvalidated for a more fundamental reason: they may simply not be true. If so, disproof would be an important contribution in itself.

At least in the deductive portions of the article, Leone and Jackson have carried economic models of political phenomena beyond conventional analyses. They suggest that both agency and legislative decisions will be strongly influenced by economic consequences, and further that it may be important to consider the distributional consequences within an industry and to distinguish short- and long-term effects. They raise two important questions that remain open: Can the behavior of political and bureaucratic man, or at least his actions in the regulatory arena, be explained as a response to economic factors? If so, can he or his constituents and pressure groups be as sophisticated in their assessments as are the models of this paper? This ambitious essay suggests that future efforts by Leone and Jackson may make an important contribution to resolving these issues.

6

Regulation and the Multiproduct Firm: The Case of Telecommunications in Canada

Melvyn Fuss
Leonard Waverman

We report here the results of a theoretical and empirical investigation of the problems of public regulation when a regulated firm produces more than one output using common production facilities. Measurement and interpretation of economies of scale become complex, especially if one wants to attribute any existing scale economies to a particular product.[1] The problem of efficient pricing in the presence of joint or common costs is also an issue of concern. These problems, and others, require consideration of the production technology and of the costs faced by the firm. The natural vehicle for such an analysis is the multiproduct cost function, since its arguments are outputs and input prices. Recent advances in the econometric literature (Diewert 1971) have made possible the use of cost functions to represent general structures of technology. The advent of multiproduct generalized cost functions could provide an important econometric supplement to cost-separation studies in regulatory hearings.[2]

We discuss theoretical problems associated with analyzing the production technology of a multiproduct firm (aggregation of output, economies of scale, economies of scope, cost separation), give a detailed econometric specification, and develop a constrained profit-maximizing model of a regulated telecommunciations firm in which the level of local service output is chosen by the regulators rather than by the firm. We apply this model to data generated by Bell Canada during the period 1952–1975.

Rate-of-return regulation creates potential difficulties for estimation of the production technology. If such regulation is effective, estimates of parameters of the production technology that ignore this fact may be biased. We demonstrate how the theory of duality between cost and production can be used to specify a multiproduct cost function and associated derived demand functions which explicitly incorporate effects of rate-of-return regulation.

The Separation of Common and Joint Costs

When firms produce two or more outputs utilizing common or joint inputs, two problems arise: the allocation of these common or joint costs to the separate outputs, and the measurement of aggregate output for the firm.

Common costs are defined as the costs of common inputs utilized by two or more outputs, so that the multiproduct transformation function is represented by

$$F(Y_1,\ldots,Y_m;X_1,\ldots,X_n) = 0, \tag{1}$$

where Y_i $(i = 1,\ldots,m)$ are outputs and X_j $(j = 1,\ldots,n)$ are inputs. Were costs not common, (1) could be rewritten as

$$Y_1 = F_1(X_1,\ldots,X_d),$$

$$Y_2 = F_2(X_{d+1},\ldots,X_h),$$

$$\ldots \tag{2}$$

$$Y_m = F_m(X_{k+1},\ldots,X_n),$$

where $j = 1,\ldots,d,\ldots,h,\ldots,k,\ldots,n$.

Joint costs as they are defined in the regulation literature occur when two or more outputs are produced in fixed proportions; it is impossible to produce some proportion λ of 1 without also producing λ of the others (Kahn 1971). The product transformation curve can then be represented as

$$F(X_1,\ldots,X_n) = \min(a_1 Y_1, a_2 Y_2,\ldots,a_m Y_m). \tag{3}$$

Note that (3) is the limiting case of (1). In the following discussion we will treat the problems of common and joint costs as the same issue, referring instead to *joint production*, as represented by equation (1). Whether costs are "joint" or whether production is characterized by fixed coefficients can be tested empirically.

When a firm produces heterogeneous products, there is no single unique index of output. For an index $h(Y)$ to be formed, the product transformation function must be written as

$$F(Y_1,\ldots,Y_m; X_1,\ldots,X_n) = F(h(Y),X_1,\ldots,X_n). \tag{4}$$

But (4) can be rewritten as $F(h(Y),g(x)) = 0$, since the existence of an output aggregate implies the existence of an input aggregate (Brown et al. 1976; Baumol and Braunstein 1977).[3] As a result, the dual joint cost function is separable in outputs. But then the relative marginal costs of the outputs are independent of input prices—a strong assumption (see Lau 1978).

Most regulated industries involve joint production. Electric utilities produce peak and off-peak kWh utilizing common generating transmission and distribution capacity. Railroads use the same roadbed for passenger and freight traffic. Telecommunications firms provide a wide variety of services: residential local switched calls, business local switched calls, residential switched toll calls, business switched toll calls, private wire service, teletypewriter exchange service, specialized common-carrier service, and a variety of broadband data services. All switched calls utilize local exchange switching equipment in common. Toll calls utilize common interoffice switching equipment and common intercity communications equipment. Business switched and nonswitched private wire services all use common intercity plant. These are but several of the many examples of joint production in the telecommunications sector.

It is difficult to find examples of true joint costs in telecommunications except in a temporal distribution sense. An increase in the number of circuits between two points provides increased capacity which is distributed between day and night-time calls in fixed proportions. But this same increase in peak circuit availability can provide a varying proportion of business and residential calls, hence the increase in plant is common to business and residential use but joint between peak and off-peak use. In the remainder of the paper when we use the term "jointness" we mean in the production sense, encompassing both common and joint costs as used in the regulation literature.

Effective regulation poses the following fundamental questions:

• What range of services is best supplied by a single firm? What are the production economies of scale (the change in average and marginal costs when firm size is increased)?[4] What are the economies of scope (the change in average and marginal costs when services are combined within a single firm)?[5] Economies of scope exist if and only if production is joint.

• What are the long-run marginal costs of producing one more unit of any one of the joint outputs $(Y_1, \ldots, Y_m)$?

The first set of analyses help determine the size of the firm and the degree of competition to be allowed;[6] the second analysis allows the examination of the efficiency of any rate structure.

Cost Functions, Economies of Scale, and Economies of Scope

The Multiproduct Cost Function
A multiproduct production process can be represented by the product transformation function

$$F(Y_1,\ldots,Y_m;X_1,\ldots,X_n) = 0, \tag{5}$$

where Y_i $(i = 1,\ldots,m)$ are outputs and X_j $(j = 1,\ldots,n)$ are inputs.[7]

In this section we consider only the case where rate-of-return regulation either is not used by the regulatory authorities or else is ineffective. In either case, we may assume that the firm pursues cost-minimizing behavior without regard to the possibilities of Averch-Johnson-type distortions. In that case, the theory of duality between cost and production (see Diewert 1971) ensures that for every transformation function of the type shown in equation (1) there exists a dual cost function of the form

$$C = C(Y_1,\ldots,Y_m;P_1,\ldots,P_n), \tag{6}$$

where $P_j(j = 1,\ldots,n)$ are the prices paid by the firm for the inputs X_j— as long as the product transformation function satisfies the usual regularity conditions (such as convex isoquants), the firm pursues cost-minimizing behavior, and the firm has no control over input prices.

Under these assumptions, the cost function is just as basic a description of the technology as the product transformation (joint production) function, and it contains all the required information, including information on jointness.

The properties of the multiproduct cost function (6) are that C is concave in P_j, linearly homogeneous in P_j, and increasing in Y_i and P_j; that $\partial C/\partial P_j = X_j$ (Shephard's lemma);[8] and that the own-price elasticities of factor demand are given by

$$\varepsilon_{jj} = P_j \frac{\partial^2 C}{\partial P_j^2} \Big/ \frac{\partial C}{\partial P_j}.$$

Economies of Scale and Incremental Costs
The fact that average cost (cost per unit of output) is not defined for multiple-output technologies makes analysis of returns to scale somewhat complex, since we can no longer just measure the effect of output increases on the average cost of production. In addition, we need to distinguish between economies of scale in some overall sense (that is, when all outputs are increased) and economies of scale associated with the expansion of a particular output (with all other outputs held constant). We begin by considering an overall measure of returns to scale.

"Overall" returns to scale can be obtained by computing

$$dC = \sum_{i=1}^{m} \frac{\partial C}{\partial Y_i} dY_i$$

or

$$d \log C = \sum_{i=1}^{m} \frac{\partial \log C}{\partial \log Y_i} \frac{dY_i}{Y_i}. \tag{7}$$

Equation (7) represents the total change in cost resulting from differential changes in the levels of the m outputs. Unfortunately, unless we add additional structure to equation (7) it is difficult to interpret changes in cost resulting from changes in outputs in terms of returns to scale. One common procedure is to assume that all outputs are increased in proportion; that is, $dY_i/Y_i = d \log Y_i = \lambda$. Then

$$\frac{d \log C}{\lambda} = \sum_{i=1}^{m} \frac{\partial \log C}{\partial \log Y_i}. \tag{8}$$

If $d \log C/\lambda > 1$, incremental overall costs are increasing and hence production is subject to decreasing returns to scale; if $d \log C/\lambda < 1$, the technology exhibits increasing returns to scale; if $d \log C/\lambda = 1$, overall constant returns to scale exist.

This overall description of returns to scale is somewhat less relevant in the multiple-output case than in the single-output case, since it requires all outputs to be increasing in strict proportion, which may not correspond to the optimal production plan. Nevertheless, the overall-returns-to-scale number can be a useful summary statistic for comparing results obtained from the present framework with returns to scale estimated from aggregate production or cost functions (that is, functions that aggregate all outputs into a single variable).

Now consider the concept of returns to scale with respect to a single output. From equation (7),

$$\frac{d \log C}{d \log Y_i}\bigg|_{Y_j, j \neq i \text{ constant}} = \frac{\partial \log C}{\partial \log Y_i}. \tag{9}$$

The term $\partial \log C/\partial \log Y_i$, the output cost elasticity, represents incremental or marginal cost in percentage terms.

It is tempting to specify that if

$$\frac{\partial \log C}{\partial \log Y_i} = \frac{Y_i}{C} \frac{\partial C}{\partial Y_i} > 1,$$

returns to scale in producing the ith output are decreasing; that if

$$\frac{\partial \log C}{\partial \log Y_i} < 1,$$

they are increasing; and that if

$$\frac{\partial \log C}{\partial \log Y_i} = 1,$$

they are constant. This specification would yield the correct trichotomy for the case of a single-output production process. However, any attempt to use this definition can lead to a conflict with the definition of overall returns to scale introduced earlier. Consider the two-output Cobb-Douglas cost function

$$C = A Y_1^{\alpha_1} Y_2^{\alpha_2}. \tag{10}$$

Overall decreasing returns to scale implies

$$\sum \frac{\partial \log C}{\partial \log Y_i} = \alpha_1 + \alpha_2 > 1. \tag{11}$$

However, $\partial \log C / \partial \log Y_i = \alpha_i$ can be < 1 while $\alpha_1 + \alpha_2 > 1$, which leads to a contradiction between our overall and the proposed output-specific returns to scale measures. Thus, we must reject the use of the individual-product cost elasticities as indicators of returns to scale. However, if one of the cost elasticities exceeds unity, the sum of them will also exceed unity and therefore no contradiction will arise.

Can we define a meaningful indicator of the potential advantages or disadvantages of output expansion? Since cost elasticity cannot be used, the remaining intuitive concept is that of changes in incremental cost. It would appear, at first glance, that decreasing incremental cost ($\partial^2 C / \partial Y_i^2 < 0$) should indicate increasing returns to scale. However, we will show that this marginal-cost concept also does not provide a solution to the problem of developing an unambigous indicator of scale economies. It can easily be shown that

$$\frac{\partial^2 C}{\partial Y_i^2} = \frac{C}{Y_i^2} \left[\frac{\partial^2 \log C}{\partial \log Y_i^2} + \frac{\partial \log C}{\partial \log Y_i} \left(\frac{\partial \log C}{\partial \log Y_i} - 1 \right) \right]. \tag{12}$$

The usual situation is that $\partial \log C / \partial \log Y_i < 1$. The more disaggregated the output vector, the more likely it is that $\partial \log C / \partial \log Y_i < 1$. If we accept this case, then an additional sufficient condition for $\partial^2 C / \partial Y_i^2 < 0$ is that $\partial^2 \log C / \partial \log Y_i^2 < 0$; that is, that cost elasticity is a decreasing function of output. In all such cases, a highly possible outcome is that marginal costs with respect to each output will decrease ($\partial^2 C / \partial Y_i^2 < 0$) and, at the same time, overall returns to scale will also decrease ($\Sigma_j (\partial \log C / \partial \log Y_i) > 1$). In addition, for any given degrees of jointness and overall returns to scale, it is possible (for the case of decreasing cost elasticity) to increase the rate at which marginal costs decline simply by further disaggregation of the outputs. These two possibilities should be sufficient warning against using any observed decreasing marginal cost as an indicator of sub-product-specific returns to scale. In fact, there exists no unambiguous measure of output-specific returns to scale except in the case of nonjoint production,[9] since separate cost functions cannot be constructed when common costs exist. Thus, we appear to be left with only the overall measure of returns to scale.[10] Unfortunately, this measure is of no value when one is attempting to evaluate the possible efficiency gains from increasing the scale of production of one of the outputs in a multiproduct production process.

Joint Production, Economies of Scope, and Subadditivity
To this point we have assumed that the production technology is truly a multiple-output one, in the sense that it is more efficient to produce the m outputs together than by separate production processes. This efficiency condition (jointness in production) is known in the industrial organization literature as *economies of scope* (see Panzer and Willig 1975, 1979; Baumol and Braunstein 1977).

For the purposes of this paper, we will say that the production technology exhibits economies of scope if

$$C(Y_1 \cdots Y_m) < C(Y_1, 0 \cdots 0) + C(0, Y_2, 0 \cdots 0) + C(0, 0, Y_3 \cdots 0)$$

$$+ \cdots + C(0, 0 \cdots 0, Y_m). \tag{13}$$

Panzer and Willig (1979) have shown that a sufficient condition for a twice-differentiable multiproduct cost function to exhibit economies of scope is that it exhibit cost complementarities, defined by

$$\frac{\partial^2 C}{\partial Y_i \partial Y_j} < 0 \qquad (i \neq j; i,j = 1,\ldots,m). \tag{14}$$

Conditions (14) provide a means of testing for the existence of economies of scope.

In a series of articles, Baumol (1977b), Baumol, Bailey, and Willig (1977), and Panzer and Willig (1977) have established the importance of "subadditivity of the cost function" as a production characteristic in the analysis of a regulated monopolist. Unfortunately, a test for subadditivity is difficult to devise, since one of the requirements is a knowledge of the cost function in the neighborhood of zero outputs. The closest we can

come is a (weak) local test in the neighborhood of the point of approximation. It can be shown that the simultaneous existence of local economies of scale and local economies of scope is sufficient to ensure local
subadditivity.

Cost Separation and Econometric Cost Functions

The transcripts of regulatory hearings in the telecommunications sector
are replete with discussions of how to allocate joint and common cost.[11,12]
In the United States, since some of the telephone plant is under state
jurisdiction and some under federal jurisdiction, it became necessary to
"separate" interstate from intrastate plant. When regulators became concerned with the structure of prices rather then just their average level,
costs of different services had to be separated. The push for entry by
specialized common carriers (SCCs) and AT&T's competitive response
prompted the F.C.C. requests for guidance from affected parties. In
Canada, competitive pressures between two transnational carriers and
suggestions of "cream skimming" and predatory pricing prompted a
lengthy cost inquiry.

Three basic separation formulas have been proposed: embedded direct
cost (EDC), long-run increamental cost (LRIC), and fully distributed
cost (FDC). These formulas are needed in order to assess "correct"
prices. The FDC method is essentially one of long-run average cost
pricing. Two methods have been proposed to fully distributed these
average costs: relative use (revenue share, for example) and historical cost
causation.[13]

The calculation of average embedded direct costs is equivalent to the
measurement of short-run variable costs. Unless there are no fixed costs,
long-run pricing at EDC will generate losses. FDC in principle takes into
account the fixed costs. However, pricing on the basis of FDC is associated
with a number of problems. Where production is characterized by long-
run returns to scale, setting price equal to average FDC is inefficient
since, for Pareto optimality, prices *ex ante* should be set equal to long-run
incremental costs. Separating common costs by some measure of relative
use is arbitrary and should not be used as a basis for price setting, since
there is in general no connection between intensity of use and cost
causation.

Cost separation is a bogus issue that exists because of regulatory
commissions' reliance on historical average costs as a guide to setting
price. But there is no method of correctly separating historical average

costs. Pricing rules based on efficiency criteria should be set at long-run incremental costs, thus avoiding any need to "separate" costs.

One must be careful in defining the long run, in order to be certain that incremental costs are measured in terms of changes in capacity output, not changes in actual output at less than capacity.[14] As an example, let us examine the data-telecommunications market. Carriers have argued that the incremental costs of data service are low since it is an adjunct to the large monopoly switched message service that must be provided for voice transmission. However, if the quality of the entire system must be increased to accommodate an acceptable level of reliability for data transmission, these upgrading costs are attributable to data-service users and should be fully charged to them alone as part of the incremental costs of the change in the system. This higher quality of service is provided jointly to all users, but quality-upgrading joint costs should be solely allocated to the data-service users.

Can econometric analysis of the retrospective cost functions of telecommunications firms provide useful information for regulatory purposes? In theory, given highly disaggregated data corresponding to true economic variables in the absence of strong time trends, long-run incremental costs could be allocated on a historical assigned-cause basis.[15]

Econometric cost function analysis can be used to examine the response of a firm at the margin; that is, at the replacement values or opportunity costs of inputs. Costs are minimized subject to current factor prices. Regulators, while allowing the firm to use opportunity costs for labor and materials inputs, insist that the firm earn its allowed rate of return on the historical cost of the capital stock, not its replacement cost. As a result, costs and prices as determined under a regime of historical-cost rate base will differ from the incremental costs and prices determined by an econometric cost function.[16]

In a period of inflation, historical costs will be less than replacement costs. Incremental costs determined econometrically will then exceed historical "incremental" costs. One of the purposes of cost separation is to estimate the relative contributions of the various services—that is, the excess of price over historical cost. Comparing actual prices (those set by regulators on the basis of historical cost) with incremental replacement costs is no guide in determining the extent of cross-subsidization inherent in the actual price structure (when replacement and historical costs differ).

Incremental replacement costs are, however, a guide to efficient pricing behavior. Where economies of scale are not present, setting the price for each service equal to the incremental replacement cost (as determined by an econometric cost function) yields the set of subsidy-free Pareto-optimal prices. If there are economies of scale and the firm is constrained to at least break even, calculating the set of Ramsey prices on the basis of these incremental replacement costs leads to the most efficient "constrained" set of prices, assuming neutrality in interpersonal comparisons (that is, where distributional consequences are disregarded).

Econometric Specification of a Joint Production Process

Profit-Maximizing Model for a Multioutput Regulated Firm
Estimates of demand elasticities indicate that regulated telecommunications firms operate some services in the region of inelastic demand.[17] But profit-maximizing monopolies will never produce where marginal revenue is negative; to do so would require setting marginal revenue equal to negative marginal costs. If marginal costs are positive, an unregulated profit-maximizing monopoly finding itself in the inelastic region of demand would raise price (lower output) to increase total revenue.[18] However, many regulated utilities are not able to lower output, since the regulators insist that certain basic services be offered at prices that force the monopolist to remain in the inelastic region. One example is passenger train service. Most railroad firms would wish to reduce passenger service and raise its price. However, regulators in North America do not permit rail companies to raise the price of this service to the profit-maximizing level, although they do require the provision of passenger seats.

All studies of the telephone industry suggest that local telephone service is characterized by inelastic demand. The observed level of local service and the corresponding price are chosen not by a profit-maximizing monopolist, but by the regulators. As a result, it is reasonable to assume that the observed level of local service is not an endogenous choice variable to the firm. Instead, we consider the level of local service exogenous to the firm.

The firm's problem is to maximize profits,

$$\pi = \Sigma q_i Y_i - C(Y_1, \ldots, Y_m; P_1, \ldots, P_n), \tag{15}$$

subject to the constraint on the provision of certain services:

$$Y_i \geq \bar{Y}_i \qquad (i \in H),$$

where H is the class of outputs constrained by the regulators, assumed to be the first H outputs. (Note that if demand were inelastic in the region of Y_i, the firm would never decide to offer more than $\bar{Y}_i$.[19])

Substituting into the profit expression, we obtain

$$\pi = \sum_{i \notin H} q_i Y_i + \sum_{i \in H} q_i \bar{Y}_i - C(\bar{Y}_1 \cdots \bar{Y}_H, Y_{H+1} \cdots Y_m, P_1 \cdots P_n).$$

For profit-maximizing behavior we have the first-order conditions

$$\frac{\partial \pi}{\partial Y_i} = q_i + Y_i \frac{\partial q_i}{\partial Y_i} - \frac{\partial C}{\partial Y_i} = 0 \qquad (i = H + 1, \ldots, m), \tag{16}$$

or[20]

$$MR_i = MC_i \qquad (i = H + 1, \ldots, m).$$

In addition, the second-order conditions for maximization require that[21]

$$\frac{\partial MR_i}{\partial Y_i} \leq \frac{\partial MC_i}{\partial Y_i}. \tag{17}$$

For observed output levels such that demand is elastic, we assume that marginal revenue is set equal to marginal cost. For output levels such that demand is inelastic, we assume that those outputs are exogenous to the firm.

The Multiple-Output Translog Cost Function

The translog cost function is becoming an increasingly popular specification of the functional form of a cost function (Brown et al. 1976; and Fuss 1977). The function is quadratic in logarithms and is one of the family of second-order Taylor-series approximations to an arbitrary cost function. The multiple-output translog cost function, assuming capital-augmenting technical change (input n), takes the form[22]

$$\log C = \alpha_0 + \sum_{i=1}^{m} \alpha_i \log Y_i + \sum_{j=1}^{n-1} \beta_j \log P_j + \beta_n \log P_n^*$$

$$+ \frac{1}{2} \sum_{i=1}^{m} \sum_{k=1}^{m} \delta_{ik} \log Y_i \log Y_k + \frac{1}{2} \sum_{j=1}^{n-1} \sum_{k=1}^{n-1} \gamma_{jk} \log P_j \log P_k$$

$$+ \frac{1}{2} \sum_{j=1}^{n} \gamma_{jn} \log P_j \log P_n^* + \sum_{i=1}^{m} \sum_{j=1}^{n-1} \rho_{ij} \log Y_i \log P_j$$

$$+ \sum_{i=1}^{m} \rho_{in} \log Y_i \log P_n^*, \tag{18}$$

where α_0, α_i, β_j, δ_{ik}, γ_{jk}, ρ_{ij} are parameters to be estimated, and $P_n^* = P_n e^{-\theta t}$ where θ is the rate of decline in the price of a nominal unit of capital due to capital-augmenting technical change. (In all the following equations, the asterisk notation is dropped unless it is important for interpretation.)

Using Shephard's lemma ($\partial C/\partial P_j = X_j$), we have

$$\frac{\partial \log C}{\partial \log P_j} = \frac{P_j X_j}{C} = M_j = \beta_j + \sum_k \gamma_{jk} \log P_k + \sum_i \rho_{ij} \log Y_i, \tag{19}$$

where $j = 1, \ldots, n$ and M_j is the cost share of the jth input.

Equations (18) and (19) make up the cost system. However, a number of features of the system reduce the number of parameters to be estimated. Since M_j is a cost share,

$$\sum_{j=1}^{n} M_j = 1;$$

this implies

$$\sum_j \beta_j = 1, \qquad \sum_j \gamma_{jk} = 0, \qquad \sum_j \rho_{ij} = 0.$$

In addition, the linear homogeneity property of cost functions outlined earlier implies the further parameter restrictions

$$\sum_k \gamma_{jk} = 0.$$

Finally, the fact that the function is a second-order approximation implies

$$\delta_{ik} = \delta_{ki}, \qquad \gamma_{jk} = \gamma_{kj}.$$

The translog cost function can be used along with the profit-maximizing conditions to generate additional equations representing the optimal choice of endogenous outputs.

Taking the derivations of the cost function with respect to endogenous outputs, we have[23]

$$\frac{\partial \log C}{\partial \log Y_i} = \frac{\partial C}{\partial Y_i}\frac{Y_i}{C} = MR_i \frac{Y_i}{C} = \frac{q_i(1 + 1/\varepsilon_i)\,Y_i}{C}, \tag{20}$$

where ε_i is the own price elasticity for the ith output. Denoting $q_i\,Y_i/C$ as R_i, the "revenue share," we obtain

$$R_i = \frac{\partial \log C}{\partial \log Y_i}\left(1 + \frac{1}{\varepsilon_i}\right)^{-1}. \tag{21}$$

For the translog system the sum of the R_i is not constrained to be unity, since the firm is not constrained to earn zero economic profits.[24] Using the translog cost function, the system of equations (21) become

$$R_i = \left(\alpha_i + \sum_k \delta_{ik} \log Y_k + \sum_j \rho_{ij} \log P_j \right) \left(1 + \frac{1}{\varepsilon_i} \right)^{-1}, \tag{22}$$

where $i = H + 1, \ldots, m$.

Factor Price Elasticity, Incremental Costs, Overall Economies of Scale, and Economies of Scope with the Translog Cost Function

It can be shown that the own price elasticity of demand for factor j can be computed as (see Berndt and Wood 1975)

$$\varepsilon_{jj} = \frac{\partial \log X_j}{\partial \log P_j} = \frac{\gamma_{jj} - M_j + M_j^2}{M_j}. \tag{23}$$

Once γ_{jj} is estimated, the above price elasticities are determined. The incremental or marginal cost elasticity of producing output i is

$$\frac{\partial \log C}{\partial \log Y_i} = \alpha_i + \sum_k \delta_{ik} \log Y_k + \sum_j \rho_{ij} \log P_j. \tag{24}$$

The incremental cost curve for output Y_i can be obtained as

$$\text{ICC}(Y_i) = \frac{C}{Y_i} \left(\alpha_i + \delta_{ii} \log Y_i + \sum_{k \neq i} \delta_{ik} \log \bar{Y}_k + \sum_j \rho_{ij} \log \bar{P}_j \right), \tag{25}$$

where $\bar{Y}_k$ and $\bar{P}_j$ are preassigned constant outputs and prices, respectively. The "overall" returns-to-scale number can be obtained from

$$\frac{d \log C}{\lambda} = \sum_i \frac{\partial \log C}{\partial \log Y_i}$$

$$= \sum_i \alpha_i + \sum_i \sum_k \delta_{ik} \log Y_k + \sum_i \sum_j \rho_{ij} \log P_j. \tag{26}$$

Economies of scope or jointness in production can only be tested in the translog framework using the approximate tests discussed by Denny and Fuss (1977). The condition is that

$$\delta_{ij} = -\alpha_i \alpha_j \qquad (i \neq j),$$

when the data have been scaled so that all $Y_i = P_j = 1$ at the point of approximation.[25]

Specialized Descriptions of Technology and the Translog Cost Function
Three specialized descriptions of technology are often assumed in the estimation of production structures. The joint production function $F(Y_1,\ldots,Y_m;X_1,\ldots,X_m) = 0$ is said to have a *separable* input-output structure if it can be written in the form

$$G(Y_1,\ldots,Y_m) = H(X_1,\ldots,X_m). \tag{27}$$

It can be shown (see Denny and Pinto 1978) that the joint cost function can then be written in the form

$$C = C(h(Y_1,\ldots,Y_m),P_1,\ldots,P_n). \tag{28}$$

It is obvious from equations (27) and (28) that the test for separability is the test for the existence of an output aggregate. Following Denny and Fuss 1977, it can be shown that the separability constraints for the translog approximation used in this paper ($m = n = 3$) are

$$\alpha_1 = \alpha_3 \frac{\rho_{11}}{\rho_{31}},$$

$$\alpha_2 = \alpha_3 \frac{\rho_{21}}{\rho_{31}},$$

$$\rho_{12} = \rho_{11} \frac{\rho_{22}}{\rho_{21}}, \tag{29}$$

$$\rho_{32} = \rho_{31} \frac{\rho_{22}}{\rho_{21}}.$$

A production function is said to be *homothetic* if input proportions are independent of scale. Shephard (1953) showed that the cost function for a homothetic production structure takes the form

$$C = g(P_1,\ldots,P_n)h(Y_1,\ldots,Y_m). \tag{30}$$

For the translog approximation used in this paper the homotheticity constraints are

$$\rho_{12} = \rho_{21} = \rho_{13} = \rho_{31} = \rho_{23} = \rho_{32} = 0. \tag{31}$$

Finally, the production structure will be of a Cobb-Douglas form if the joint cost function can be written as

$$C = AP_1^{\beta_1}P_2^{\beta_2}P_3^{\beta_3}Y_1^{\alpha_1}Y_2^{\alpha_2}Y_3^{\alpha_3}. \tag{32}$$

For the translog function used in this paper the Cobb-Douglas constraints are

$$\delta_{ik} = \rho_{ij} = \gamma_{jk} = 0 \qquad (i,j,k, = 1, 2, 3). \tag{33}$$

Data

Data pertaining to Bell Canada's operations during the period 1952–1975 were used to estimate the equations of our model. Bell Canada is the single largest telecommunications firm in Canada, serving in 1975 close to 8 million telephones in the provinces of Ontario and Quebec. For the majority of services offered, no competition is allowed. However, there is a range of so-called competitive services, such as data transmission (where competition with one other firm, Canadian National/Canadian Pacific Telecommunications, has always existed).

The basic source of all our data is a Bell Canada submission to the Canadian Radiotelevision and Telecommunication Commission entitled Response to Interrogatories of the Province of Ontario, Item 101, 12 February 1977, that presents constant-dollar revenues, skill-weighted manhours, net value of capital, and the associated prices. (This is referred to hereafter as the BCS.)

Output Data

The BCS gives both constant-dollar (1967 base) and current-dollar revenues for local services, directory advertising, and three subdivisions of message toll (intra-Bell, Trans-Canada and adjacent members, U.S. and overseas). Also included are other toll revenues and miscellaneous revenues. We used three output measures: local services, message toll services, and what we label competitive services (the remaining three services).[26] The aggregate measure of message toll output was derived as a Divisia index of the three constant-dollar subaggregates using arithmetic weights. The implicit price index for the toll aggregate service was determined from the division of current-dollar revenue by the Divisia quantity index.

An aggregate measure of the quantity of competitive services was computed in a similar fashion by calculating a Divisia quantity index of the directory advertising, other tolls, and miscellaneous services. The implicit price index was formed as above—by dividing total current-dollar revenue from the three services by the quantity index.

Input Data

The BCS lists four separate factors: cost of materials, services, rent, and supplies; indirect taxes; manhour input; and capital input. We call the first two groups *materials* and form the aggregate price index as a Divisia index (arithmetic weights) of the separate components. Table 6 of the BCS provides a series called "Labour Value, Adjusted for Quality," in constant 1967 dollars. An earlier memorandum indicates that the method of adjusting for quality consists of weighting actual man-hours in each of twenty-eight labor categories by the ratio of the average total hourly remuneration of that specific group in the base year to the average remuneration for all groups (the Kendrick method; see Olley 1970). All hours attributable to contruction are excluded, as are sick leave, vacations and holidays. This series represents the quantity of labor input for our study.

Because we could not acquire a comparable "adjusted" series for the nominal expenditure on labor, we used nominal labor expenditures as reported in Bell Canada annual reports. As these expenditures included management salaries, sick pay, vacation pay, and services not included in the quantity index, the implicit price index was slightly greater than unity in 1967. We normalized the labor price series to be unity in 1967.

Table 7 of the BCS includes a series entitled "Total Average Net Stock of Physical Capital in 1967 Values." The earlier Olley (1970) memorandum describes the process that generated this capital series. For each year from 1920 on, the age distribution of capital in place was determined in each of six categories (buildings, central office equipment, station equipment, outside plant, furniture and office equipment, and motor vehicles). Constant-dollar values were determined by reflating the physical stock by a Laspeyres price index (1967 = 1.0) for each capital type. Cash, accounts receivable, and short-term assets less short-term liabilities were excluded. Total net value of the capital stock in any year is the sum of the six individual constant-dollar categories.

The user cost of capital (P_k) for our study is calculated as

$$P_k = P_I(i + \delta),$$

where i is the expected long-run real after-tax rate of return applicable to Bell Canada (assumed to be constant at 6 percent), δ is the rate of real economic depreciation (from the BCS), and P_I is the telephone plant price index (from the BCS).

We have assumed that the expected real rate of return was constant over the period. Attempting to incorporate an increasing real rate led to implausible results. We chose 6 percent as the real rate, but also examined the effects of the alternative assumptions of 5 percent and 7 percent. Jenkins (1972, 1977) estimated the actual real after-tax rate of return for a wide cross-section of Canadian firms over the 1953–1973 period. The average rate was 6 percent. For the communications sector, the 1965–1969 average real rate was 5.2 percent including capital gains and 7 percent excluding capital gains. For the 1965–1974 period Jenkins estimated the average rate, excluding capital gains, to be 7.2 percent for the communications sector.

Empirical Results

Estimation Procedure

For both the demand functions and the augmented-cost-equations system the method of estimation was iterative three-stage least squares, an asymptotically efficient simultaneous-equations procedure. The instrumental variables used for the right-hand-side endogenous variables were formed from the exogenous variables of the two systems: local service output, input prices, and real income.

Estimates of Elasticities in Demand

We estimated log-linear demand functions of the form

$$\log Y_{it} = a_i + b_i \log(q_{it}/\text{CPI}_t) + d_i \log N_t, \qquad (34)$$

where Y_{it} ($i = 1,2,3$) are per capita outputs of local service, toll service, and competitive services, respectively; q_{it} ($i = 1,2,3$) are the corresponding output prices; CPI_t is the consumer price index; and N_t is real per capita disposable income in Bell Canada's operating territory.[27]

Equations (34) can be viewed as first-order approximations to arbitrary demand functions. We have also assumed that the service in question is weakly separable from all other goods and services in the individual's utility or production functions, and that the aggregate price index of these other commodities can be adequately represented by the consumer price index.

The three estimated demand functions are

$$\log Y_{1t} = -0.489 - 0.721 \log(q_{1t}/\text{CPI}_t) + 0.443 \log N_t; \quad R^2 = 0.804,$$
$$\phantom{\log Y_{1t} =} (0.209) \quad (0.264) \qquad\qquad (0.264)$$

$$\log Y_{2t} = -1.902 - 1.435 \log(q_{2t}/\text{CPI}_t) + 1.095 \log N_t; \quad R^2 = 0.934,$$
$$\phantom{\log Y_{2t} =} (1.01) \quad (0.451) \qquad\qquad (0.450)$$

$$\log Y_{3t} = -1.261 - 1.638 \log(q_{3t}/\text{CPI}_t) + 0.890 \log N_t; \ R^2 = 0.780.$$
$$(0.200) \quad (0.166) \qquad\qquad (0.047)$$

(Standard errors of coefficients are given in parentheses.)

The above results confirm one of the assumptions of the previous sections: that Bell Canada operates in the inelastic region of the demand curve for local services. Therefore, we will assume in the augmented cost model estimated below that the level of the local service output (Y_1) is exogenous to the firm's profit-maximizing output choice decision.

Estimation of the Augmented Model

The system of equations consisting of the cost function (18), the cost-share equations (19), and the revenue-share equations (22) was estimated using the data described in the previous section. The estimated elasticities for toll (-1.435) and competitive services (-1.638) were used as extraneous estimates in the revenue-share equations.

Parameter estimates are given in table 6.1, along with the corresponding standard errors. Goodness-of-fit statistics are given in table 6.2. The ceofficient representing capital-augmenting technical change, θ indicates that augmenting technical change resulted in an annual decrease of 6.7 percent in the effective price of a nominal unit of capital. The rate of total cost diminution is given by $\partial \log C/\partial t = \theta M_n$, where M_n is the cost share of capital. The rate is 3.0 percent at the point of approximation (1964), and ranges from 2.3 percent in 1952 to 3.4 percent in 1975.

Table 6.3 presents the own-price elasticities of demand for the three factors for the beginning, midpoint, and terminal years, and table 6.4 gives the cross-price elasticities for the middle year. Note the fall in the capital own-price elasticity over time, the rise in the labor own-price elasticity, and the constancy of the materials own-price elasticity. These trends are due to the trends in Bell Canada's cost shares. To demonstrate this fact, we note that the own-price elasticity (ε_{ii}) is calculated as

$$\varepsilon_{ii} = \frac{\delta_{ii} + M_i^2 - M_i}{M_i}.$$

The derivative of the ith own-price elasticity with respect to share M_i is

$$\frac{\partial \varepsilon_{ii}}{\partial M_i} = 1 - \frac{\gamma_{ii}}{M_i^2}.$$

Since γ_{ii} is a constant, the elasticity will fall as the share increases and increase as the share falls—a property of any translog cost function.

Table 6.1 Parameter estimates for the augmented translog joint-cost function.

	Coefficient	Standard Error
α_0	0.0140	0.985
θ	0.0668	0.009
α_1	0.7521	0.332
α_2	0.3732	0.099
α_3	0.2295	0.057
β_1	0.0348	0.334
β_2	0.5008	0.326
β_3	0.4644	0.145
δ_{11}	0.1130	0.071
δ_{12}	-0.0857	0.022
δ_{13}	-0.0369	0.001
δ_{22}	0.0479	0.009
δ_{23}	-0.0061	0.003
δ_{33}	0.1662	0.002
γ_{11}	-0.0505	0.047
γ_{12}	0.0659	0.044
γ_{13}	-0.0154	0.024
γ_{22}	-0.1251	0.049
γ_{23}	0.0592	0.025
γ_{33}	-0.0435	0.031
ρ_{11}	0.1210	0.052
ρ_{12}	-0.0671	0.051
ρ_{13}	-0.0539	0.031
ρ_{21}	-0.0276	0.012
ρ_{22}	0.0349	0.013
ρ_{23}	-0.0073	0.012
ρ_{31}	-0.0369	0.007
ρ_{32}	0.1444	0.007
ρ_{33}	0.0225	0.007

Table 6.2 Goodness-of-fit statistics for augmented model.

Equation	R^2	SEE[a]
Cost function	0.9991	0.013
Capital cost share	0.9471	0.014
Labor cost share	0.9592	0.012
Toll revenue "share"	0.5260[b]	0.008
Competitive revenue "share"	0.9602	0.004

a. SEE: Standard error of estimate.
b. The toll revenue share is approximately constant (at 0.34), which accounts for the low R^2. The standard error of the estimate, 0.008, indicates a high degree of explanation in spite of the low R^2.

Table 6.3 Own-price elasticities of factor demand.

	Capital	Labor	Materials
1952	−0.800	−0.807	−1.04
1964	−0.671	−0.989	−1.02
1975	−0.589	−1.11	−1.05

Table 6.4 Own- and cross-price elasticities of factor demand (1964).

	Capital	Labor	Materials
Capital	−0.671	0.508	0.163
Labor	0.627	−0.989	0.363
Materials	0.365	0.658	−1.02

Note: In order to interpret the numbers, apply the convention that the effect of a change in the price of capital is contained in the first row, the effect of a change in the price of labor is contained in the second row, etc. Thus, the first row consists of elasticities of the form $d\log X_i/d\log P_k$ ($i = K, L, M$).

As the cross-price elasticities indicate, all three inputs are substitutes, with output held constant. Thus, the cost-function concavity conditions will be satisfied at the point of approximation, 1964.

Tests of the Structure of Production
Table 6.5 summarizes the tests of the various specialized production structures discussed above. The tests were performed using the likelihood-ratio-test. The likelihood-ratio-test statistic, $-2\log(L_1/L_0)$, is distributed asymptotically as χ_r^2; where L_0 and L_1 are the values of the unconstrained and constrained likelihood functions, respectively, and r is the number of additional restrictions contained in the null hypothesis (the degrees of freedom of the test). Since we view the translog cost function as a second-order approximation, the tests presented in table 6.5 are approximate (see Denny and Fuss 1977).[28] The point of approximation chosen was

Table 6.5 Tests of the production structure.

Structure	Log Likelihood	Test Statistic $[-2\log(L_1/L_0)]$	Degrees of Freedom	Critical Value (5%)
Joint cost function (maintained hypothesis)	464.48		98	
Homotheticity	441.96	44.96	6	12.59
Cobb-Douglas[a]	n.c.[b]	n.c.	15	n.c.
Separability	450.04	28.88	4	9.49
Nonjointness (lack of economies of scope)	1952: 462.47	4.02	3	7.82
	1964: 464.07	0.62	3	7.82
	1975: 462.83	3.10	3	7.82
Constant returns to scale	1952: 461.84	5.28[c]	1	3.84
	1964: 464.47	0.73	1	3.84
	1975: 463.26	2.44	1	3.84

a. The Cobb-Douglas structure is a special case of the homothetic structure, and therefore is rejected along with the homothetic structure.
b. Not computed.
c. The rejection of constant returns to scale is a rejection in favor of decreasing returns to scale.

the middle year of the sample, 1964. Since the tests depend on the point of approximation, when a null hypothesis was not rejected tests were also performed using the initial year (1952) and the final year (1975) as points of approximation. Thus, three test statistics appear in table 6.5 for the nonjointness and constant-returns-to-scale hypotheses.

From the results contained in table 6.5 we can reject homotheticity, the Cobb-Douglas structure, and separability into outputs and inputs as descriptions of the telecommunications production structure. The rejection of separability is particularly important, since all previous estimates utilize this assumption (see, for example, Dobell et al. 1972; Vinod 1976a,b). A surprising result is the acceptance of nonjointness, which indicates a lack of economies of scope. We can take a closer look at this test by recalling that economies of scope imply $\partial^2 C / \partial Y_i \partial Y_j < 0$. It can easily be shown that

$$\frac{\partial^2 C}{\partial Y_i \partial Y_j} = \frac{C}{Y_i Y_j} \left(\frac{\partial \log C}{\partial \log Y_i} \frac{\partial \log C}{\partial \log Y_j} + \frac{\partial^2 \log C}{\partial \log Y_i \partial \log Y_j} \right). \tag{35}$$

If we scale the data so that the point of approximation is characterized by $P_j = Y_i = 1$ $(i,j = 1,2,3)$, then equation (35) is negative if $\alpha_i \alpha_j + \delta_{ij} < 0$ $(i,j = 1,2,3)$. Table 6.6 presents the estimate of $\alpha_i \alpha_j + \delta_{ij}$ and the associated approximate standard errors underlying the test of the null hypothesis when 1964 is the point of approximation.

Table 6.6 Estimated jointness parameters.

Formula	Estimate	Standard Error
$\alpha_1\alpha_2 + \delta_{12}$	-0.016	0.021
$\alpha_1\alpha_3 + \delta_{13}$	0.002	0.009
$\alpha_2\alpha_3 + \delta_{23}$	-0.002	0.003

Although none of the estimates of $\partial^2 C / \partial Y_i \partial Y_j$ is significantly different from zero, the point estimates of $\partial^2 C / \partial Y_1 \partial Y_2$ and $\partial^2 C / \partial Y_2 \partial Y_3$ are negative. Thus, there is some weak evidence of cost complementarities between local and toll services, and between toll and competitive services. The lack of cost complementarity between local and competitive services is reasonable, in that competitive services consist primary of private line services, which in Canada are not interconnected with the local switched network.

The hypothesis that production is subject to constant returns to scale is not rejected, except at the beginning of the sample period, where there exists evidence of decreasing returns to scale. The test statistic for the middle year (1964) is 0.13, which compares with a 5 percent critical value of 3.84. This implies that the contant-returns-to-scale hypothesis is a close description on the technology at the point of approximation usually chosen in studies that use translog functions.

We stated above that economies of scope and economies of scale are sufficient conditions for subadditivity. Since neither characteristic is strongly supported by our results, there is also no real evidence to support the contention that Bell Canada's production process is subadditive. However, we must emphasize again that our test is local, and hence not really suitable. In any case, necessary conditions cannot be investigated within our framework.

Overall Scale Elasticity

The overall scale elasticity (SE) can be measured as

$$SE = \left(\frac{d\log C}{d\lambda}\right)^{-1} = \left(\sum_i \frac{\partial \log C}{\partial \log Y_i}\right)^{-1},$$

where λ is a proportionate increase in outputs (see Panzer and Willig 1975). Table 6.7 presents the estimated scale elasticity and approximate standard errors for 1952, 1964, and 1975.[29] The point estimates indicate decreasing returns for the first half of the period and increasing returns for the latter half of the period, but (as shown by the tests in table 6.5)

Table 6.7 Estimated scale elasticity (SE).

	SE	Standard Error
1952	0.845	0.068
1964	1.02	0.064
1975	1.15	0.093

are not estimated accurately enough to cause a rejection of the constant-returns-to-scale hypothesis for the latter period.

The monotonic rising trend in the returns-to-scale parameter is highly suspect. When we used a rising real rate of return instead of the constant 6 percent that yields the results of table 6.7, the parameter estimates indicated implausible scale elasticities (negative in some years, impossibly high in other years). Moreover, the estimates of scale elasticities presented in table 6.7 are sensitive to changes in the assumed real constant rate of return. Lowering the rate to 5 percent increased the scale elasticity somewhat (to 0.912 in 1952, 1.06 in 1964, and 1.20 in 1975); however, none of the values was significantly different from unity. Increasing the assumed rate to 7 percent lowered the estimate of scale elasticity (to 0.867 in 1952, 0.981 in 1964, and 1.12 in 1975); none of these estimates was significantly different from 1.0 except for the 1952 estimate.

There are two likely sources of the problems: incorrect specification of technical change, and omission of capacity-utilization measures. None of the data available to us allowed us to overcome these problems. Technical change is likely to be both factor-specific and neutral. When we tried to incorporate both Hicks neutral and factor-augmenting technical changes, the variance-covariance matrix of the estimating equations became ill-conditioned. This problem highlights the difficulty of separating measures of scale elasticity from general measures of the rate of technical progress in a highly trended time series.[30]

Measures of capacity utilization have both theoretical and empirical limitations. An aggregate output cannot be defined unless the production function can be separated into inputs and outputs. Thus, capacity output can only be defined under an assumption that has been rejected by our empirical results. One could, however, define capacity in terms of the physical limitations of utilizing capital stock. We had no information that would have allowed us to account for changes in capital-stock utilization. The inability to correct for changes in capacity utilization creates problems for the measurement of production characteristics, particularly economies of scale. If the utilization rate fell monotonically throughout the period, perhaps because of capital expansion involving lumpy expenditures on increasingly larger units, the inability to account for capacity utilization would bias the measure of scale elasticity upward.

The omission of some sources of technical change could also incorrectly attribute to scale expansions in output that should be attributable to changes in technology. Even with these two problems, which we feel bias the estimates of scale elasticity upward in the latter part of the sample period, no statistically significant economies of scale were found.

Incremental Costs and Their Relationships to Output Prices

Incremental cost curves for each of the three output can be estimated using equation (25). With the midsample (1964) observations taken as the fixed values of input prices and irrelevant outputs, the incremental cost curves were found to be downward-sloping for all three outputs.[31] Since the incremental cost elasticities are increasing for all three outputs $(\partial^2 \log C / \partial \log Y_i^2 = \delta_{ii} > 0)$, at some output level incremental costs must increase. For all three services the regions of increasing incremental costs occur at output levels greater than that observed in the sample. We arbitrarily doubled each of the three outputs, and reestimated the incremental cost elasticities assuming that the observed relationship between output and costs still held. Marginal-cost curves continued to fall at these higher outputs.

We do not find it very useful to compare incremental costs with prices charged for these services for the purposes of examining relative contributions and "cream-skimming" as usually defined in regulatory hearings. As we indicated previously, these incremental costs are based on replacement or opportunity cost concepts, while the firm is regulated on a historical capital cost basis. Prices could then be below these incremental opportunity costs but be above historical fully allocated average costs as determined in regulatory hearings. Valuing inputs at opportunity costs (replacement value) might indicate losses when compared with actual revenue even though the firm was earning its allowed rate of return on its rate base. In our study, only the cost of capital and the value of the capital input exhibit differences between historical and opportunity costs. Though the firm has to pay each unit of labor the opportunity cost in each year, regulators do not allow the firm to revalue its capital (or rate base) every year on the basis of replacement value and the opportunity cost of capital.

However, it is of some interest to compare output price with incremental

Table 6.8 Actual prices and incremental costs (replacement value).

	Local Services		Toll Services		Competitive Services	
	Price	IC^a	Price	IC	Price	IC
1952	0.92	2.16	1.05	0.40	0.78	0.32
1964	1.00	1.73	1.04	0.34	1.00	0.41
1975	1.18	1.48	1.19	0.22	1.56	0.30

Note: The index is 1967 = 1.0.
a. Incremental cost.

cost for the purposes of evaluating the efficiency aspects of rate setting. Table 6.8 compares prices and marginal costs, where the opportunity cost of capital used in the calculations is the nominal after-tax realized rate of return.

In all years of the sample, the actual price for local service was below the measured incremental replacement cost for that service. In all years, the actual prices for both toll and competitive services were substantially above the marginal costs of these respective services. If there were indeed no economies of scale, marginal-cost pricing would cover all costs. Pricing at the marginal costs of the services would substantially lower the prices for toll and competitive services and increase the price of local service. If there were increasing returns to scale, marginal-cost pricing could not cover all costs. We cannot calculate the second-best set of Ramsey prices, constraining the firm to break even, since one of the three services was estimated to have a constant elasticity of demand less than unity imply negative marginal revenue.[32]

Sensitivity of the Empirical Results to Alternative Elasticity Assumptions
The extraneous demand elasticities are estimated from rather *ad hoc* specifications. We therefore investigated the sensitivity of all our empirical results to alternative estimates of demand elasticities. We increased the absolute value of the point estimates of toll-service and competitive-service demand elasticities by two standard deviations. The adjusted demand elasticities are −2.30 for toll service and −2.03 for competitive services. The parameter estimates did change, but the characteristics of production did not change in any significant way. The estimates of the scale elasticity fell marginally (0.98 in 1964 as compared with 1.02 with the lower demand elasticities; 1.10 in 1975 as compared with 1.14 for our base-case results).

The Behavior of the Multiproduct Firm Subject to Rate-of-Return Regulation—A Duality Approach

Behavioral Model

Since 1966, Bell Canada has been subject to regulation limiting the maximum rate of return that may be earned on invested capital. It is well known that rate-of-return regulation can bias the choice of inputs away from the cost-minimizing mix. This hypothesis (known as the Averch-Johnson, or A-J effect) has been tested, somewhat inconclusively, by Spann (1974), Peterson (1975), and Cowing (1978), among others. If the hypothesis is correct, then parameters (and hence technological characteristics estimated from econometric cost functions) will be biased owing to misspecification of the behavioral model. In this section we demonstrate the way in which the A-J effect can be explicitly incorporated into econometric cost functions and the derived cost-share and revenue-share equations. A unique feature of the derivation is the extensive use of modern duality theory.[33] Suppose the product transformation function is

$$F(Y_1,\ldots,Y_m;K,X_2,\ldots,X_n) \leqslant 0, \tag{36}$$

where $K = X_1$ is the capital stock used to determine the allowed return. Then the firm's problem is to maximize

$$\sum_{i=1}^{m} q_i Y_i - \sum_{j=2}^{n} p_j X_j - p_k K \tag{37}$$

subject to (36) and

$$\Sigma q_i Y_i - \Sigma p_j X_j \leqslant sK, \tag{38}$$

where q_i ($i = 1,\ldots,m$) are endogenous output prices and s is the allowed rate of return. The appropriate Lagrangian expression is

$$\mathscr{L} = \sum_i q_i Y_i - \sum_j p_j X_j - p_k K + \lambda_1 \left(sK - \sum_i q_i Y_i + \sum_j p_j X_j \right)$$

$$+ \lambda_2 [-F(Y_1,\ldots,Y_m;K,X_2,\ldots,X_n)]. \tag{39}$$

If production is technologically efficient and the firm earns exactly the allowed rate of return, (36) and (38) become equalities. Further, if we assume that the optimal solution results in nonzero Y_i and X_j for all i and j, then the first-order Kuhn-Tucker conditions for a maximum of (37) subject to (36) and (38) will involve no inequalities. These conditions are

$$\frac{\partial \mathscr{L}}{\partial X_j} = -p_j(1-\lambda_1) - \lambda_2 \frac{\partial F}{\partial X_j} = 0 \qquad (j = 2,\ldots,n), \tag{40}$$

$$\frac{\partial \mathscr{L}}{\partial K} = -(p_k - \lambda_1 s) - \lambda_2 \frac{\partial F}{\partial K} = 0, \tag{41}$$

and

$$\frac{\partial \mathscr{L}}{\partial Y_i} = \left(q_i + Y_i \frac{\partial q_i}{\partial Y_i} \right)(1-\lambda_1) - \lambda_2 \frac{\partial F}{\partial Y_i} = 0$$

or

$$\tag{42}$$

$$\mathrm{MR}_i(1-\lambda_1) - \lambda_2 \frac{\partial F}{\partial Y_i} = 0,$$

where MR_i is the marginal revenue of the ith output.
Differentiating (39) with respect to λ_1 and λ_2 gives

$$\frac{\partial \mathscr{L}}{\partial \lambda_1} = sK - \sum_i q_i Y_i - \sum_j p_j X_j = 0 \tag{43}$$

and

$$\frac{\partial \mathscr{L}}{\partial \lambda_2} = -F(Y_1,\ldots,Y_m;K,X_2,\ldots,X_n) = 0. \tag{44}$$

From (40) and (41) we obtain

$$\frac{\partial F}{\partial X_g} \bigg/ \frac{\partial F}{\partial X_l} = \frac{p_g(1-\lambda_1)}{p_l(1-\lambda_1)} = \frac{p_g^*}{p_l^*} \qquad (g,l = 1,\ldots,n), \tag{45}$$

and

$$\frac{\partial F}{\partial X_g} \bigg/ \frac{\partial F}{\partial K} = \frac{p_g(1-\lambda_1)}{p_k - \lambda_1 s} = \frac{p_g^*}{p_k^*} \qquad (g = 1,\ldots,n), \tag{46}$$

where p_g^*, p_l^*, and p_k^* are shadow prices of the inputs. Equations (45) and (46) state that in the optimal solution the firm sets the marginal rate of technical substitution equal to the ratio of shadow prices. But this condition is just the usual cost-minimization condition, except for the fact that the prices are shadow prices instead of market prices. The firm can be viewed as acting *as if* it minimized cost subject to the shadow prices. Therefore, by solving equations (43)–(46) we can obtain the producer's constrained multiproduct cost function,

$$C^* = C^*(p_1^*,\ldots,p_n^*, Y_1,\ldots,Y_m). \tag{47}$$

Alternatively, utilizing the theory of duality between production and cost, we can start with the cost function (47) and assume that the producer acts *as if* he minimizes cost subject to the outputs and shadow prices appearing in (47). We know from the marginal conditions (45) and (46) that this basic duality property is not affected by the use of shadow prices for the inputs. Of course, the p_j^* are endogenous. However, the point of the above analysis is to demonstrate that we can treat the producer as behaving as if the p_j^* were exogenous. The endogenous nature of p_j^* will be taken into account in equations (56)–(58). Using Shephard's lemma once again, we have

$$\frac{\partial C^*}{\partial p_j^*} = X_j \qquad (j = 1,\ldots,n). \tag{48}$$

Equation (48) will be used to generate the cost-share equations for the rate-of-return-regulated firm.

From the above analysis it is clear that equations (43)–(46) determine the cost-minimization solution subject to the production technology and the rate-of-return constraints. We will now show that equation (42), which determines the choice of Y_i, is just the marginal-cost-equals-marginal-revenue condition necessary for profit maximization.

From the technology constraint we obtain

$$\sum_{i=1}^{m} \frac{\partial F}{\partial Y_i} dY_i + \frac{\partial F}{\partial K} dK + \sum_{j=2}^{n} \frac{\partial F}{\partial X_j} dX_j = 0. \tag{49}$$

Using (40) and (41), equation (42) becomes

$$\sum_{i=1}^{m} \frac{\partial F}{\partial Y_i} dY_i - \frac{1}{\lambda_2}(p_k - \lambda_1 s)dK - \frac{1}{\lambda_2} \sum_{j=2}^{n} p_j(1 - \lambda_1)dX_j = 0,$$

or

$$\lambda_2 \sum_{i=1}^{m} \frac{\partial F}{\partial Y_i} dY_i - \left[\left(p_k dK + \sum_{j=2}^{n} p_j dX_j \right) - \lambda_1 \left(sdK + \sum_{j=2}^{n} p_j dX_j \right) \right] = 0. \tag{50}$$

Since

$$C = p_k K + \sum_{j=2}^{n} p_j X_j,$$

we have

$$dC = p_k dK + \sum_{j=2}^{n} p_j dX_j. \tag{51}$$

In addition, from (43),

$$s\,dK + \Sigma p_j dX_j = d(\Sigma q_i Y_i) = dR. \tag{52}$$

Now suppose that only Y_i changes, so that $dY_k = 0\,(k \neq i)$. Then equation (50) becomes, using (51) and (52),

$$\lambda_2 \frac{\partial F}{\partial Y_i} dY_i - (dC - \lambda_1 dR) = 0, \tag{51'}$$

where

$$dR = d(\Sigma q_i Y_i) \qquad (dY_k = 0, k \neq i).$$

We can write equation (51) in the form

$$\lambda_2 \frac{\partial F}{\partial Y_i} = \frac{dC}{dY_i} - \lambda_1 \frac{dR}{dY_i} = \mathrm{MC}_i - \lambda_1 \mathrm{MR}_i. \tag{52'}$$

Substituting for $\lambda_2 \partial F/\partial Y_i$ in equation (42), we obtain

$$\mathrm{MR}_i(1 - \lambda_1) - [\mathrm{MC}_i - \lambda_1 \mathrm{MR}_i] = 0,$$

or

$$\mathrm{MR}_i = \mathrm{MC}_i. \tag{53}$$

Thus, equation (42) is just the MR = MC condition in somewhat disguised form.

The above interpretation of the first-order conditions suggests that the overall optimization problem can be subdivided into two sequential problems. First, for any outputs, minimize cost subject to the technology and rate-of-return constraints. This defines the output expansion path in terms of shadow-price tangency conditions from equations (40), (41), (43), and (44). Second, conditional on the optimal input proportions, choose outputs so as to equate marginal revenue to marginal cost (from equation (42)).

Because a sequential analysis can be applied in the case of rate-of-return regulation, the approach used in the earlier sections of this paper is relevant. That is, first use the cost function to obtain the input demand equations and then use the profit-maximizing conditions to determine the optimal Y_i.

The constrained cost function C^* can be written as

$$C^* = p_k^* K + \sum_{j=2}^{n} p_j^* X_j, \tag{54}$$

where it is understood that K and X_j are optimal (cost-minimizing) inputs, given p_k, p_j, s, and Y_i. C^* can also be written as

$$C^* = (p_k - \lambda_1 s) K + \sum_{j=2}^{n} p_j (1 - \lambda_1) X_j$$

$$= p_k K + \sum_{j=2}^{n} p_j X_j - \lambda_1 \left(sK + \sum_{j=2}^{n} p_j X_j \right)$$

$$= C(p_k, p_2, \ldots, p_n, s, Y_1, \ldots, Y_m) - \lambda_1 \Sigma q_i Y_i, \qquad (55)$$

or

$C = C^* + \lambda_1 \Sigma q_i Y_i$, where C depends only on observable variables which are exogenous to the cost-minimization problem. Now

$$\frac{\partial C}{\partial p_l} = \sum_j \frac{\partial C^*}{\partial p_j^*} \frac{\partial p_j^*}{\partial p_l} + \frac{\partial C^*}{\partial p_k^*} \frac{\partial p_k^*}{\partial p_l} + \left(\Sigma q_i Y_i \right) \frac{\partial \lambda_1}{\partial p_l} \qquad (l = 2, \ldots, n), \qquad (56)$$

where we have explicitly recognized the endogenous nature of p_j^*, p_k^*, and λ_1.

Taking derivatives of (55) and substituting in (56) yields

$$\frac{\partial C}{\partial p_l} = X_l (1 - \lambda_1) - \left(\sum_j p_j X_j \right) \frac{\partial \lambda_1}{\partial p_l} - sK \frac{\partial \lambda_1}{\partial p_l} + \left(\Sigma q_i Y_i \right) \frac{\partial \lambda_1}{\partial p_l}$$

$$= X_l (1 - \lambda_1) - \frac{\partial \lambda_1}{\partial p_l} \left(sK + \sum_j p_j X_j - \sum_i q_i Y_i \right)$$

$$= X_l (1 - \lambda_1), \text{ using equation (43).}$$

Thus we have a modified Shephard's lemma:

$$\frac{\partial C}{\partial p_j} = X_j (1 - \lambda_1) \qquad (j = 2, \ldots, n). \qquad (57)$$

We can obtain additional components of the factor-demand equations by differentiating C with respect to p_k and s:

$$\frac{\partial C}{\partial p_k} = \sum_j \frac{\partial C^*}{\partial p_j^*} \frac{\partial p_j^*}{\partial p_k} + \frac{\partial C^*}{\partial p_k^*} \frac{\partial p_k^*}{\partial p_k} + \left(\Sigma q_i Y_i \right) \frac{\partial \lambda_1}{\partial p_k}$$

$$= -\frac{\partial \lambda_1}{\partial p_k} \left(\sum_j p_j X_j \right) + K - \frac{\partial \lambda_1}{\partial p_k} (sK) + \left(\Sigma q_i Y_i \right) \frac{\partial \lambda_1}{\partial p_k}$$

$$= K, \qquad (58)$$

$$\frac{\partial C}{\partial s} = \sum_j \frac{\partial C^*}{\partial p_j^*} \frac{\partial p_j^*}{\partial s} + \frac{\partial C^*}{\partial p_k^*} \frac{\partial p_k^*}{\partial s} + \left(\sum_i q_i Y_i\right) \frac{\partial \lambda_1}{\partial s}$$

$$= -\frac{\partial \lambda_1}{\partial s}\left(\sum p_j X_j\right) - \lambda_1 K - \frac{\partial \lambda_1}{\partial s}(sK) + \left(\sum q_i Y_i\right) \frac{\partial \lambda_1}{\partial s}$$

$$= -\lambda_1 K. \tag{59}$$

In summary, we can generate the input demand functions and the Lagrangian multiplier from the cost function using the modified Shephard's lemma:

$$\frac{\partial C}{\partial p_j} = X_j(1 - \lambda_1) \qquad (j = 2,\ldots,n),$$

$$\frac{\partial C}{\partial p_k} = K, \tag{60}$$

$$\frac{\partial C}{\partial s} = -\lambda_1 K.$$

This last result was also derived by Peterson (1975), who apparently did not recognize the additional behavioral equations that could be obtained from the cost function.

Actual estimating equations can be formed by noting that

$$X_j/X_l = \frac{\partial C}{\partial p_j} \bigg/ \frac{\partial C}{\partial p_l}, \tag{61}$$

which eliminates the unknown Lagrangian multiplier λ_1. This multiplier can be obtained from the above equations as

$$\lambda_1 = -\frac{\partial C}{\partial s} \bigg/ \frac{\partial C}{\partial p_k}. \tag{62}$$

The remaining equations in the profit-maximizing model can be obtained from the equations $\partial R/\partial Y_i = \partial C/\partial Y_i$, where C is defined as in (55).

The Translog Econometric Model Under Rate-of-Return Constraint
The cost function can be written in the form

$$C = C(p_k, p_2, \ldots, p_n, s, Y_1, \ldots, Y_m). \tag{63}$$

For ease of notation, let $p_k = p_1$ and $s = p_{n+1}$. Then the translog approximation to the cost function (63) is

$$\log C = \alpha_0 + \alpha_T T + \sum_{i=1}^{m} \alpha_i \log Y_i + \sum_{j=1}^{n+1} \beta_j \log p_j$$

$$+ \tfrac{1}{2} \sum_{i=1}^{m} \sum_{k=1}^{m} \delta_{ik} \log Y_i \log Y_k$$

$$+ \tfrac{1}{2} \sum_{j=1}^{n+1} \sum_{k=1}^{n+1} \log p_j \log p_k$$

$$+ \sum_{i=1}^{m} \sum_{j=1}^{n+1} \rho_{ij} \log Y_i \log p_j. \tag{64}$$

The cost-share equations become

$$\frac{\partial \log C}{\partial \log p_j} = \frac{p_j (1 - \lambda_1) X_j}{C}$$

$$= (1 - \lambda_1) M_j$$

$$= \beta_j + \sum_{k=1}^{n+1} \gamma_{jk} \log p_k + \sum_{i=1}^{m} \rho_{ij} \log Y_i \qquad (j = 2, \dots, n), \tag{65}$$

$$\frac{\partial \log C}{\partial \log p_1} = \frac{p_1 X_1}{C}$$

$$= M_1$$

$$= \beta_1 + \sum_{k=1}^{n+1} \gamma_{1k} \log p_k + \sum_{i=1}^{m} \rho_{i1} \log Y_i, \tag{66}$$

$$\frac{\partial \log C}{\partial \log p_{n+1}} = \frac{p_{n+1}(-\lambda_1 X_1)}{C}$$

$$= -\lambda_1 M_{n+1}$$

$$= \beta_{n+1} + \sum_{k=1}^{n+1} \gamma_{n+1,k} \log p_k + \sum_{i=1}^{m} \rho_{i,n+1} \log Y_i, \tag{67}$$

where $M_{n+1} = p_{n+1} X_1 / C$ is the allowed rate-of-return "cost share."

The cost system to be estimated consists of equations (64) and (66) and equations of the form

$$\frac{M_j}{M_2} = \frac{\beta_j + \sum_{k=1}^{n+1} \gamma_{jk} \log p_k + \sum_{i=1}^{m} \rho_{ij} \log Y_i}{\beta_2 + \sum_{k=1}^{n+1} \gamma_{2k} \log p_k + \sum_{i=1}^{m} \rho_{i2} \log Y_i} \qquad (j = 3, \dots, n). \tag{68}$$

Once the parameters have been estimated, λ_1 can be obtained from the ratio of (66) and (67). In addition to the cost-share equations, we have, as before, the revenue "share" equations obtained from the $MC_i = MR_i$ optimality conditions:

$$R_i = \frac{q_i Y_i}{C}$$

$$= \left(\alpha_i + \sum_{i=1}^{m} \delta_{ik} \log Y_k + \sum_{j=1}^{n+1} \rho_{ij} \log p_j \right) \left(1 + \frac{1}{\varepsilon_i} \right)^{-1}, \tag{69}$$

where ε_i is the own-price elasticity of demand.

Conclusions

Two important issues in regulation are the extent to which a utility is a natural (that is, competition-excluding) monopoly and the appropriate rate structure to be used by a multioutput regulated firm. Both issues require a knowledge of the firm's production technology. We believe that the most appropriate vehicle with which to estimate technology with these issues in mind is the multioutput cost function. We have estimated this function for Bell Canada, assuming no Averch-Johnson distorting effect.

A number of interesting empirical results emerge. First, the estimates of the overall scale elasticity are not sufficiently precise to enable one to reject the hypotheses of increasing, constant, or decreasing returns in scale. Second, we have not been able to reject the hypothesis of nonjoint production. The hypotheses of separability between outputs and inputs, homotheticity, and a Cobb-Douglas framework were, however, all rejected. Third, if the underlying technology is in fact a constant-returns-to-scale technology, efficient (marginal cost) pricing would lead to an increase in local-service rates and a decrease in toll-service and competitive-service rates.

The rejection of the most commonly specified functional forms suggests a need to use flexible forms, such as the translog form, in any estimation of telecommunications technology. However, for such an application a more extensive data base than the one available to us is desirable. This is demonstrated by the fact that our results are not as robust in the face of alternative assumptions as we would have preferred. What is needed is time-series data for a cross-section of telephone companies. The need for this more extensive data base is particularly obvious when one contemplates the estimation of the multioutput cost-function model which takes into account Averch-Johnson effects.

We thank the University of Toronto Institute for Policy Analysis for providing computer funds, and Angelo Molino for excellent research assistance.

Notes

1. For attempts to define multiproduct scale economies see Baumol and Braunstein 1977, Baumol 1977, and Panzar and Willig 1978.

2. For an application of multiproduct cost functions to U.S. railroad data see Brown et al. 1976.

3. This proof is taken from Brown et al. 1976, p. 9.

4. We are ignoring for the moment the problems of defining economies of scale, of measuring output for a firm producing a number of products, and of defining average cost.

5. Baumol et al. (1976) and Baumol and Braunstein (1977) refer to this change as "economies of scope," such as the economies of integrating a number of products within a firm.

6. They only help since the benefits of a single firm must be compared to the benefits of competition, product diversity, innovation, and cost minimization.

7. In the case of a single output, $m = 1$ and equation (1) can be solved explicitly as $Y_1 = f(X_1, \ldots, X_n)$, which is the usual form of the production function.

8. For an introduction to duality theory and the use of Shephard's lemma see Baumol 1977a, chap. 14.

9. If production is not joint, then

$$C(Y_1, \ldots, Y_m; P_1, \ldots, P_n) = \sum_{i=1}^{m} C^i(Y_i, P_1, \ldots, P_n)$$

(see Hall 1973). In this case the multiple-output technology is just a collection of single-output technologies, and

$$\frac{\partial \log C}{\partial \log Y_i} = \frac{\partial \log C^i}{\partial \log Y_i}$$

is an unambiguous measure of returns to scale.

10. Panzar and Willig (1978) developed a measure of product-specified economies of scale which may provide a solution to the consistency problem. However, their measure requires knowledge of the cost function in the region where one or more outputs are zero, and such output levels are generally unobservable.

11. See Kahn 1970, p. 53; FCC docket 20003 (Cost Separation); FCC docket 18128 (Telepek); FCC Docket 19919; Canadian Transport Commission "Cost Inquiry."

12. We are indebted to M. A. Schankerman for a memorandum entitled "Contributions and Cream-Skimming in Telecommunications Services."

13. The FCC in 1967 allocated the costs of local loops and switches to inter- and intrastate service by their relative minutes of use. When this formula resulted in "too low" a figure for interstate use, it was multiplied by three to reflect the higher "value" of interstate service (Kahn 1970, p. 153). Actually, to utilize demand elasiticities to determine the

"opportunity costs" of various joint services may be correct. However, demand studies indicate that the demand for interstate service is more elastic than that for intrastate service. Efficient pricing rules would suggest a relative decrease in the price for interstate service.

14. Economies of fill are not related in any way to long-run economies of scale.

15. In the above example, econometric analysis could associate the upgrading changes in cost with the data users if residential voice traffic did not increase at the same time. However, were business and residential traffic to increase by the same amount, system-upgrading costs would be associated with both types of demand. The typical time-series data used in studies of the telecommunications sector, including data available to us, are too highly aggregated and time-trended to permit these causal types of relationships to be estimated with any degree of precision. The required information would be time-series, cross-sectional data for a number of telephone companies.

16. One cannot use some historical embedded average cost of capital in econometric analysis, since the firm does not face these average embedded costs at the margin. Maximizing profits dependent on these embedded costs would yield the incorrect factor proportions and output decisions based on actual current market prices.

17. See Dobell et al. 1972; Waverman 1977; Houthakker and Taylor 1970.

18. This result is correct as long as demand complementarities among the monopolist's products are not sufficiently strong that an increase in the price of the product with inelastic demand so reduces demand for other products that the monopolist's total revenue falls.

19. See note 18 for an applicable qualification.

20. In the case of substitutability or complementarity among the monopolist's products, marginal revenue would be given by

$$\text{MR}_i = q_i + \sum_j Y_j \frac{q_j}{Y_i}.$$

Since our empirical demand functions did not indicate the existence of the required interrelationships, this more general case has been relegated to a note.

21. In the actual estimation, the stability conditions

$$\frac{\partial \text{MR}_i}{\partial Y_i} < \frac{\partial \text{MC}_i}{\partial Y_i}$$

were satisfied at all data points.

22. We attempted to incorporate Hicks's neutral technical change both instead of and in addition to capital-augmenting technical change. The attempts proved unsuccessful.

23. It can be shown that if demand interdependence is present,

$$\frac{\partial \log C}{\partial \log Y_i} = \frac{q_i Y_i}{C} \left[1 + \sum_j \left(\frac{1}{\varepsilon_{ij}}\right) \left(\frac{q_j Y_j}{q_i Y_i}\right) \right],$$

where ε_{ij} is the cross-price elasticity of demand for product Y_i with respect to price q_j.

24. Since C is based on opportunity or replacement cost while the firm's actual revenue is constrainted by historical cost, $\sum_i R_i$ can be less than C with the firm still earning its allowed rate of return.

25. See Denny and Pinto 1978. A more detailed description of this test is provided below.

26. The three subcategories contained in the aggregate "competitive" service are other toll (private line, data communications, broadband, TWX); miscellaneous (consulting and other services), and directory advertising. Directory advertising was spun off to form a

separate company at the end of 1971. Our estimation procedure took this exogenous shift in revenues into account.

27. Although we attempted other formulations incorporating cross-elasticity effects, none of these attempts proved successful. There was no indication of significant interdependence among the demands for the three services.

28. The tests for homotheticity and the Cobb-Douglas structure are also exact in the sense that they do not depend on the point of approximation.

29. Standard errors were calculated as linear approximations. See Kmenta 1971, p. 444.

30. The measures of cost-diminution technical change and returns to scale are both monotonically trended. However, their combined effect on total factor productivity is to produce an almost constant rate. Ohta (1974) showed that the rate of total factor productivity can be measured as $\varepsilon_{CY}^{-1} \cdot \varepsilon_{C_t}$, where ε_{CY} is the scale elasticity and ε_{C_t} is the rate of total cost diminution. The resulting rates of total factor productivity are 2.7 percent in 1952, 2.9 percent in 1964, and 3 percent in 1975.

31. We reemphasize that a falling incremental cost curve is not necessarily associated with overall increasing returns to scale.

32. Only if an even number of services were subject to inelastic demands would we be able to calculate a Ramsey price vector. The solution, of course, is to relax the assumption of constant demand elasticities so that increasing the price of local services will eventually place the product in an estimated elastic demand region.

33. The approach taken in this section is similar to that used by Cowing (1978). However, we make more explicit use of duality theory to obtain the estimating equations, and do not need to assume profit-maximizing behavior with respect to the production of all outputs.

References

Baumol, W. J. 1977a. *Economic Theory and Operations Analysis*, fourth edition. Englewood Cliffs, N.J.: Prentice-Hall.

———. 1977b. "On the Proper Cost Tests for Natural Monopoly in a Multiproduct Industry." *American Economic Review* 67: 809–822.

Baumol, W. J., and Braunstein, Y. M. 1977. "Empirical Study of Scale Economies and Production Complementarity: The Case of Journal Publication." *Journal of Political Economy* 85: 1037–1048.

Baumol, W. J., Bailey, E. E., and Willig, R. D. 1977. "Weak Invisible Hand Theorems on the Sustainability of Prices in a Multiproduct Monopoly." *American Economic Review* 67: 350–365.

Berndt, E. R., and Wood, D. W. 1975. "Technology, Prices and Derived Demand for Energy." *Review of Economics and Statistics* 57: 259–268.

Brown, R., Caves, D., and Christensen, L. 1976. Estimating Marginal Costs for Multi-Product Regulated Firms. Social Systems Research Institute working paper 7609, University of Wisconsin, Madison.

Cowing, T. 1978. "The Effectiveness of Rate-of-Return Regulation: An Empirical Test using Profit Functions." In M. Fuss and D. McFadden (eds.), *Production Economics: A Dual Approach to Theory and Applications*. Amsterdam: North-Holland.

Denny, M., and Fuss, M. 1977. "The Use of Approximation Analysis to Test for Separability and the Existence of Consistent Aggregates." *American Economic Review* 67: 404–418.

Denny, M., and Pinto, C. 1978. "An Aggregate Model with Multi-Product Technologies." In M. Fuss and D. McFadden (eds.), *Production Economics: A Dual Approach to Theory and Applications.* Amsterdam: North-Holland.

Diewert, W. E. 1971. "An Application of the Shephard Duality Theorem: A Generalized Leontief Production Function." *Journal of Political Economy* 79: 481–507.

Dobell, A. R., Taylor, L. D., Waverman, L., Liu, T. H., and Copeland, M. D. G. 1972. "Communications in Canada." *Bell Journal of Economics and Management Science* 3: 179–219.

Fuss, M. A. 1977. "The Demand for Energy in Canadian Manufacturing: An Example of the Estimation of Production Structures with Many Inputs." *Journal of Econometrics* 5: 89–116.

Hall, R. E. 1973. "The Specification of Technologies with Several Kinds of Outputs." *Journal of Political Economy* 81: 878–892.

Houthakker, H. S., and Taylor, L. D. 1970. *Consumer Demand in the United States.* 2nd edition. Cambridge, Mass.: Harvard University Press.

Jenkins, G. P. 1972. Analysis of Rates of Return from Capital in Canada. PhD. diss., Dept. of Economics, University of Chicago.

————. 1977. Capital in Canada: Its Social and Private Performance 1965–1974. Economic Council of Canada discussion paper 98.

Kahn, A. E. 1970, 1971. *The Economics of Regulation.* 2 vols. New York: Wiley.

Kmenta, J. 1971. *Elements of Econometrics.* New York: Macmillan.

Lau, L. J. 1978. "Applications of Profit Functions." In M. Fuss and D. McFadden (eds.), *Production Economics: A Dual Approach to Theory and Applications.* Amsterdam: North-Holland.

Ohta, M. 1974. "A Note on the Duality between Production and Cost Functions: Rate of Return to Scale and Rate of Technical Progress." *Economic Studies Quarterly* 25: 63–65.

Olley, R. E. 1970. Productivity Gains in a Public Utility—Bell Canada 1952 to 1967. Paper presented at the annual meeting of the Canadian Economics Association.

Panzar, J. C., and Willig, R. D. 1975. Economics of Scale and Economies of Scope in Multi-Output Production. Bell Laboratories discussion paper 33.

————. 1979. Economies of Scope, Product Specific Economies of Scale, and the Multi-product Competitive Firm. Bell Laboratories economics discussion paper 152.

Peterson, H. C. 1975. "An Empirical Test of Regulatory Effects." *Bell Journal of Economics* 6: 111–126.

Spann, R. 1974. "Rate of Return Regulation and Efficiency in Production: An Empirical Test of the Averch-Johnson Thesis." *Bell Journal of Economics and Management Science* 5: 38–52.

Vinod, H. D. 1976a. "Application of New Ridge Regression Methods to a Study of Bell System Scale Economies." *Journal of the American Statistical Association* 71: 929–933.

————. 1976b. Bell Scale Economies and Estimation of Joint Production Functions. Bell Laboratories, Holmdel, N.J. Submitted in the Fifth Supplemental Response, FCC docket 20003.

Waverman, L. The Demand for Telephone Services in Britain. Mimeographed. University of Toronto Institute for Policy Analysis.

Comment

Ronald Braeutigam

The article by Fuss and Waverman represents a major step forward in empirical research in the telephone industry. Their study generates a number of interesting conclusions, but even more important is the fact that it applies solid theoretical and empirical techniques to a difficult problem. The use of a flexible-form cost function and the theory of duality enables the authors to test a number of propositions which earlier studies have employed as maintained hypotheses. In addition, the econometric methods used in the paper are novel applications of well-known techniques, generally well justified, and help to identify areas where future research may lead to an even better understanding of the underlying technology.

Among the most interesting empirical results are the following. The authors cannot reject the null hypothesis that there are constant returns to scale in the industry. Neither can they reject the null hypothesis that there are no economies of scope. They do reject the proposition that the production function is homothetic, as well as the separability of inputs and outputs. The authors have also integrated a technical-change coefficient in their analysis, and conclude that capital-augmented technical change helped to reduce total cost at an annual rate of about 3 percent over the period 1952–1975. Finally, they have produced estimates of marginal cost for three types of services: local service, message toll, and "competitive" services (private line, broadband, and TWX). They suggest that local-service tariffs have been less than marginal cost for the period 1952–1975, while the tariffs for the other two service categories have exceeded marginal costs. They conclude that more efficient pricing would therefore result from some increase in local-service tariffs and some decrease in the other tariffs.

The techniques and the conclusions both represent important contributions to our understanding of the technology of telecommunications. Additionally, they provoke the reader to ask a number of questions which it may now be possible to answer with the advances in technique that are used in the article.

Usefulness of Cost Data

It is interesting that Canadian regulators are involved in a cost inquiry much like the American FCC docket 18128. The alternatives they are investigating have familiar names: embedded direct cost (EDC), long-run incremental cost (LRIC), and fully distributed cost (FDC). The most useful applications of a cost function of the sort estimated by Fuss and Waverman are in the determination of marginal and total costs, rather than in the calculation of the three aforementioned costs. The authors do not claim that the translog function will aid in the quest for EDC and FDC methodologies. However, they do attempt to describe an incremental cost function, and certain problems arise in the process. In equation (25) they state that the "incremental cost curve for output Y_i can be obtained as

$$ICC(Y_i) = \frac{C}{Y_i}\left(\alpha_i + \delta_{ii}\log Y_i + \sum_{k \neq i} \delta_{ik}\log \bar{Y}_k + \sum_j \rho_{ij}\log \bar{P}_j\right),$$

where $\bar{Y}_k$ and $\bar{P}_j$ are preassigned constant outputs and prices, respectively," and where C is total cost and the parameters α_i, δ_{ii}, δ_{ik}, and ρ_{ij} are estimated.

Fuss and Waverman have used the terms "incremental cost" and "marginal cost" interchangeably. They are correct in describing equation (25) as a local description of the *marginal* cost of producing Y_i. However, it is necessary to point out that the *incremental* cost of producing Y_i is usually defined in regulatory circles as the difference in cost incurred when producing Y_i at some level, as opposed to producing a zero level of Y_i. Formally, this concept of incremental cost is represented for a two-product case as

$$ICC^*(Y_1) = C(Y_1, Y_2) - C(0, Y_2),$$

where the level of Y_2 remains unchanged and factor prices are held constant and therefore suppressed in the definition of $ICC^*(Y_1)$.

There is a relationship between the ICC used by Fuss and Waverman and the more conventional ICC^*. In particular, if the estimated parameters of the translog function (α_i, δ_{ii}, δ_{ik}, and ρ_{ij}) were constant over the range of output of Y_i from zero to $\hat{Y}_i$, then

$$ICC^*(\hat{Y}_i) = \int_{Y_i=0}^{\hat{Y}_i} ICC(Y_i)dY_i + F_i,$$

where, in addition to the variables already defined, F_i represents a fixed cost that is not incurred unless Y_i is positive.

The distinction between ICC*($\hat{Y}_i$) and ICC($\hat{Y}_i$) emphasizes two major points about the translog function. First, since it is a Taylor-series approximation of a function, it will generally be accurate only locally. The parameters α_i, δ_{ii}, δ_{ik}, and ρ_{ij} will generally not be constant as Y_i varies from zero to $\hat{Y}_i$. Second, the translog function cannot accommodate a zero as one of its arguments (in particular, $Y_i = 0$), since it involves a logarithm of zero. Moreover, if avoidable fixed costs are attributable to a service (such as F_i in the example above), the cost function is not continuous at $Y_i = 0$. If it is not continuous, then neither is it differentiable at $Y_i = 0$.

Fuss and Waverman are aware of these limitations. They note that the local nature of the estimation prohibits their testing for subadditivity in the cost function. Our purpose here is simply to point out why one will not be able to infer the usual kind of incremental cost information referred to by regulators—ICC*—from the estimated cost function.

Joint Production and Economies of Scope

One part of the article that may cause some confusion is the treatment of "joint production." The authors describe joint production as meaning that the production function can be written as (equation (3))

$$F(X_1,\ldots,X_n) = \min(a_1 Y_1, a_2 Y_2,\ldots,a_m Y_m),$$

but cannot be written as (equation (2))

$$Y_1 = F_1(X_1,\ldots,X_d)$$

$$Y_2 = F_2(X_{d+1},\ldots,X_h)$$

$$Y_m = F_m(X_{h+1},\ldots,X_n),$$

where the Y variables refer to output levels and the X variables to input levels. In other words, the authors are characterizing a joint production process as one in which each input cannot be uniquely attributed to the production of a particular output.

The first point needing clarification involves the statement that "economies of scope exist if and only if production is joint." Economies of scope may exist in some cases without joint production; thus the "only if" part of the statement does not appear to be true. For example, consider the following cost function:

$$C = 10 + Y_1 + Y_2.$$

Note that the process involves costs which cannot all be attributed unambiguously to individual outputs, but production is not joint. However, also note that

$$C(4,5) = 19,$$

$$C(0,5) = 15,$$

$$C(4,0) = 14.$$

Thus,

$$C(4,5) < C(0,5) + C(4,0),$$

and the cost function does exhibit economies of scope, even though production is not joint.

The second point involves the statement that "economies of scope imply $\partial^2 C/\partial Y_i \partial Y_j < 0$." The implication is not generally true of cost functions. For example, consider the cost function

$$C = F + Y_1 + Y_2,$$

where F is a fixed, shared cost. Then

$$C(Y_1, Y_2) = F + Y_1 + Y_2 < C(0, Y_2) + C(Y_1, 0) = 2F + Y_1 + Y_2$$

and there are economies of scope, even though $\partial^2 C/\partial Y_1 \partial Y_2 \not< 0$.

Model Specification

At the heart of the article is an estimation of a translog cost function. The theoretical basis for the work is presented clearly. Specifically, it is assumed that the firm minimizes total cost in producing any observed vector of output, with no effect to the contrary such as an Averch-Johnson bias. The importance of this assumption is recognized explicitly by the authors, and a theoretical discussion of the A-J variation is presented in the concluding section. With this in mind, we confine our comments to the cost-minimizing model estimated in the article.

Those who have worked with translog cost functions are no doubt familiar with the property that the number of parameters to be estimated increases rapidly as the number of outputs and factor prices increases. Some aggregation is needed to make the model tractable. For example, the thought of having a translog function that includes factor prices for each of the twenty-eight types of labor mentioned in the paper boggles the mind! While one might like to see how the empirical results are affected by, for example, using four or five outputs instead of three, the authors are constrained by the amount of data they have available. In light of this, the categories of outputs chosen seem reasonable.

We address two areas of specification here. The first involves the following statement:

For observed output levels such that demand is elastic, we assume that marginal revenue is set equal to marginal cost. For output levels such that demand is inelastic, we assume that those outputs are exogenous to the firm.

In other words, Fuss and Waverman have run a set of separate regressions to determine the demand schedules for each of the three output categories selected, and then calculated an elasticity of demand for each. They find that local service had an inelastic demand, and conclude that price (or quantity) regulation has in effect made the level of local service exogenous to the firm.

They find the other two service categories to have elastic demands, and therefore conclude that these output levels are endogenous to the firm, determined by profit-maximizing behavior (setting the marginal revenue equal to the marginal cost) in each market. There exists the uncomfortable possibility that regulators have specified the price (or quantity) level in each market at a level such that marginal cost exceeds marginal revenue, where the marginal revenue remains positive. Restated, the observation of a nonnegative marginal revenue is a *necessary*, but not *sufficient* condition for the profit-maximizing behavior assumed by the authors. (This assumes that the outputs are not complements; the issue of cross elasticities of demand will be addressed below.) Fuss and Waverman could have reinforced the validity of their endogeneity assumptions in these two markets with some additional institutional description about the way in which the regulatory process does in fact work.

A second potential problem of specification arises from the estimation of the log-linear demand functions used to provide additional information for the estimation of the cost function itself. Fuss and Waverman have assumed that each service "is weakly separable from all other goods and services in the individual's utility or production functions, and that the aggregate price index of these other commodities can be adequately represented by the consumer price index." Specifically, they have assumed that the cross-elasticities of demand among the three types of services are zero. This may or may not be true in the Canadian industry. It is an empirical matter that preferably should be tested rather than asserted as a maintained hypothesis. For example, competitive services may be imperfect substitutes for message toll services, at least for some users. Also, local service may exhibit some complementarity with respect to message toll services. At least in principle, if these complementarities were strong enough, then the observation of an inelastic demand for local service would not necessarily mean that the level of local service is exogenously specified. (This possibility is recognized in note 18, but the empirical test for demand complementarity is not made.)

More broadly, Fuss and Waverman employ a set of revenue-share equations (equation 22) as part of the system used to estimate the cost function. The revenue-share equations do not admit the possibility of cross-elasticities of demand; consequently, the model may be misspecified. In summary, the effects of this could range from incorrect assumptions about the endogeneity or exogeneity of each of the various services to incorrectly specified revenue-share equations. Both could alter the estimates of the coefficients of the cost function.

Pricing and Economic Efficiency

Fuss and Waverman note that the price for local service appears to be less than the incremental (or, as I have argued above, the marginal) cost, over the time period in question. For the message toll and competitive services the reverse is suggested. If there are no economies of scale (a possibility not rejected in the paper), then in the quest for economically efficient prices we need not worry about second best. If we were to set prices equal to marginal costs, then the firm would break even and economic efficiency would be maximized.

If there are economies of scale, then second best may be of interest. Fuss and Waverman state that second-best (Ramsey-optimal) prices cannot be calculated since local service has a constant elasticity of demand whose absolute value is less than unity. This by itself does not appear to be a problem. It is true that the log-linear specification of demands used by the authors does assume a constant elasticity of demand. Assume for the moment that there are zero income effects (an assumption contradicted by the empirical results in the article) and zero cross-elasticities of demand. Then, at a Ramsey optimum, two conditions would hold:

$$\Pi = 0$$

and

$$\left(\frac{p^i - MC^i}{p^i}\right)\varepsilon_i = \left(\frac{p^j - MC^j}{p^j}\right)\varepsilon_j \quad \text{for all } i \text{ and } j,$$

where

Π = overall level of profit for the firm,
p^i = price of ith service,
MC^i = marginal cost of ith service,
ε^i = price elasticity of demand for ith service.

The constant-elasticity assumptions would simply require that the percentage deviations of price from marginal cost—the term $(p^i - MC^i/p^i)$—would be proportional in each market. The fact that the absolute value of the price elasticity in any market is less than unity does not preclude the determination of Ramsey-optimal prices.

The general assertion of Fuss and Waverman that the calculation of second-best prices may not be possible is correct. The estimates of parameters may not be constant over the range of outputs between the prevailing levels and the second-best levels. The calculation would be complicated further by the existence of nonzero income effects, as indicated by the present estimates, and by nonzero cross-elasticities of demand, if they exist.

Conclusion

The analysis of Fuss and Waverman casts doubt on a number of prior studies of the telephone industry, many of which have assumed unrealistic and restrictive production functions (such as the Cobb-Douglas, a form they reject), and most of which have characterized telephone operations with a single, highly aggregated output. They have shown how it is possible to apply flexible-form cost functions to the telephone industry, and have suggested that, at least in the Canadian case, there is a real question as to whether the industry is a natural monopoly. Perhaps more data and further refinement in the estimating techniques will enable us to say more about that question. However, the present work alone has considerably advanced the state of the art of empirical work in the telecommunications industry.

Comment

Bridger M. Mitchell

Melvyn Fuss and Leonard Waverman have given us a stimulating article, reemphasizing the importance of closely examining the behavior of the multiple-product firm and focusing our attention on the central difficulties of analyzing common costs in a regulated market. Their analytic methods —particularly when developed in more ex:ensive form—promise to be a welcome addition to the economists' tool kit for addressing public-policy issues of rate structure, entry and competition, and the appropriate extent of monopoly supply. However, the article falls short of providing empirical results bearing on the policy questions that arise in regulation of the telecommunications sector.

I will briefly review Fuss and Waverman's methodology, and will comment on the appropriateness of their data as well as their modeling of regulatory constraints and of demand. I will then suggest how their econometric methods might be combined with an alternative procedure for estimating joint cost functions, an approach that holds greater promise for empirically establishing the long-run parameters of the production technology in the telecommunications sector.

The Model

Fuss and Waverman assume that three aggregate services (Y_i) are produced from three aggregated inputs (X_j) by a general multiproduct transformation function with convex isoquants:

$$F(Y,X) = 0, \qquad Y = (Y_1, Y_2, Y_3), \quad X = (X_1, X_2, X_3). \tag{1}$$

Provided that input prices (p) are exogenous, a cost-minimizing firm will have the dual cost function

$$C(Y,p), \qquad p = (p_1, p_2, p_3), \tag{2}$$

which embodies all of the technical information contained in (1).

Fuss and Waverman particularize this model by specifying (2) to be a general quadratic function in the logarithms of total cost, output, and price variables (the so-called translog cost function). They assume that the firm sells its services at uniform prices q, and maximizes profits

$$\Pi = \sum q_i Y_i - C \qquad (3)$$

subject to a regulatory constraint to be specified. This behavior implies a particular structure for the cost shares,

$$\frac{p_j X_j}{C} = f_j(Y,p), \qquad j = 1,2,3 \qquad (4)$$

and the "revenue shares" of the outputs

$$\frac{q_i Y_i}{C} = g_i(Y,p,\eta), \qquad \eta = (\eta_1,\eta_2,\eta_3), \qquad i = 1,2,3. \qquad (5)$$

In their application of this model the authors simultaneously estimate the parameters of the seven equations in (2), (4), and (5) by iterated three-stage least squares, assuming that technological change is Hicks-neutral and that per capita income and Y_1 (local telephone service) are exogenous variables. The demand elasticities, η_2 and η_3, for the endogenous outputs, Y_2 and Y_3, are estimated from independent demand equations.

The principal empirical findings are that

• the overall returns-to-scale elasticity is not significantly different from unity,
• incremental costs are falling for all services,
• all inputs are substitutes,
• there is a lack of economies of scope, and
• price is below incremental cost for local service.

Data

Fuss and Waverman use annual time-series data for Bell Canada for the period 1952–1975. Output is aggregated into three services: local (Y_1), toll (Y_2), and "competitive" (Y_3). The last category includes private-line, data, TWX, and wide-area telephone service (WATS) as well as directory advertising. For Y_2 and Y_3, constant-dollar quantity indices were available, and prices (q_2,q_3) were computed as implicit indices from the ratios of current revenues and the quantity indices. The output measure for local service (which is unexplained) could be either the number of main telephone stations or the quantity of local calls. Since flat-rate charges were in effect for most customers during this period, it would be inappropriate to use demand estimates based on an average price per call.

Inputs are similarly aggregated into three broad categories—materials, labor, and capital—by constructing annual price indices for each category.

The time-series nature of the data employed by the authors poses a fundamental question for the interpretation of their results: Are year-to-year changes in total cost, factor cost shares, and output prices a reliable basis for estimating the long-run multiproduct production function? Unfortunately, annual data are dominated by short-run behavior and often reflect disequilibrium conditions. This extremely capital-intensive industry is characterized by lumpy and large-scale investment projects requiring years for systemwide installation. Capacity utilization ("fill") shows significant annual variation. Moreover, the structure of the firm's output prices is not readily adjusted to reflect year-to-year changes in both demand conditions and relative prices of inputs. Finally, the precision of the parameter estimates is restricted by the limited variation in prices, factor shares, and output proportions observed in time-series data. At best, then, the data used by the authors could enable them to estimate the local properties of *short-run* cost and production functions.

Regulatory Constraint

The impact of regulation on the multiproduct firm is a challenging topic, one worthy of extended investigation. Although the Fuss-Waverman article represents a start in this direction, it does not reach the goal of analyzing the effect of regulation on a utility's actual behavior.

To formally introduce regulation into a model of a profit-maximizing multiproduct firm, the authors take two approaches. The first, used in their empirical work, is to assume that regulation constrains the price of one output (local service) and leaves the firm free to set the levels of the remaining prices. Fuss and Waverman choose local service as the exogenous output because their demand equation obtains an inelastic price coefficient, and the model cannot function with negative marginal revenue. The authors' alternative approach, which they develop theoretically for the translog cost function, is to assume that the firm is subject to classic rate-of-return regulation on total invested capital.

The difficulty, of course, is that regulators exert (or attempt to exert) control at many points. Indeed, the accounting procedures for separating common costs between services are intended to influence the rate levels of several services, and it is possible that such price regulation would force a regulated monopoly to operate at inelastic levels of demand in all markets. However, in an aggregative model one hesitates to use up more than one degree of freedom to specify the regulatory constraint, and there is no readily-available theory of regulators' preferences to specify the degree of price control exerted in each market. It would, therefore, be interesting to have the results of the authors' second approach —for a profit-maximizing firm constrained only by rate-of-return regulation—to examine how closely such a firm's output prices resemble those observed in the data.

Finally, the authors note that rate-of-return regulation was imposed on Bell Canada in the middle of the sample period. Did this change in the firm's regulatory environment influence its costs and product behavior?

Demand

Fuss and Waverman estimate a log-linear equation for the quantity of each of the three aggregate telecommunication services as a function of each service's own price and of real income per capita. The authors' cursory attention to the demand side of the market—they suggest that their equations be regarded as first-order approximations to arbitrary demand functions—stands in sharp contrast to their systematic development of the implications of joint products on the supply side. In principle, the demands for local, toll, and "competitive" services are interdependent and must be represented in the form of a joint demand function,

$$D(Y,p) = 0. \tag{6}$$

Several types of interdependencies are likely to be important for the particular output aggregates Fuss and Waverman use. First, the price of local service is both the cost to the customer of local calling and the price of access to obtain toll services, since he must first have a local telephone in order to place long-distance calls. The demand for toll services will, therefore, be a function of both local- and toll-service prices, especially for high-volume toll users who must purchase additional local lines in order to obtain access to the toll network. Second, some of the competitive services, particularly WATS, are close substitutes for message-toll service for high-volume users. The demands for Y_2 and Y_3 should, therefore, each be functions of both q_2 and q_3. Finally, telephone service has long been recognized as a case in which important externalities exist in the demand functions of individual consumers. In the demands for both local service and message toll service, the number of persons connected to the telephone network positively affects the demand for access as well as the number of calls at given prices. This externality, when incorporated into the firm's profit-maximizing calculus, can result in positive marginal revenues from supplying local service even when the demand function is apparently inelastic.

A satisfactory empirical investigation of the system of demand equations relevant to the Fuss-Waverman production structure will be a challenging undertaking. Over the period 1952–1975 important structural changes have occurred in telephone services. The introduction of direct distance dialing and of off-peak discount rates for toll calls has had a pronounced effect in stimulating message-toll traffic. Similarly, the availability of WATS and discount rates for bulk toll service and the recent emergence of competitive carriers for specialized intercity services have affected the conventional message-toll market as well as the market for other telecommunication services. Realistic estimates of the demand structure will need to incorporate at least the basic nature of these trends.

One can well sympathize with the authors for avoiding the additional difficulties posed by the simultaneity of demand and cost functions in a complete representation of their model. Nevertheless, it is clear that if the multiproduct firm's price policy is endogenous in its production decisions, then one may not without further investigation assume that prices are predetermined in using market data to estimate the system of demand equations that it faces.

An Alternative Approach

As an alternative to the direct econometric estimation of production or cost functions for the multiproduct firm, one may incorporate the major characteristics of the firm's joint production technology into a *process model*. In the telephone industry such an approach has been developed by S. C. Littlechild ("Peak-Load Pricing of Telephone Calls," *Bell Journal of Economics and Management Science* 1 (1970): 191–210). A process model incorporates multiple outputs Y_i and a technology consisting of items of equipment K_j with maximal capacities K_j. In such a model, particular pieces of equipment are in common use for multiple outputs. For example, K_1, the local loop and switch, provides capacity that is shared between local and toll services. The capacity constraints are that usage, when summed over the set of outputs B_j that use each item of equipment, not exceed the available capacity,

$$\sum_{i \in B_j} Y_i \leqslant \bar{K}_j. \tag{7}$$

Each item of equipment is associated with a long-run cost function that, in general, may incorporate economies of scale and factor substitution,

$$c_j(K_j,p). \tag{8}$$

When a particular set of regulatory constraints is imposed, the process model is optimized for a specified objective function. For example, the firm may be assumed to maximize profits:

$$\Pi = \sum_i q_i Y_i - \sum_j c_j(K_j,p). \tag{9}$$

As outputs, the process model yields the quantities and prices of market services, the levels of inputs, and the shadow price of each service. An important feature of the process-model approach is that the shadow prices may be interpreted as the long-run marginal costs of expanding the output of each service.

It is possible to combine the econometric and process approaches. Beginning with the process model, one may vary the input prices orthogonally over a wide range to generate minimum-cost solutions for joint production. (The model may also be used to introduce new technologies, different regulatory constraints, or the entry of competitors). The prices and outputs of these solutions constitute pseudodata that embody the firm's long-run responses to differing market conditions. One can then use these pseudodata to econometrically estimate a smooth multiple-output cost or production function, such as the translog function. Such a function will summarize the production technology into a small number of parameters representing the degree of scale economies, the nature of input substitution, and the character of expansion paths. This alternative approach of combining process information with econometric specifications avoids many of the problems inherent in time-series data, including multicollinearity, limited sample variation in key variables, and the presence of disequilibrium behavior.

J. M. Griffin's initial study of multi-output production in the electric power industry ("Long-run Production Modeling with Pseudo Data: Electric Power Generation," *Bell Journal of Economics* 8 (1977): 112–127) suggests that the psuedodata approach can elucidate policy questions that depend on the empirical measurement of long-run parameters. Although Fuss and Waverman's time-series analysis does not yield reliable information on these questions, the application of their methodology in conjunction with a process model is a promising line of future inquiry.

This comment is an elaboration of my discussion of the paper "Multiproduct, Multiinput Cost Functions for a Regulated Utility: The Case of Telecommunications in Canada," by Melvyn Fuss and Leonard Waverman, presented at the conference. Preparation of these remarks has been supported by a fellowship from the German Marshall Fund and by National Science Foundation grant APR 77-16286 to the Rand Corporation.

7

Open Entry and Cross-Subsidization in Regulated Markets

Kenneth C. Baseman

Decisions by the Federal Communications Commission and other regulatory agencies to encourage competition in regulated markets have led to extensive consideration of the problem of cross-subsidization. In particular, the FCC has concerned itself (in docket 18128) with whether American Telephone and Telegraph could increase prices in its monopoly MTS-WATS markets in order to finance "unfair" competition against firms competing with AT&T in other markets.[1] The same issue arises in postal service. The U.S. Postal Service is a monopoly carrier for first class mail and competes with various firms in parcel delivery.

AT&T's position before the FCC and Congress is one which I suspect many economists would find appealing, at least at first blush:[2] that as long as revenues in competitive markets cover incremental costs, the pricing structure cannot be said to involve cross-subsidization even though the resulting prices exclude potential competitors from markets nominally open to entry. Revenues in excess of incremental cost in competitive markets allow those markets to make some contribution toward covering costs that are common to the provision of both competitive and monopoly services. Therefore, prices charged to consumers of monopoly services can be lower than if joint provision of the various services were not allowed. Further, consumers of competitive services are better off than if the monopolist's price were disallowed, since that price is lower than the price competing firms can offer. Therefore, correct application of the incremental-cost test ensures that consumers in all markets are better off with joint provision of the services.

My argument is that the above position, despite its intuitive appeal, is incorrect. I shall demonstrate that the combination of franchise monopoly markets and an incremental-cost pricing rule in competitive markets cannot be expected, in general, to lead the industry to the most efficient market structure. In particular, it will be shown that the above set of rules may allow the multiproduct firm to successfully monopolize both its own franchise monopoly markets and the competitive markets even when joint production is absolutely inefficient. In such situations, the price in the monopoly markets will be seen to lie above the cost of serving those markets alone. The results are then interpreted as statements about cross-subsidization by reference to Faulhaber's (1975a) game-theoretic approach to cross-subsidization.

A Simple Numerical Example

Suppose we have two products for which the demands are perfectly price-inelastic, and that the cost functions are

$C(q_1,0) = 40,$

$C(0,q_2) = 40,$

$C^m(q_1,q_2) = 90.$

Let S denote an input, used by the joint monopolist, that is necessary for the production of either service. Expenditures on S are common costs for the joint monopolist. Let A_i denote inputs that are used only in the production of service i. Expenditures on A_i are attributable to service i. Suppose all input prices equal unity.

Now let the two-product monopolist's most efficient input choice, with respect to his joint-production technology, be

$S = 50,$

$A_1 = 20,$

$A_2 = 20.$

Let service 2 be the joint monopolist's franchise monopoly market. The incremental cost of additionally serving market 1 is given by

$$C^m(q_1,q_2) - C^m(0,q_2) = 90 - 70 = 20. \tag{1}$$

The monopolist can clearly pick p_1^m to satisfy an incremental-cost rule, while beating the competition in market 1 by choosing p_1^m such that

$20 < p_1^m < 40.$

To satisfy a break-even constraint, the monopolist then chooses p_2^m to satisfy

$$90 - p_1^m = p_2^m > 50. \tag{2}$$

The final result is a joint monopoly over both markets, with total costs 10 above what they would be with separate production.

Now suppose that the monopolist's cost-minimizing input choice, using the joint production technology, is given by

$S = 8,$

$A_1 = 42,$

$A_2 = 42.$

Since the incremental cost of serving market 1 is now 42, it would appear that an inefficient joint monopoly could not pass an incremental-cost test. However, suppose that the elasticity of substitution between the inputs S and A_i is greater than zero (that is, suppose we are not dealing with a fixed-proportions technology). Then an inefficient joint monopoly may be feasible. Suppose that one of the points on the monopolist's isoquant is

$S = 20,$

$A_1 = 38,$

$A_2 = 38.$

Total costs are now 96, reflecting the fact that we have moved away from the cost-minimizing point for joint production. However, since A_1 is less than 40, joint monopoly can now be successful.

In remainder of the article I will distinguish, as was done above, between two types of inefficient joint monopoly: type 1, in which the monopolist's cost-minimizing input choice, using the joint-production technology, allows him to pass an incremental-cost test, and type 2, in which the joint monopolist cannot pass an incremental-cost test using the cost-minimizing input combination for joint production, but input substitutability allows the joint monopolist to serve both markets while satisfying an incremental-cost pricing rule.

More Examples of Inefficient Joint Monopoly

In this section, a two-product model will be used to further develop the notion of inefficient joint monopoly. The assumptions of the model, except for subadditivity and the specification of the monopolist's cost function, match the assumptions made in Faulhaber's (1975a) work on cross-subsidization.

Assumptions

A1. The demand functions are given by

$$q_i = q_i(p_1, p_2) \qquad (i = 1,2),$$

with

$$\frac{\partial q_i}{\partial p_i} < 0, \qquad \frac{\partial q_i}{\partial p_j} \geq 0.$$

A2. The cost functions for independent production of the two commodities are given by $C^1(q_1,0)$ and $C^2(0,q_2)$. The cost functions exhibit nonincreasing average cost:

$$\frac{d(C^i(q_i)/q_i)}{dq_i} \leq 0.$$

A3. The joint monopolist's cost function is given by

$$C^m(q_1,q_2) = \min_{S, A_1, A_2} C^m(S, A_1, A_2; q_1, q_2, p_{A_1}, p_{A_2}, p_S), \qquad (3)$$

where S, A_1, and A_2 retain their definitions from the preceding section. The underlying production function is given by

$$q_1^m = q_1^m(S, A_1),$$

$$q_2^m = q_2^m(S, A_2).$$

The isoquants for the above production functions are convex:[3]

$$\left.\frac{dS}{dA_i}\right|_{dq_i=0} < 0, \qquad \left.\frac{d^2S}{dA_i^2}\right|_{dq_i=0} > 0.$$

A4. The overall cost function is superadditive:

$$C^m(q_1,q_2) > C^1(q_1,0) + C^2(0,q_2).$$

A5. The monopolist is confined to price pairs for which $\partial \pi^m/\partial p_i > 0$ $(i = 1,2)$. The monopolist's $\pi^m = 0$ locus might look something like that depicted in figure 7.1. Price pairs along the arc AB satisfy $\partial \pi^m/\partial p_i > 0$. The assumption is plausible in that, even if the firm is indifferent to whether or not its prices lie on an undominated portion of the $\pi^m = 0$ locus, the regulator will attempt to force the firm toward the "low" price pairs on AB. In addition, along any $\pi^m = k > 0$ locus, a profit-maximizing monopolist faced with either direct or indirect competition (in the form of a substitute product offered by a competing firm) has an incentive to choose the "low" price pairs for which $\partial \pi^m/\partial p_i > 0$.

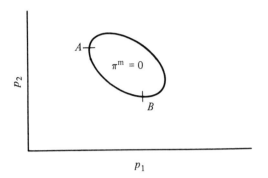

Figure 7.1 Region of non-negative profit for a two-product monopolist.

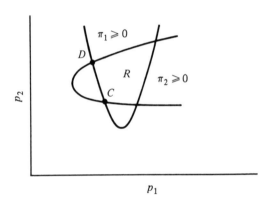

Figure 7.2 Regions of non-negative profit for two single-product firms.

We are also assuming that, at the noncooperative zero-profit equilibrium for separate production, $\partial \pi^i / \partial p_i > 0$ for $i = 1,2$. This would be the case if the profit functions $\pi^i(p_i;p_j)$ were concave in their own prices. Figure 7.2 shows regions of non-negative profits are shown for firms producing independently (with $\partial q^i / \partial p_j > 0$ and decreasing average costs). At C, a price increase by either firm would yield it positive profits. At any other zero-profit solution for the two firms, such as D, $\partial \pi^i / \partial p_i < 0$ for at least one of the firms (in this case it is firm 2). C dominates other solutions to $\pi^i(p_1,p_2) = 0$ for $i = 1,2$, since, at the other solutions, entry would force price reductions in at least one of the markets.

We know from assumption A4 that the joint monopolist will lose money at (p_1^c,p_2^c), since the two independent firms just break even at that point and the monopolist incurs larger costs to produce the same outputs. Denote by L the joint monopolist's losses at (p_1^c,p_2^c). R^m is the monopolist's revenue function. Thus,

$$\pi^m(p_1^c, p_2^c) = R^m(p_1^c, p_2^c) - C^m(q_1^c(p_1^c, p_2^c), q_2^c(p_1^c, p_2^c)) = L < 0. \quad (4)$$

Now assume that market 2 is a franchise monopoly market for our joint monopolist, but that entry is allowed in market 1. Can the joint monopolist, given a franchise monopoly in market 2 and an incremental-cost pricing rule in market 1, find a price pair that yields non-negative profits? That price pair (p_1^m, p_2^m) must satisfy the following conditions.

i. $p_1^m \leq p_1^*$, where p_1^* is the lowest price, given p_2^m, at which a firm serving only market 1 can break even.[4] A profit-maximizing monopolist will always choose to satisfy this requirement with equality. This can be most easily seen by referring back to figure 7.1. Positive profits occur for the monopolist at price pairs in the interior of $\pi^m = 0$. Thus, if our monopolist starts at some price pair on AB and finds his p_1^m more than sufficient to prevent entry in market 1, he can increase profits by increasing p_1^m. Thus, condition i is replaced by condition i':

i'. $p_1^m = p_1^*$. This result, which means that for a given value of p_2^m profits are maximized at p_1^*, will simplify the analysis, since p_1^* can be derived implicitly from p_2^m and we need deal with only the single decision variable p_2^m.

ii. $p_1^m q_1^m \geq p_{A_1} A_1$. This is the incremental-cost pricing rule.

iii. $\pi^m(p_1^m, p_2^m) \geq 0$.

The entry-deterring price[5] in market 1, p_1^*, is given implicitly by

$$p_1^* = p_1 \mid R^1(p_1, p_2^m) - C^1(q_1(p_1, p_2^m)) = 0. \quad (5)$$

The derivative dp_1^*/dp_2^m is

$$\frac{dp_1^*}{dp_2^m} = -\frac{\partial R^1}{\partial p_2^m} - \frac{\partial C^1}{\partial q_1}\frac{\partial q_1}{\partial p_2} \bigg/ \frac{\partial R^1}{\partial p_1^*} - \frac{\partial C^1}{\partial q_1}\frac{\partial q_1}{\partial p_1^*}$$

$$= -\left(p_1^* - \frac{\partial C^1}{\partial q_1}\right)\frac{\partial q_1}{\partial p_2} \bigg/ \frac{\partial R^1}{\partial p_1^*} - \frac{\partial C^1}{\partial q_1}\frac{\partial q_1}{\partial p_1^*} \leq 0. \quad (6)$$

The denominator in the expression above is equal to $\partial \pi^1/\partial p_1^* > 0$ for $p_1^* \leq p_1^c$. The numerators are non-negative, being the product of two non-negative terms. Assumption A2 requires $\partial C^1/\partial q_1 \leq C^1(q_1)/q_1$, and equation (5) requires $p_1^* = C^1(q_1)/q_1$. Therefore, $p_1^* \geq \partial C^1/\partial q_1$. Also, $\partial q_1/\partial p_2 \geq 0$ by assumption A1.

We now examine a candidate price vector $(p_1^*, \bar{p}_2^m)$ to see if the joint monopolist can satisfy conditions i' through iii. At $(p_1^*, \bar{p}_2^m)$ the joint monopolist's profits are

$$\pi^m(p_1^*,\bar{p}_2^m) = R^m(p_1^*,\bar{p}_2^m) - C^m(q_1(p_1^*,\bar{p}_2^m),q_2(p_1^*,\bar{p}_2^m)). \tag{7}$$

The change in the joint monopolist's profits when he moves from ($p_1^* = p_1^c,p_2^c$) to ($p_1^*,\bar{p}_2^m$) is given by

$$\int_{p_2^c}^{\bar{p}_2^m} \frac{d\pi^m}{dp_2^m}dw,$$

where w is a dummy variable of integration.
The total derivative $d\pi^m/dp_2^m$ is

$$\frac{d\pi^m}{dp_2^m} = \frac{\partial^+\pi^m}{\partial p_1^*}\frac{dp_1^*}{dp_2^m} + \frac{\partial^+\pi^m}{\partial p_2^m}. \tag{8}$$

A necessary condition for a successful joint monopoly is that equation (8) be positive. If the monopolist cannot obtain an increase in profits via an increase in p_2^m,[6] his initial losses (L) can never be overcome.

For given specifications of the demand and cost functions, equation (8) can be either positive or negative. Large unexploited monopoly profits in the franchise monopoly market will help the joint monopolist, since then $\partial\pi^m/\partial p_2^m$ will be large. Similarly, large losses in market 1, given dp_1^*, will tend to hurt the joint monopolist. Large substitution effects (in demand) and substantial scale economies for independent production of service 1 will hurt the joint monopolist, since these factors make $|dp_1^*/dp_2^m|$ large.

When demands are independent or when independent production is done at constant cost, then $dp_1^*/dp_2^m = 0$ and equation (8) reduces to

$$\frac{d\pi^m}{dp_2^m} = \frac{\partial\pi^m}{\partial p_2^m}. \tag{9}$$

This result is highly intuitive. Independent demands or constant costs imply that changes in p_2^m will not affect the entry-preventing price in market 1. Therefore, the only things that affect profits when p_2 changes are the changes in costs and revenues in market 2.

We are now ready to complete the analysis. Type 1 joint monopoly will obtain if

$$\int_{p_2^c}^{\bar{p}_2^m} \frac{d\pi^m}{dp_2^m}dw - L \geq 0 \tag{10}$$

and

$$P_{A_1}A_1 \leq p_1^*\bar{q}_1^m. \tag{11}$$

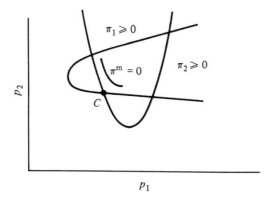

Figure 7.3 A case where joint monopoly cannot succeed.

When equation (11) is not satisfied by the joint monopolist's cost-minimizing input choices, given $\bar{q}_1^m$ and $\bar{q}_2^m$, the monopolist can turn to type 2 monopolization. Let the joint monopolist substitute away from A_1 and toward S until the point is reached (if one exists) where $p_{A_1}A_1 = p_1^*\bar{q}_1^m$. Denote by $\hat{A}_1$ the largest value of A_1 satisfying the incremental-cost constraint. Because the monopolist's isoquants are assumed to be convex, the total costs of supplying the two markets will increase with this substitution. Denote by ΔC^m the change in costs:

$$\Delta C^m = \min_{A_2,S} C^m(A_2,S;\hat{A}_1,\bar{q}_1^m,\bar{q}_2^m) - \min_{A_1,A_2,S} C^m(A_1,A_2,S;\bar{q}_1^m,\bar{q}_2^m) > 0. \quad (12)$$

Of course, the larger the elasticity of substitution, the smaller ΔC^m will have to be in order to satisfy the incremental-cost pricing rule.
The joint monopolist will now succeed if

$$\int_{p_2^c}^{\bar{p}_2^m} \frac{d\pi^m}{p_2^m}\,dw - L - \Delta C^m \geq 0. \quad (13)$$

The various possibilities for success or failure of inefficient joint monopoly can be diagramed. Demands are assumed to be substitutes in these figures. Figure 7.3 depicts a case where joint monopoly cannot succeed. The $\pi^m = 0$ locus lies "northeast" of the point C because of the superadditivity assumption. Joint monopoly cannot succeed, because the undominated portion of the $\pi^m = 0$ locus lies entirely within the $\pi_1 \geq 0$ region. At any price pair chosen by the monopolist, a firm offering only service 1 can successfully underprice p_1^m.

Figure 7.4 illustrates a situation where joint monopoly might succeed. Because a $\pi^m = k$ locus passes outside $\pi_1 \geq 0$, price pairs (such as point

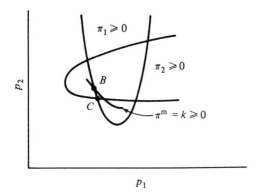

$\pi_1 \geqslant 0$

$\pi_2 \geqslant 0$

B

$\pi^m = k \geqslant 0$

C

p_2

p_1

Figure 7.4 A case where joint monopoly might succeed.

B) can be chosen at which a firm serving only market 1 will not be viable. If at any such point revenues exceed incremental costs, type 1 joint monopoly is possible. If the incremental-cost rule is not satisfied at B, the monopolist can attempt to satisfy the rule by substituting away from A_1. If there exists an $\hat{A}_1$ that satisfies the rule, and if $k \geq \Delta C^m$, then a type 2 joint monopoly could survive.

Type 1 versus Type 2 Joint Monopolies

I have found it convenient for heuristic purposes to define two different types of joint monopolies. Both types (not just type 2) depend crucially on the assumption of variable proportions. If it is true that joint production is necessarily inefficient, then a cost-minimizing monopolist will forgo joint production and operate two subsidiaries that produce their services independently. Costs will be higher than under independent production by separate firms, owing to the presumably small costs of operating the holding company. To get from the holding company to a case of type 1 joint monopoly, the monopolist must substitute away from attributable inputs toward common inputs; otherwise the incremental-cost pricing constraint can never be satisfied. This is not to say that the distinction is purely heuristic. Type 1 joint monopolies could occur whenever a monopolist fails to minimize costs, so long as the failure is biased in the "right" direction. The failure could either be inadvertent (that is, a result of x-inefficiency) or deliberate. There are reasons why the monopolist might choose a technology other than the cost-minimizing one. For example, Averch-Johnson input distortion and rate-base padding are both due to decisions by the monopolist to choose input combinations

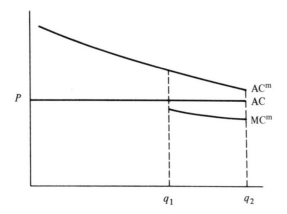

Figure 7.5 The case of an inefficient single-product monopoly.

that do not minimize costs. The profitability of such choices, of course, depends upon the monopolist's being subject to a rate-of-return constraint and not a break-even constraint.

The incentive the monopolist will have to monopolize both markets (in either the type 1 or the type 2 case) also follows from the fact that the profit constraint is given in the form of a limit on the allowed rate of return. Averch and Johnson (1962) demonstrated that so long as the allowed rate of return exceeds the cost of capital and additional profits can be drawn from a monopoly market, a regulated monopolist will find it profitable to serve additional markets even if incremental costs are not covered in those markets. Serving such markets increases the size of the rate base, thereby allowing total profits to rise. The monopolist can cover any "losses" in competitive markets with additional revenues drawn from the monopoly market.

The Results in Terms of Cost Functions

The results in the preceding sections can be illustrated by looking directly at the cost functions. In figure 7.5 we assume that the monopolist has a franchise monopoly over the first q_1 units of output, but that for subsequent units $(q_2 - q_1)$ competition is allowed. The minimum-average-cost curve is shown as AC. The inefficient monopolist's average-cost curve is AC^m. The incremental cost for the monopolist of producing $q_2 - q_1$ (the area under MC^m) is less than the constant incremental cost of those units when produced by another firm. The inefficient monopolist can thus serve both markets. The market will look like a natural monopoly market to a regulator who does not have knowledge of the full technology set.

A similar result can be obtained in the multiproduct case. The assumption that the joint monopolist is inefficient is stated algebraically as

$$C^m(q_1,q_2) > C^1(q_1) + C^2(q_2),$$

$$C^m(q_1,0) > C^1(q_1),$$

$$C^m(0,q_2) > C^2(q_2).$$

If the joint monopolist passes an incremental-cost test in market 1 and the monopolist chooses p_1^m to "just" deter entry, we have

$$C^m(q_1,q_2) - C^m(0,q_2) \leq p_1^m q_1^m = C^1(q_1),$$

or

$$C^m(q_1,q_2) \leq C^m(0, q_2) + C^1(q_1)$$

or

$$C^m(q_1,q_2) < C^m(q_1,0) + C^m(0,q_2).$$

The monopolist's chosen technology will appear to be subadditive, although the cost-minimizing technology is not. A regulator without knowledge of the full technology set will think he is dealing with a two-product natural monopoly.

These results are not surprising. Under an incremental-cost test, incremental costs for each service will not sum up to total costs whenever the average cost function is declining or, with several products, when the cost function is subadditive. There will be a residual of common costs that cannot be attributed to any service and that reflect the fact that production of larger outputs allows the firm to realize lower average costs of production. The substitution away from attributable inputs toward common inputs thus requires the choice of a cost function that is "more subadditive" than the cost function associated with the cost-minimizing technology.

Inefficient Joint Monopoly and Cross-Subsidization

Readers familiar with Faulhaber's work on cross-subsidization have no doubt recognized that the prices charged by our joint monopolist are not subsidy-free. Faulhaber's basic insight is that cross-subsidization can be neatly and elegantly analyzed by employing the theory of cooperative games. The "players" of the game are the consumers in each market. Joint monopoly production is the outcome of that game if the monopolist chooses a price vector satisfying the core conditions. Among the core conditions are the requirements that $p_i^m \leq p_i^c$—that is, the monopolist must "beat" the prices available to each "player" if independent production is chosen. Our joint monopolist clearly does not satisfy the core conditions, since $p_2^m > p_2^c$. The price in market 2 is above "stand alone" cost, and service 2 users are subsidizing consumers of service 1. The franchise-monopoly rule prevents the consumers in market 2 from withdrawing from the joint monopolist's "coalition." Even though joint monopoly is inefficient and the prices are outside the core of the cooperative game, a "cooperative" solution—joint monopoly—is forced upon the users of service 2.

Open Entry

We have seen that a franchise monopolist can be inefficient and still compete successfully in other markets even when subject to an incremental-cost pricing rule in competitive markets. In addition, an incremental-cost pricing rule gives a franchise monopolist an incentive to choose inefficient technologies if his cost-minimizing joint technology does not allow him to satisfy an incremental-cost pricing rule in competitive markets. In either case, because resources are wasted in supplying the franchise-monopoly market, a natural policy implication is that the monopoly market ought to be opened up to entry. Work by Panzar and Willig (1977a) indicates that such a market test may backfire. A "true" natural monopoly may be unsustainable if entry restrictions are lifted.

Sustainability

Panzar and Willig (1977a) have demonstrated that the assumption that the cost function is subadditive (the "natural monopoly" assumption) is not sufficient to guarantee that a monopolist will be able to profitably maintain production of the full set of outputs if free entry is allowed. A natural monopoly, when faced with entry, may be forced to reduce its product offerings or face elimination from the market.

In the one-product case, if natural monopoly is unsustainable the effect of an open-entry rule will be a reduction in output. In the multiproduct case, when natural monopoly is unsustainable and entry is allowed, the

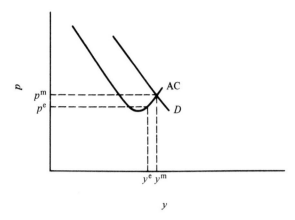

Figure 7.6 The case of an unsustainable single-product natural monopoly.

resulting equilibrium will feature fewer products. In either case, welfare (total surplus) could increase or decrease if entry is allowed and the natural monopoly is unsustainable. Thus, under certain circumstances, entry restrictions may be required in order to achieve the welfare maximum.

The sustainability models thus appear to raise troublesome policy questions concerning the role of entry restrictions in regulated markets. Many regulated markets exhibit declining average-cost curves and possible economies of joint production, which may give rise to sustainability problems. This is especially true where some sort of "networking" is present, as in telecommunications, mail service, power distribution, and transportation. In such instances there may be economies from the joint provision of several "links" in the network.

The question Panzar and Willig pose is: Under what conditions can a natural monopolist choose a price vector that guarantees that a potential entrant can anticipate only negative profits if entry is attempted? No consideration is given to the joint monopolist's reaction to attempted entry. The justification for this assumption, and the implications of relaxing the assumption, will be considered later in this article.

Sustainability with One Product

The "natural monopoly" assumption does not require the average cost curve to be monotonically decreasing. Figure 7.6 depicts a cost curve that satisfies the subadditivity assumption that the cheapest way to produce the output y^m is production by only one firm. In such a situation, where the average-cost curve turns up, the natural monopoly will be unsustainable. For example, an entrant, by choosing p^e, can supplant the original monopolist. Of course, if the average-cost curve is monotonically decreasing, the natural monopoly will be sustainable. This result was first pointed out by Faulhaber (1975b).

Sustainability with Two Products

(Note: Some cases considered by Panzar and Willig are not treated in this section. "Cooperative" entry and the case of independent demands will be discussed later.)

The monopolist's outputs are denoted by the vector $y^m = (y_1^m, y_2^m)$. The monopoly prices are $p^m = (p_1^m, p_2^m)$. The demand functions are given by

$$y_i^m = Q^i(p^m) \qquad (i = 1,2)$$

with

$$\frac{\partial Q^i}{\partial p_i} < 0, \qquad \frac{\partial Q^i}{\partial p_j} > 0.$$

The multiproduct minimum cost function is $C(y^m)$. This cost function is assumed to exhibit multiproduct scale economies characterized by least ray average cost; $(1/\lambda)C(\lambda y^m) > C(y^m)$ for $0 < \lambda < 1)$. In addition, the average incremental cost of each output, with the amount of the other service held constant, is assumed to be declining.

The cost functions available to firms producing only one of the two products are $C(y_1,0)$ and $C(0,y_2)$. These cost functions are assumed to exhibit declining average costs. Costs are assumed to be subadditive:

$$C(y^m) = C(y_1^m, y_2^m) < C(y_1,0) + C(0,y_2). \tag{13}$$

The monopolist's chosen price vector is sustainable against an entrant offering only one of the products if and only if

$$p_i^e y_i^e - C(y_i^e) < 0 \qquad (i = 1,2),$$

where $p_i^e \leq p_i^m$ and $y_i^e \leq Q^i(p_i^e, p_j^m)$.

Panzar and Willig derived seven necessary conditions for the sustainability of the monopolist's price and output choice. Among those conditions, in addition to subadditivity and cost minimization by the monopolist, are the following:

- p^m is undominated; that is, there cannot exist a $(p_1^e, p_2^e) \leq (p_1^m, p_2^m)$ with $\pi(p^e) \geq 0$.
- $p_i^m y_i^m < C(y_i^m)$ for $i = 1, 2$. If this condition did not hold, then an entrant could offer y_i^m at p_i^m and earn non-negative profits.

The second condition is related to Faulhaber's application of the theory of cooperative games to the problem of cross-subsidization. Multiproduct monopoly can be viewed as the core outcome of a cooperative cost game in which the "players" are the consumers of each service (one "player" is associated with each service). Denote by E_i the revenue allocation ("imputation") assigned to each customer group. The core conditions require that revenues cover costs, or

$$\sum_{i=1}^{2} E_i \geq C(y^m),$$

and that no customer group be charged more than its "stand-alone" costs, or

$$E_i < C(y_i^m) \qquad (i = 1, 2).$$

The second condition requires that the imputation $E = (p_1^m y_1^m, p_2^m y_2^m)$ be in the core of the cost game. Clearly, it is first required that the cost game possess a nonempty core.[7] Panzar and Willig show that the assumption of weak cost complementarities is sufficient to ensure that the core of the cost game is nonempty. Weak cost complementarities require that the marginal cost of one service not increase with increased output of any other service.

Given a nonempty core to the cost game, the second condition plus $\pi^m \geq 0$ require that the market revenues lie in that core. This means that the demand functions must lie "out" far enough so that the monopolist can cover its costs (for example, if all demands are zero, market revenues are clearly outside the core). In addition, market demands allowing $\pi^m \geq 0$ must contain some points that allow the monopolist to price below stand-alone cost in both markets. Panzar and Willig provide some examples which indicate that, when the demands are insufficient to support independent production of the two commodities, the monopolist, in order to serve both products, may have to set price above stand-alone cost in one of the markets. In this section I shall be concerned only with sustainability problems that arise when the second condition is satisfied.[8] (Sustainability problems when that condition is not satisfied are discussed briefly below.)

The crux of the sustainability problem lies in the twin assumptions

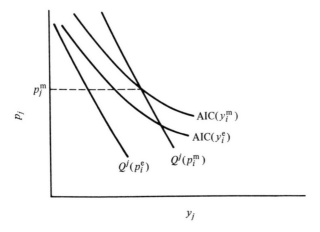

Figure 7.7 The case of an unsustainable natural monopoly that cannot recover the incremental costs of providing a substitute service.

of single-product economies of scale (for both entrant and monopolist) and demand substitutability. The first of these effects allows the potential entrant, facing p^m, to contemplate a substantial price cut in one of the markets. The potential entrant, looking only at the demand for one of the products, enters if $\pi^e \geq 0$ can be achieved (the market demand curve lies above his average cost curve). This gives a new $p_i = p_i^e$. The question, for the sustainability calculation, is whether the monopolist could have chosen a vector $p^m = (p_i^e, p_j^m)$ that would have yielded non-negative profits. Such a choice may not have been feasible. The lower price for service i implies that the demand curve for substitute service j will have shifted "backward." At lower outputs, the joint monopolist's average incremental cost (AIC) of providing service j will increase. If the average incremental cost of providing service j increases "fast" enough, and the demand curve shifts back "far" enough, there may be no points in common that allow the monopolist to recover the incremental costs of providing service j. Such a situation is depicted in figure 7.7.

The move from (p_i^m, y_i^m) to (p_i^e, y_i^e) has two effects. AIC_j shifts down, because production of service j is now complemented by larger production of service i.[9] The demand curve for service j shifts back because the products are substitutes. As drawn, the new demand curve lies nowhere above the new AIC curve, so the natural monopoly is unsustainable. Moreover, by subadditivity, the average-cost curve for a firm supplying only service j lies above AIC_j. Thus, service j will not be provided at all. The total surplus forgone in market j is the area above p_j^m and below $Q^j(p_i^e)$. If this forgone surplus exceeds the gains in surplus in market i,

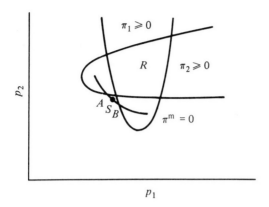

Figure 7.8 A sustainable natural monopoly.

then the decision to allow entry will have resulted in a decline in welfare.

In the sustainability calculation, then, the presence of strong product-specific scale economies for both the entrant and the joint monopolist, and a large cross-price elasticity of demand tend to favor the entrant over the monopolist. On the other side, of course, large economies of joint production tend to favor the joint monopolist.

The sustainability problem is further illustrated in figures 7.8 and 7.9. Figure 7.8 depicts a sustainable natural monopoly. The region of prices that could simultaneously support independent production of both services is denoted R. By subadditivity, the $\pi^m = 0$ locus must lie "southwest" of R. The sustainable range of prices lies on the arc AB. From any point on that arc (such as the point S), price reductions for either service cannot move an entrant into a region of non-negative profits.

Figure 7.9 shows an unsustainable natural monopoly. An entrant in market 2 can, by a large price reduction, come to rest in the $\pi_2 \geq 0$ region, thus successfully supplanting the original monopolist. The point M satisfies all the necessary conditions for sustainability. However, M is unsustainable against, for example, the point E.

Sustainability with Monopoly Reaction

That a monopolist does not react when entry occurs is a very tenuous assumption. Panzar and Willig justify the use of the Cournot-Nash assumption with regard to prices as follows:

...the Cournot-Nash expectation need not be self-fulfilling. Competitive entry would plunge the previously breaking-even monopoly

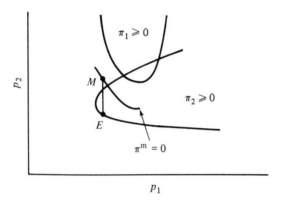

Figure 7.9 An unsustainable natural monopoly.

into the red and would necessitate changes in its prices. However, if the entrant is "small" relative to the industry, the magnitude of these required adjustments will also be "small" and may hence be justifiably ignored by the entrant. Also, the entrant may believe that the regulator would insure that the price adjustments would not be retaliatory with respect to the entrant's product lines, and that instead the monopolist's losses would be recovered from changes in prices of services only tangentially related to the entrant's offerings. (Panzar and Willig 1977a, p. 4.)

The second of these reasons is plausible enough. Regulators have the power to forbid price reactions, and occasionally have been known to exercise that power. However, in two of the three versions of the sustainability models presented by Panzar and Willig the entrants are quite large. With several products, scale economies, and declining average incremental cost, the entrant must supply more of the product than the original monopolist had chosen to provide. In the single-product case, with a U-shaped average cost curve, the subadditivity assumption requires that the entrant be at least half the size of the original firm. Successful entry at a smaller scale would violate the subadditivity assumption, implying that we were not dealing initially with a natural monopoly. Only in the case where the monopolist cannot find (or is not allowed by the regulator to choose) a price vector satisfying the core conditions can a small-scale entrant be successful. Discussion of this last case is deferred until later in the article.

With a large-scale entrant it is reasonable to ask whether the regulator would or should disallow a price reaction by the monopolist when entry occurs. The costs of disallowing monopoly reaction can be enormous, quite apart from sustainability issues. Suppose an entrant can produce the monopolist's output at a cost only slightly less than that of the monopolist. If we allow entry and disallow a monopoly price reaction, the total cost to society of obtaining (approximately) the monopolist's original output will be the entrant's total costs plus the monopolist's fixed costs. Also, given the general dissatisfaction with industry performance in markets where regulators have restricted price reductions by firms of roughly equal size, such as airlines, it is at least worth taking a look at what happens in the sustainability problem when the monopolist is allowed to react to a large-scale entrant.

With regard to the first reason given in the quote above, there is something inherently incongruous about an entrant small enough to be ignored and large enough to drive the monopolist from one of his markets. Admittedly, the two-product case exaggerates the effect of entry, since in that case successful entry means that the monopoly disappears. However, even in the *n*-product case, where the effect of entry in any one market may only be to force the monopolist to offer a smaller product set, the assumption that the monopolist will not react is noticeably at variance with the behavior of real-world regulated monopolies.

What I propose to examine is the short-run profit-maximizing response of the monopolist to attempted entry. It will turn out, not surprisingly, that the range of situations under which monopoly production is sustainable is enlarged substantially. As in the Panzar-Willig model, sustainable natural monopoly production can be viewed as a Nash equilibrium, although in this case it is the monopolist's reaction function and not his price against which the entrant holds the Cournot-Nash expectation. The monopolist's reaction function will be derived by solving for his profit-maximizing (loss-minimizing) price and quantity choices, given the price and quantity choices of the entrant.

To examine the short run aspects of the problem we need to specify in more detail the monopolist's cost function. Let the cost function be given by

$$C(y_1^m, y_2^m) = \min_{F, F_1, F_2, V, V_1, V_2} C(F, F_1, F_2, V, V_1, V_2; y_1^m, y_2^m, \text{input prices}),$$
(14)

where F and V are the fixed and variable inputs that are common costs for both services and F_i and V_i are the fixed and variable inputs used specifically in providing service i. The incremental, or attributable, cost of providing service i is denoted by IC^i.

In the short run, the monopolist finds himself already having chosen F, F_1, F_2, and V.[10] We retain the assumption that $p_2^m y_2^m < C(y_2^m)$. However, given the single-product scale economies, the entrant can contemplate offering service 2 at a price lower than the monopolist's current price. Since the entrant must exploit economies of scale in order to enter, he is also offering to supply a larger quantity than that provided by the monopolist. Thus, if the monopolist is to supply any of service 2 at all, he must at least match the entrant's price.[11]

The monopolist's profit-maximization problem[12] is given by

$$\text{maximize}_{p_1^m, p_2^m, y_1^m, y_2^m} \pi^m = \sum_{i=1}^{2} [p_i^m y_i^m - IC^i(y_i^m)] - \text{other costs}$$

$$(p_2^e - p_2^m \geq 0)$$

and

$$Q^i(p_1^m, p_2^m) - y_i^m \geq 0 \qquad (i = 1,2).$$

The second of the above constraints indicates that the monopolist's output choice is limited to outputs that can be sold. The Lagrangian for the optimization problem is

$$\mathcal{L} = \pi^m + \sum_{i=1}^{2} \lambda_i [Q^i(p_1^m, p_2^m) - y_i^m] + \mu(p_2^e - p_2^m). \tag{15}$$

The Kuhn-Tucker necessary conditions for an interior solution are

$$\frac{\partial \mathcal{L}}{\partial p_2^m} = y_2^m + \lambda_1 \frac{\partial Q^1}{\partial p_2^m} + \lambda_2 \frac{\partial Q^2}{\partial p_2^m} - \mu = 0, \tag{16}$$

$$\frac{\partial \mathcal{L}}{\partial p_1^m} = y_1^m + \lambda_1 \frac{\partial Q^1}{\partial p_1^m} + \lambda_2 \frac{\partial Q^2}{\partial p_1^m} = 0, \tag{17}$$

$$\frac{\partial \mathcal{L}}{\partial y_1^m} = p_1^m - \frac{\partial IC^1}{\partial y_1^m} - \lambda_1 = 0, \tag{18}$$

$$\frac{\partial \mathcal{L}}{\partial y_2^m} = p_2^m - \frac{\partial IC^2}{\partial y_2^m} - \lambda_2 = 0, \tag{19}$$

$$\frac{\partial \mathcal{L}}{\partial \lambda_i} = Q^i - y_i^m \geq 0, \qquad \lambda_i \geq 0, \qquad \lambda_i(Q^i - y_i^m) = 0, \tag{20}$$

$$\frac{\partial \mathcal{L}}{\partial \mu} = p_2^e - p_2^m \geq 0, \qquad \mu \geq 0, \qquad \mu_i(p_2^e - p_2^m) = 0. \tag{21}$$

Successful entry requires $\lambda_2 = 0$; otherwise $Q^2 - y_2^m = 0$ (the monopolist serves the entire market). We then know immediately from equation (19) that the monopolist will set price equal to marginal cost in market 2.

With $\lambda_2 = 0$, equation (17) becomes

$$y_1^m + \lambda_1 \frac{\partial Q^1}{\partial p_1^m} = 0. \tag{22}$$

Since $\partial Q^1/\partial p_1^m < 0$ and $y_1^m > 0$ at an interior solution, equation (22) requires $\lambda_1 > 0$, which carries the unsurprising implication that in a market unthreatened by entry the monopolist supplies the entire available demand.

Equation (13) can be rewritten as

$$\mu = y_2^m + \lambda_1 \frac{\partial Q^1}{\partial p_2^m} > 0, \tag{23}$$

which implies, from (21), that the monopolist sets $p_2^m = p_2^e$.

Equations (19) and (21) taken together then yield

$$p_2^m = \frac{\partial IC^2}{\partial y_2^m} = p_2^e. \tag{24}$$

The monopolist's short-run profit-maximizing response to entry is thus to match the entrant's price and choose the output level at which short-run marginal cost equals that price.

Of course, in addition to the Kuhn-Tucker necessary conditions, the monopolist's price and output choices must satisfy the standard loss-minimization conditions for continued production:

$$p_i^m y_i^m \geq p_{V_i} V_i \qquad (i = 1,2)$$

and

$$\sum_{i=1}^{2} p_i^m y_i^m \geq p_V V + p_{V_1} V_1 + p_{V_2} V_2,$$

where the p_Vs are the variable input prices.

The effect of the monopolist's short-run response to entry is illustrated in figure 7.10. We begin with the monopolist choosing an initial vector of outputs and prices. The point M, with $\hat{p}_2^m$ and $\hat{y}_2^m$, is assumed to represent the solution in market 2 to that problem. The choice of $\hat{y}_2^m$ and the inputs necessary to produce it also allow us to specify the short-run average-incremental-cost (AIC_{sr}), average-variable-incremental-cost $(AVIC_{sr})$, and marginal-cost (MC_{sr}) curves shown in the figure.

To position the demand curve for service 2 requires some statement

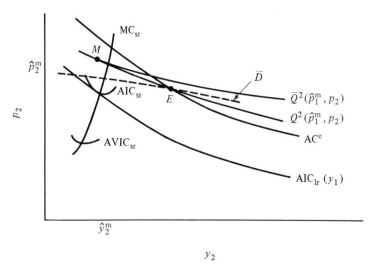

Figure 7.10 Monopolist's short-run response to entry.

about the monopolist's postentry choice of p_1^m. In general, the sign of dp_1^m/dp_2 is indeterminate.[13] The monopolist, when faced with announced entry at p_2^e, could choose to raise, lower, or hold constant p_1^m. To make things as simple as possible, I will assume that p_1^m is held constant at $\hat{p}_1^m$. Therefore, the demand curve for service 2 will not shift as a result of entry at p_2^e.[14] By the Panzar-Willig criteria, successful entry would be observed whenever the market demand curve lay above the entrant's average-cost curve. For example, at E in figure 7.10 successful entry would be feasible.

Successful entry, given the monopolist's short-run reaction, requires that the residual demand available to the entrant lie someplace above his average-cost curve. The residual demand is given by the horizontal distance between the market demand curve and the monopolist's short-run marginal-cost curve.[15] The $\bar{Q}^2$ market demand curve allows successful entry at E. The residual demand available to the entrant is shown as the dashed line $\bar{D}$.

Given successful entry in market 2, one can easily verify that, even with reaction by the monopolist, sustainability is not ensured and entry may reduce welfare. All one has to do when constructing the demand and cost curves for market 1 is to make sure the long-run AIC^1 curve lies well out from the origin and the postentry demand curve is tucked just inside it, thereby ensuring the long-run infeasibility of continued service in market 1 and the loss of large amounts of surplus.

Thus, even though the monopolist's short-run profit-maximizing response to entry increases the likelihood of sustainability (because larger unserved market demands are required for successful entry), that response by no means ensures sustainability. The troublesome policy issues concerning open entry remain unanswered, at least on an *a priori* basis.

Sustainability with Monopoly Reaction and One Product
The monopolist's reaction to entry in the one-product case is less obvious. Recall that for a single-product natural monopoly to be unsustainable the average-cost curve must turn up. This implies that the entrant will be offering to supply an output less than the monopolist's original output (Panzar and Willig refer to this as "cooperative" entry). Unfortunately, in this case we will not be able to derive the monopolist's reaction function from the new firm's entry "offer." We were able to do so in the preceding section because the entrant had to offer to supply an output larger than the joint monopolist's original output. The monopolist then took the entrant's price as given and chose that quantity which equated his marginal cost to the entrant's announced price. With cooperative entry, we (and the entrant) must make an assumption about the monopolist's reaction.

Suppose the monopolist chooses to react along his short-run marginal cost curve by, again, accepting the entrant's price and setting quantity so as to equate his marginal cost to the entrant's price. This reaction will

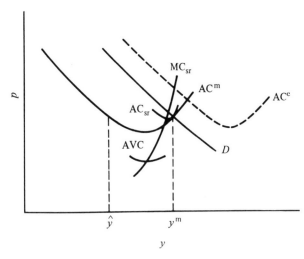

Figure 7.11 Monopolist's reaction ensures sustainability of a single-product natural monopoly.

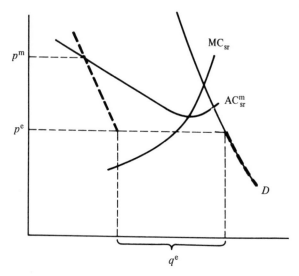

Figure 7.12 Monopoly reaction in the one-product case.

deter entry if costs are subadditive over the market range (and not just up to the monopolist's output) and if the monopolist's minimum average variable cost is less than his minimum average cost. Figure 7.11 shows such a situation. We can check for subadditivity by constructing a new average-cost curve, denoted AC^e, from a vertical axis at $\hat{y}$, the output at which average cost is equal to the average cost at y^m. As long as the demand curve lies below AC^e, costs are subadditive over the market range. Monopoly reaction along the short-run marginal-cost curve then deters entry by leaving the entrant a residual demand $(D - MC_{sr})$ that is less than $D - \hat{y}$.

Reaction along the short-run marginal-cost curve is not necessarily the monopolist's profit-maximizing response to entry. To see this examine figure 7.12, which shows the demand curve (the discontinuous dashed line) facing the monopolist when an entrant offers to sell q^e units at price p^e. If the monopolist matches or beats p^e, the market demand is his. His profit-maximizing choice is, then, to match p^e and choose quantity as described above. However, an alternative strategy that might yield higher profits (or lower losses) would be to set p^m above p^e and allow the entrant to sell q^e units. This price increase, coupled with a substantial reduction in output, could allow the original firm to break even. The entrant would of course raise his price to match p^m; but if he cannot increase output much past q^e in the short run, this strategy might work for the monopolist.

I suspect that this result is somewhat unlikely and, in any event, clearly undesirable. The regulator could effectively block it by not allowing the monopolist to decrease output and increase price in response to entry. Such a policy would force the monopolist to react along his short-run marginal-cost function. The sustainability of socially desirable natural monopolies would then be ensured as long as p^e remained greater than the monopolist's minimum average variable cost.

Sustainability and Entry Restrictions

We have seen that the Panzar-Willig approach to sustainability problems can be extended to allow consideration of a monopolist's short-run profit-maximizing response to entry. Those authors mention that further insight into sustainability could, and should, be obtained through a dynamic version of the model and through consideration of nonlinear prices.[16]

The range of policy options when sustainability is a problem can also be expanded. The sustainability problem is "merely" another case where market demand is insufficient to support continued production.[17] One policy solution to that problem is to impose entry restrictions or minimum price regulation in other markets, so that sufficient excess revenues can be generated to pay for production in the unsustainable market.

Another policy option is the imposition of a set of taxes and subsidies. A subsidy, defined either as a certain amount per unit of output or as a percentage of revenues, could be offered to any firm willing to serve the otherwise unsustainable market. Presumably, given the economies of joint production, the market will be served by our joint monopolist. The revenues to finance this subsidy would come from a set of taxes, defined in a similar manner, on the remaining products in the industry. Competition for these remaining markets is thereby feasible, with the lowest-cost producer serving each market. If the remaining markets do in fact make up a natural monopoly, then it can be preserved without resort to entry restrictions. Of course, running such a program would have its costs. However, there are also social costs—which could be very large—to protecting an inefficient joint monopolist behind a wall of entry restrictions.

Sustainability in Intercity Telecommunications: A Short Case Study

The particularly vexatious aspect of the sustainability problem is the fact that optimal resolution of the public-policy issues may require knowledge of the behavior of demand and cost functions outside the range of observed price and output choices. This would certainly be true if one tried to assess whether large-scale entry were feasible in any market, since the answer to that question depends on the behavior of demand and cost cruves beyond the range of current observations.

Fortunately, we may often be able to say something about what happens in markets where, if entry restrictions were to be lifted, production might be infeasible, We will often have observations on the long-run average-cost cruve in such markets. If forgone scale economies are "small" as output is reduced, then sustainability problems cannot be expected to arise. Either production remains feasible over widely varying outputs (in which case a natural monopoly will be sustainable) or, if natural monopoly is unsustainable, the forgone surplus in the "lost" market will tend to be "small." Thus, the welfare calculation, in which these losses must be balanced against the welfare gains in the market where entry occurs, will tend to favor the postentry world.

An argument along these lines can be put forth in the area of intercity telecommunications. Waverman (1975) argued convincingly that economies of scale for microwave transmission are exhausted at output levels well below the observed outputs of many telecommunications links.[18] In addition, our observation of the market responses of many commercial telecommunications users to the FCC's "above 890" decision[19] verify that microwave scale economies are small enough so that large individual commercial users, given appropriate prices, can "go it alone" with private microwave.[20] Finally, the demand for private line service is a derived demand for telecommunications as an input. Since telecommunications expenditures are typically a small fraction of total cost for a firm, one would expect the demand for private line service to be quite price-inelastic. Combined, these factors suggest that any forgone surplus would be small if open entry in public message-toll service rendered unsustainable the continued provision of private line service.

Even without monopoly reaction, the increased surplus accompanying successful entry in message-toll service would be quite large. For example, if the scale elasticity for independent production were 1.3, the initial MTS price advantage over independent production were 10 percent, and the demand function were linear, increased surplus in MTS would be half the product of the 10 percent price reduction and an output increase of one-third. With monopoly reaction, the surplus would be larger, since the market demand would have to be larger in order to accommodate the entrant. If the monopolist's short-run marginal-cost curve were roughly vertical, an output increase of 133 percent would be required to overcome the initial 10 percent monopoly advantage.

To carry this multiproduct interpretation of each telecommunications link one step further, one can ask why the cost function might be subadditive. The most plausible reason is economies of scale in transmission. The various services share the same transmission facilities.[21] For a given level of transmission capacity, the joint monopolist, especially at the *ex ante* planning stage,[22] can freely alter the mix between private line and message toll service without forgoing transmission scale economies. Thus, as the product mix is varied, the average incremental cost of transmission capacity for each service will not change. Therefore, the joint monopolist will not, for reasons arising from the transmission technology, run into a declining average-incremental-cost curve when performing the *ex ante* adjustment in output mix necessary to deter entry. This implies that sustainability problems should never arise for private line service, since the joint monopolist is offering message toll service in addition to private line service and thus will always be "farther down" the transmission average-cost curve than any potential entrant offering only private line service.

Sustainability problems could conceivably arise in message toll service, since, in addition to transmission, a switching technology must be employed in order to route each call to the desired destination. The threat of entry in private line service may force the joint monopolist to reduce private-line prices. Some users will then shift at least part of their demands from MTS to private-line service. If there are economies of scale in switching, this demand shift away from MTS will force the joint monopolist "backward and up" along a declining average-incremental-cost curve for message toll service. In a qualitative sense, at least, the stage has been set for the possible infeasibility of continued provision of message toll service.

Such an outcome is not to be expected. A very substantial body of message-toll users would not contemplate using private lines at any conceivable price for private-line service as long as message-toll service was available at current prices. The move to private line requires a large enough demand along any one route to cover the costs of a dedicated circuit. Residential toll users, with small individual demands along any one route, will prefer MTS to private-line service, even given drastic price reductions for private line, if a switching technology is available which allows the pooling of their individual demands at prices close to current MTS prices. We can infer that such a technology is available from the variety of switched private-line services currently offered, at small scales of production, by the specialized common carriers.

Of particular relevance is MCI's "Execunet" service, which is a very close substitute for AT&T's message-toll service. Execunet is a switched service, and an Execunet subscriber can place a call to any phone on the public network in any city served by MCI. Execunet is offered at a scale that is minuscule in comparison with the scale realized by AT&T for message-toll service on the same routes.[23] I do not have market-share figures for each firm on a route-by-route basis, but the national totals give some idea of relative magnitudes. In the fiscal year ending March 31, 1977, MCI's Execunet sales were $28 million (*Telecommunications Reports* 1977). AT&T's message-toll revenues in 1975 were $12.9 billion, of which WATS accounted for $1.4 billion (FCC 1975). Admittedly, these figures overstate the relative size of AT&T, since MCI does not offer service on most routes served by AT&T. However, MCI does serve most high-density routes, and even if one assumes that AT&T derives only 10 percent of its revenues from routes also served by MCI, MCI's market share is only 2.1 percent. In addition, at this point the example is biased against the probability that message-toll service can be provided at a small scale by a joint monopolist also offering private-line service, since MCI's private-line volume is but a tiny fraction of AT&T's. Thus, MCI offers Execunet even though, by hypothesis,[24] it must forgo scale economies in both transmission and switching. The joint monopolist facing entry in private-line service would be forgoing only whatever scale economies there are in switching as he attempted to market both services.

An alternative view of the intercity telecommunications market definition is that only one product—transmission capacity—is being provided. The observed rate differentials for a circuit between A and B are then viewed as evidence of price discrimination. In this one-product world, nonincreasing average cost is then sufficient for the sustainability of each link. Scale elasticities greater than unity have been found in virtually every empirical investigation of telecommunications, so the assumption is certainly defensible. However, even if subadditivity holds but nonincreasing average cost does not, natural monopoly will generally be sustainable if the monopolist reacts along his short-run marginal-cost curve.

If each link is sustainable, can sustainability problems arise across links? The answer would appear to be no as long as the costs of serving a collection of links are subadditive, as long as weak cost complementarities hold across links (that is, the marginal cost of serving link i does not increase with increased output on link j), and as long as market revenues are in the core. The demands for service along different links are arguably independent. The demand is for service between A and B; the consumer is indifferent to the prices charged on other routes, since a call to C cannot be substituted for the desired call to B.

Under these assumptions, proposition 3 of Panzar and Willig 1977a applies and the natural monopoly network will be sustainable. Since each link considered alone is sustainable, successful entry on any one link would require that the lower post entry price pull in consumers from other links. Independent demand implies that consumers will not move across links. Thus, the natural monopoly network will be sustainable.

We are left with what could be a source of sustainability problems in telecommunications. AT&T currently averages its message-toll rates, with prices on high-density routes set above "cost" and prices on low-density routes set below "cost." It may be that AT&T, in attempting to restructure its rates when faced with an open-entry rule, would be unable to find an initial price vector satisfying the core conditions. In other words, consumers on low-density routes might be unwilling to pay prices high enough to cover the average incremental cost of being served. Whether this is a realistic possibility I cannot say, since the size of the subsidies arising from nationwide rate averaging is unknown. The size of those subsidies will depend on the "true" scale elasticity for telecommunications and on the demand mix of toll users along low-density routes. The latter factor is important because a toll user along a low-density route could experience lower toll prices under an open-entry rule if a large enough fraction of his toll calls were to be carried over high-density routes.

If toll service in some rural areas proves to be either infeasible or much more expensive under an open-entry rule, then some source of subsidy for those consumers may be desirable. As I indicated earlier, there are ways of providing that subsidy while still allowing entry.

The views expressed are those of the author and should not be taken as representing official views or positions of the U.S. Department of Justice. John Hoven, Richard Ippolito, Bruce Owen, Robert Reynolds, James Rosse, and Lee Sparling provided helpful comments at various stages in my research on these issues. The author is solely responsible for any errors.

Notes

1. MTS: message-toll service. WATS: wide-area telephone service. AT&T no longer has a *de jure* monopoly on MTS. The D.C. Court of Appeals overturned the FCC's Execunet

decision. Execunet is a close substitute for MTS offered by MCI. The FCC had disallowed MCI's Execunet tariff on the grounds that MCI had not been authorized to offer public switched service.

2. Before the FCC, in docket 18128, AT&T proposed as a pricing standard the "Baumol burden test," which is an extension of the simple incremental-cost test. The "burden test" shares the deficiencies of the incremental-cost test.

3. The convexity of the isoquants ensures that the second-order necessary and sufficient conditions for the monopolists's cost-minimization problem are satisfied.

4. I assume that if $p_1^m = p_1^*$ the joint monopolist will satisfy the entire demand. This assumption is made for convenience only. Alternatively, I could require $p_1^m < p_1^* - \varepsilon$ and carry the ε throughout the analysis.

5. p_1^* is the entry-deterring price in a "friction-free" world without entry barriers. With entry barriers, the entry-deterring price will exceed p_1^*.

6. When equation (8) is negative the opposite strategy of increasing p_2^m will not aid the monopolist, since then p_1^m must increase in the face of competition in market 1.

7. The assumption of subadditivity is sufficient to guarantee a nonempty core in the two-player game. With more than two players, weak cost complementarities are required.

8. The distinction between the two sources of unsustainability becomes blurred when consideration is given to the monopolist's reaction to entry. In the Panzar-Willig world, if the second condition is not satisfied natural monopoly can be displaced by local price changes. With monopoly reaction a large price cut is needed for successful entry whether or not the initial prices are in the core.

9. Alternatively, AIC_j need not shift down if $C_{ij} = 0$ over the range of output changes being considered. In that case, the source of the economics of joint production is a savings in the inframarginal fixed or startup costs when two services are produced jointly rather than separately. Thus, although the increasing output of service i may dictate larger fixed expenditures by the monopolist, the increased use of fixed inputs generates no additional cost complementarities.

10. To make things simple I am assuming that F and V come in fixed proportions. This is the case if a fixed maintenance program must be followed to keep a unit of F operating efficiently.

11. Again, I am assuming that at $p_2^m = p_2^c$ the monopolist can supply as much of good 2 as he chooses. The alternative, requiring $p_2^m \leq p_2^c - \varepsilon$, yields equivalent results but is less convenient.

12. The monopolist's problem and solution are precisely the same as the Panzar-Willig "cooperative" entrant's solution to the problem of what prices and outputs to choose if entry is considered at less than the monopolist's existing output and the monopolist's average-cost curve is declining.

13. dp_1^m/dp_2 is obtained by totally differentiating equation (17) and solving for dp_1^m/dp_2.

14. $p_1^m \gtreqless p_1^m$ would imply $Q^2(p_1^m, p_2^c) \gtreqless Q^2(\hat{p}_1^m, p_2^c)$.

15. For prices less than the monopolist's minimum AVIC, the entire market demand is available to the entrant.

16. I have looked at the sustainability problem with nonlinear prices, but have been unable to generate any clear-cut results. It is clear that some price discrimination scheme would, *ceteris paribus*, increase the likelihood of markets, unthreatened by entry, being served by the monopolist. However, the effects of nonlinear pricing strategies are unclear in markets where entry is threatened. The monopolist, by appropriate use of declining

block-rate tariffs, can inch down the demand curve, leaving a smaller residual demand for the entrant. However, once the monopolist has positioned himself, the entrant now has the more powerful tools of price discrimination to get at the available residual demand. The net effects on the likelihood of entry (and the probability of sustainability problems) are ambiguous.

17. Regulators now deal routinely with such situations. An example is subsidized air service on low-density routes.

18. Waverman's work indicates that microwave scale economies are exhausted somewhere between 1,000 and 4,000 voice circuits, with a cost premium of only a few percent at around 600 circuits. A 100-circuit system could be constructed at a cost premium of about 60 percent. By way of comparison, AT&T's L4 cable system has a capacity of 32,400 circuits.

19. The "above 890" decision allowed telecommunications users, for the first time, to build and operate their own microwave communications systems.

20. AT&T's response to the "above 890" decision was a substantial price reduction (the "Telpak" tariffs) to large-volume private-line customers. As a result, there has been very little investment in private microwave systems beyond that observed before the Telpak tariffs became effective.

21. If the various services do not share transmission facilities, as would be the case with physically separate analog and digital transmission systems, then one must search elsewhere for a source of subadditivity.

22. The substitution can also occur after the system is in place. AT&T currently transfers existing circuits back and forth between message-toll and private-line service.

23. MCI's operation at a small scale is not inconsistent with scale economies in telecommunications. AT&T's rates may be set above "cost" on the high-density routes over which the firms compete.

24. That is, here we are assuming, for the sake of argument, that the "cream skimming" explanation of MCI's entry is valid. An alternative view, held by MCI and other specialized common carriers, is that their entry can be defended because their costs, even at very low scale, are lower than AT&T's.

References

Areeda, Phillip, and Turner, Donald F. 1975. "Predatory Pricing and Related Practices under Section 2 of the Sherman Act." *Harvard Law Review* 88: 697–733.

Averch, Harvey, and Johnson, L. L. 1962. "Behavior of the Firm under Regulatory Constraint." *American Economic Review* 52: 1053–1069.

Baumol, William, Bailey, Elizabeth, and Willig, Robert. 1977. "Weak Invisible Hand Theorems on the Sustainability of Multiproduct Monopoly." *American Economic Review* 67: 809–822.

Faulhaber, Gerald. 1975a. "Cross-Subsidization: Pricing in Public Enterprise." *American Economic Review* 65: 966–977.

———. 1975b. Increasing Returns to Scale: Optimality and Equilibrium. Ph.D. diss., Princeton University.

Federal Communications Commission. 1976. Recommended decision, docket 18128.

———. 1975. *Common Carrier Statistics*.

———. 1976. Report of domestic telecommunications policies, docket 20003.

Kahn, Alfred E. 1970. *The Economics of Regulation*, vol. 1. New York: Wiley.

Panzar, John C., and Willig, Robert D. 1977a. "Free Entry and the Sustainability of Natural Monopoly." *Bell Journal of Economics* 8: 1–22.

————. 1977b. "Economies of Scale in Multi-Output Production." *Quarterly Journal of Economics* 91: 481–494.

Scherer, F. M. 1977. "Predatory Pricing and the Sherman Act: A Comment." *Harvard Law Review* 89: 869–890.

Seneca, Rosalyn. 1973. "Inherent Advantage, Costs and Resource Allocation in the Transportation Industry." *American Economic Review* 63: 945–956.

Spence, Michael. 1977. "Entry, Capacity, Investment and Oligopolistic Pricing. *Bell Journal of Economics* 8: 534–544.

Telecommunications Reports 43 (no. 25): 13.

Waverman, Leonard. 1975. "The Regulation of Intercity Telecommunications." In Almarin Phillips (ed.), *Promoting Competition in Regulated Markets*. Washington, D.C.: Brookings Institution.

Comment

William J. Baumol

My comments are devoted primarily to the first portion of Kenneth
Baseman's illuminating article—the portion dealing with appropriate
tests of cross-subsidization rather than that devoted to the issue of sustainability. This part of his article is entirely critical in character, seeking
to demonstrate weaknesses in the incremental-cost and burden-test
approaches to the construction of criteria of cross-subsidization. As a
general comment, one might have wished that the author had gone
beyond mere criticism, and that he had offered some counterproposals
—tests that in his view are more effective than those to which he objects.
Such an attempt to approach issues more constructively is, of course,
always to be encouraged.

In my view, however, an alternative criterion of cross-subsidization
may not be necessitated by the paper's criticisms. This is not meant to
deny that the analysis has brought to our attention a substantial policy
issue. Indeed, the issue implicitly raised has probably been important
throughout economic history. That issue is governmental grant of
monopoly in cases where it cannot be justified by superior performance
—a topic that has loomed large in the economic literature since the
publication of *The Wealth of Nations*. What I will undertake to show
is that it is this issue, and *not* the adequacy of the proposed tests of cross-
subsidization, with which Baseman's analysis deals. Rather, I will show
that in the circumstances envisioned in the paper the marginal-cost test
of cross-subsidization performs exactly as one would wish it to, and that
the problem the examples raise is that of a monopoly franchise unjusti-
fiably granted.

While the paper presents a number of variants of its argument on
cross-subsidization, I will deal only with the simplest example, since it
brings out the issues so clearly.

In the example in question, Baseman examines a case in which there
are diseconomies of scope—it is more expensive to have a single firm
produce both of two commodities than to have the same quantities produced separately by two specialized firms. The monopolist's total cost
of producing the two items together is 90, and the incremental cost of
each item is only 20. Each item can be produced by a specialized com-

petitor at a total cost of 40. The unspecialized firm has a monopoly franchise in commodity 2 and therefore fears no competition in this market. It sets a price of, say, 35 for the competitive product, good 1, thoroughly exceeding its incremental cost, and covers the remainder of its 90 cost by charging a price of 55 for its monopoly product, good 2, thereby depriving the consumers of the opportunity of buying the good from a specialized firm at 40. Clearly, the consumers of good 2 are burdened by the arrangement.

But the story, as told so far, obscures the true source of the burden. To make the issue clear, instead of considering only the case in which there is a monopoly franchise, let us examine two possibilities: that in which entry is prevented by law (the monopoly franchise) and that in which entry is free. In each case we contrast the results of an incremental-cost floor for competitive product 1 with those of a full-cost floor for that product, where for illustration it is assumed that consumers of each good must then be charged half their 90 total cost (each must pay 45). The results are summarized in the following table.

	Incremental-Cost Pricing		Full-Cost Pricing	
	P_1	P_2	P_1	P_2
Legal monopoly in market 2	35	55	45	70
Free entry in market 2	35	?	45	?

Consider first what happens if there is a legal monopoly franchise in good 2. Under the incremental-pricing regime, as before, the consumers of good 1 pay 35 and the consumers of good 2 pay the residue, 55. But with full-cost pricing the firm loses its market for good 1, and customers of the monopolized product will then have to pay both the fixed cost, 50, and the incremental cost, 20. That is, the monopoly product's cost will rise from 55 to 70, because of the loss of the contribution of 15 in excess of incremental cost which product 1 would otherwise have provided.

Now consider the case where entry is free. Then, if in order to meet competition in product 1 the unspecialized firm charges 35 for that product under an incremental-cost floor, it will simply be unable to maintain its market for product 2, for either it will charge 55 and lose that market to an entrant or it will charge less than 40 and go broke. Ultimately, the unspecialized firm will be driven from both markets, for it cannot survive serving only market 1 at a price of 35.

With entry, the same will happen under full-cost pricing. Indeed, what must ultimately happen with free entry is that the unspecialized firm will be unable to remain in either market, and that is just as the public welfare requires.

Arithmetic arguments can be confusing, yet it is easy to draw a number of general conclusions from this discussion:

• The consumer is obviously poorly served in the case illustrated in the Baseman paper, but this is because the firm has been granted a monopoly in a market where there is no cost justification for such a grant. Thus, under an incremental-cost regime customers are not as well off as they might otherwise be. But they are worse off still under full-cost pricing, which forces *both* customer groups to pay more than under incremental-cost pricing.

• If despite the absence of any cost justification the government is determined to impose a monopoly in market 2, then the issue is what pricing scheme minimizes the resulting damage. It is easy to see that it is the incremental pricing scheme.

• Under these circumstances it is simply wrong to say that incremental pricing introduces cross-subsidization by the customers of the monopoly product. Given the idiotic decision to impose the monopoly in market 2, under a ceiling on total company profits the customers of the monopoly product are better off when the competitive product 1 is sold at any price above incremental cost that is low enough to keep the competitive market for the unspecialized firm, for then the competitive-market sales make a net financial contribution to the company and consumer payments for the monopoly product must be reduced accordingly.

• Most important for the current discussion, pricing based on an incremental-cost test achieves the right results in either of the two cases, the case in which the monopoly is imposed in market 2 and the case where it is not. In the first case it saves money for both customer classes; in the second case it drives the unspecialized firm out of business, as it deserves because of its relative inefficiency.

I conclude from all this that tests of cross-subsidization can and must be incremental in character. To say that the sale of a product benefits from a cross-subsidy means that its sale is at the expense of the customers of other products. But if the product in question contributes net revenues in excess of its net incremental costs, then surely its market is not being served at the expense of the customers of other products, whether or not those other products have a protected monopoly.

Finally, I should like to emphasize the desirability of further work on both subjects raised by the discussion: criteria that can be used to identify which products do merit a monopoloy franchise, and further sharpening of the tests of cross-subsidization. With regard to the latter, while I believe firmly that appropriate tests will have to be based on a comparison of incremental revenues and costs, there is, as always, room for further improvement in the testing procedures that have so far been designed. I hope that the author of the article will turn his considerable abilities to these issues.

I thank the National Science Foundation for its support of the writing of these comments.

Comment

John C. Panzar

My comments will deal with the second half of Mr. Baseman's article, in which he discusses some alternative approaches to the theory of monopoly sustainability and some of the policy issues involved.

The author's exposition of the essence of the sustainability problem for the two-product case is intuitive and concise. I was particularly intrigued with his diagrammatic use of the average-incremental-cost curve to show why the monopolist may not be able to match the price cut of a single-product entrant and still break even (figure 7.7). This device is a useful complement to the Panzar-Willig price-space diagram of figure 7.9. The use of such a price-quantity diagram also makes clearer the structural similarity of the sustainability problem to the literature on entry deterrence. Since the bulk of the paper's analytics are devoted to Baseman's attempt to develop an alternative to the Nash behavioral assumption underlying the Panzar-Willig analysis of sustainability, it may be worthwhile to develop a little perspective on this issue.

Anytime one attempts to model a potential entrant's decision problem, it is necessary to make some assumption about what the entrant perceives will be the response of the monopolist to his entry. The limit-pricing theory of Bain and Sylos, for example, was based upon the entrant's assuming that the monopolist would keep his output constant in the face of entry. The theoretical results of such models are, of course, quite sensitive to the behavioral assumptions employed, and debates in the literature tend to focus upon whether one assumption is more or less "reasonable" than another.

When discussing a regulated industry, it would seem that such debates are beside the point, since postentry price responses can be controlled by the regulator. In principle, allowable price responses can therefore be known objectively by all potential entrants, and the nature of such allowable responses becomes an important policy issue. In this light, it becomes evident that the policy tradeoff between the salutary stimulus that free entry may provide for efficiency and innovation and the possibility of wasteful, duplicating entry cannot be analyzed independently of regulatory price-response policy. Two extreme examples should help clarify this point:

• "Predatory pricing," if allowed as a response to entry, may deter many entrants who in fact possess superior technology or products.
• Welcoming entrants into the regulatory "fold" through favorable price adjustments will certainly lead to wasteful entry. (In Baseman's figure 7.8, even the point S may not be sustainable if the entrant perceives that the regulator will allow it and the original monopolist to "come to rest" at the southwest corner of R.)

The sustainability discussion of Panzar and Willig, then, is best interpreted as an analysis of the potential problems with a policy of free entry *given* that the regulator does not allow a price response—the simplest such regulatory policy to analyze. It demonstrated that there may indeed be serious problems with a policy of open entry under that condition. Therefore, an important direction for additional research is to examine open entry and sustainability under meaningful alternative assumptions about the responses to entry the regulatory will allow the monopolist to make. The goal of such analyses would, of course, be to determine whether or not a proposed policy tends to make sustainability problems more or less severe. While I believe Baseman's model to be a step in this right direction, I do have a few comments to make about his analysis and choice of regulatory scenario.

Baseman assumes that the entrant expects the regulator to allow the monopolist to respond to entry in a manner that maximizes his profits in the short run. In the light of the above discussion, is this an interesting policy alternative to analyze? In the first place, it is difficult to reconcile the short-run behavior of the monopolist with the (presumably) long-run concerns of the entrant. Perhaps the entrant is only interested in earning some short-run profit, but unless for some unexplained reason the technology he uses is extremely fungible he must also consider the possibility of losing some of his investment when the monopolist makes his long-run response. Put another way, what is the regulator's policy to be toward the (initial) monopolist in the long run? Will he prevent the monopolist from adjusting his input choices indefinitely? Baseman is not at all clear on these points.

Second, would it ever make sense for the regulator to adopt such a policy? Baseman raises this question in connection with the no-response scenario, but offers little in the way of justification for his own model in this regard. Presumably, the fact that regulation is effective means that there are unexploited profits to be had, even in the short run. This might induce some form of collusion between the monopolist and potential entrants, since tolerating some entry in market 2 may provide the opportunity to reap large profits in market 1.

Finally, Baseman's basic conclusion that "the monopolist's short-run profit-maximizing response to entry increases the likelihood of sustainability (because larger unserved market demands are required for successful entry)" depends upon the assumption that the monopolist does not choose to raise the price in the unthreatened market. If he did, the market demand for service 2 might shift out far enough so that even the entrant's residual demand would exceed the original (constant p_1) market demand. In view of this difficulty and the above discussion about unexploited profits, it may be more interesting to analyze the model by explicity assuming that the regulator allows the monopolist to change only the price in the service threatened by entry. Unfortunately, if the monopoly *is* unsustainable, it is easy to show that the monopolist cannot lose part of market 2 and break even in the long run without raising the price in market 1. While hardly conclusive, Baseman's discussion has indicated the usefulness of modeling alternative price responses to entry in a sustainability framework.

Another potential policy option for dealing with the sustainability problem that Baseman mentions only briefly involves taxes and subsidies. I find this concept quite intriguing analytically, so let me briefly elaborate. Consider the unsustainable situation depicted in figure 7.9. If it is required that any firm serving market 2 pay a (lump sum) penalty and that an equal bonus be paid to any firm offering to serve market 1, the $\Pi^2 \geq 0$ set will "shrink" and the $\Pi^1 \geq 0$ set will expand, without affecting the $\Pi^m = 0$ locus. (Baseman discusses per-unit or *ad valorum* taxes and subsidies, which, while they may be easier to administer, introduce an additional price distortion into the analysis.) It is at least possible that the situation of figure 7.9 may thereby be "transformed" into that of figure 7.8, which would lead to the emergence of a region of sustainable prices. The same scheme could also be used, in principle, to allow movement from one sustainable price vector to a socially preferred, but previously unsustainable, set of prices (for example, in figure 7.8, from S to a point to the left of A). These possibilities are illustrated in the accompanying diagrams. In (a), there are initially no sustainable price vectors. However, after the imposition of an appropriate tax-and-subsidy scheme has shifted the $\Pi^1 = 0$ and $\Pi^2 = 0$ loci to the positions indicated by the dashed lines, all prices on the $\Pi^m = 0$ locus are sustainable. In (b), a tax-and-subsidy policy has shifted the sustainable region from BCD to ABC, allowing the regulator to choose a price vector between A and B if he finds it to be socially desirable.

I shall conclude with a few remarks about the policy implications of

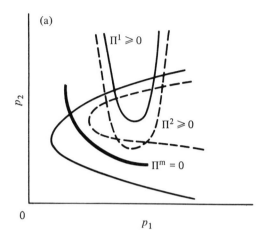

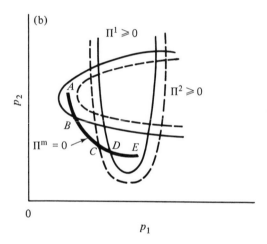

Movement to previously unsustainable prices.

Baseman's analysis. Baseman's heuristic empirical argument suggests that sustainability is not likely to be a problem in intercity telecommunications. Even if his perceptions are correct, there is a great need for additional empirical work in this area on which to base intelligent policy analysis. The knowledge that there exist one or more sustainable price vectors is, in and of itself, of little use to the policymaker. The relevant question is whether or not there are any socially desirable prices which are sustainable. If not, the decisionmaker faces a tradeoff between the benefits resulting from a policy of open entry and the concomitant loss of pricing flexibility. The important insights to be gained from Baseman's paper are that the terms of this policy tradeoff may be improved through the implementation of appropriate tax-and-subsidy schemes and through alternative regulatory policies toward allowable postentry responses by the multiproduct monopolist.

The views expressed in this comment are solely those of the author and do not necessarily reflect those of Bell Laboratories or the Bell System.

8

Current Developments in the Economics of Regulation

Sam Peltzman

The economics of regulation seems to have arrived at a crossroads. Activity in the field is burgeoning and threatening to burst the boundaries established by theoretical insights that just yesterday seemed adequate to guide research for some time. My task here will be to step back and try to set some of the new work in a longer perspective, a perspective which I think indicates that we ought to be cautious about what to expect from it.

I find it useful, like so many who are charged with summarizing the work of academic conferences, to proceed taxonomically, So, I will organize my remarks around three principles that I believe are suggested by the history of the economics of regulation. The first of these is that the theory seems to move in waves, in the sense that once-respected theoretical insights seem easily superseded by new ones. This partly reflects the muddled state of the field, where normative and positive issues tend to get indiscriminately run together and a common theoretical bond is lacking. The first identifiable wave, which held center stage up to about 1960, is sometimes called the "public-interest" view. It can be found in one form or another in the seminal work of Hotelling (1938) and in generations of text books on public utilities. The focus is on market failure, typically of the natural monopoly variety, as the stimulus for regulation. While the public-interest view of regulation as guardian against monopolistic inefficiency always viewed itself as more proscriptive than descriptive, it did claim some practical insights. Surely a finding that, for example, electric rates were not held down by regulation would represent a loss of innocence.

When the work initiated by Stigler and Friedland (1962) began revealing that regulation did not work as the public-interest view held that it should or did, the way was prepared for a new generalization: the cartel or "capture" view of regulation, whereby compact interest groups, usually of producers rather than consumers, were held to dominate regulatory decisionmaking. The public-interest view became more clearly a normative paradigm. Its underlying welfare economics remained a valid way of organizing discussion about what regulators ought to be doing, but any belief that regulators often did what they should was now severely tempered. For about a decade the capture model provided a major framework for the positive analysis of regulatory behavior. This work is not yet complete, as evidenced by Leone and Jackson's intriguing attempt to bring out the rent-generating elements for producers in pollu-tion-control regulation (a form of regulation that appears, on its surface, to cut against the producer's interest). Nevertheless, the simple, straight-forward view of regulation as a cartel enforcement device now is coming under serious question. Perhaps this is due partly to the lavish growth of forms of regulation that, like pollution control, seems to require much excavation before any cartelizing element emerges. More likely, it is due to a growing recognition that very substantial rent-dissipating elements (such as the perpetuation of excess capacity in railroads, which Levin's article documents so well) were an integral part, and not merely a side-show, of regulatory activity in areas where the producer-protection model seemed most fruitful (for example, transportation).

While it may be premature to call it a new wave, this conference seems to confirm what is at least a new ripple. For want of a better term, I will call it "creeping realism" ("creeping" both because it is not a radical break with either the public-interest or producer-interest models and because, as I will argue, its analytical structure is so unevenly balanced that walking straight will be difficult). What it seems to me the creeping-realism literature is trying to do is to integrate some of the newer econom-ics of political decisionmaking with some of the elements of the older normative economics of regulation. The older welfare economics is invoked to rationalize one or another form of regulatory intervention, but the resulting real-world institution then must bend to the realities of politics. And politics means coalition-building and log-rolling, so that nothing so simple as a "public" interest or a "producer" interest is going to predominate.

It is best to let a more precise characterization of this literature emerge from a few examples provided by this conference. The article of Leone and Jackson is a good starting point. Somewhere in freshman or sopho-more economics the normative rationale for pollution control is typically spelled out, and then later our charges are told that the way regulators actually do things leaves much to be desired. Leone and Jackson see more here than a confused attempt to control pollution. If this were the whole story, we should see congressmen from districts with large paper mills (an industry with large pollution-control costs) opposing increased restrictions. They do not. Why not? Possibly they are implicitly bought off by the design of the regulation, the very design that seems laden with inefficiency to the conventional analyst. Leone and Jackson then find empirical support for this possibility. In effect, the regulators levy a higher implicit tax on new entrants than on established mills. With just a little growth in demand, the net effect of the regulation is to generate nontrivial rents for established mills. Thus, a potentially antagonistic and powerful interest is brought within the coalition served by the regulators. Of course, potential entrants are hurt, but you will not find the Association of Potential New Entrants listed in the Washington telephone directory.

Sometimes creeping realism means a partial revival of a public-interest, or at least a non-producer-interest, view. For example, minimum capital requirements have long been recognized as a potential restriction of entry. Munch and Smallwood and their discussants focus on the possible benefits for consumers of insurance, who might otherwise be left stranded in a bankruptcy. In effect, the minimum capital requirement substitutes for the high costs facing the untutored consumer in evaluating the financial capacity of the insurer.

The last example I want to cite is the article of Willig and Bailey. Their wholly normative paper breaks with the venerable tradition of separating allocative from distributive issues. They want to guide a regulator who wishes to set prices that take simultaneous account of efficiency and income distribution norms. What about the old story that redistribution is better done by explicit money transfers than by the Public Service Commission? Willig and Bailey are silent on this. Though I am persuaded by Gary Becker's (1976) argument that the old story is wrong, I suspect that Willig and Bailey's silence is deliberate. For all our past hand-wringing about how messy it is, regulators persist in allowing distributive considerations to intrude on, and even dominate, their pricemaking. Even the pure theorist, Willig and Bailey seem to be saying, had better adjust to this reality.

The approach of Willig and Bailey illustrates my second principle of the economics of regulation, which is that practice leads theory. The full-blown development of the welfare economics of natural monopoly lagged the growth of electricity and telephone regulation. The capture models lagged the most notable empirical counterparts—ICC regulation of trucking, organization of the Civil Aeronautics Board, oil import quotas, and so on. The creeping-realism literature seems to be lagging two events, one practical and the other intellectual. The practical antecedent seems to be the growth of the whole panoply of safety, environmental, and consumer-information regulation, whose very existence or whose practice has often proved difficult to rationalize theoretically. The intellectual precursor seems to be the perceived difficulties with earlier models about which one or another theory did seem to have a lot to say. For example, if as the capture model holds the ICC is in business to organize a trucking cartel and enforce rate-making collusion among the railroads, why does it harm both captors by perpetuating excess railroad capacity?

Of course, intellectual and real-world developments are related here. The newer forms of regulation, such as consumer protection and pollution control, began their great growth at about the same time the capture model was making its biggest splash in academia. However, the Second Principle was at work, and most students of regulation did not rush to apply the capture model to the new regulations. Instead, they seemed willing, for a time, to try to understand the new regulations within the framework of the older public-interest model. When it became clear that the newer agencies were no more dedicated to Pareto optimality than their ancestors, the first reaction in the literature (still the dominant one) was to tell the new regulators to mend their ways. Kneese's 1971 work on the potential gains from effluent fees comes immediately to mind. The next reaction was more analytical. Much of what I have called creeping realism seems to be focusing on the new regulation. It seems to say that if the public-interest model doesn't explain how the new regulation works and if the capture model has been found wanting in explaining important aspects of the behavior of those agencies to which it seems most applicable, we now have all the more reason to develop a new synthesis.

However, we ought to embrace any new model of regulation with some caution. Implicit in much of what I have so far said is, perhaps, another principle of the economics of regulation: that the currently fashionable theory is usually wrong, or at least misleading. This conference provided more examples of this Third Principle than I have already touched upon. For example, none of the literature spawned by Stigler and Friedland argued very strenuously against the notion that natural-monopoly problems were an initial impetus to regulation of utilities. The story seemed to be that once the clamor for regulation had been heeded, the industry was able to assert itself in the mundane activity of the new agencies. However, Jarrell (1978) argued that the facts are more compatible with the view that industry interest was present at the creation of these agencies as well. The article of Fuss and Waverman, though working from a much different perspective, also ends up questioning the natural-monopoly rationale for telecommunications regulation. The elaboration of the producer interest in pollution regulation by Leone and Jackson serves to update this story.

As I have pointed out, the producer-protection model has met its own share of skepticism, both at this conference and elsewhere. Levin's article adds new insights into work begun by Keeler (1974), Friedlaender (1971), and others. But, these have a common theme. The ICC's attempt to preserve excess capacity in railroading is an integral part of its history, and not some aberration of a cartel manager manque. It constitutes a huge tax on the wealth of railroad owners for the benefit of a few shippers. Moreover, Keeler pointed out that U.S. railroads are not alone in facing such a tax. Similarly, Munch and Smallwood's discussion of the potential benefits to at least some consumers of capital requirements was echoed at the conference in discussions of similar benefits from more explicit entry control, like licensing. Occupational licensure may have been the first form of regulation to which economists applied the producer-protection model. Adam Smith deserves paternity here, as in much else. His descendants, like Friedman and Kuznets and Kessel, gave the model considerable empirical content. However, the realist challenge intrudes here too. The potential empirical importance of a consumer interest in shaping licensing regulation was debated at the conference and is the subject of ongoing work by Holen, Leffler, and Gaston and Carroll. It is, however, too early to tell whether this work will end up confirming my Third Principle, which is that the predominant licensing-as-cartel model is wrong.

However, if that principle has any validity, I believe that its lesson may be especially important for the new realist literature, as well as for some of the more institutionally innocent work that seeks new applications for market-failure models. The realist literature seems to be organizing around the following pattern: Select an area where producer protection has seemed important (for example, licensing, minimum price, or entry regulation); then show that there is a potential market failure that makes it credible for a coalition of producers and consumers, not merely the producers alone, to seek regulation. Or, reverse the pattern: Select an area, such as pollution, where market failure had seemed the most compelling force for regulation; then show how regulation of the market failure can be structured to serve a producer interest at the same time, and thereby enhance the political survival value of the regulatory institutions. This is an interesting research strategy that, I believe, deserves encouragement. Indeed, I have argued elsewhere (1976) that diversification of the interest groups served by a regulatory agency, rather than specialization, ought to be the common pattern.

There appears to be a dangerous asymmetry in the way this research is carried out: One part of the model (the cartel element) gets serious analytical treatment, while the other (market failure) is hardly developed beyond the point of vague possibility. Needless to say, the danger of this asymmetry increases with the emphasis placed on market failure as the source of regulation.

I can best elaborate on this sweeping claim by making another: Conjuring up rationales for regulation is too easy a sport; perhaps it deserves a Pigovian tax. On a few minutes' notice, any competent economist could apply an externalities model to fashions in clothing, a natural-monopoly model to stereo equipment (after all, don't they advertise amplifiers powerful enough to drive all the speakers on your block?), or a producer-protection model to laws against heroin. The only reason for taking some applications more seriously than others is our sense of their empirical importance. This, I would argue, is precisely what led us 10 or 15 years ago to take producer protection seriously as an important element in regulatory behavior. From the beginning the focus of that literature was on the importance of the measurable features of that phenomenon, not simply on the legal possibilities embedded in, say, the Civil Aeronautics Act or the Interstate Commerce Acts; so the literature developed by estimating the number of firms excluded from one or another market (for example, Jordan's work on airlines), the size of rents to existing firms (Friedman and Kuznets [1954] on the AMA), the gap between competitive and regulated prices (Keeler [1972] on the CAB). The range of sophistication in this literature is, to be sure, very wide, but most of it seemed to point in the same direction of pinning down the empirical magnitudes. And the increased technical virtuosity seems to have resulted in better or more credible estimates of the size of the regulatory effects. Perhaps the air-transportation literature, starting from Keyes's work in the early 1950s, best illustrates these points. By now any new entrant to any part of the capture literature is conditioned to worry not only about the potential or directional effect of regulation, but about its size. Note, for example, the procedure of Leone and Jackson. After stating the rather novel possibility that the EPA is creating positive rather than negative producer rents, they immediately give a crude estimate of magnitudes (capital gains of $200 million versus losses of about 1 percent of this). Had the numbers been reversed, I doubt that the theoretical possibility would be given much attention.

This degree of concern for empirical relevance does not, however, seem to carry over to our treatment of market-failure issues. To be sure, some of the relevant issues have received analytically sophisticated treatment attentive to empirical importance. A case in point is the treatment of scale economies in two of the articles presented here. Levin's on railroad costs makes precise the nature of economies of scale in this industry, and then proceeds to measure the magnitude of the costs of excess capacity resulting from restrictions on exit when there are traffic-density economies. The compelling result is not the theoretical possibility of suppressed density economies, but their very large magnitude. Similarly, the main motive to Fuss and Waverman's work seems to be concern with the extent of scale economies in telecommunications; that is, with how the economies can be measured in the multiproduct-firm, and how big the economies are. Again, the interesting result is the sense of empirical proportions conveyed by the work—the suggestion that scale economies may not be so extensive as heretofore believed. Both these articles add to previous work. Examples that come to mind are Keeler's (1972) and Friedlaender's (1971) work on railroad costs, in the case of Levin, and Christensen and Greene's (1976) work on electric utilities, in the case of Fuss and Waverman. However, even in the economies-of-scale literature no one will accuse us of great haste in this search for empirical relevance. Public utility commissions were being created for almost a century before this empirical literature became established, textbooks were written about their operation, and Hotelling made it evident in the title that his classic article on optimal pricing applied to railroad and utility rates. This whole enterprise was based on a presumed but undemonstrated belief in the importance of scale economies in particular activities.

Much of the current discussion of newly fashionable market failures seems to be at a similar stage of development. To be sure, vague beliefs are now enshrined in jargon and clothed in formal models which give them the correct ritual flavor and exclude the uninitiated. Perhaps a card-carrying member of the profession should not oppose this too loudly or even be entirely cynical about it. There is, after all, a gain in precision in talking about failure of information and insurance markets instead of about the cheated consumer. My worry is that the professional discussion here does not seem to be leading toward the next question: How important are the problems being discussed? Here, I would refer the reader back to Noll and Joskow's summary of the literature on health, safety, and performance standards. They review a welter of possible problems with unregulated markets that have cropped up in this literature, and a modest number of attempts to evaluate the effects of regulation. But they are as struck as I am by the lack of work on the empirical importance of the theoretical problems. At this stage in the development of economics, one should have hoped that the empirical question would be given priority. It does, after all, matter for how seriously we want to pursue the theoretical enterprise whether 1 percent or 50 percent of the sales of some product generated negative consumer surplus, just as it ought to have mattered to the early public-utility economists whether the output elasticity of total costs was 0.95 or 0.25. Nor do I mean to imply by this lapse into jargon that the theoretical enterprise has to be held captive to a sophisticated technology of data production and analysis. Precise point estimates are not required for getting at gross magnitudes. But, at least in the safety-health literature, we have not begun to find out if the theoretical problems we explore are worth talking about.

The literature on environmental externalities also falls into the "newly fashionable" category, and the situation here is a little better than in safety and health. The work by Lave and Seskin (1970) on health effects of pollution and that of Ridker (1967) and Crocker (1971) on land values is a start at defining the scope of the problem. But, again, compare the attention to this basic part of the problem with that given to theoretical problems which implicitly assume that there is a substantial problem. I refer here to the literature cited by Noll and Joskow on such matters as optimal control mechanisms for pollution and the attendant general equilibrium consequences. Similarly, the bulk of applied research on pollution control tends to avoid the issue of how important pollution externalities are, choosing instead to focus on such matters as the costs of various abatement policies. If someone today asserted that any substantial reduction in pollution would have trivial benefits, or that the resources spent in the name of pollution control had trivial effects on pollution, there would be no substantial concrete basis for laughing him out of court. Given this state of affairs, we may be seriously compromising our knowledge about pollution regulation. For all we know, this regulation may be only the disguised form of entry control Leone and Jackson describe, or a WPA project for the suppliers of control equipment, or something else that would call for a fundamentally different analytical framework than we have so far brought to bear on pollution regulation.

My point here is not to propose radically alternative models, since that would implicitly decide the crucial empirical issues. Instead, I am suggesting that, before we push our normative models into the newer areas of regulation or try to marry the normative models with economic analyses of politics, we not rush past an essential question: Are the welfare problems we are invoking trivial or sizable? We may well conclude that there is more reason to spend analytical energy on the externalities of automobile pollution than, say, those of automobile colors, in much the same way that we were able to conclude that there were at least some interesting scale-economy problems in regulated utilities. However, the justification for taking this sort of risk is much weaker today than it was fifty or one hundred years ago, when the tools of empirical analysis were far less developed.

I do not want to minimize the difficulties inherent in assessing the magnitude of the problems on which we focus our analysis. One need only read the discussion surrounding the Fuss-Waverman paper to see that there are still many difficulties to the measuring of scale economics. The corresponding measurement problems in the newer areas of regulation are going to be even more formidable, because we will not typically have something like balance sheets and income-expense accounts to start from. However, the biggest challenge, I suspect, will be to our imagination and flexibility in using analytical tools that we already have. If this is right, then I am more optimistic than Noll and Joskow, at least about the potential for success.

To be more concrete, let me give a couple of examples of how we might frame questions that could get us closer to discovering the size of some of the problems I have mentioned.

• Are consumers behaving in a way consistent with the story that a big problem exists? For at least some goods there will be some objective measure of performance: accident frequencies of cars, failure propensities of insurers, injury frequencies of various occupations. Given these (or, more precisely, the relevant exogenous components), we can ask whether the good products or jobs sell at a premium to the bad and by how much relative to an independent estimate of the extra costs of the bad product. We will have an interesting problem if this premium is small, or if the good products do not drive out the bad.

• Does the political process act as if the problem is large or small? By now we are sufficiently wary not to take at face value the nominal intent of regulation. Nor can we easily interpret departures from this intent. Thus, suppose we found that, long after the establishment of a well-financed and amply empowered Consumer Protection Agency, as many consumers were being cheated or maimed as before. This could mean that the cheating and maiming was so small as to be practically irreducible. It could also mean that the title of the agency was hiding its objectives. If we found a large physical reduction in consumer fraud or injury, we would still have to evaluate its economic significance.

No study of the political process or the markets it regulates can escape such interpretive problems. Still, I believe we can gain something by looking for consistencies or regularities in political behavior, because the political process should not be expected to be indifferent to dead-weight losses in unregulated markets. These may be tolerated or even encouraged because they help "buy" another objective, but no rational model of political behavior would hold the dead-weight losses to be a good in and of themselves. Thus, if the dead-weight losses are large enough and inherent in unregulated markets, we ought to expect a consistent political response.

To uncover this consistency, I believe that the economics of regulation will have to give up some of its provincial focus on American institutions. The simple fact that many jurisdictions seem to persist in leaving large parts of transportation unregulated is telling (if crude) evidence that unregulated markets do not systematically generate large dead-weight losses. This is not to say that if regulation were ubiquitous the converse would be demonstrated. It could be that the forces making for regulation in the United States are so universally powerful that they can always overcome dead-weight losses of their own making. However, ubiquitous regulation would, I think, force us to take more seriously than otherwise the potential problems with unregulated transportation markets raised by advocates of regulation. My suggestion is that international comparisons of regulatory institutions can be a useful check or a crude screening device for selecting problems that may be worth pursuing. For example, we will take the possibility of market failure in electricity and telecommunications more seriously if every important country intervenes in these markets with seemingly appropriate institutions; we will be more skeptical if there is the same variety as in transportation. In view of the potential payoff to a modest analytical effort, there seems to me to be considerable scope for pursuing international institutional comparisons. If I am right, this strategy can also have obviously valuable spinoffs—for example, comparisons of the effects of apparently similar institutions.

These examples are more illustrations of a point than an agenda. The point is that deficiencies of data or analytical technique are not great enough to justify our neglect of the crucial empirical issues which have so far been ignored in analyses of the newer regulatory institutions. If this is so, perhaps we ought to impose that Pigovian tax on further proliferation of normative models or on their incipient marriage to the economics of politics until we begin redressing this neglect.

Such a reallocation of effort is not, of course, a substitute for a generally useful theory of regulatory behavior. It is entirely possible that when that theory is written it will so restructure our analysis of the regulatory process that the welfare problems that now tend to hold center stage will be pushed off to the side. We might, in hindsight, regret the time spent in worrying about their size. However, even though such a theory does not yet exist, research on specific forms of regulation has to look for some theoretical grounding. This is now being done by extending traditional normative models to the newer forms of regulation and by implicitly inserting specific allocative outcomes into the relevant objective function of regulators. Meanwhile, a good deal of the theoretical work on regulation has a similar motivation.

The promise of these analyses, either in enhancing our current understanding of regulation or in leading to a richer theory, rests on the importance of the problems around which they are organized. This is why I believe it is especially timely to divert some analytical energy to discovering the importance of these problems.

The increasing scope and spread of regulation and its impact on academic research make it almost obligatory for me to discuss policy issues. While my primary purpose in criticizing some of the focus of current research is to point out the unmet intellectual challenge, there are also related policy issues. At least some of the recent research seems to want to breach the wall between allocative and distributive issues that has stood so long in academic discussions of regulatory issues. The reasons for this are debatable, but, whatever their source, the infirmities of "make price equal marginal cost and send a check to the losers" advice are heeded at several points in these articles. Bailey and Willig discard this paradigm at the formal level, since their model starts with a marriage of allocative and distributive objectives as a given for the regulator. If one thing is clear from the discussion of excess capacity in railroads, it is the practical failure of our traditional advice. Finally, one of the motives to the marriage of the economics of regulation and the economics of politics is recognition of the practical link between economics and politics in regulatory policy.

The inference I choose to draw from the practical failure and the perhaps impending intellectual disintegration of the traditional policy advice of regulatory economists is that policy advice is not our strong point. An earlier generation of economists, with fewer policy problems tempting them, might have told us to stick to organizing the facts of the world intelligibly and systematically. If we follow this advice well, our impact on policy may increase. Since the impact is so small now and since "Policy Implications" is likely to remain the traditional conclusion to papers on regulation, this is a fairly safe prediction. Here again we are forced to proceed on less firm theoretical ground than we would like. This means that one day we may find out that the very categories in which we communicate with policymakers have little relevance for them. However, for now, any economist who wants to do "policy-relevant" work is forced to run that risk. If costs and benefits of the type we usually focus on are relevant for policy, the policymakers will inevitably have to deal with their magnitudes. Here I believe, economists have started to develop a methodology that can substantially reduce these policy-information costs.

In may cases the policymaker will, at least crudely, "know the score" without our help. Bankruptcies of short-haul, low-density railroads will, for example, get part of Levin's message across. However, consider the position of a politician whose constituency is not directly affected by the problems of short-haul, low-density railroads. He or she may be reluctant to vote for subsidizing these railroads, but fearful that without a "yea" vote a massive disaster will befall a political ally from another district. For such a swing voter, the sort of information provided by Levin's work, which pins down the consequences of the existing policy, can be far more valuable than *a priori* arguments about the desirability of free entry and exit. The other side of this is that policymakers looking for the "facts" will have to rely heavily on economists in these matters. The sport we have developed of debunking purely technical attempts at getting the "facts" is symptomatic. No competitor has succeeded in challenging our ability to organize data around a consistent theoretical superstructure in matters relevant for social policy.

Perhaps a better example of the policy payoff of our giving empirical content to theoretical issues is the current state of airline regulation. Congressional acceptance of deregulation and increased implementation of the basic principles of competition by the CAB provide a rare example of political endorsement of the professional consensus. But the professional consensus, backed by *a priori* arguments about lack of scale economies in the business and perhaps a few casual observations about experience in deregulated markets, was achieved well before policy began changing. What I want to suggest is that it took the weight of a fairly extensive empirical literature, able to generalize from the experience of deregulated markets and make precise the range of effects to be expected from deregulation, before policy changed—or at least before politicians felt able to use the work of economists to press for a change in policy.

Let me quickly recognize some of the risks of generalizing from this correlation between the flowering of an empirical literature and a shift in policy:

• The number of "swing" legislators susceptible to academic evidence is probably unusually large in the particular case of airlines, since the industry interest is not great in many congressional districts.

• The literature here is unusually well developed. One thinks immediately of the work of Keyes (1952), Caves (1962), Jordan (1970), Eads (1975), Keeler (1972), Douglas and Miller (1974), and the CAB's own economics staff, and fears that the list is incomplete. The quantity is matched by quality, and this combination may well be unmatched in the literature on the economic effects of regulation.

• There is probably by now a professional consensus, backed by a growing empirical literature, that regulation of exit from railroading is very costly. However, there has been little change in policy.

• Policy has changed in the same direction as a professional consensus, which had no strong empirical base. I am thinking here of the deregulation of stock-brokerage commissions. My casual judgment is that most economists would have "voted" with the Securities and Exchange Commission on this in the belief that the industry was structurally competitive. However, even if this is so, the direct role of economists in the process was peripheral.

In view of all these cross-currents, I am left less with any strong conclusions than with a tentative hypothesis: that the impact of economists on policy is indirect, and that the empirical support for their arguments weighs more heavily on policymakers than the arguments themselves. The justification for providing some future historian of ideas with more data with which to test this hypothesis is partly to make the sample more representative, but mainly because I think the choices are limited. The gap between theoretical possibility and empirical grounding has become so great in so much of regulatory economics that achieving a professional consensus, not to mention professional development, is going to compel us to look harder and harder at just how the world really works.

References

Becker, G. 1976. Comment. *Journal of Law and Economics* 29: 245–248.

Caves, R. 1962. *Air Transport and Its Regulations: An Industry Study*. Cambridge, Mass.: Harvard University Press.

Christensen, L., and Greene, W. 1976. "Economies of Scale in the U.S. Power Industry." *Journal of Political Economy* 84: 655–676.

Crocker, T. 1971. "Externalities, Property Rights and Transaction Costs." *Journal of Law and Economics* 14: 451–464.

Douglas, G., and Miller, J. 1974. *Economic Regulation of Domestic Air Transport*. Washington, D.C.: Brookings Institution.

Eads, G. 1975. "Competition in the Domestic Trunk Airline Industry: Too Much or Too Little? In A. Phillips (ed.), *Promoting Competition in Regulated Markets*. Washington, D.C.: Brookings Institution.

Friedlaender, A. 1971. "The Social Costs of Railroad Regulation." *American Economic Review* (Papers and Proceedings) 61: 226–234.

Friedman, M., and Kuznets, S. 1954. *Income from Independent Professional Practice*. New York: National Bureau of Economic Research.

Gaston, R., and Carroll, S. 1977. New Approaches and Empirical Evidence on Occupational Licensing and the Quality of Service Received. Department of Economics, University of Tennessee, Knoxville. Mimeographed.

Holen, A. 1977. The Economics of Dental Licensing. Center for Naval Analyses, Washington, D.C. Mimeographed.

Hotelling, H. 1938. "The General Welfare in Relation to Problems of Taxation and Railway and Utility Rates." *Econometrica* 6: 242–269.

Jarrell, G. 1978. "The Demand for State Regulation of the Electric Utility Industry." *Journal of Law and Economics* 21: 269–296.

Jordan, W. 1970. *Airline Regulation in America: Effects and Imperfections*. Baltimore: Johns Hopkins University Press.

Keeler, T. 1972. "Airline Regulation and Market Performance." *Bell Journal of Economics and Management Science* 3: 399–423.

———. 1974. "Costs, Returns to Scale and Excess Capacity." *Review of Economics and Statistics* 56: 201–208.

Kessel, R. 1958. "Price Discrimination in Medicine." *Journal of Law and Economics* 1. 20–53.

Keyes, L. 1952. *Federal Control of Entry into Air Transportation*. Cambridge, Mass.: Harvard University Press.

Kneese, A. 1971. "Environmental Pollution Economics and Policy." *American Economic Review* (Papers and Proceedings) 61: 153–166.

Lave, L., and Seskin, E. 1970. "Air Pollution and Human Health." *Science* 169: 723–730.

Leffler, K. 1978. "Physician Licensure: Competition and Monopoly in American Medicine." *Journal of Law and Economics* 21: 165–186.

Peltzman, S. 1976. "Toward a More General Theory of Regulation." *Journal of Law and Economics* 29: 211–239.

Ridker, R. 1967. *Economic Costs of Air Pollution*. New York: Praeger.

Stigler, G., and Friedland, C. 1962. "What Can Regulators Regulate: The Case of Electricity." *Journal of Law and Economics* 5: 1–15.

Authors and Discussants

Authors

Elizabeth E. Bailey
Civil Aeronautics Board

Kenneth C. Baseman
Department of Justice

Melvyn Fuss
University of Toronto

John E. Jackson
University of Michigan

Paul L. Joskow
Massachusetts Institute of Technology

Robert A. Leone
Harvard Business School

Richard C. Levin
Yale University

Patricia Munch
Rand Corporation

Roger C. Noll
California Institute of Technology

Sam Peltzman
University of Chicago

Dennis Smallwood
University of California, San Diego

Leonard Waverman
University of Toronto

Robert D. Willig
Princeton University

Discussants

William J. Baumol
Princeton University and
New York University

Ronald Braeutigam
Northwestern University

Alfred E. Kahn
Cornell University

Alvin K. Klevorick
Yale University

Allan V. Kneese
University of New Mexico

Howard Kunreuther
University of Pennsylvania

Michael P. Lynch
Federal Trade Commission

Bridger M. Mitchell
International Institute of Management
and Rand Corporation

Almarin Phillips
University of Pennsylvania

John C. Panzar
Bell Telephone Laboratories, Inc.

Richard Schmalensee
Massachusetts Institute of Technology

George J. Stigler
University of Chicago

Richard Zeckhauser
Harvard University

Index